CASE CLOSED

VOLUME 62

Gosho Aoyama

Case Briefing:

Subject:
Occupation:
Special Skills:
Equipment:

Jimmy Kudo, a.k.a. Conan Edogawa
High School Student/Detective
Analytical thinking and deductive reasoning, Soccer
Bow Tie Voice Transmitter, Super Sneakers,
Homing Glasses, Stretchy Suspenders

The subject is hot on the trail of a pair of suspicious men in black when he is attacked from behind and administered a strange substance which physically transforms him into a first grader. When the subject confides in the eccentric inventor Dr. Agasa, they decide to keep the subject's true identity a secret for the safety of everyone around him. Assuming the new identity of first-grader Conan Edogawa, the subject continues to assist the police force on their most baffling cases. The only problem is that most crime-solving professionals won't take a little kid's advice!

Table of Contents

CONFIDEN

CASE CLOSED

Volume 62
Shonen Sunday Edition

Story and Art by GOSHO AOYAMA

MEITANTEI CONAN Vol. 62
by Gosho AOYAMA
© 1994 Gosho AOYAMA
All rights reserved.
Original Japanese edition published by SHOGAKUKAN.
English translation rights in the United States of America, Canada,
the United Kingdom and Ireland arranged with SHOGAKUKAN.

Translation
Tetsuichiro Miyaki

Touch-up & Lettering
Freeman Wong

Cover & Graphic Design
Andrea Rice

Editor
Shaenon K. Garrity

Printed in the U.S.A.

Published by VIZ Media, LLC
P.O. Box 77010
San Francisco, CA 94107

10 9 8 7 6 5 4 3 2 1
First printing, April 2017

FALSE FRIENDSHIP

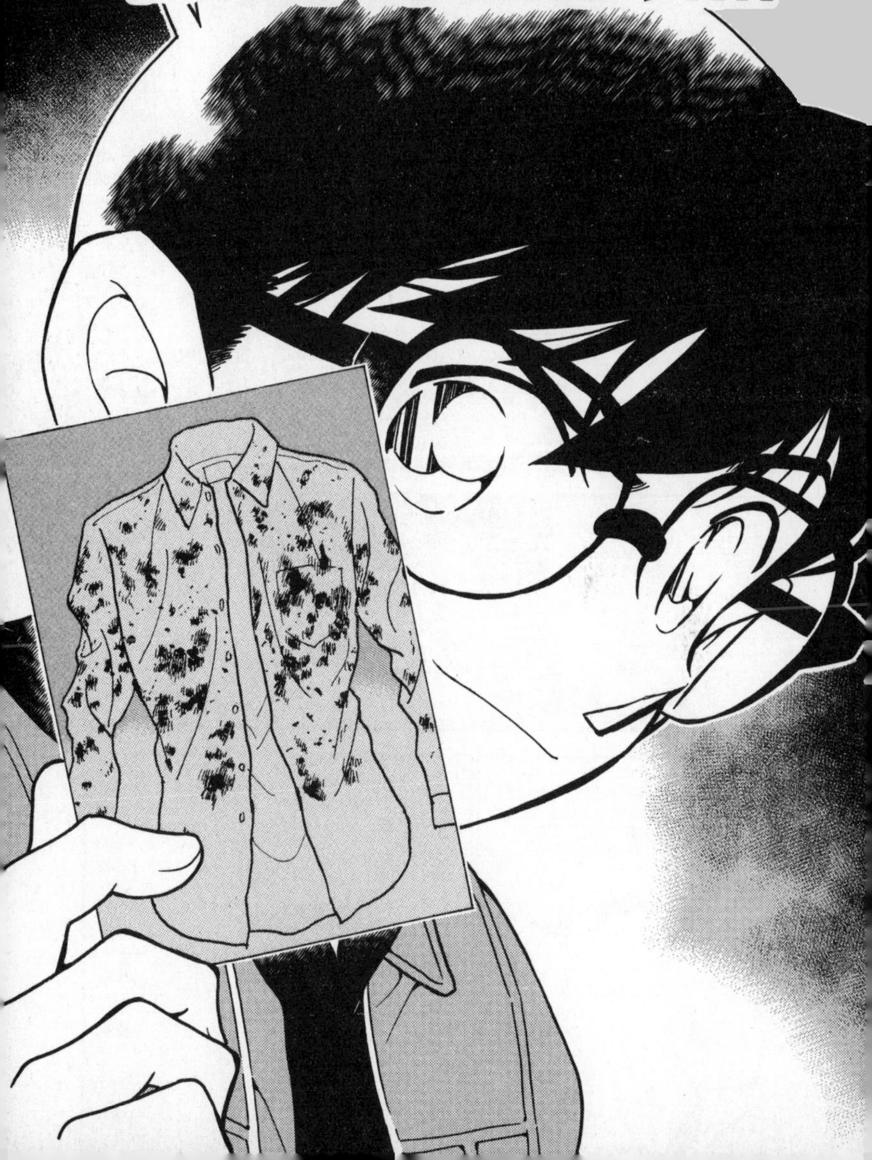

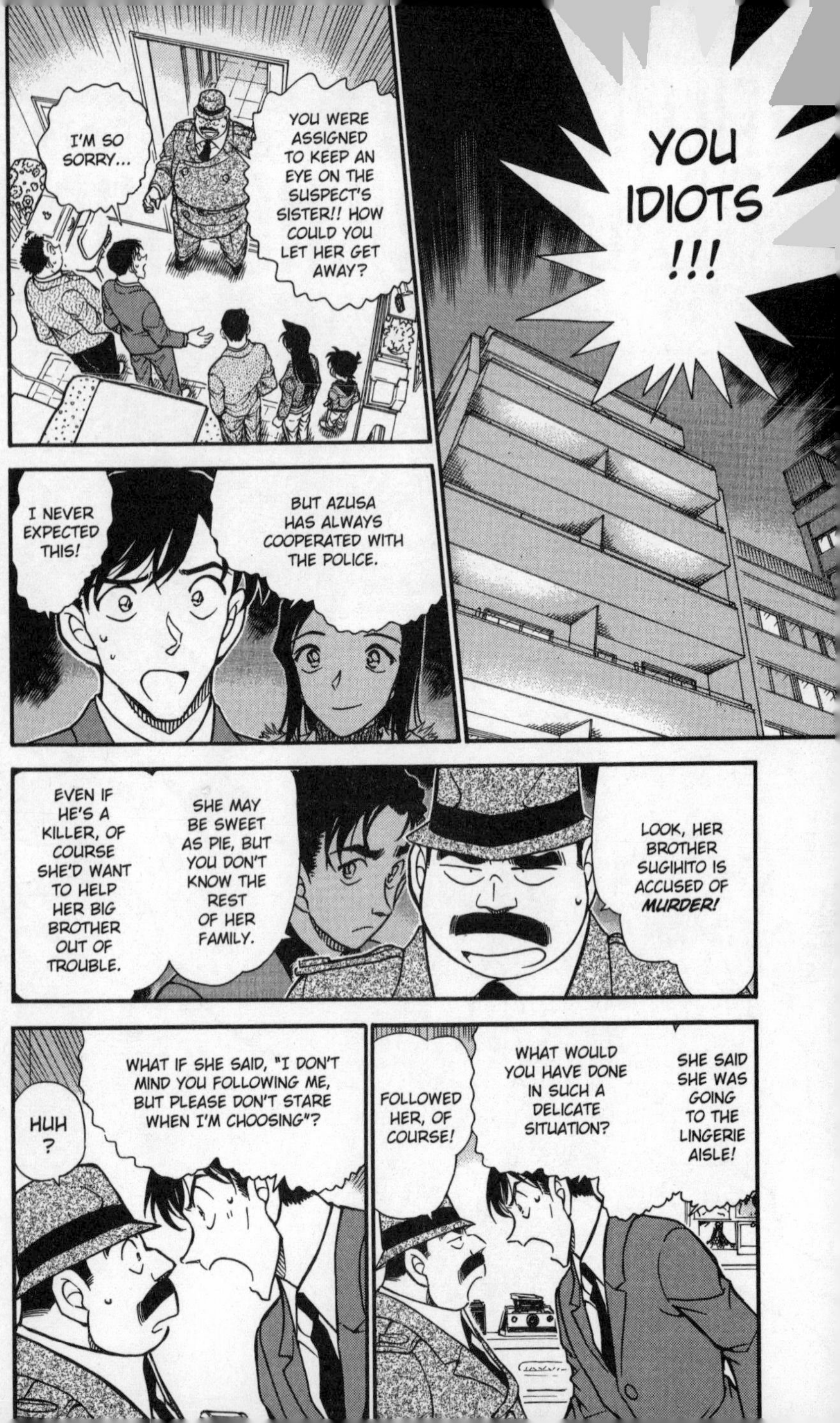
YOU IDIOTS!!!
YOU WERE ASSIGNED TO KEEP AN EYE ON THE SUSPECT'S SISTER!! HOW COULD YOU LET HER GET AWAY?
I'M SO SORRY...
BUT AZUSA HAS ALWAYS COOPERATED WITH THE POLICE.
I NEVER EXPECTED THIS!
LOOK, HER BROTHER SUGIHITO IS ACCUSED OF ***MURDER!***
SHE MAY BE SWEET AS PIE, BUT YOU DON'T KNOW THE REST OF HER FAMILY.
EVEN IF HE'S A KILLER, OF COURSE SHE'D WANT TO HELP HER BIG BROTHER OUT OF TROUBLE.
SHE SAID SHE WAS GOING TO THE LINGERIE AISLE!
WHAT WOULD YOU HAVE DONE IN SUCH A DELICATE SITUATION?
FOLLOWED HER, OF COURSE!
WHAT IF SHE SAID, "I DON'T MIND YOU FOLLOWING ME, BUT PLEASE DON'T STARE WHEN I'M CHOOSING"?
HUH ?

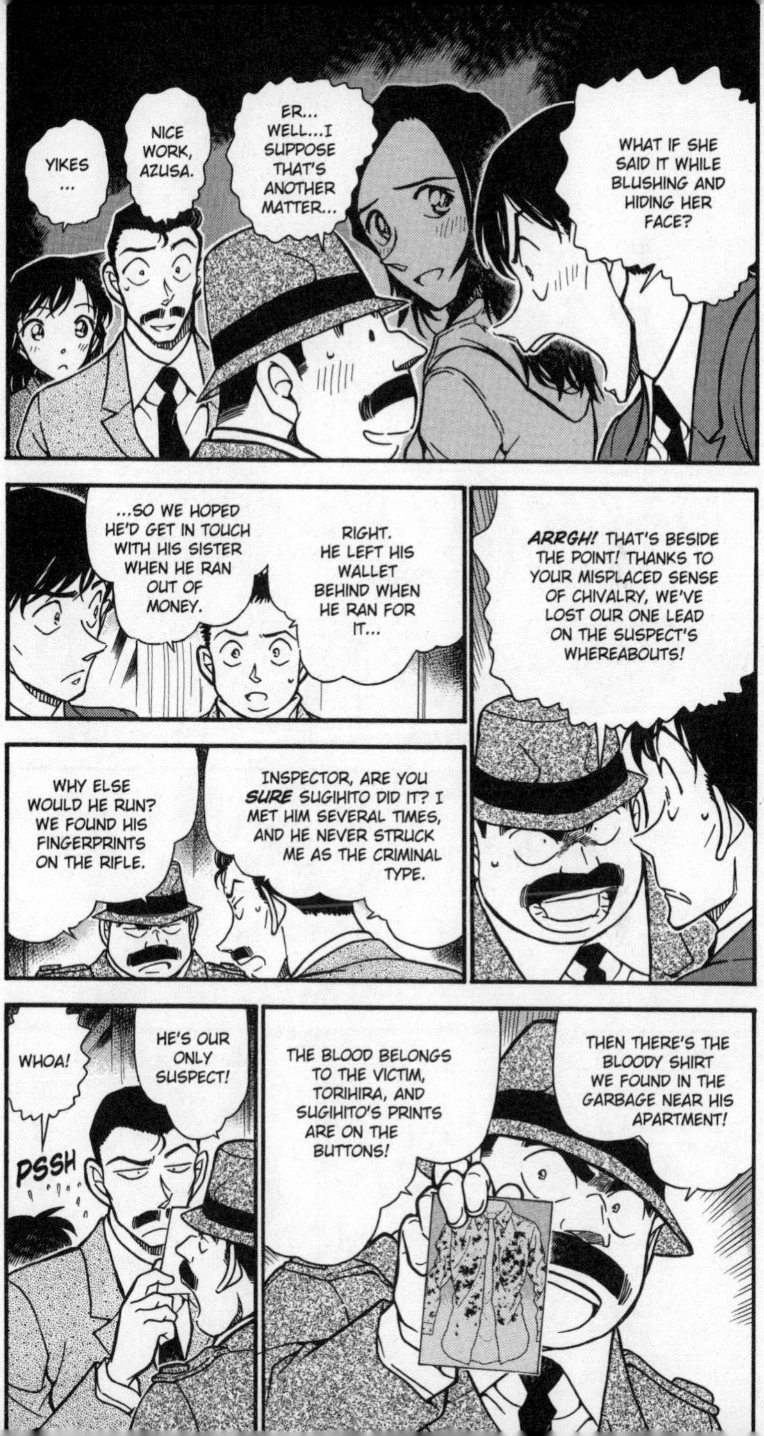
WHAT IF SHE SAID IT WHILE BLUSHING AND HIDING HER FACE?
ER... WELL...I SUPPOSE THAT'S ANOTHER MATTER...
NICE WORK, AZUSA.
YIKES ...
ARRGH! THAT'S BESIDE THE POINT! THANKS TO YOUR MISPLACED SENSE OF CHIVALRY, WE'VE LOST OUR ONE LEAD ON THE SUSPECT'S WHEREABOUTS!
RIGHT. HE LEFT HIS WALLET BEHIND WHEN HE RAN FOR IT...
...SO WE HOPED HE'D GET IN TOUCH WITH HIS SISTER WHEN HE RAN OUT OF MONEY.
INSPECTOR, ARE YOU *SURE* SUGIHITO DID IT? I MET HIM SEVERAL TIMES, AND HE NEVER STRUCK ME AS THE CRIMINAL TYPE.
WHY ELSE WOULD HE RUN? WE FOUND HIS FINGERPRINTS ON THE RIFLE.
THEN THERE'S THE BLOODY SHIRT WE FOUND IN THE GARBAGE NEAR HIS APARTMENT!
THE BLOOD BELONGS TO THE VICTIM, TORIHIRA, AND SUGIHITO'S PRINTS ARE ON THE BUTTONS!
HE'S OUR ONLY SUSPECT!
WHOA!
PSSH

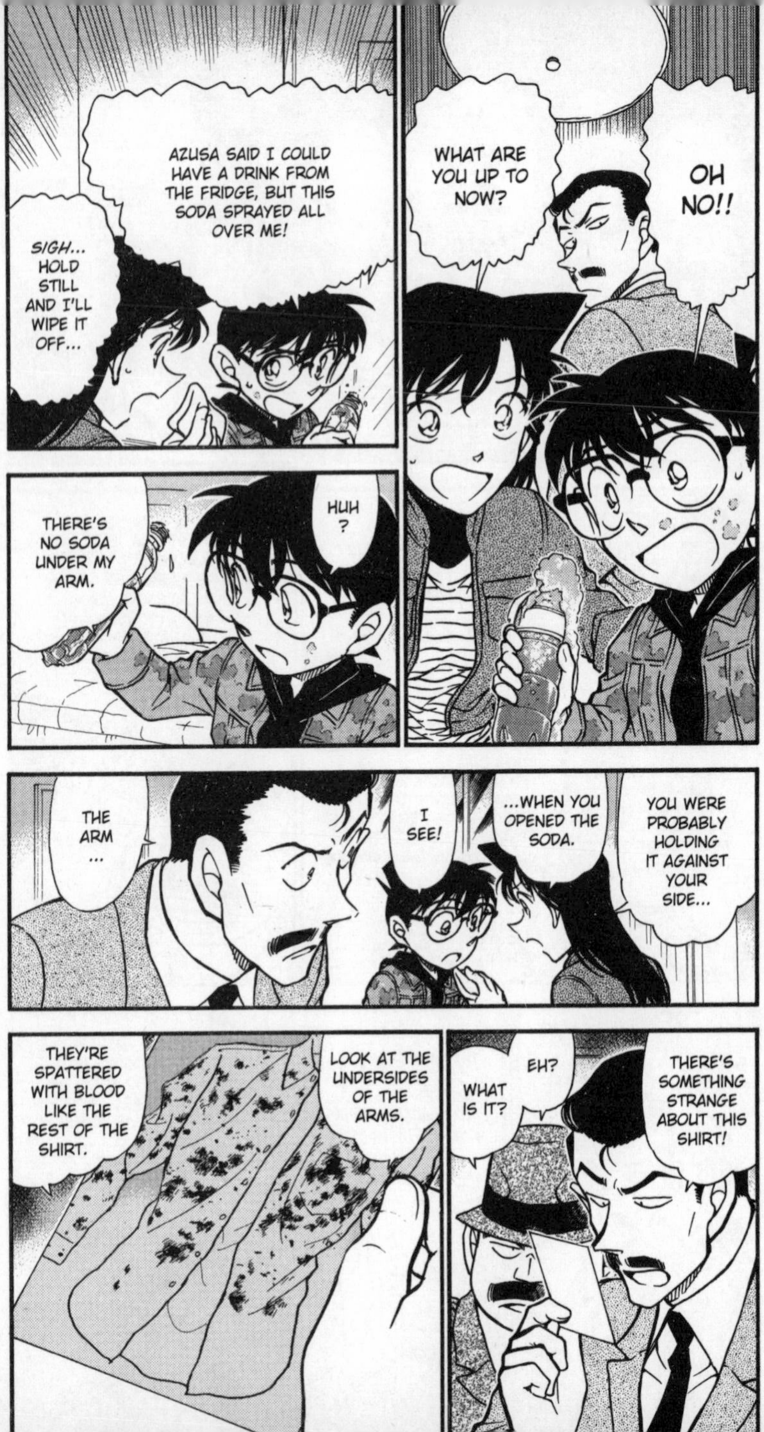
OH NO!!
WHAT ARE YOU UP TO NOW?
AZUSA SAID I COULD HAVE A DRINK FROM THE FRIDGE, BUT THIS SODA SPRAYED ALL OVER ME!
SIGH... HOLD STILL AND I'LL WIPE IT OFF...
HUH?
THERE'S NO SODA UNDER MY ARM.
YOU WERE PROBABLY HOLDING IT AGAINST YOUR SIDE...
...WHEN YOU OPENED THE SODA.
I SEE!
THE ARM ...
THERE'S SOMETHING STRANGE ABOUT THIS SHIRT!
EH?
WHAT IS IT?
LOOK AT THE UNDERSIDES OF THE ARMS.
THEY'RE SPATTERED WITH BLOOD LIKE THE REST OF THE SHIRT.

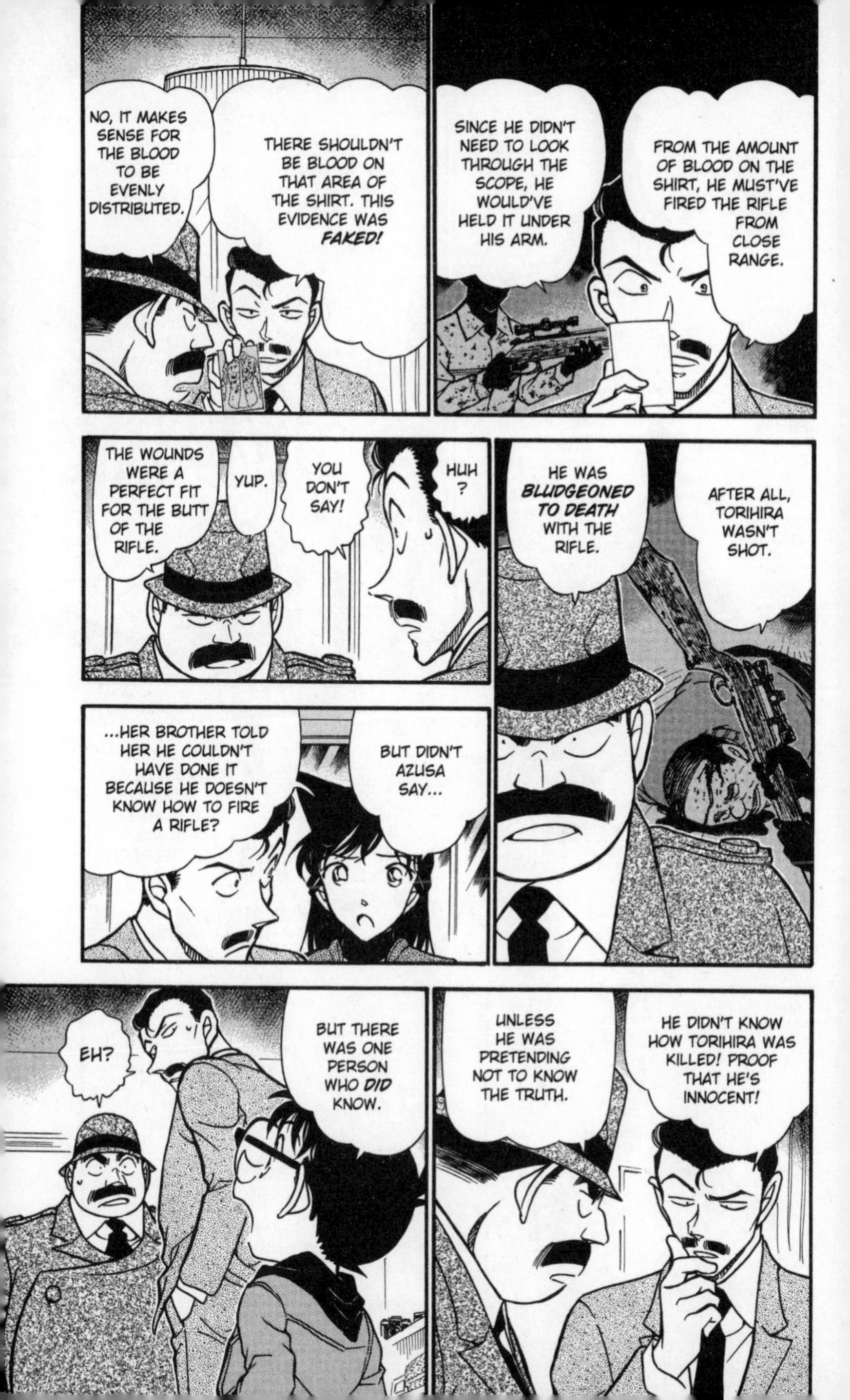
FROM THE AMOUNT OF BLOOD ON THE SHIRT, HE MUST'VE FIRED THE RIFLE FROM CLOSE RANGE.
SINCE HE DIDN'T NEED TO LOOK THROUGH THE SCOPE, HE WOULD'VE HELD IT UNDER HIS ARM.
THERE SHOULDN'T BE BLOOD ON THAT AREA OF THE SHIRT. THIS EVIDENCE WAS *FAKED!*
NO, IT MAKES SENSE FOR THE BLOOD TO BE EVENLY DISTRIBUTED.
AFTER ALL, TORIHIRA WASN'T SHOT.
HE WAS *BLUDGEONED TO DEATH* WITH THE RIFLE.
HUH?
YOU DON'T SAY!
YUP.
THE WOUNDS WERE A PERFECT FIT FOR THE BUTT OF THE RIFLE.
BUT DIDN'T AZUSA SAY...
...HER BROTHER TOLD HER HE COULDN'T HAVE DONE IT BECAUSE HE DOESN'T KNOW HOW TO FIRE A RIFLE?
HE DIDN'T KNOW HOW TORIHIRA WAS KILLED! PROOF THAT HE'S INNOCENT!
UNLESS HE WAS PRETENDING NOT TO KNOW THE TRUTH.
BUT THERE WAS ONE PERSON WHO *DID* KNOW.
EH?

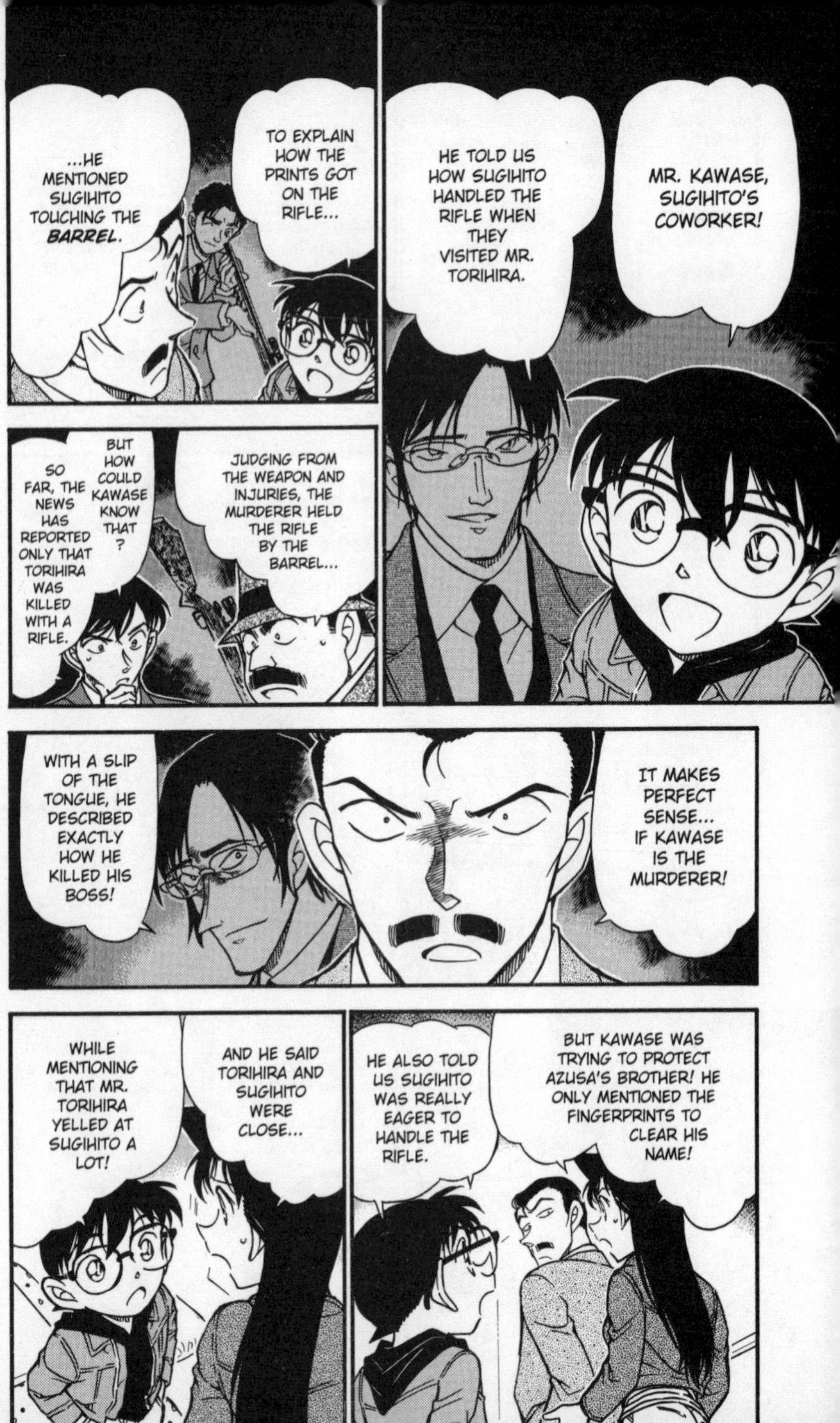
MR. KAWASE, SUGIHITO'S COWORKER!
HE TOLD US HOW SUGIHITO HANDLED THE RIFLE WHEN THEY VISITED MR. TORIHIRA.
TO EXPLAIN HOW THE PRINTS GOT ON THE RIFLE...
...HE MENTIONED SUGIHITO TOUCHING THE ***BARREL***.
JUDGING FROM THE WEAPON AND INJURIES, THE MURDERER HELD THE RIFLE BY THE BARREL...
BUT HOW COULD KAWASE KNOW THAT?
SO FAR, THE NEWS HAS REPORTED ONLY THAT TORIHIRA WAS KILLED WITH A RIFLE.
IT MAKES PERFECT SENSE... IF KAWASE IS THE MURDERER!
WITH A SLIP OF THE TONGUE, HE DESCRIBED EXACTLY HOW HE KILLED HIS BOSS!
BUT KAWASE WAS TRYING TO PROTECT AZUSA'S BROTHER! HE ONLY MENTIONED THE FINGERPRINTS TO CLEAR HIS NAME!
HE ALSO TOLD US SUGIHITO WAS REALLY EAGER TO HANDLE THE RIFLE.
AND HE SAID TORIHIRA AND SUGIHITO WERE CLOSE...
WHILE MENTIONING THAT MR. TORIHIRA YELLED AT SUGIHITO A LOT!

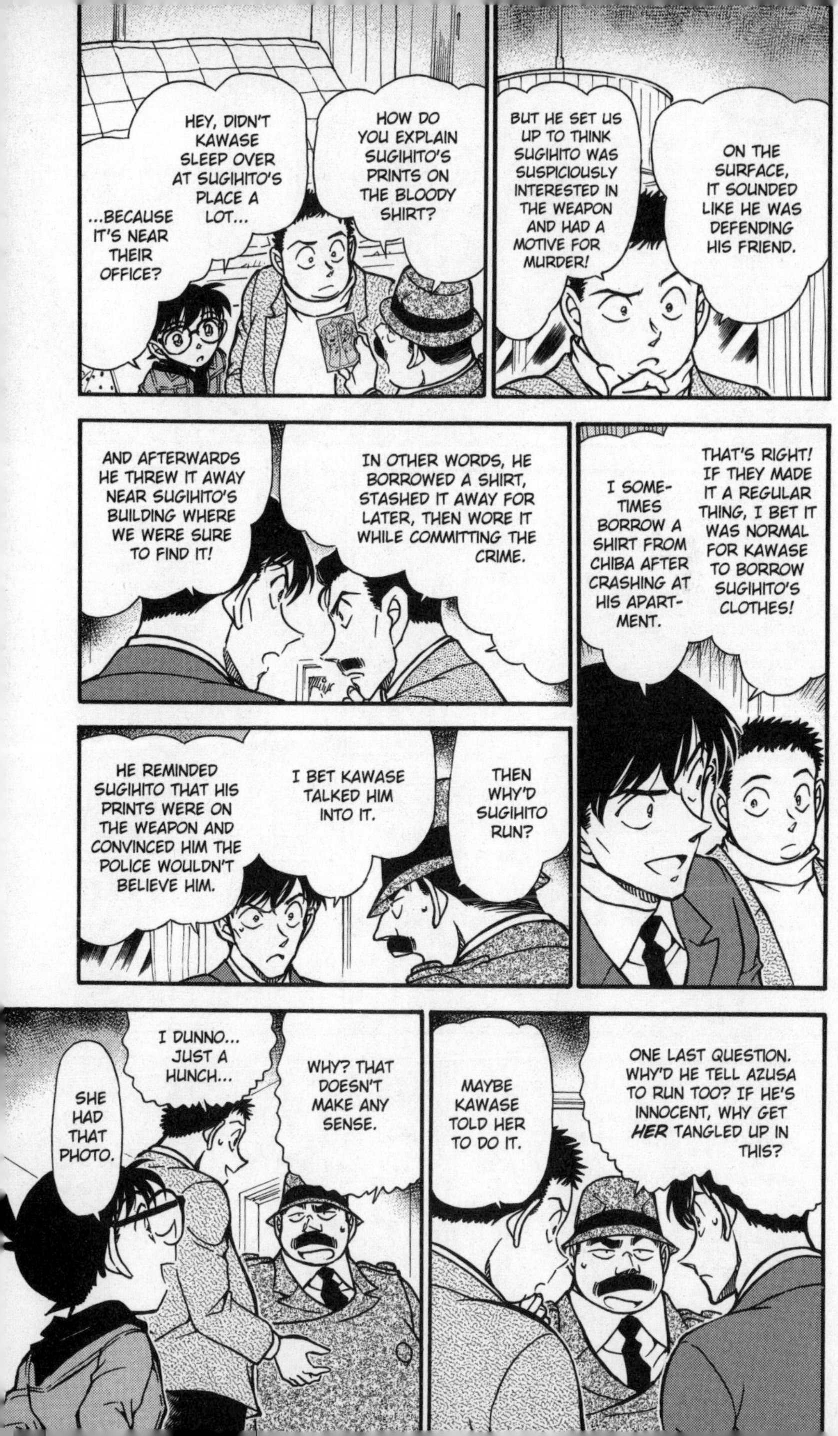
ON THE SURFACE, IT SOUNDED LIKE HE WAS DEFENDING HIS FRIEND.
BUT HE SET US UP TO THINK SUGIHITO WAS SUSPICIOUSLY INTERESTED IN THE WEAPON AND HAD A MOTIVE FOR MURDER!
HOW DO YOU EXPLAIN SUGIHITO'S PRINTS ON THE BLOODY SHIRT?
HEY, DIDN'T KAWASE SLEEP OVER AT SUGIHITO'S PLACE A LOT...
...BECAUSE IT'S NEAR THEIR OFFICE?
THAT'S RIGHT! IF THEY MADE IT A REGULAR THING, I BET IT WAS NORMAL FOR KAWASE TO BORROW SUGIHITO'S CLOTHES!
I SOMETIMES BORROW A SHIRT FROM CHIBA AFTER CRASHING AT HIS APARTMENT.
IN OTHER WORDS, HE BORROWED A SHIRT, STASHED IT AWAY FOR LATER, THEN WORE IT WHILE COMMITTING THE CRIME.
AND AFTERWARDS HE THREW IT AWAY NEAR SUGIHITO'S BUILDING WHERE WE WERE SURE TO FIND IT!
THEN WHY'D SUGIHITO RUN?
I BET KAWASE TALKED HIM INTO IT.
HE REMINDED SUGIHITO THAT HIS PRINTS WERE ON THE WEAPON AND CONVINCED HIM THE POLICE WOULDN'T BELIEVE HIM.
ONE LAST QUESTION. WHY'D HE TELL AZUSA TO RUN TOO? IF HE'S INNOCENT, WHY GET **HER** TANGLED UP IN THIS?
MAYBE KAWASE TOLD HER TO DO IT.
WHY? THAT DOESN'T MAKE ANY SENSE.
I DUNNO... JUST A HUNCH...
SHE HAD THAT PHOTO.

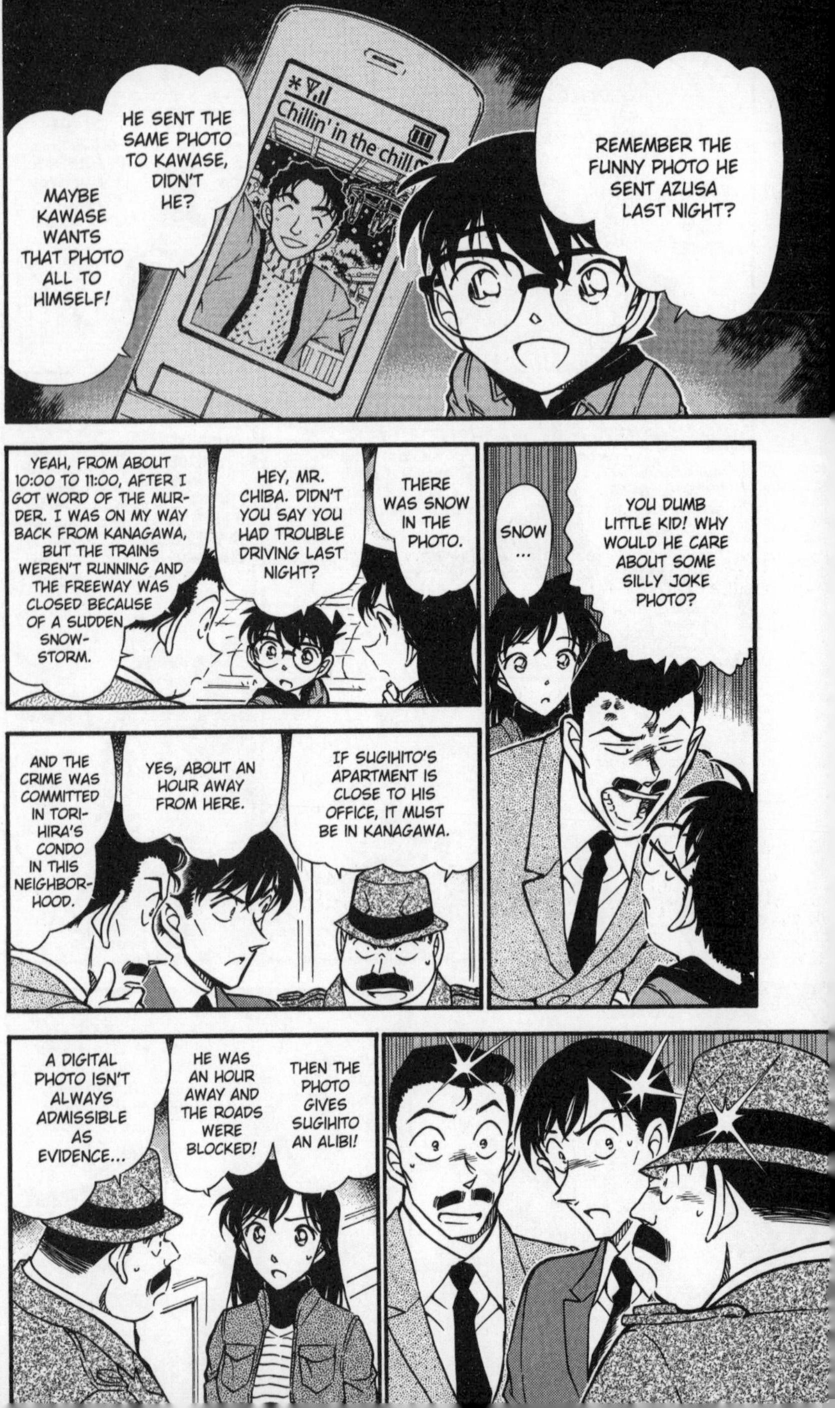
REMEMBER THE FUNNY PHOTO HE SENT AZUSA LAST NIGHT?
Chillin' in the chill
HE SENT THE SAME PHOTO TO KAWASE, DIDN'T HE?
MAYBE KAWASE WANTS THAT PHOTO ALL TO HIMSELF!
YOU DUMB LITTLE KID! WHY WOULD HE CARE ABOUT SOME SILLY JOKE PHOTO?
SNOW ...
THERE WAS SNOW IN THE PHOTO.
HEY, MR. CHIBA. DIDN'T YOU SAY YOU HAD TROUBLE DRIVING LAST NIGHT?
YEAH, FROM ABOUT 10:00 TO 11:00, AFTER I GOT WORD OF THE MURDER. I WAS ON MY WAY BACK FROM KANAGAWA, BUT THE TRAINS WEREN'T RUNNING AND THE FREEWAY WAS CLOSED BECAUSE OF A SUDDEN SNOWSTORM.
IF SUGIHITO'S APARTMENT IS CLOSE TO HIS OFFICE, IT MUST BE IN KANAGAWA.
YES, ABOUT AN HOUR AWAY FROM HERE.
AND THE CRIME WAS COMMITTED IN TORIHIRA'S CONDO IN THIS NEIGHBORHOOD.
THEN THE PHOTO GIVES SUGIHITO AN ALIBI!
HE WAS AN HOUR AWAY AND THE ROADS WERE BLOCKED!
A DIGITAL PHOTO ISN'T ALWAYS ADMISSIBLE AS EVIDENCE...

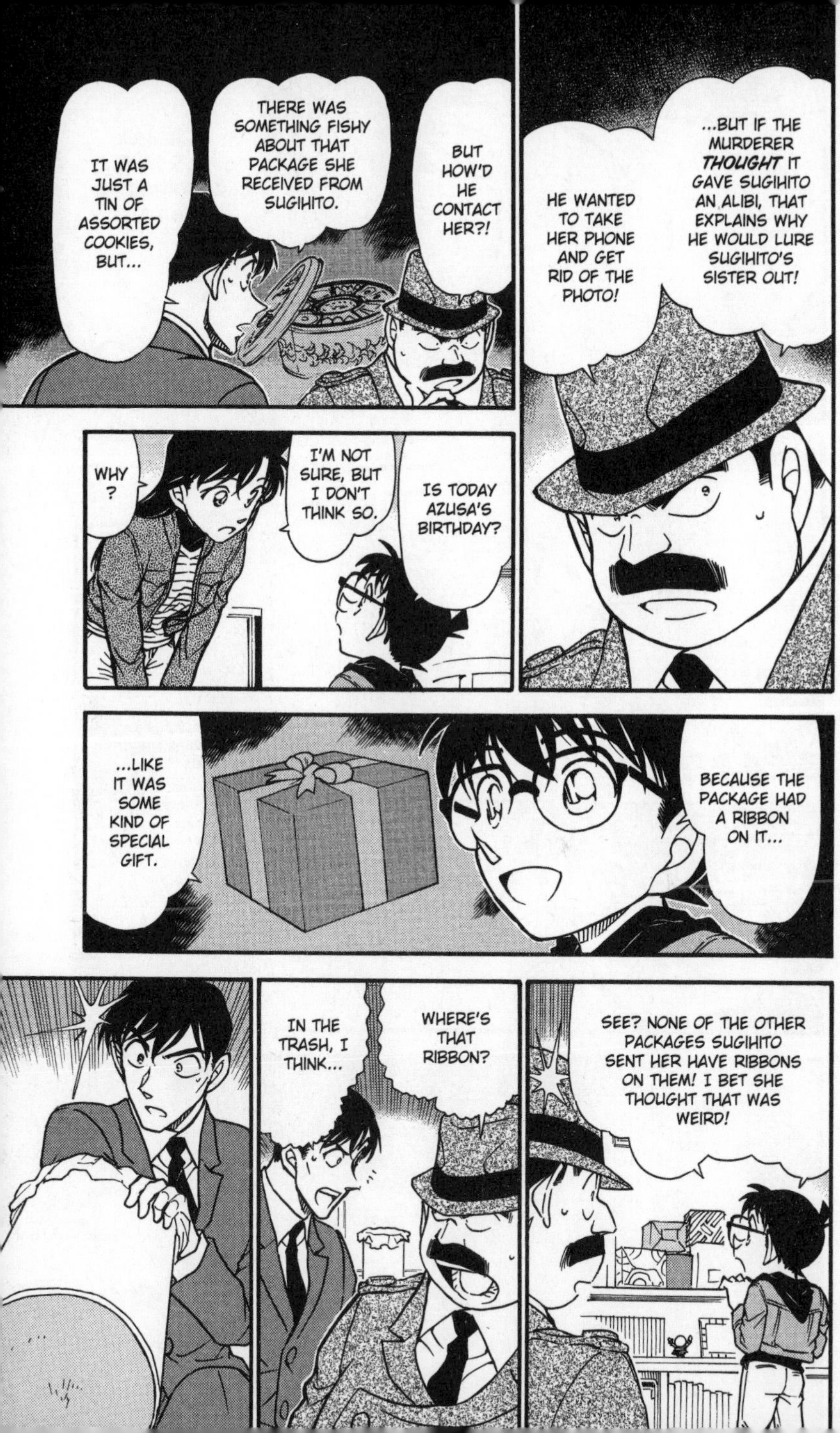
...BUT IF THE MURDERER THOUGHT IT GAVE SUGIHITO AN ALIBI, THAT EXPLAINS WHY HE WOULD LURE SUGIHITO'S SISTER OUT!
HE WANTED TO TAKE HER PHONE AND GET RID OF THE PHOTO!
BUT HOW'D HE CONTACT HER?!
THERE WAS SOMETHING FISHY ABOUT THAT PACKAGE SHE RECEIVED FROM SUGIHITO.
IT WAS JUST A TIN OF ASSORTED COOKIES, BUT...
IS TODAY AZUSA'S BIRTHDAY?
I'M NOT SURE, BUT I DON'T THINK SO.
WHY?
BECAUSE THE PACKAGE HAD A RIBBON ON IT...
...LIKE IT WAS SOME KIND OF SPECIAL GIFT.
SEE? NONE OF THE OTHER PACKAGES SUGIHITO SENT HER HAVE RIBBONS ON THEM! I BET SHE THOUGHT THAT WAS WEIRD!
WHERE'S THAT RIBBON?
IN THE TRASH, I THINK...

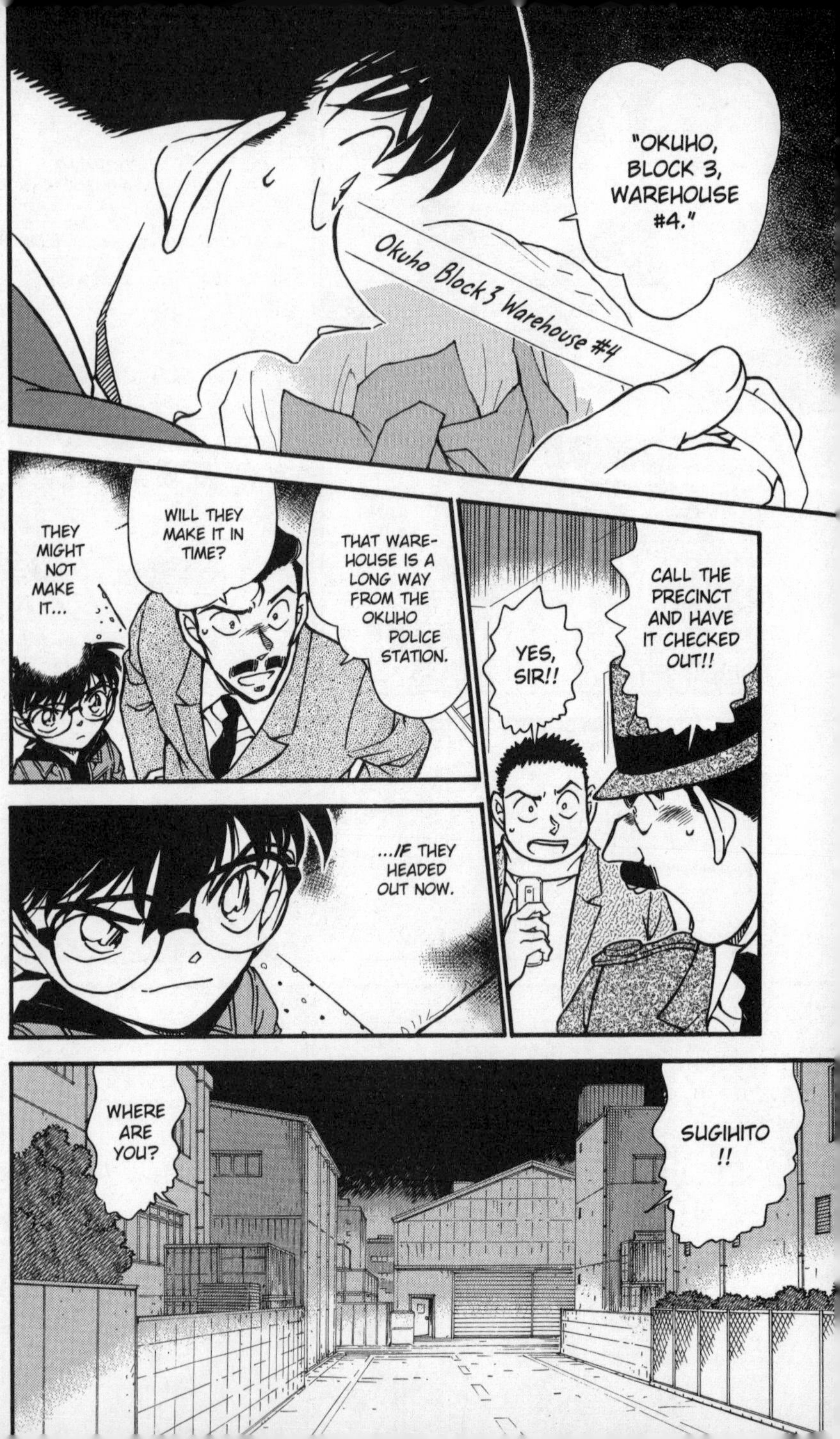
"OKUHO, BLOCK 3, WAREHOUSE #4."
Okuho Block 3 Warehouse #4
CALL THE PRECINCT AND HAVE IT CHECKED OUT!!
YES, SIR!!
THAT WARE-HOUSE IS A LONG WAY FROM THE OKUHO POLICE STATION.
WILL THEY MAKE IT IN TIME?
THEY MIGHT NOT MAKE IT...
...*IF* THEY HEADED OUT NOW.
SUGIHITO!!
WHERE ARE YOU?

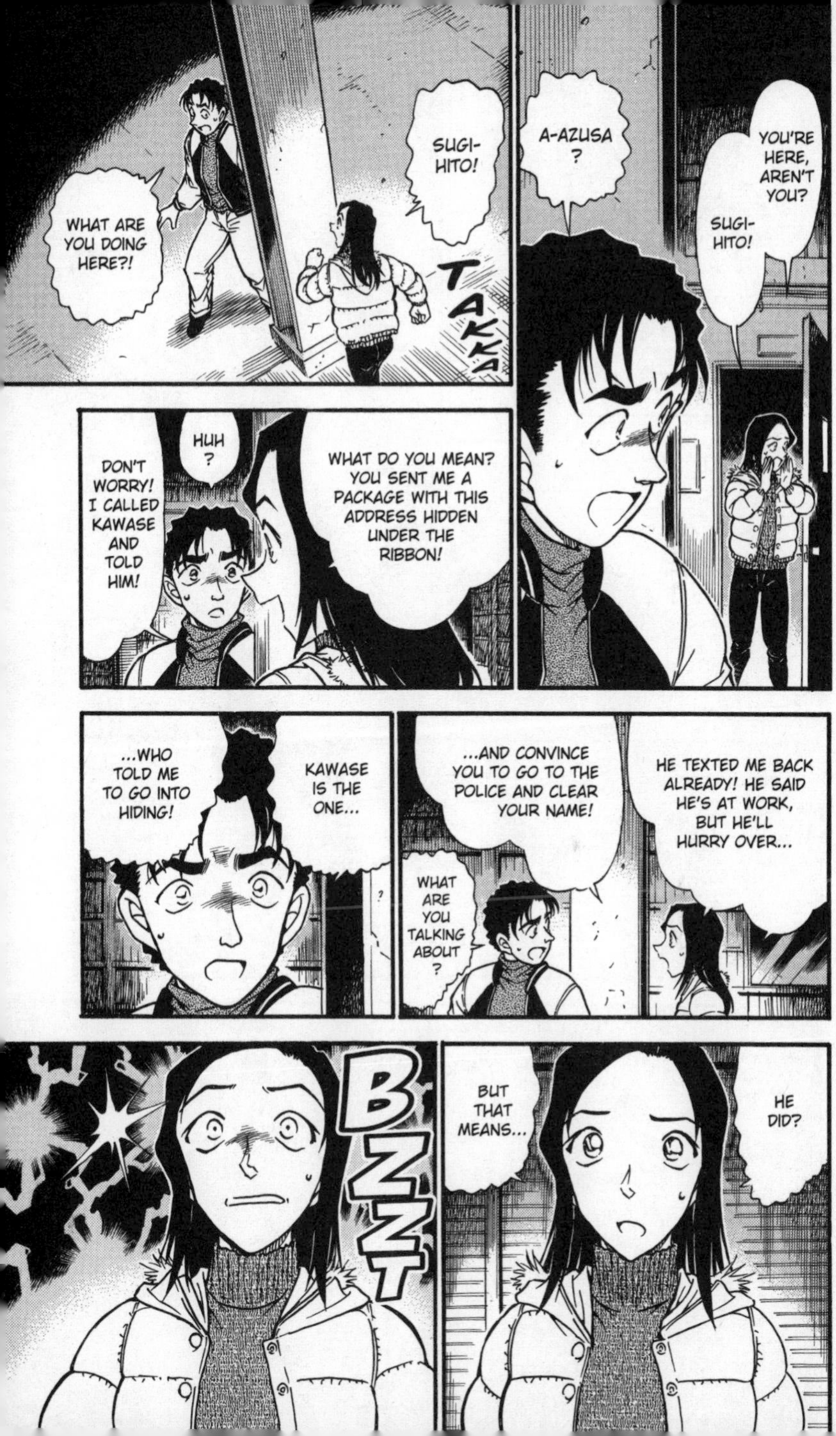
YOU'RE HERE, AREN'T YOU?
SUGI-HITO!
A-AZUSA?
SUGI-HITO!
TAKKA
WHAT ARE YOU DOING HERE?!
WHAT DO YOU MEAN? YOU SENT ME A PACKAGE WITH THIS ADDRESS HIDDEN UNDER THE RIBBON!
HUH?
DON'T WORRY! I CALLED KAWASE AND TOLD HIM!
HE TEXTED ME BACK ALREADY! HE SAID HE'S AT WORK, BUT HE'LL HURRY OVER...
...AND CONVINCE YOU TO GO TO THE POLICE AND CLEAR YOUR NAME!
WHAT ARE YOU TALKING ABOUT?
KAWASE IS THE ONE...
...WHO TOLD ME TO GO INTO HIDING!
HE DID?
BUT THAT MEANS...
BZZT

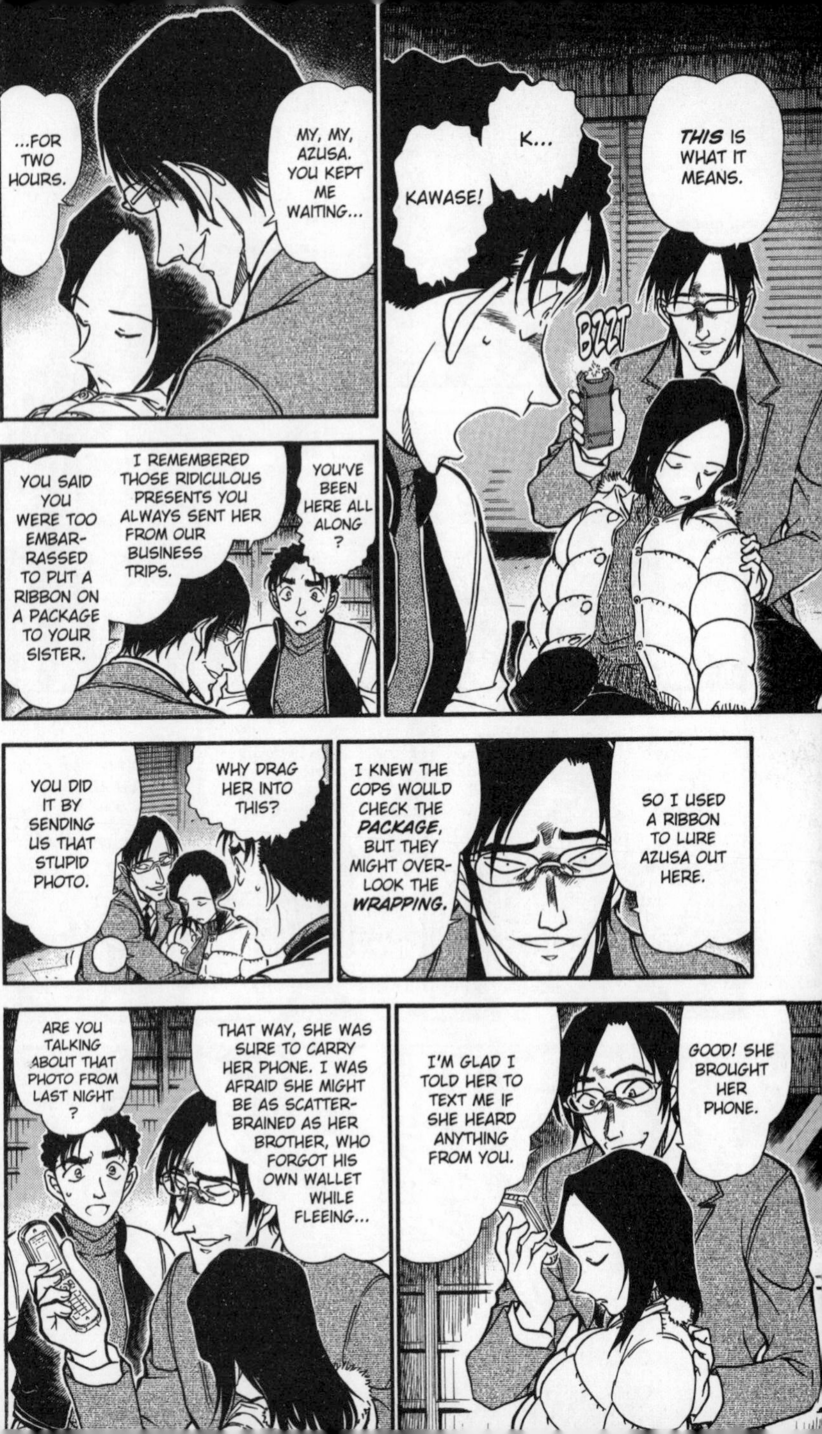
THIS IS WHAT IT MEANS.
K...
KAWASE!
BZZZT
MY, MY, AZUSA. YOU KEPT ME WAITING...
...FOR TWO HOURS.
YOU'VE BEEN HERE ALL ALONG?
I REMEMBERED THOSE RIDICULOUS PRESENTS YOU ALWAYS SENT HER FROM OUR BUSINESS TRIPS.
YOU SAID YOU WERE TOO EMBARRASSED TO PUT A RIBBON ON A PACKAGE TO YOUR SISTER.
I KNEW THE COPS WOULD CHECK THE PACKAGE, BUT THEY MIGHT OVERLOOK THE WRAPPING.
SO I USED A RIBBON TO LURE AZUSA OUT HERE.
WHY DRAG HER INTO THIS?
YOU DID IT BY SENDING US THAT STUPID PHOTO.
GOOD! SHE BROUGHT HER PHONE.
I'M GLAD I TOLD HER TO TEXT ME IF SHE HEARD ANYTHING FROM YOU.
THAT WAY, SHE WAS SURE TO CARRY HER PHONE. I WAS AFRAID SHE MIGHT BE AS SCATTERBRAINED AS HER BROTHER, WHO FORGOT HIS OWN WALLET WHILE FLEEING...
ARE YOU TALKING ABOUT THAT PHOTO FROM LAST NIGHT?

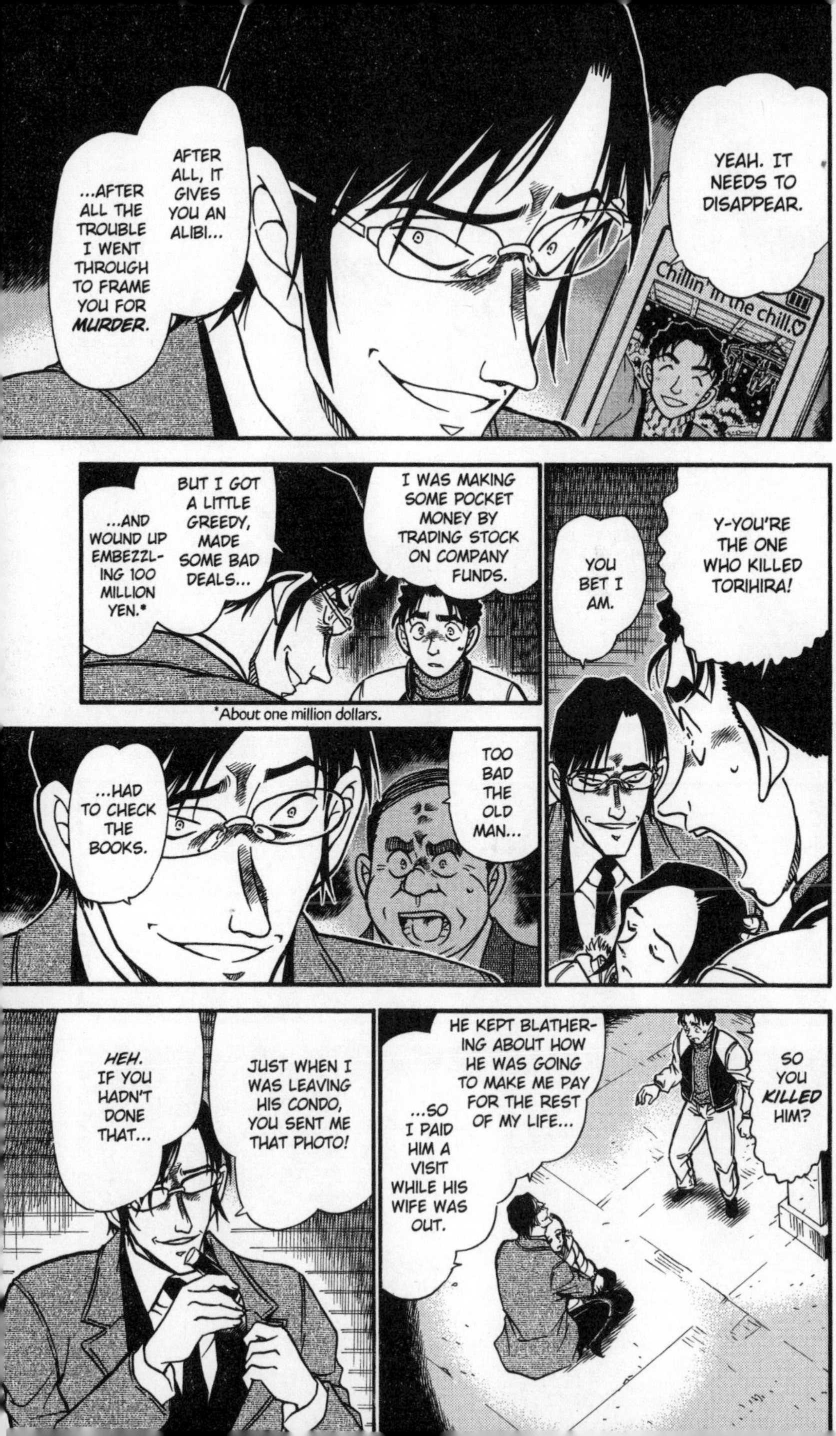
YEAH. IT NEEDS TO DISAPPEAR.
AFTER ALL, IT GIVES YOU AN ALIBI...
...AFTER ALL THE TROUBLE I WENT THROUGH TO FRAME YOU FOR **MURDER**.
Chillin' in the chill.♡
Y-YOU'RE THE ONE WHO KILLED TORIHIRA!
YOU BET I AM.
I WAS MAKING SOME POCKET MONEY BY TRADING STOCK ON COMPANY FUNDS.
BUT I GOT A LITTLE GREEDY, MADE SOME BAD DEALS...
...AND WOUND UP EMBEZZLING 100 MILLION YEN.*
*About one million dollars.
TOO BAD THE OLD MAN...
...HAD TO CHECK THE BOOKS.
SO YOU **KILLED** HIM?
HE KEPT BLATHERING ABOUT HOW HE WAS GOING TO MAKE ME PAY FOR THE REST OF MY LIFE...
...SO I PAID HIM A VISIT WHILE HIS WIFE WAS OUT.
JUST WHEN I WAS LEAVING HIS CONDO, YOU SENT ME THAT PHOTO!
HEH. IF YOU HADN'T DONE THAT...

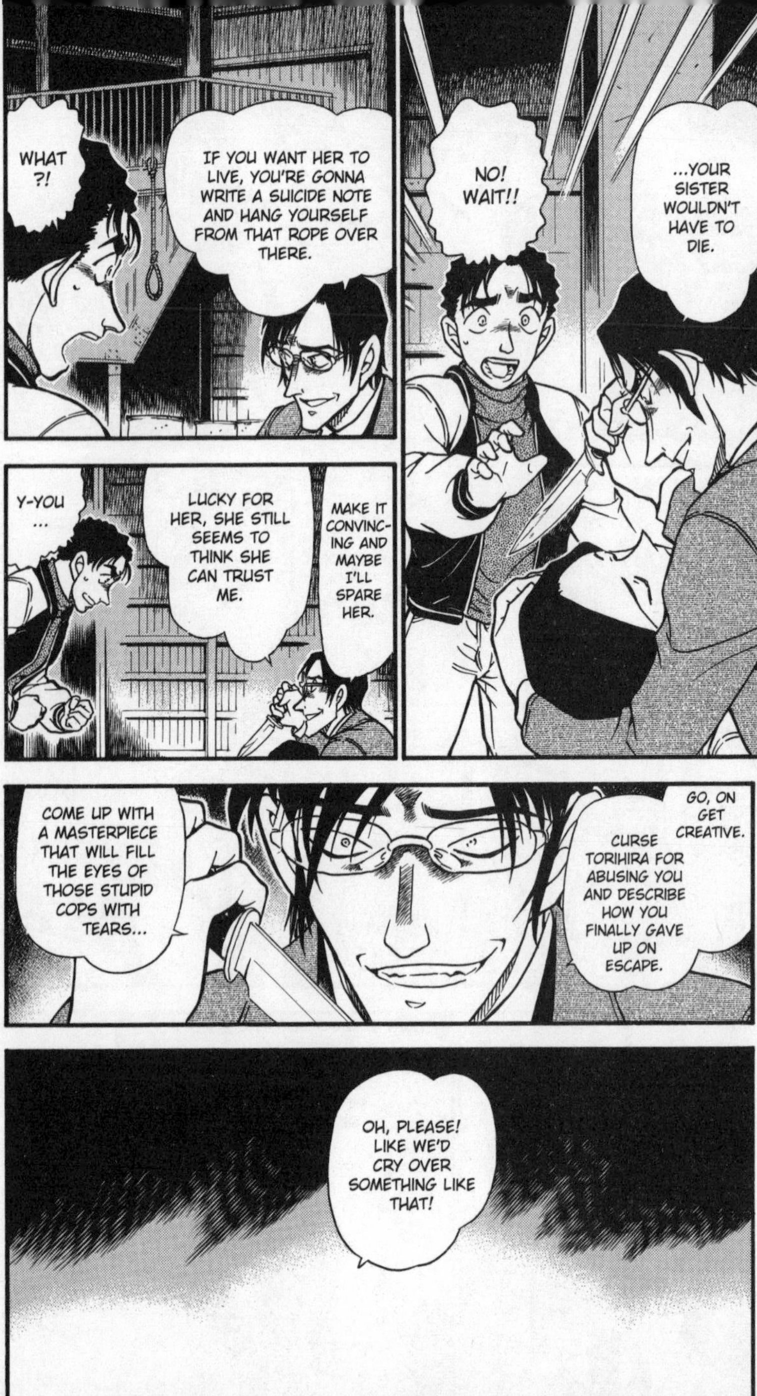
...YOUR SISTER WOULDN'T HAVE TO DIE.
NO! WAIT!!
IF YOU WANT HER TO LIVE, YOU'RE GONNA WRITE A SUICIDE NOTE AND HANG YOURSELF FROM THAT ROPE OVER THERE.
WHAT ?!
MAKE IT CONVINC-ING AND MAYBE I'LL SPARE HER.
LUCKY FOR HER, SHE STILL SEEMS TO THINK SHE CAN TRUST ME.
Y-YOU ...
GO, ON GET CREATIVE.
CURSE TORIHIRA FOR ABUSING YOU AND DESCRIBE HOW YOU FINALLY GAVE UP ON ESCAPE.
COME UP WITH A MASTERPIECE THAT WILL FILL THE EYES OF THOSE STUPID COPS WITH TEARS...
OH, PLEASE! LIKE WE'D CRY OVER SOMETHING LIKE THAT!

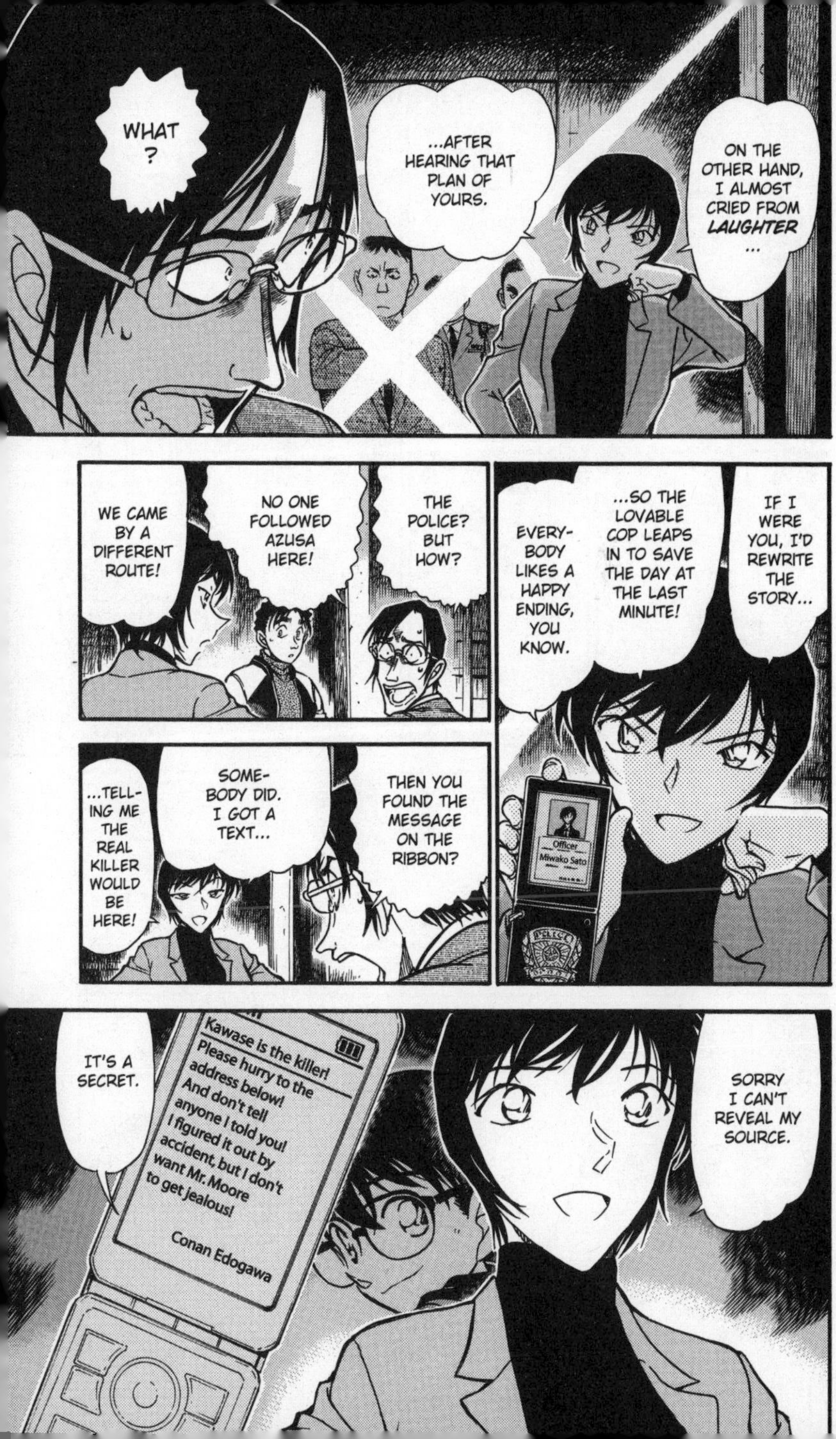
ON THE OTHER HAND, I ALMOST CRIED FROM *LAUGHTER* ...
...AFTER HEARING THAT PLAN OF YOURS.
WHAT ?
IF I WERE YOU, I'D REWRITE THE STORY...
...SO THE LOVABLE COP LEAPS IN TO SAVE THE DAY AT THE LAST MINUTE!
EVERY-BODY LIKES A HAPPY ENDING, YOU KNOW.
Officer
Miwako Sato
THE POLICE? BUT HOW?
NO ONE FOLLOWED AZUSA HERE!
WE CAME BY A DIFFERENT ROUTE!
THEN YOU FOUND THE MESSAGE ON THE RIBBON?
SOME-BODY DID. I GOT A TEXT...
...TELL-ING ME THE REAL KILLER WOULD BE HERE!
SORRY I CAN'T REVEAL MY SOURCE.
Kawase is the killer! Please hurry to the address below! And don't tell anyone I told you! I figured it out by accident, but I don't want Mr. Moore to get jealous!
Conan Edogawa
IT'S A SECRET.

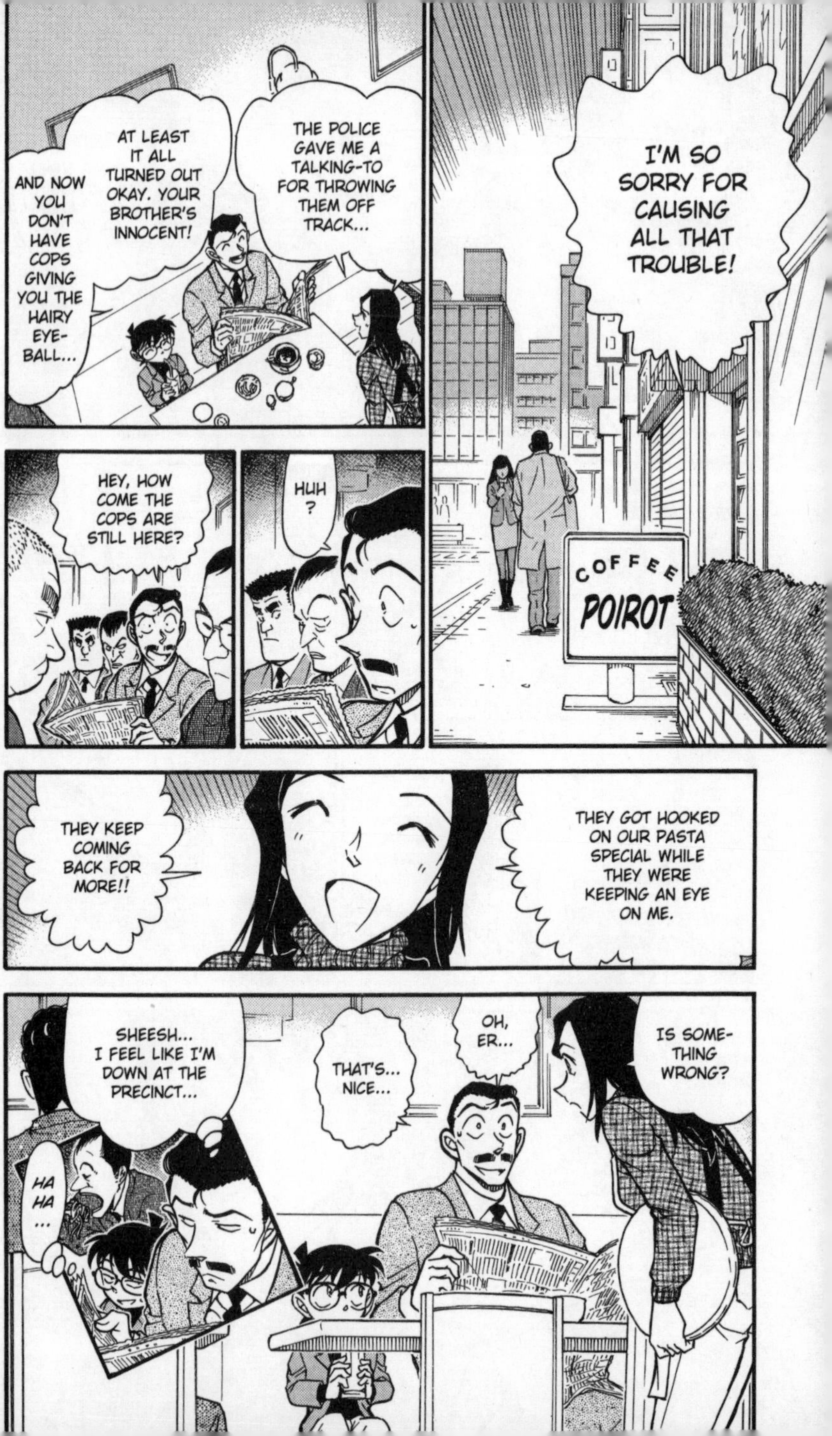
I'M SO SORRY FOR CAUSING ALL THAT TROUBLE!
COFFEE POIROT
THE POLICE GAVE ME A TALKING-TO FOR THROWING THEM OFF TRACK...
AT LEAST IT ALL TURNED OUT OKAY. YOUR BROTHER'S INNOCENT!
AND NOW YOU DON'T HAVE COPS GIVING YOU THE HAIRY EYE-BALL...
HUH?
HEY, HOW COME THE COPS ARE STILL HERE?
THEY GOT HOOKED ON OUR PASTA SPECIAL WHILE THEY WERE KEEPING AN EYE ON ME.
THEY KEEP COMING BACK FOR MORE!!
IS SOME-THING WRONG?
OH, ER...
THAT'S... NICE...
SHEESH... I FEEL LIKE I'M DOWN AT THE PRECINCT...
HA HA ...

FILE 2: THE WINGS OF ICARUS

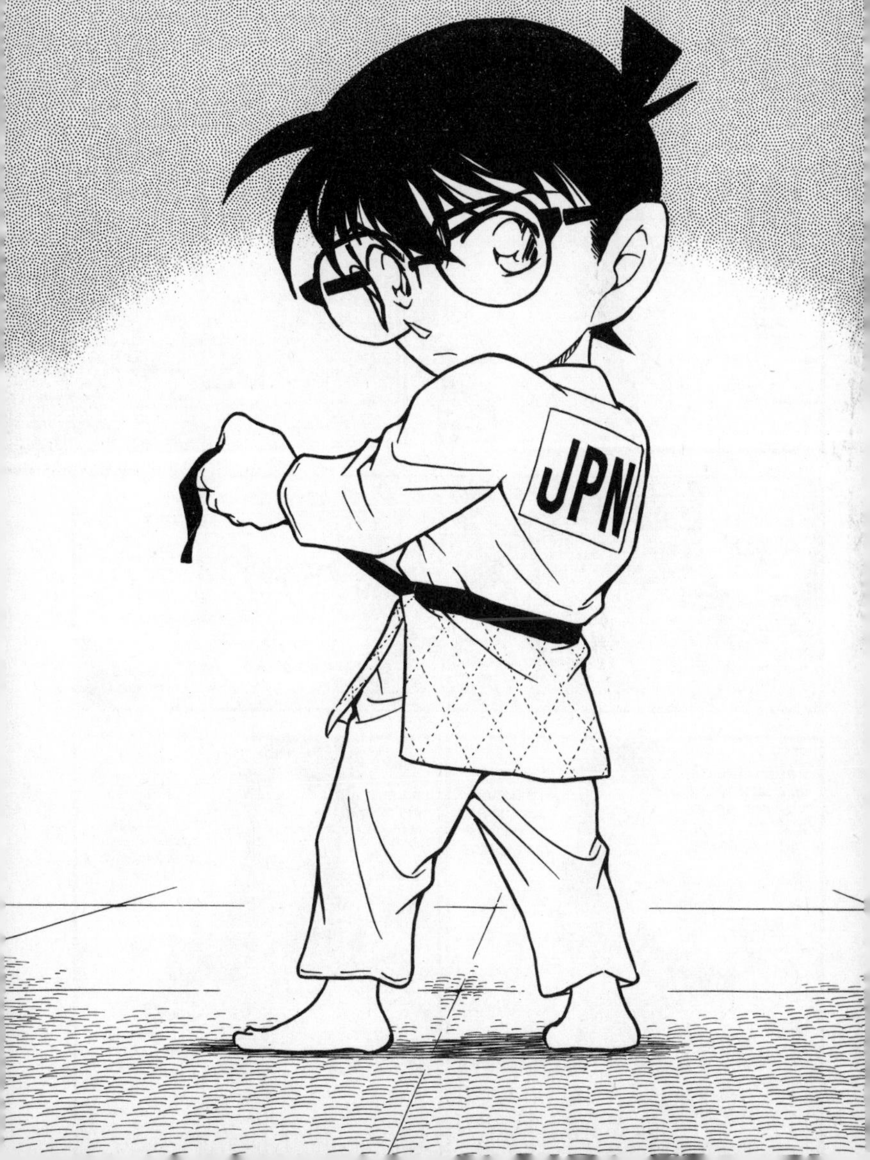
JPN

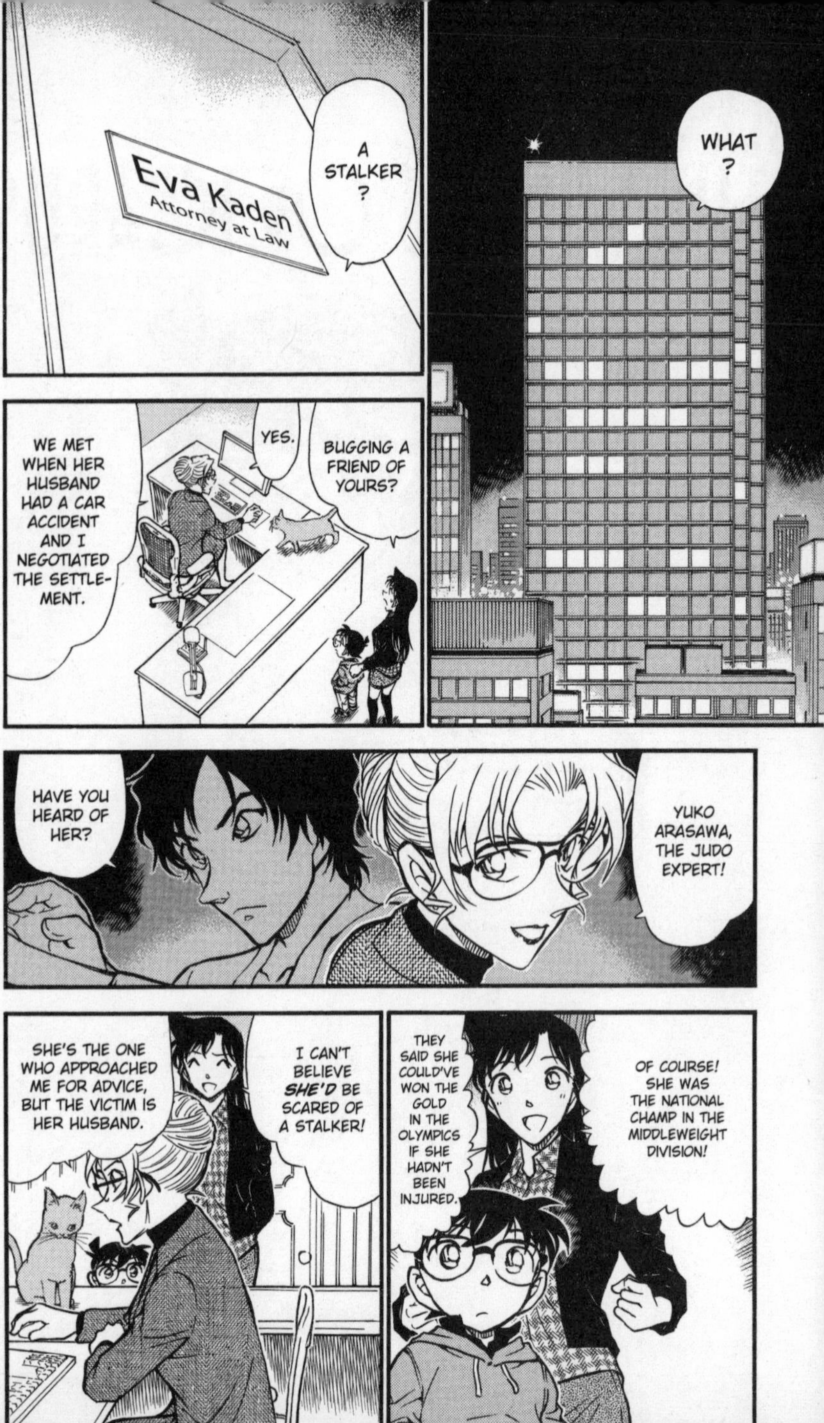
WHAT?
Eva Kaden
Attorney at Law
A STALKER?
BUGGING A FRIEND OF YOURS?
YES.
WE MET WHEN HER HUSBAND HAD A CAR ACCIDENT AND I NEGOTIATED THE SETTLEMENT.
YUKO ARASAWA, THE JUDO EXPERT!
HAVE YOU HEARD OF HER?
OF COURSE! SHE WAS THE NATIONAL CHAMP IN THE MIDDLEWEIGHT DIVISION!
THEY SAID SHE COULD'VE WON THE GOLD IN THE OLYMPICS IF SHE HADN'T BEEN INJURED.
I CAN'T BELIEVE *SHE'D* BE SCARED OF A STALKER!
SHE'S THE ONE WHO APPROACHED ME FOR ADVICE, BUT THE VICTIM IS HER HUSBAND.

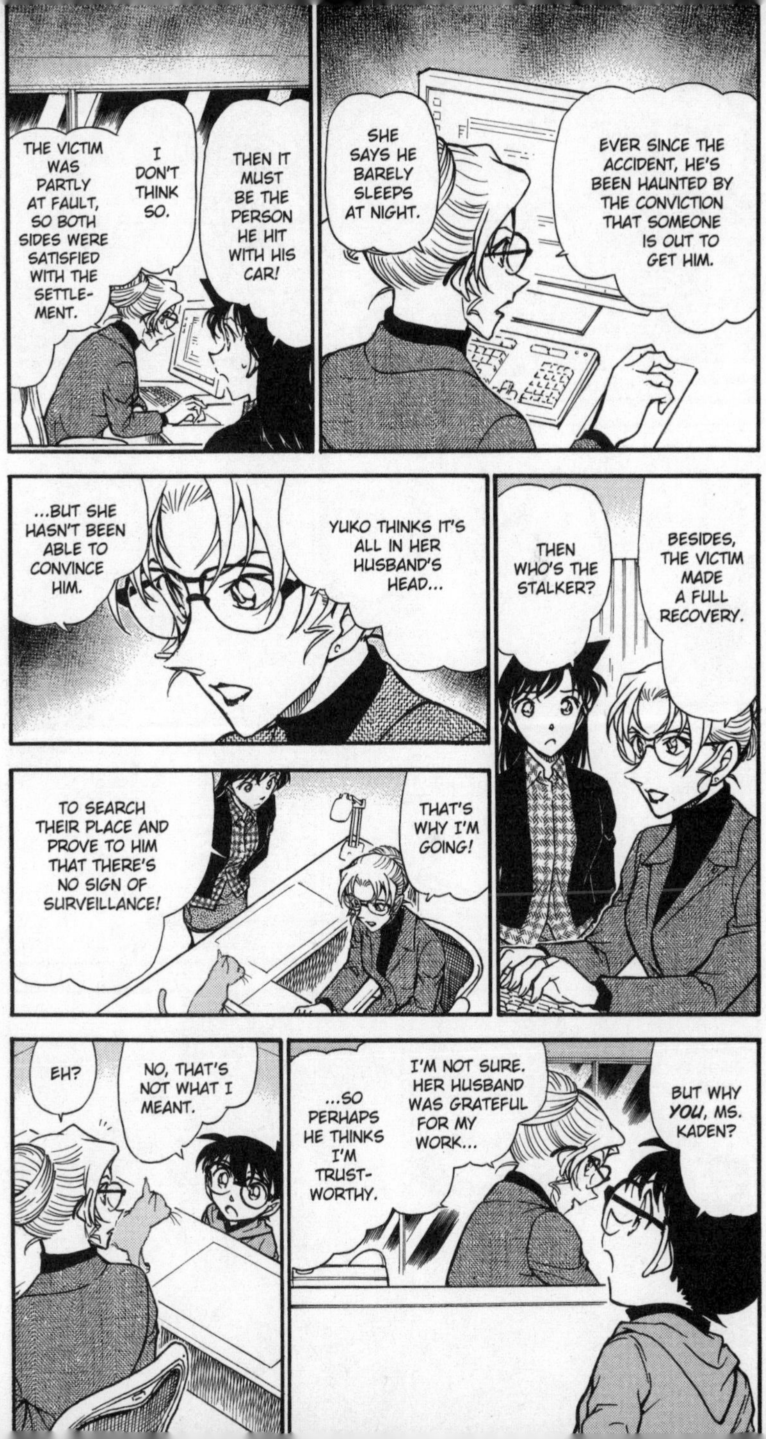
EVER SINCE THE ACCIDENT, HE'S BEEN HAUNTED BY THE CONVICTION THAT SOMEONE IS OUT TO GET HIM.
SHE SAYS HE BARELY SLEEPS AT NIGHT.
THEN IT MUST BE THE PERSON HE HIT WITH HIS CAR!
I DON'T THINK SO.
THE VICTIM WAS PARTLY AT FAULT, SO BOTH SIDES WERE SATISFIED WITH THE SETTLEMENT.
BESIDES, THE VICTIM MADE A FULL RECOVERY.
THEN WHO'S THE STALKER?
YUKO THINKS IT'S ALL IN HER HUSBAND'S HEAD...
...BUT SHE HASN'T BEEN ABLE TO CONVINCE HIM.
THAT'S WHY I'M GOING!
TO SEARCH THEIR PLACE AND PROVE TO HIM THAT THERE'S NO SIGN OF SURVEILLANCE!
BUT WHY *YOU*, MS. KADEN?
I'M NOT SURE. HER HUSBAND WAS GRATEFUL FOR MY WORK...
...SO PERHAPS HE THINKS I'M TRUST-WORTHY.
NO, THAT'S NOT WHAT I MEANT.
EH?

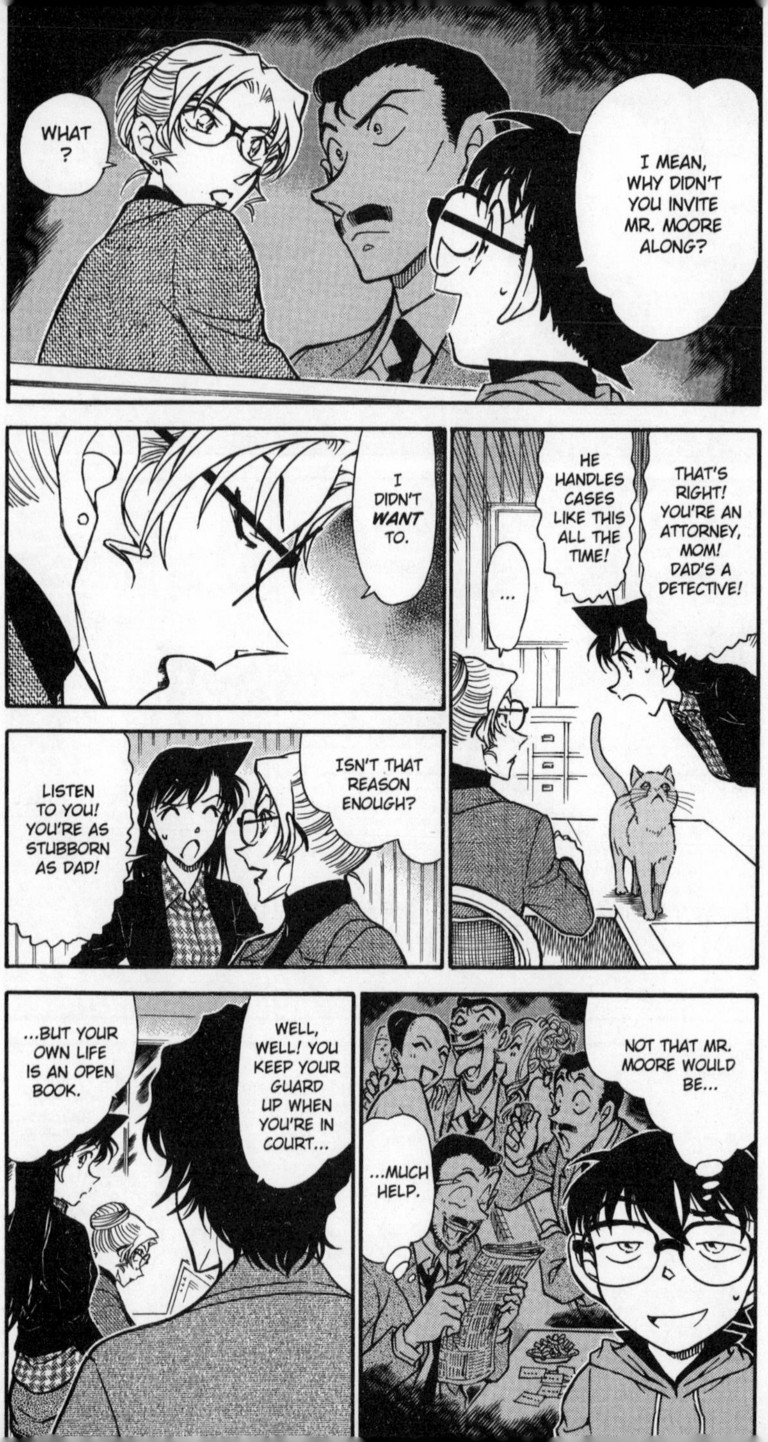
I MEAN, WHY DIDN'T YOU INVITE MR. MOORE ALONG?
WHAT?
THAT'S RIGHT! YOU'RE AN ATTORNEY, MOM! DAD'S A DETECTIVE!
HE HANDLES CASES LIKE THIS ALL THE TIME!
...
I DIDN'T *WANT* TO.
ISN'T THAT REASON ENOUGH?
LISTEN TO YOU! YOU'RE AS STUBBORN AS DAD!
NOT THAT MR. MOORE WOULD BE...
...MUCH HELP.
WELL, WELL! YOU KEEP YOUR GUARD UP WHEN YOU'RE IN COURT...
...BUT YOUR OWN LIFE IS AN OPEN BOOK.

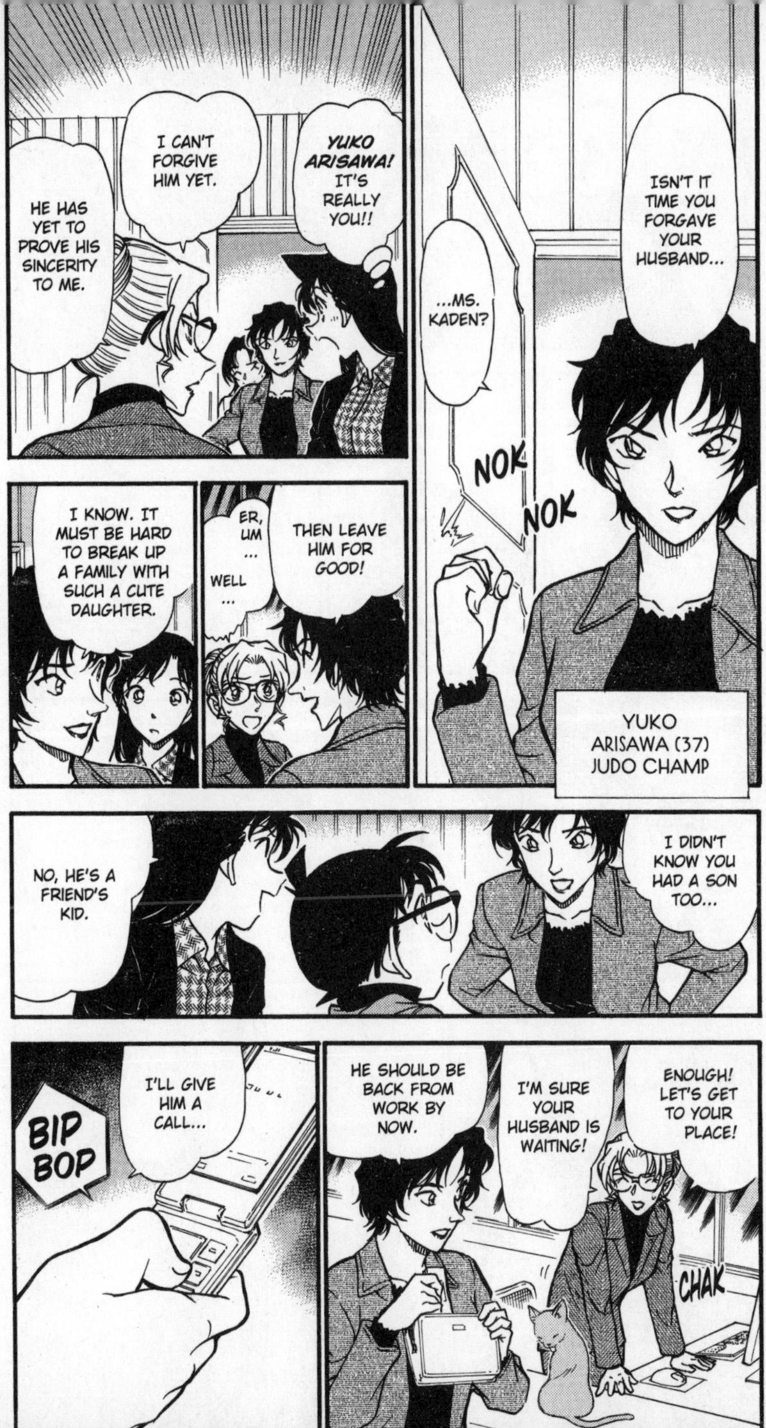
ISN'T IT TIME YOU FORGAVE YOUR HUSBAND...
...MS. KADEN?
NOK
NOK
YUKO ARISAWA (37) JUDO CHAMP
YUKO ARISAWA! IT'S REALLY YOU!!
I CAN'T FORGIVE HIM YET.
HE HAS YET TO PROVE HIS SINCERITY TO ME.
THEN LEAVE HIM FOR GOOD!
ER, UM ... WELL ...
I KNOW. IT MUST BE HARD TO BREAK UP A FAMILY WITH SUCH A CUTE DAUGHTER.
I DIDN'T KNOW YOU HAD A SON TOO...
NO, HE'S A FRIEND'S KID.
ENOUGH! LET'S GET TO YOUR PLACE!
I'M SURE YOUR HUSBAND IS WAITING!
HE SHOULD BE BACK FROM WORK BY NOW.
CHAK
I'LL GIVE HIM A CALL...
BIP BOP

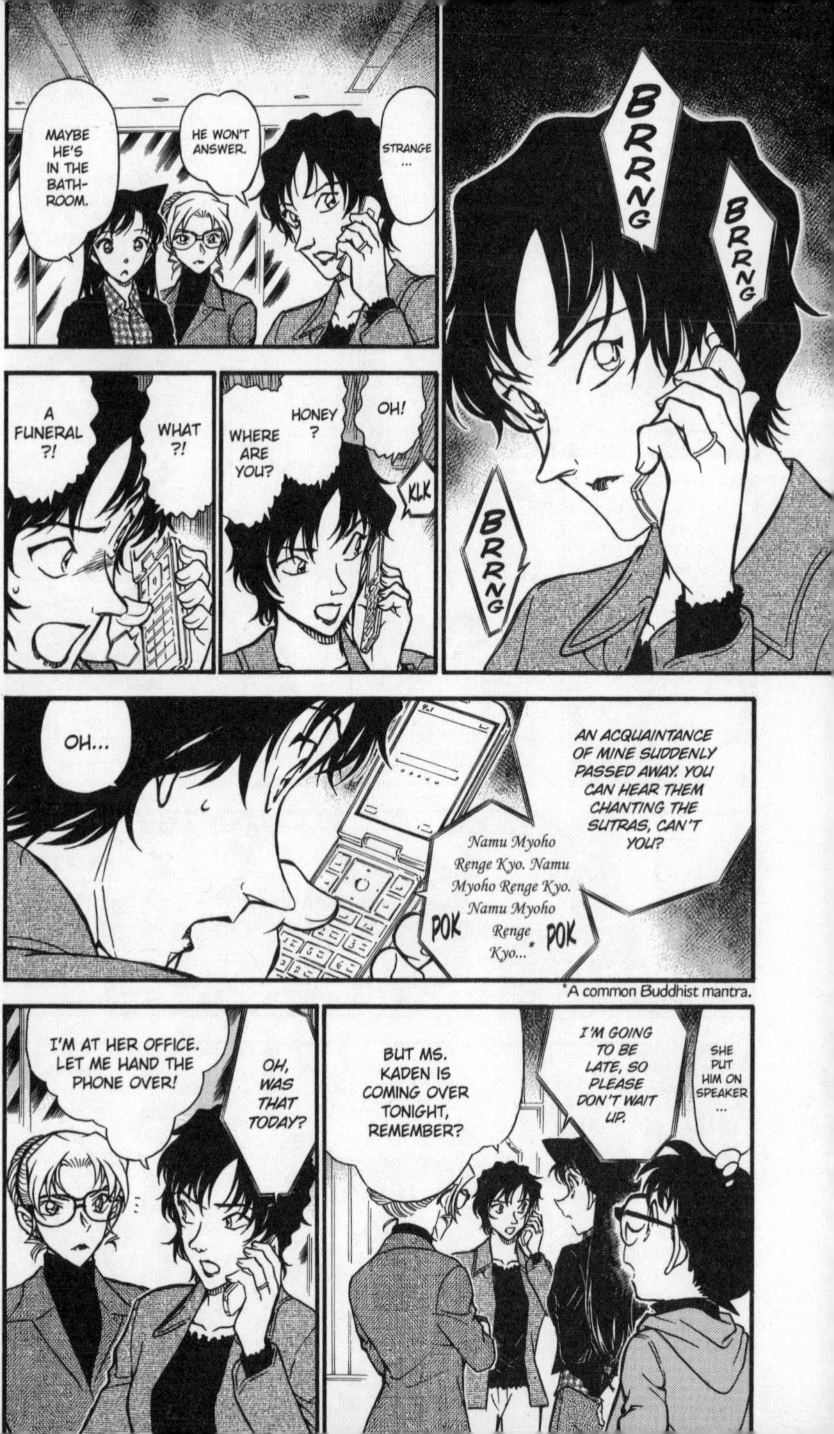
BRRNG
BRRNG
BRRNG
STRANGE ...
HE WON'T ANSWER.
MAYBE HE'S IN THE BATH-ROOM.
KLK
OH!
HONEY ?
WHERE ARE YOU?
WHAT ?!
A FUNERAL ?!
AN ACQUAINTANCE OF MINE SUDDENLY PASSED AWAY. YOU CAN HEAR THEM CHANTING THE SUTRAS, CAN'T YOU?
Namu Myoho Renge Kyo. Namu Myoho Renge Kyo. Namu Myoho Renge Kyo...*
POK
POK
OH...
*A common Buddhist mantra.
SHE PUT HIM ON SPEAKER ...
I'M GOING TO BE LATE, SO PLEASE DON'T WAIT UP.
BUT MS. KADEN IS COMING OVER TONIGHT, REMEMBER?
OH, WAS THAT TODAY?
I'M AT HER OFFICE. LET ME HAND THE PHONE OVER!

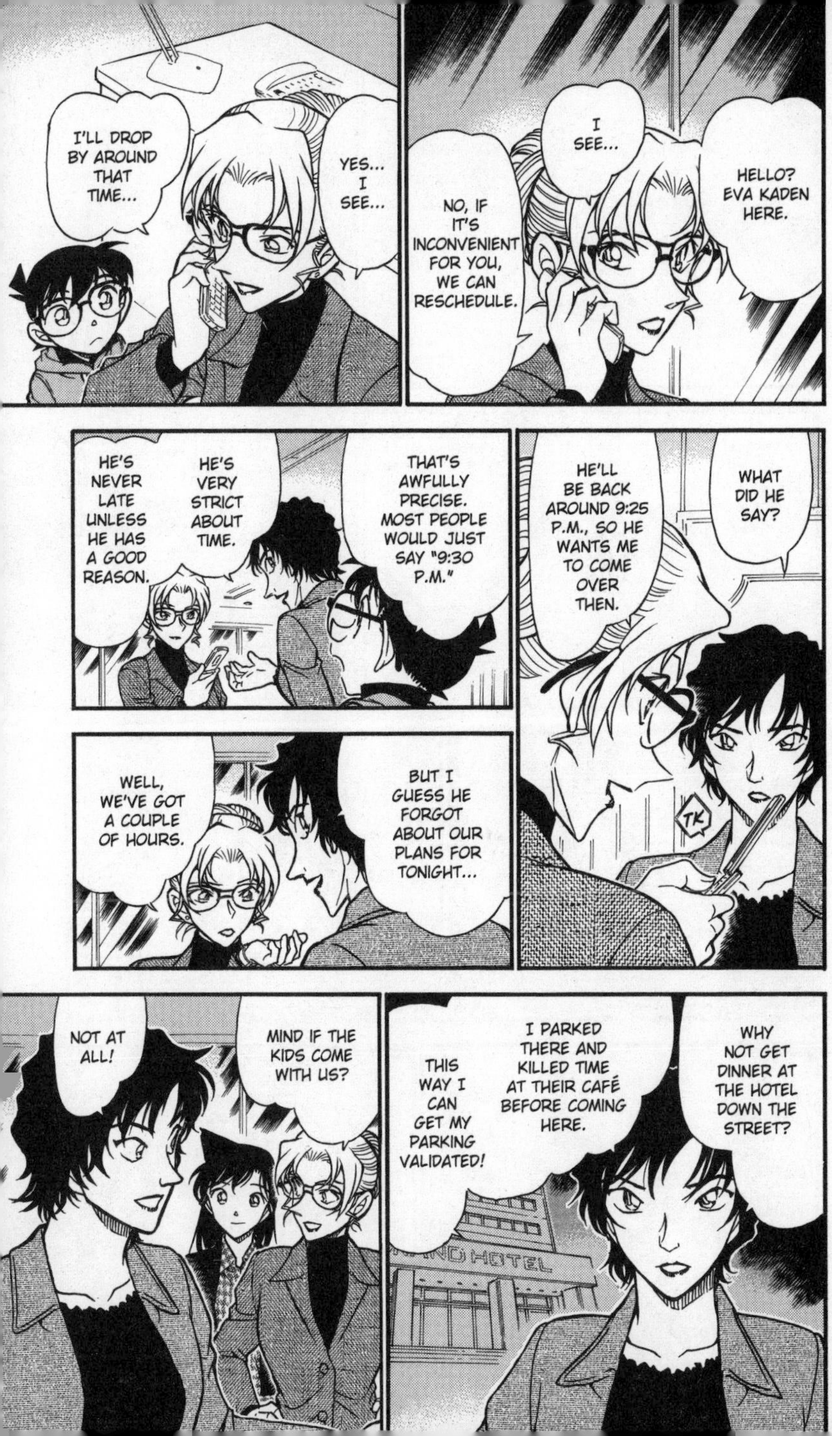
HELLO? EVA KADEN HERE.
I SEE...
NO, IF IT'S INCONVENIENT FOR YOU, WE CAN RESCHEDULE.
YES... I SEE...
I'LL DROP BY AROUND THAT TIME...
WHAT DID HE SAY?
HE'LL BE BACK AROUND 9:25 P.M., SO HE WANTS ME TO COME OVER THEN.
TK
THAT'S AWFULLY PRECISE. MOST PEOPLE WOULD JUST SAY "9:30 P.M."
HE'S VERY STRICT ABOUT TIME.
HE'S NEVER LATE UNLESS HE HAS A GOOD REASON.
BUT I GUESS HE FORGOT ABOUT OUR PLANS FOR TONIGHT...
WELL, WE'VE GOT A COUPLE OF HOURS.
WHY NOT GET DINNER AT THE HOTEL DOWN THE STREET?
I PARKED THERE AND KILLED TIME AT THEIR CAFÉ BEFORE COMING HERE.
THIS WAY I CAN GET MY PARKING VALIDATED!
MIND IF THE KIDS COME WITH US?
NOT AT ALL!

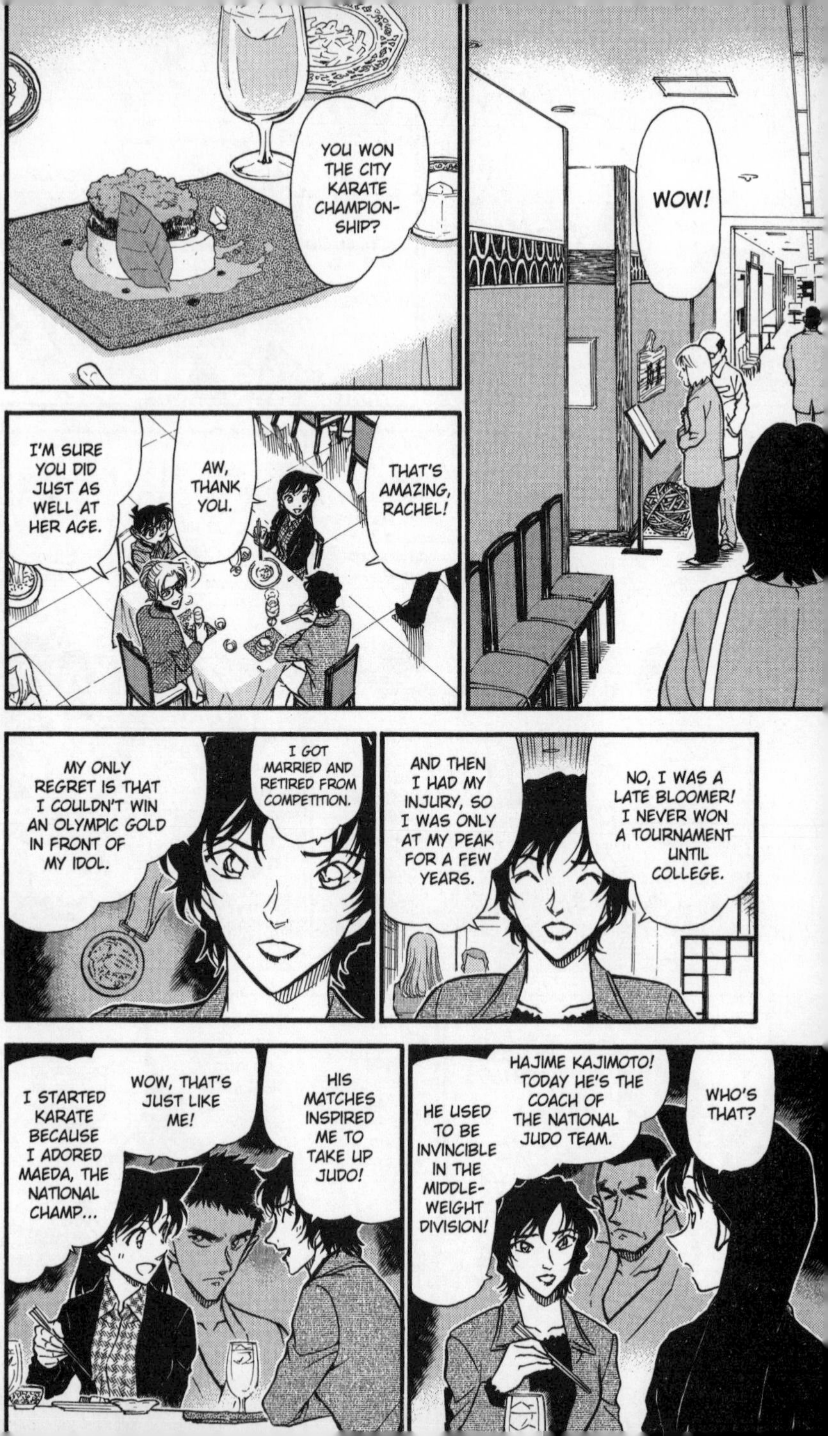
WOW!
YOU WON THE CITY KARATE CHAMPIONSHIP?
THAT'S AMAZING, RACHEL!
AW, THANK YOU.
I'M SURE YOU DID JUST AS WELL AT HER AGE.
NO, I WAS A LATE BLOOMER! I NEVER WON A TOURNAMENT UNTIL COLLEGE.
AND THEN I HAD MY INJURY, SO I WAS ONLY AT MY PEAK FOR A FEW YEARS.
I GOT MARRIED AND RETIRED FROM COMPETITION.
MY ONLY REGRET IS THAT I COULDN'T WIN AN OLYMPIC GOLD IN FRONT OF MY IDOL.
WHO'S THAT?
HAJIME KAJIMOTO! TODAY HE'S THE COACH OF THE NATIONAL JUDO TEAM.
HE USED TO BE INVINCIBLE IN THE MIDDLE-WEIGHT DIVISION!
HIS MATCHES INSPIRED ME TO TAKE UP JUDO!
WOW, THAT'S JUST LIKE ME!
I STARTED KARATE BECAUSE I ADORED MAEDA, THE NATIONAL CHAMP...

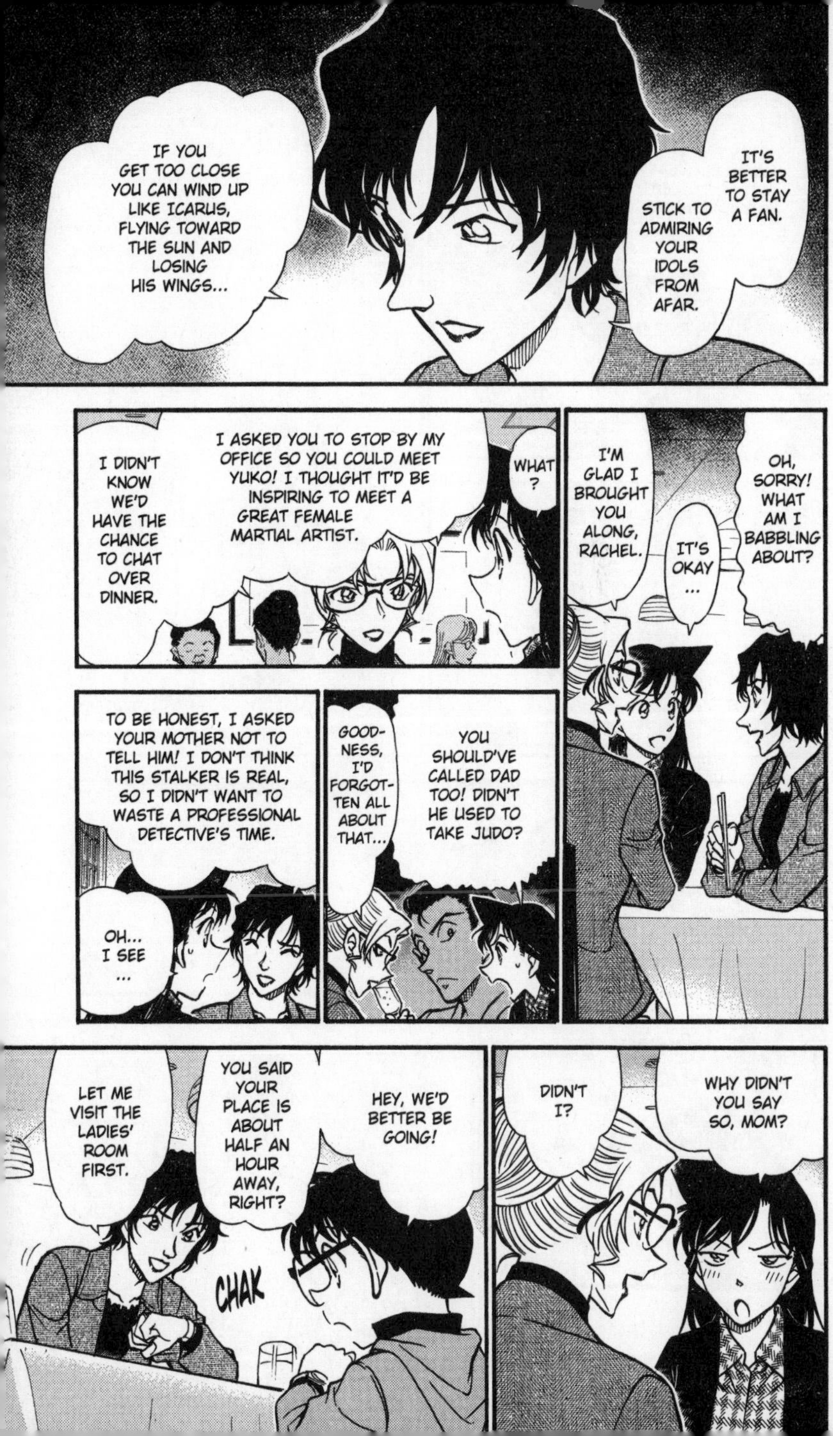
IT'S BETTER TO STAY A FAN.
STICK TO ADMIRING YOUR IDOLS FROM AFAR.
IF YOU GET TOO CLOSE YOU CAN WIND UP LIKE ICARUS, FLYING TOWARD THE SUN AND LOSING HIS WINGS...
OH, SORRY! WHAT AM I BABBLING ABOUT?
IT'S OKAY...
I'M GLAD I BROUGHT YOU ALONG, RACHEL.
WHAT?
I ASKED YOU TO STOP BY MY OFFICE SO YOU COULD MEET YUKO! I THOUGHT IT'D BE INSPIRING TO MEET A GREAT FEMALE MARTIAL ARTIST.
I DIDN'T KNOW WE'D HAVE THE CHANCE TO CHAT OVER DINNER.
YOU SHOULD'VE CALLED DAD TOO! DIDN'T HE USED TO TAKE JUDO?
GOODNESS, I'D FORGOTTEN ALL ABOUT THAT...
TO BE HONEST, I ASKED YOUR MOTHER NOT TO TELL HIM! I DON'T THINK THIS STALKER IS REAL, SO I DIDN'T WANT TO WASTE A PROFESSIONAL DETECTIVE'S TIME.
OH... I SEE...
WHY DIDN'T YOU SAY SO, MOM?
DIDN'T I?
HEY, WE'D BETTER BE GOING!
YOU SAID YOUR PLACE IS ABOUT HALF AN HOUR AWAY, RIGHT?
CHAK
LET ME VISIT THE LADIES' ROOM FIRST.

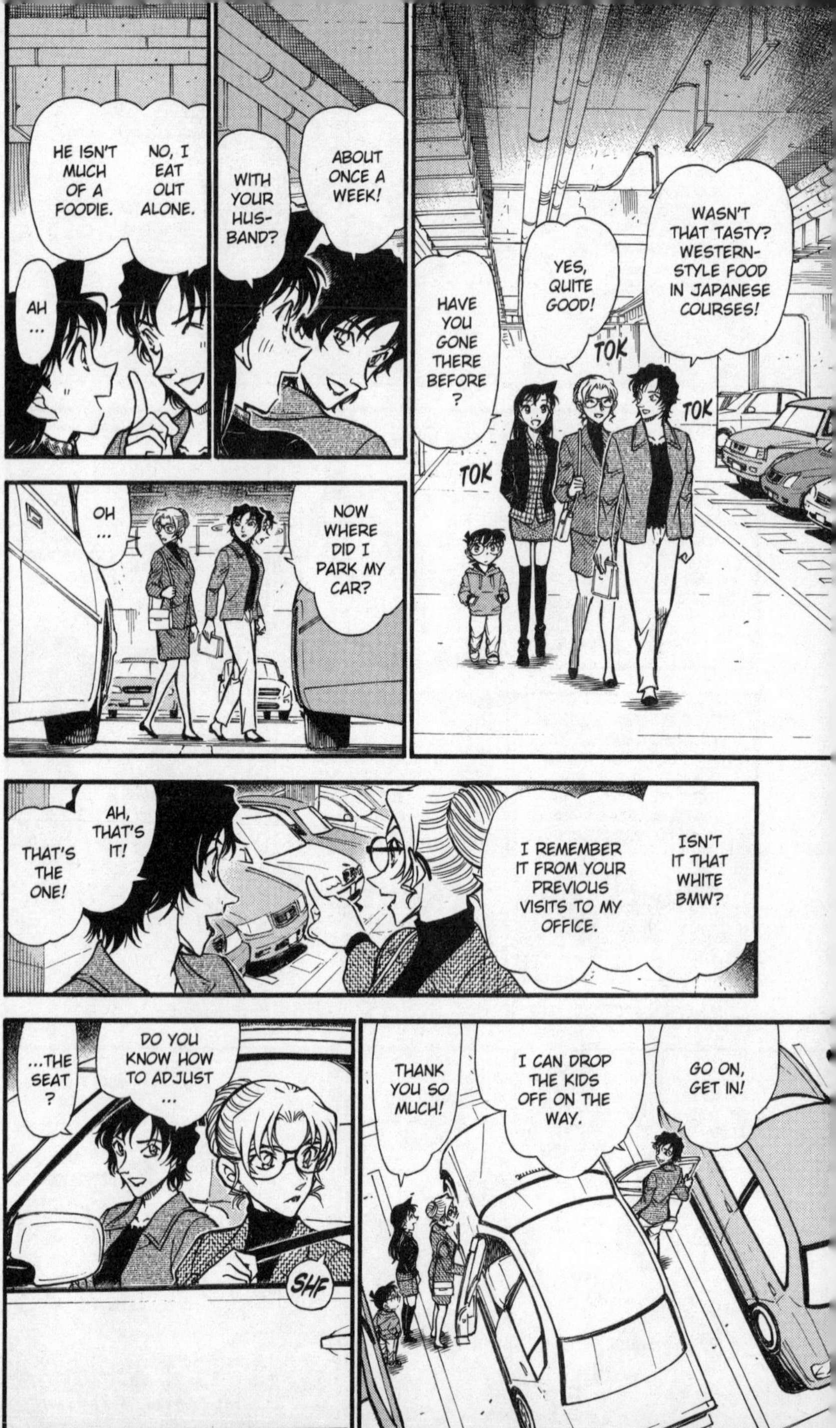
WASN'T THAT TASTY? WESTERN-STYLE FOOD IN JAPANESE COURSES!
YES, QUITE GOOD!
TOK
TOK
HAVE YOU GONE THERE BEFORE?
TOK
ABOUT ONCE A WEEK!
WITH YOUR HUS-BAND?
NO, I EAT OUT ALONE.
HE ISN'T MUCH OF A FOODIE.
AH ...
NOW WHERE DID I PARK MY CAR?
OH ...
ISN'T IT THAT WHITE BMW?
I REMEMBER IT FROM YOUR PREVIOUS VISITS TO MY OFFICE.
AH, THAT'S IT!
THAT'S THE ONE!
GO ON, GET IN!
I CAN DROP THE KIDS OFF ON THE WAY.
THANK YOU SO MUCH!
DO YOU KNOW HOW TO ADJUST ...
...THE SEAT?
SHF

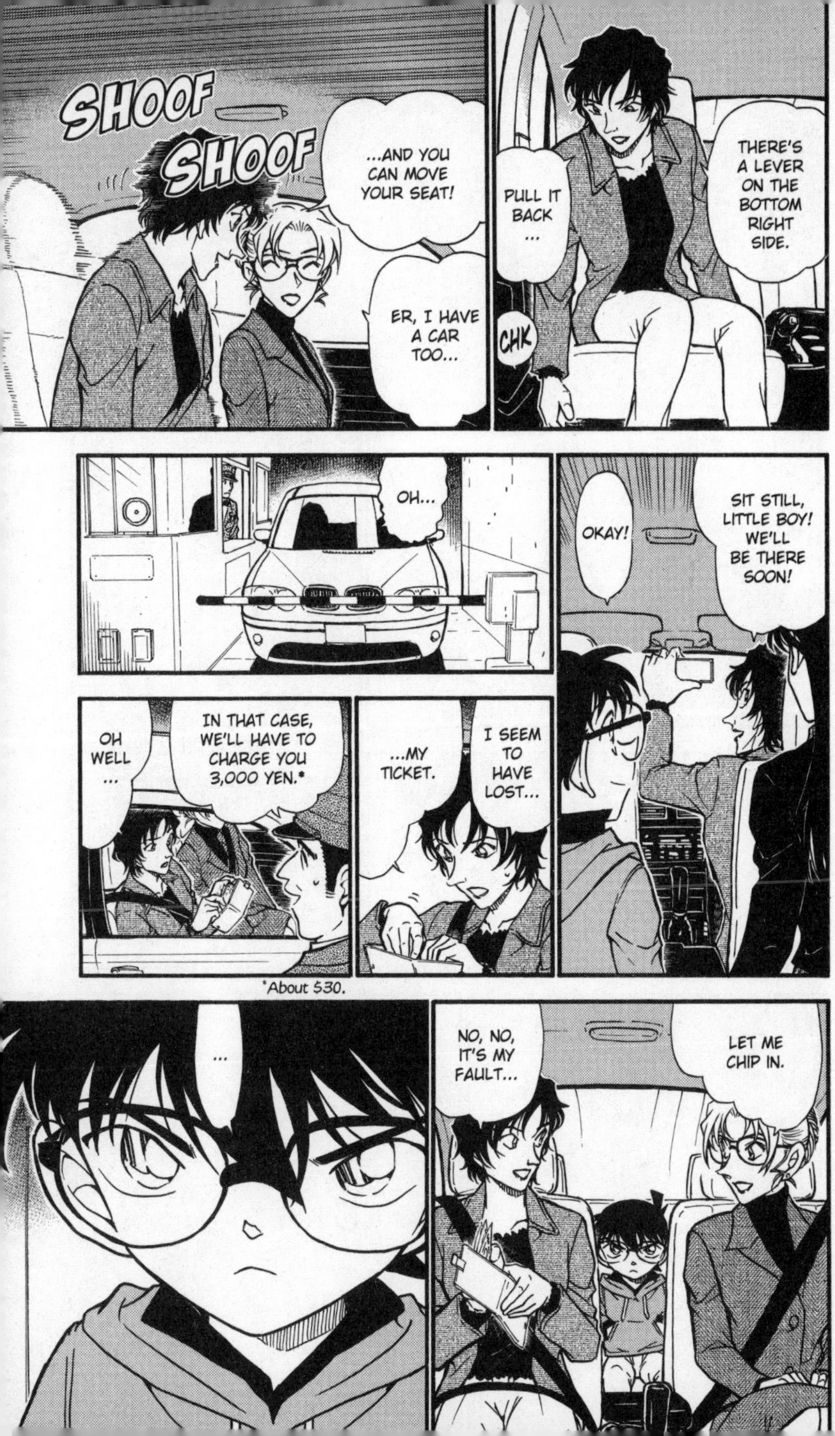
THERE'S A LEVER ON THE BOTTOM RIGHT SIDE.
PULL IT BACK ...
CHK
...AND YOU CAN MOVE YOUR SEAT!
SHOOF
SHOOF
ER, I HAVE A CAR TOO...
SIT STILL, LITTLE BOY! WE'LL BE THERE SOON!
OKAY!
OH...
I SEEM TO HAVE LOST...
...MY TICKET.
IN THAT CASE, WE'LL HAVE TO CHARGE YOU 3,000 YEN.*
OH WELL ...
LET ME CHIP IN.
NO, NO, IT'S MY FAULT...
...

*About $30.

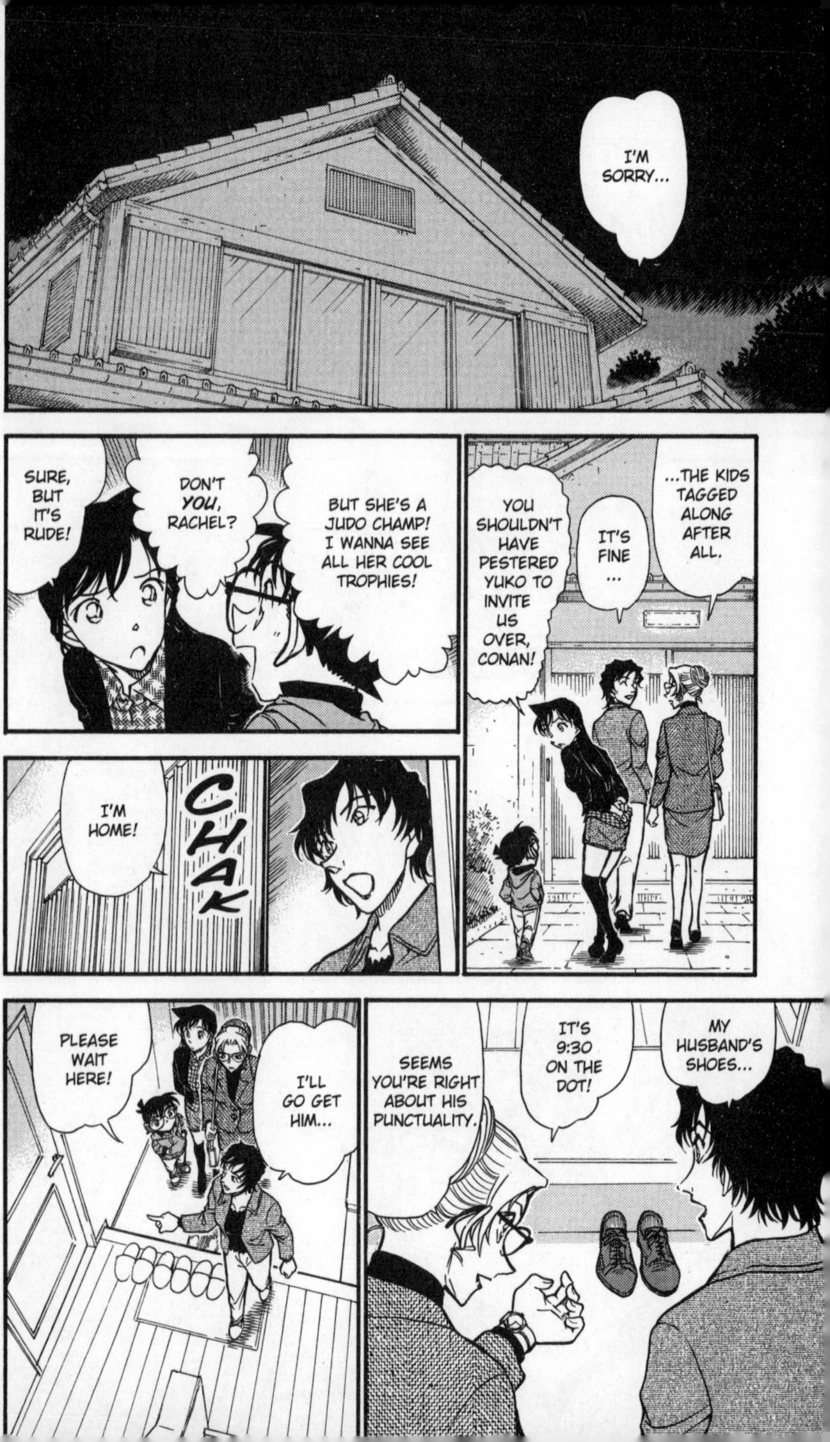
I'M SORRY...
...THE KIDS TAGGED ALONG AFTER ALL.
IT'S FINE ...
YOU SHOULDN'T HAVE PESTERED YUKO TO INVITE US OVER, CONAN!
BUT SHE'S A JUDO CHAMP! I WANNA SEE ALL HER COOL TROPHIES!
DON'T *YOU*, RACHEL?
SURE, BUT IT'S RUDE!
CHAK
I'M HOME!
MY HUSBAND'S SHOES...
IT'S 9:30 ON THE DOT!
SEEMS YOU'RE RIGHT ABOUT HIS PUNCTUALITY.
I'LL GO GET HIM...
PLEASE WAIT HERE!

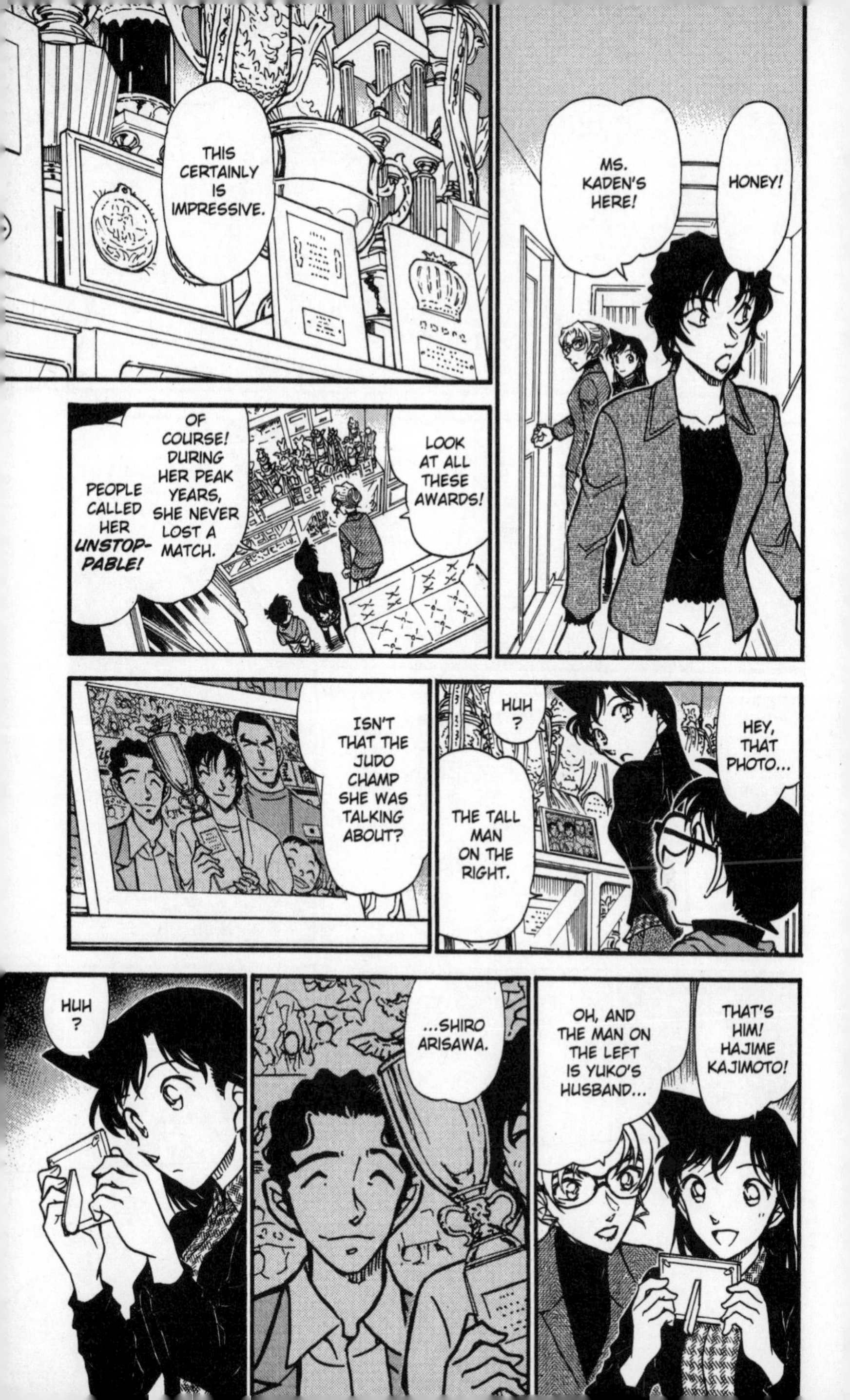
HONEY!
MS. KADEN'S HERE!
THIS CERTAINLY IS IMPRESSIVE.
LOOK AT ALL THESE AWARDS!
OF COURSE! DURING HER PEAK YEARS, SHE NEVER LOST A MATCH.
PEOPLE CALLED HER *UNSTOPPABLE!*
HEY, THAT PHOTO...
HUH?
THE TALL MAN ON THE RIGHT.
ISN'T THAT THE JUDO CHAMP SHE WAS TALKING ABOUT?
THAT'S HIM! HAJIME KAJIMOTO!
OH, AND THE MAN ON THE LEFT IS YUKO'S HUSBAND...
...SHIRO ARISAWA.
HUH?

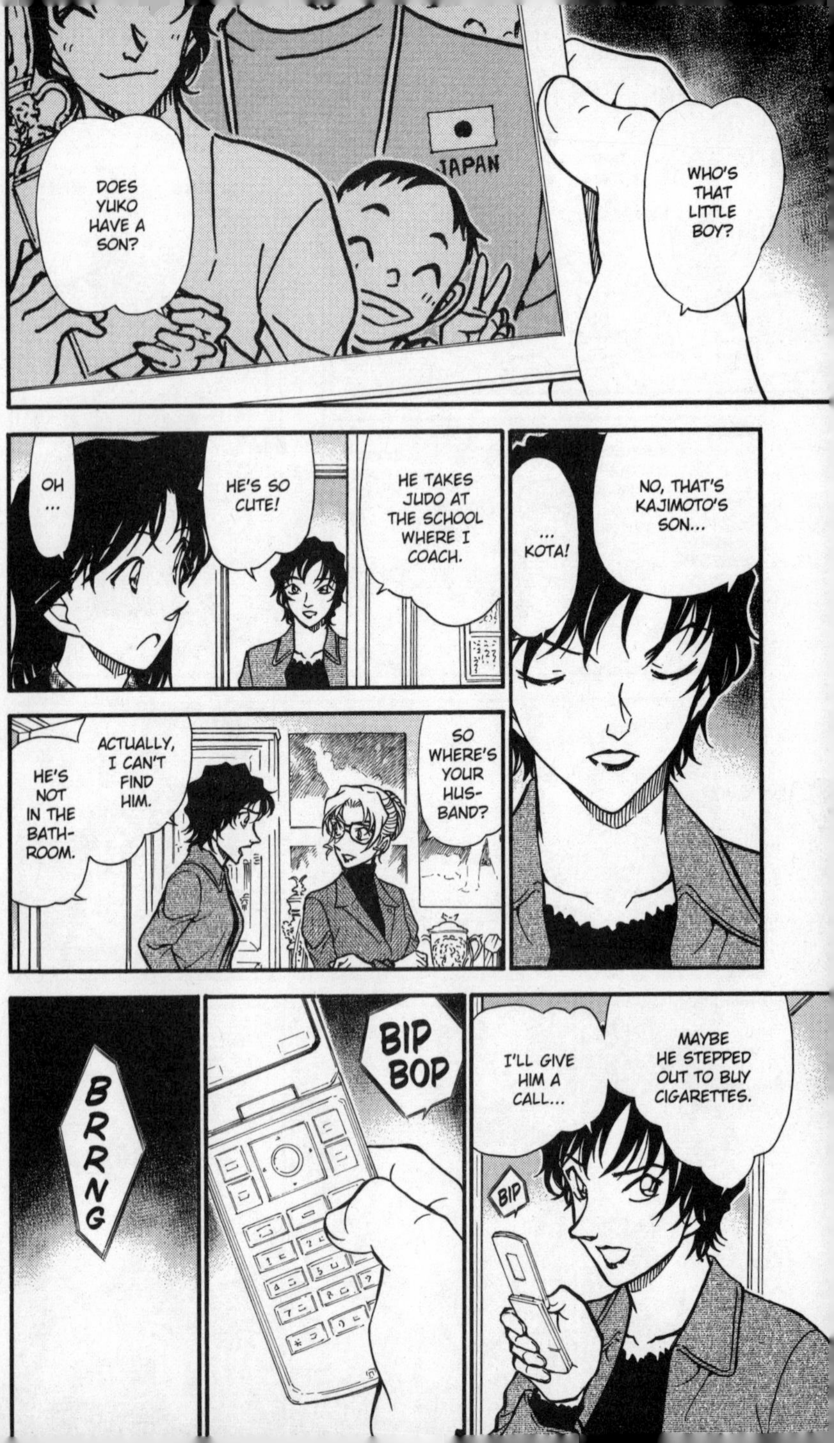

JAPAN
WHO'S THAT LITTLE BOY?
DOES YUKO HAVE A SON?
NO, THAT'S KAJIMOTO'S SON...
... KOTA!
HE TAKES JUDO AT THE SCHOOL WHERE I COACH.
HE'S SO CUTE!
OH ...
SO WHERE'S YOUR HUSBAND?
ACTUALLY, I CAN'T FIND HIM.
HE'S NOT IN THE BATHROOM.
MAYBE HE STEPPED OUT TO BUY CIGARETTES.
I'LL GIVE HIM A CALL...
BIP
BIP BOP
BRRNG

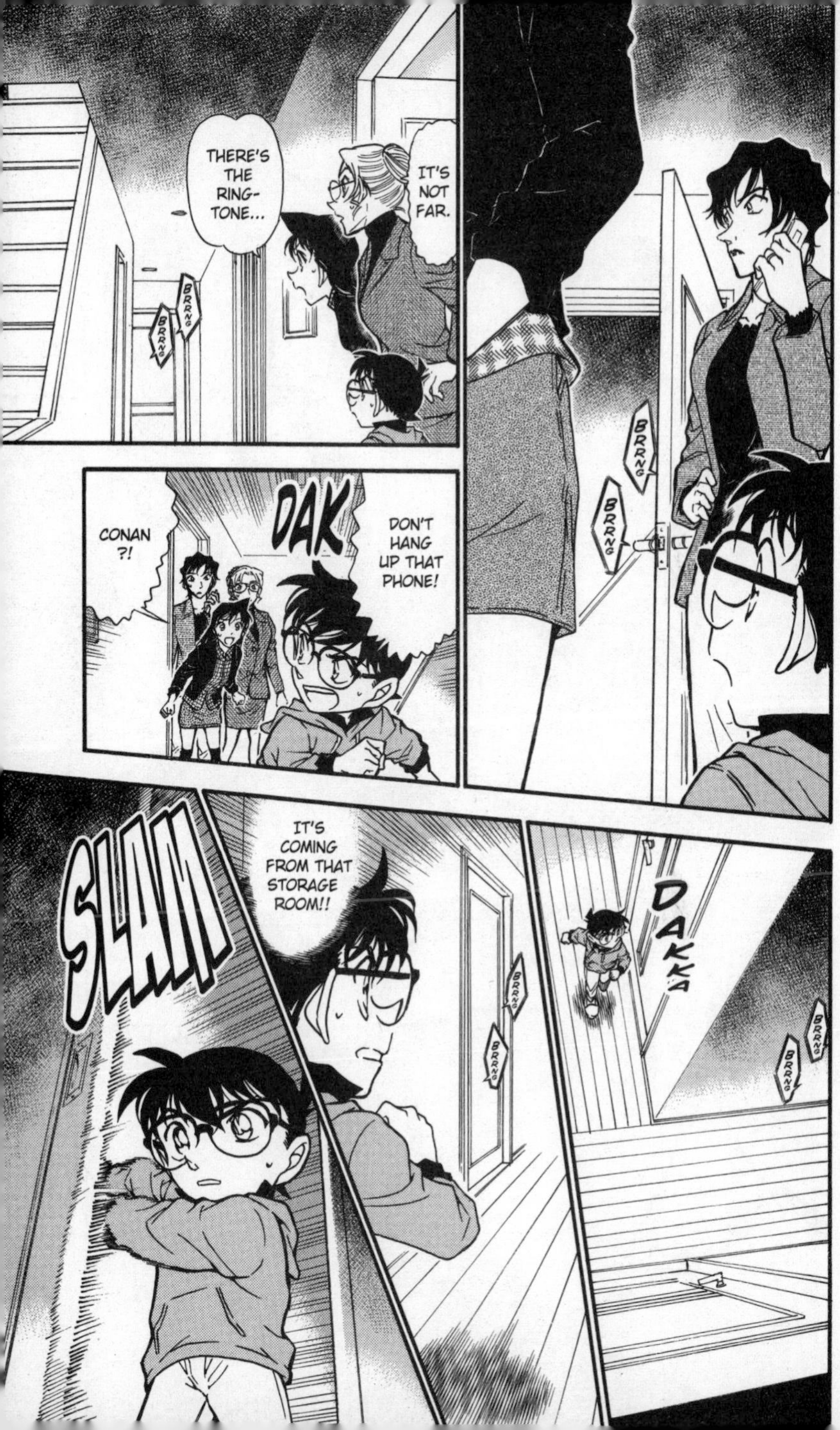
BRRNG
BRRNG
IT'S NOT FAR.
THERE'S THE RING-TONE...
BRRNG
BRRNG
DON'T HANG UP THAT PHONE!
DAK
CONAN ?!
BRRNG
BRRNG
DAKKA
IT'S COMING FROM THAT STORAGE ROOM!!
BRRNG
BRRNG
SLAM

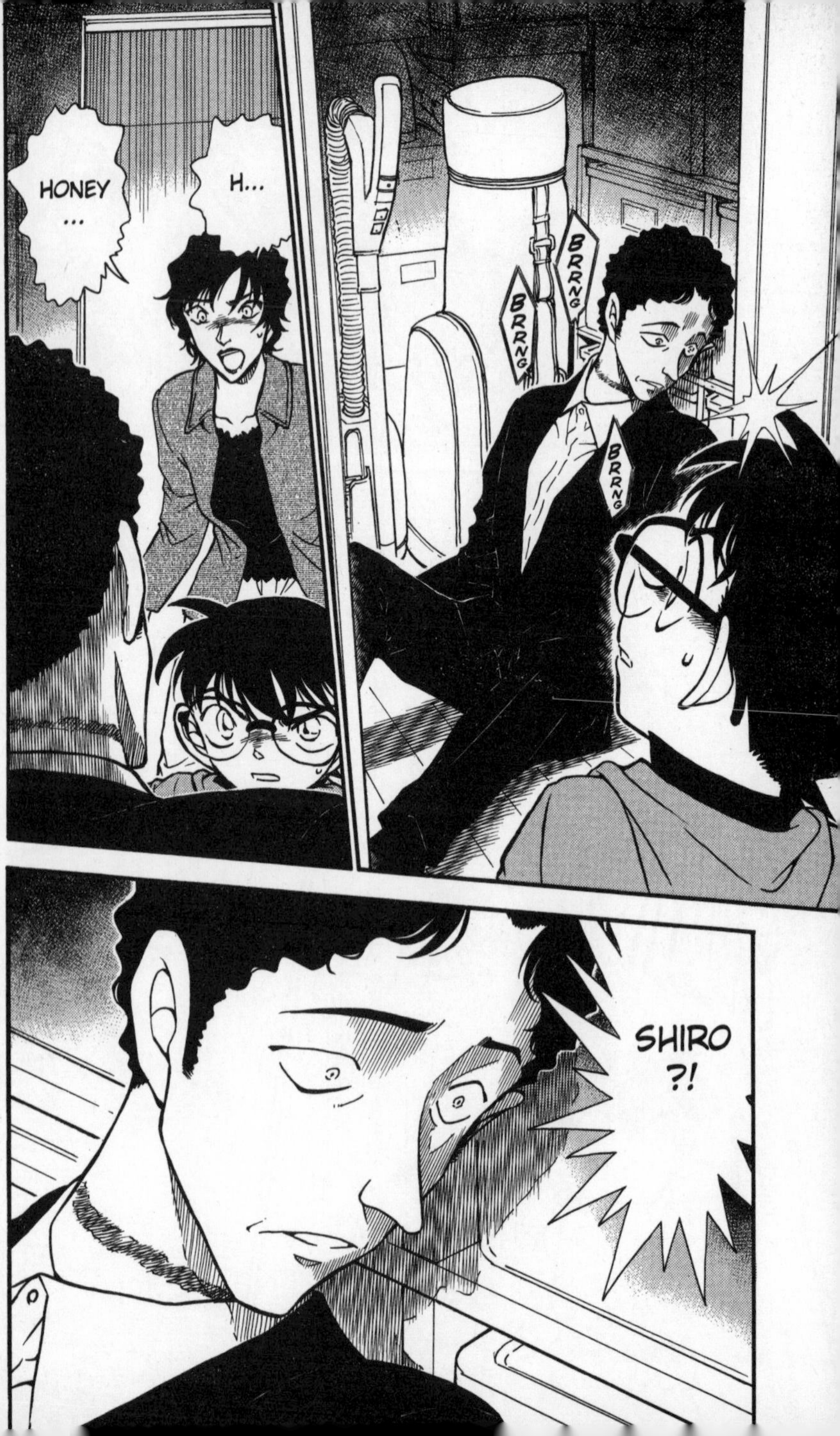
BRRNG
BRRNG
BRRNG
H...
HONEY ...
SHIRO ?!

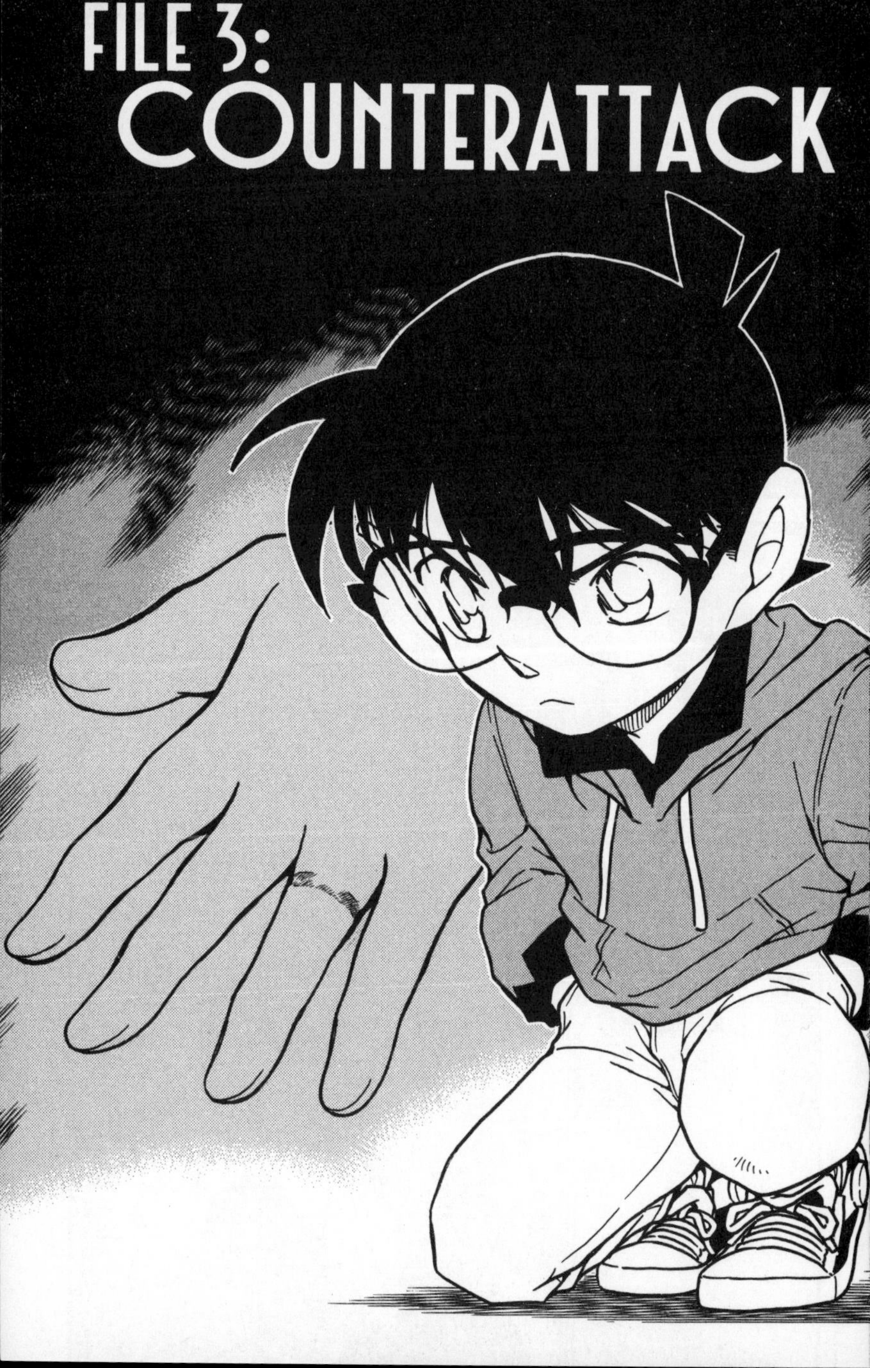
FILE 3:
COUNTERATTACK

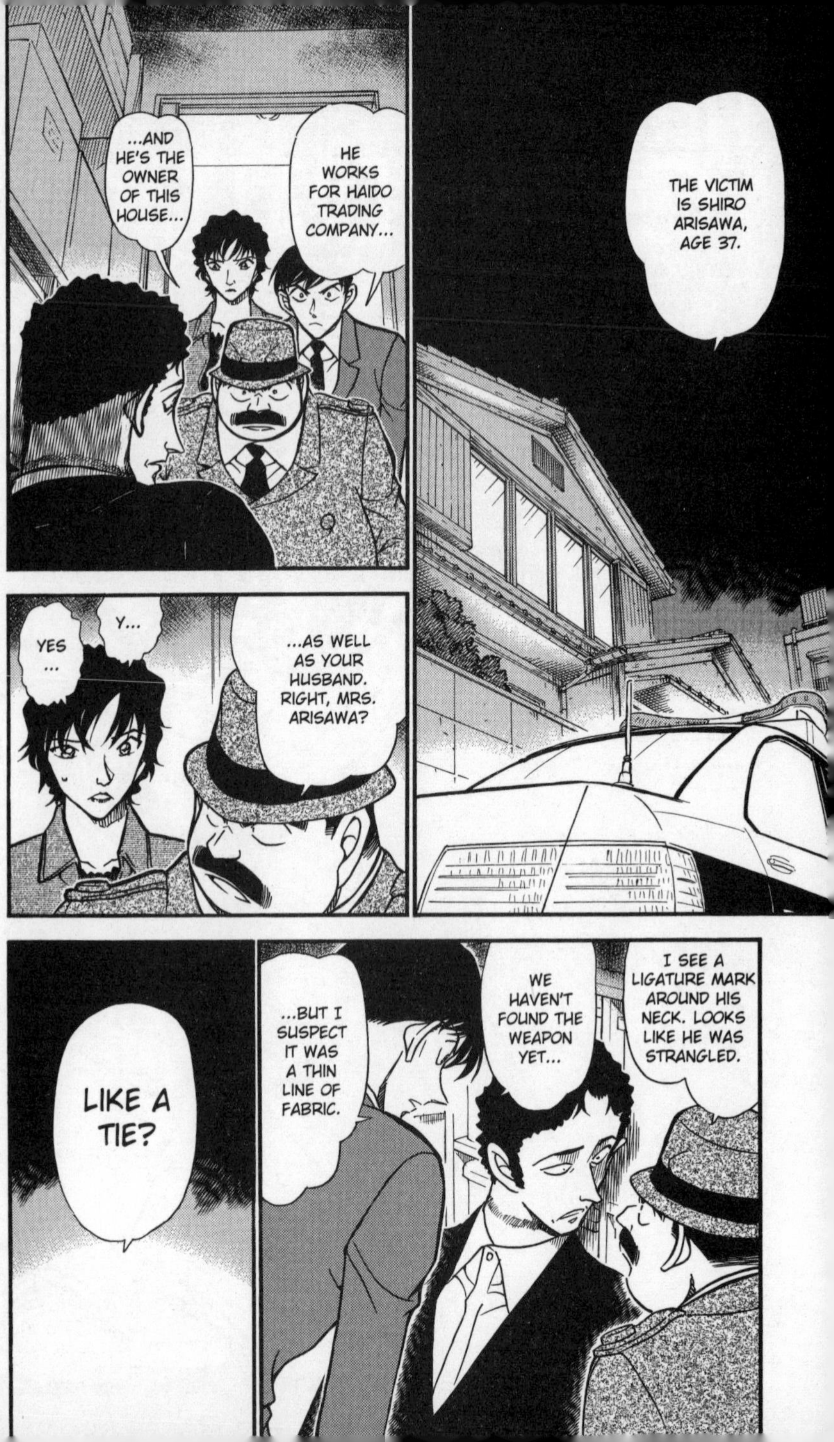
THE VICTIM IS SHIRO ARISAWA, AGE 37.
HE WORKS FOR HAIDO TRADING COMPANY...
...AND HE'S THE OWNER OF THIS HOUSE...
...AS WELL AS YOUR HUSBAND. RIGHT, MRS. ARISAWA?
Y...
YES ...
I SEE A LIGATURE MARK AROUND HIS NECK. LOOKS LIKE HE WAS STRANGLED.
WE HAVEN'T FOUND THE WEAPON YET...
...BUT I SUSPECT IT WAS A THIN LINE OF FABRIC.
LIKE A TIE?

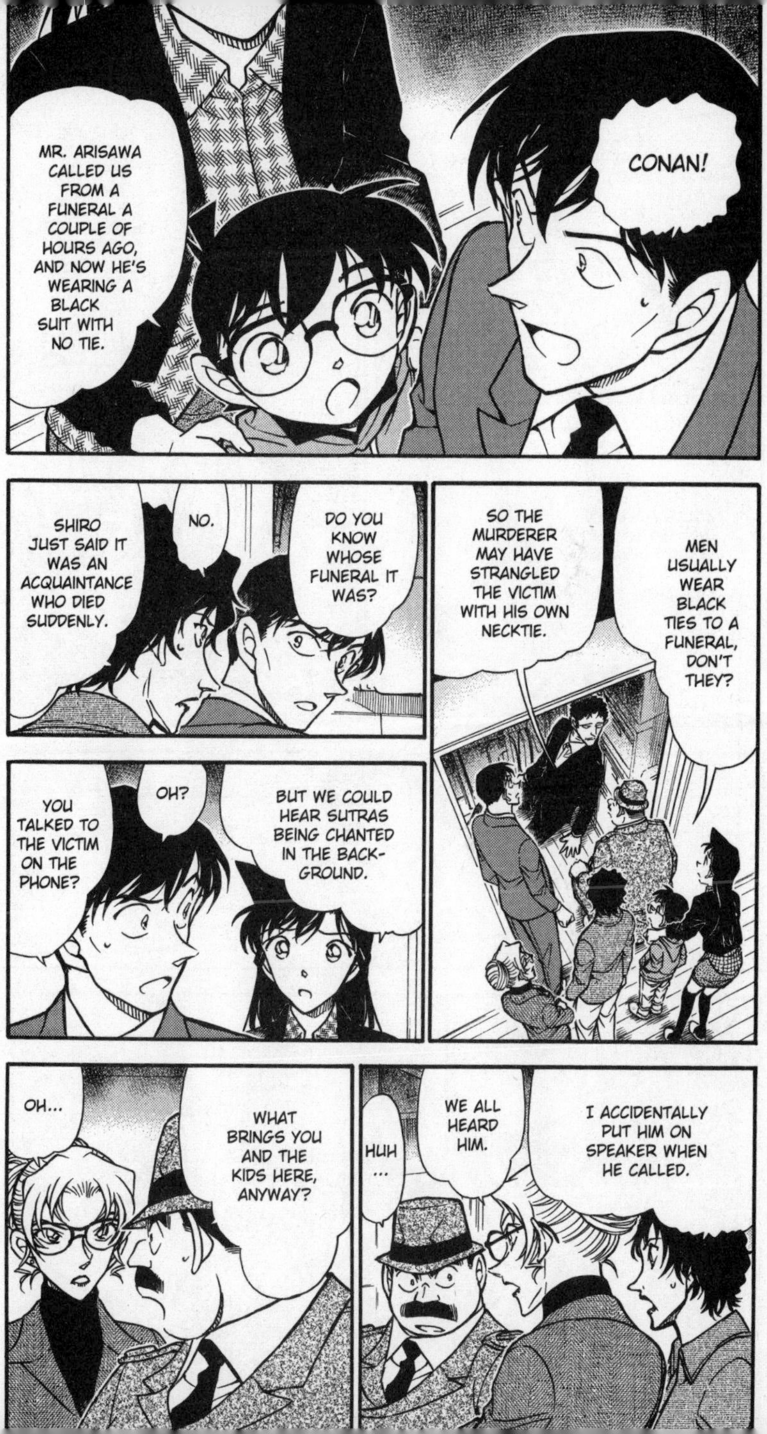
CONAN!
MR. ARISAWA CALLED US FROM A FUNERAL A COUPLE OF HOURS AGO, AND NOW HE'S WEARING A BLACK SUIT WITH NO TIE.
MEN USUALLY WEAR BLACK TIES TO A FUNERAL, DON'T THEY?
SO THE MURDERER MAY HAVE STRANGLED THE VICTIM WITH HIS OWN NECKTIE.
DO YOU KNOW WHOSE FUNERAL IT WAS?
NO.
SHIRO JUST SAID IT WAS AN ACQUAINTANCE WHO DIED SUDDENLY.
BUT WE COULD HEAR SUTRAS BEING CHANTED IN THE BACK-GROUND.
OH?
YOU TALKED TO THE VICTIM ON THE PHONE?
I ACCIDENTALLY PUT HIM ON SPEAKER WHEN HE CALLED.
WE ALL HEARD HIM.
HUH ...
WHAT BRINGS YOU AND THE KIDS HERE, ANYWAY?
OH...

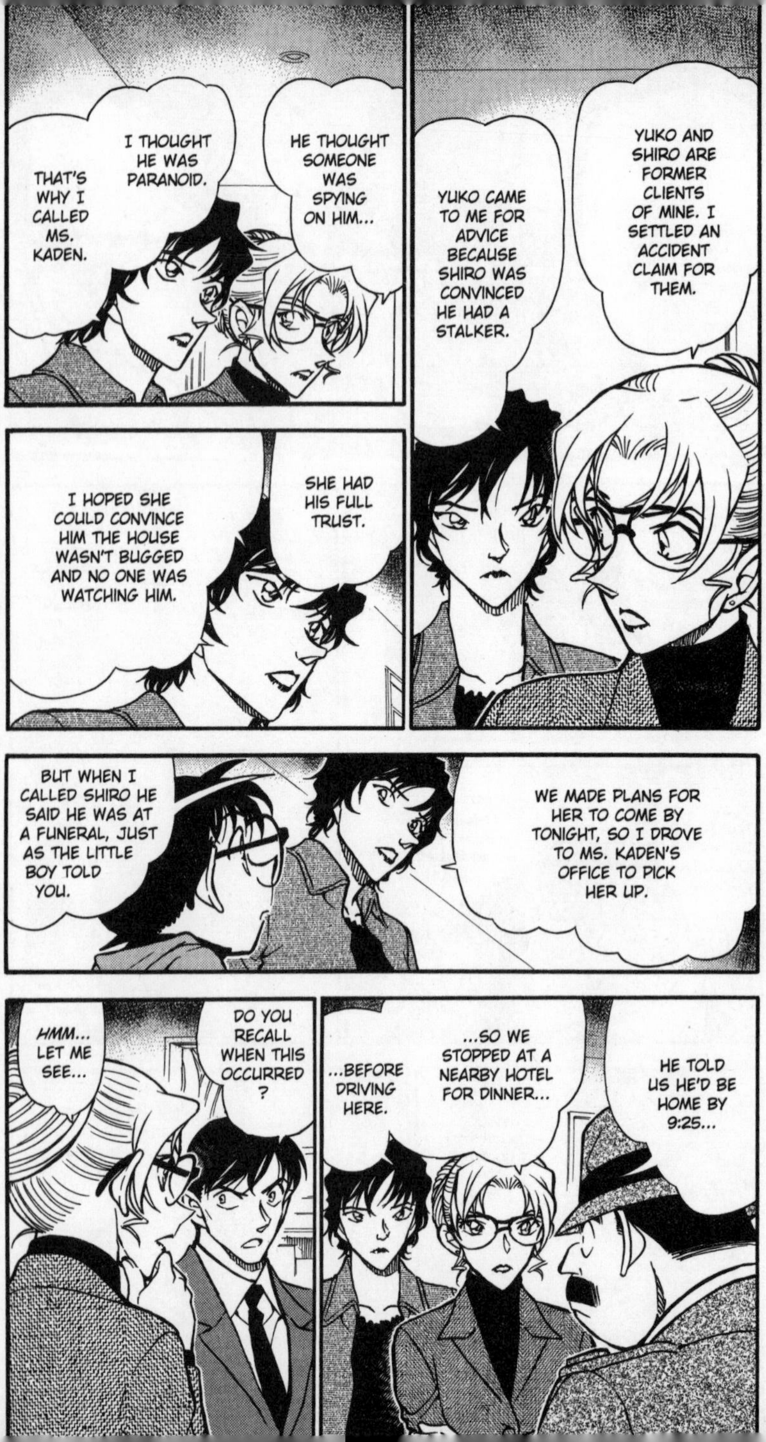
YUKO AND SHIRO ARE FORMER CLIENTS OF MINE. I SETTLED AN ACCIDENT CLAIM FOR THEM.
YUKO CAME TO ME FOR ADVICE BECAUSE SHIRO WAS CONVINCED HE HAD A STALKER.
HE THOUGHT SOMEONE WAS SPYING ON HIM...
I THOUGHT HE WAS PARANOID.
THAT'S WHY I CALLED MS. KADEN.
SHE HAD HIS FULL TRUST.
I HOPED SHE COULD CONVINCE HIM THE HOUSE WASN'T BUGGED AND NO ONE WAS WATCHING HIM.
WE MADE PLANS FOR HER TO COME BY TONIGHT, SO I DROVE TO MS. KADEN'S OFFICE TO PICK HER UP.
BUT WHEN I CALLED SHIRO HE SAID HE WAS AT A FUNERAL, JUST AS THE LITTLE BOY TOLD YOU.
HE TOLD US HE'D BE HOME BY 9:25...
...SO WE STOPPED AT A NEARBY HOTEL FOR DINNER...
...BEFORE DRIVING HERE.
DO YOU RECALL WHEN THIS OCCURRED?
HMM... LET ME SEE...

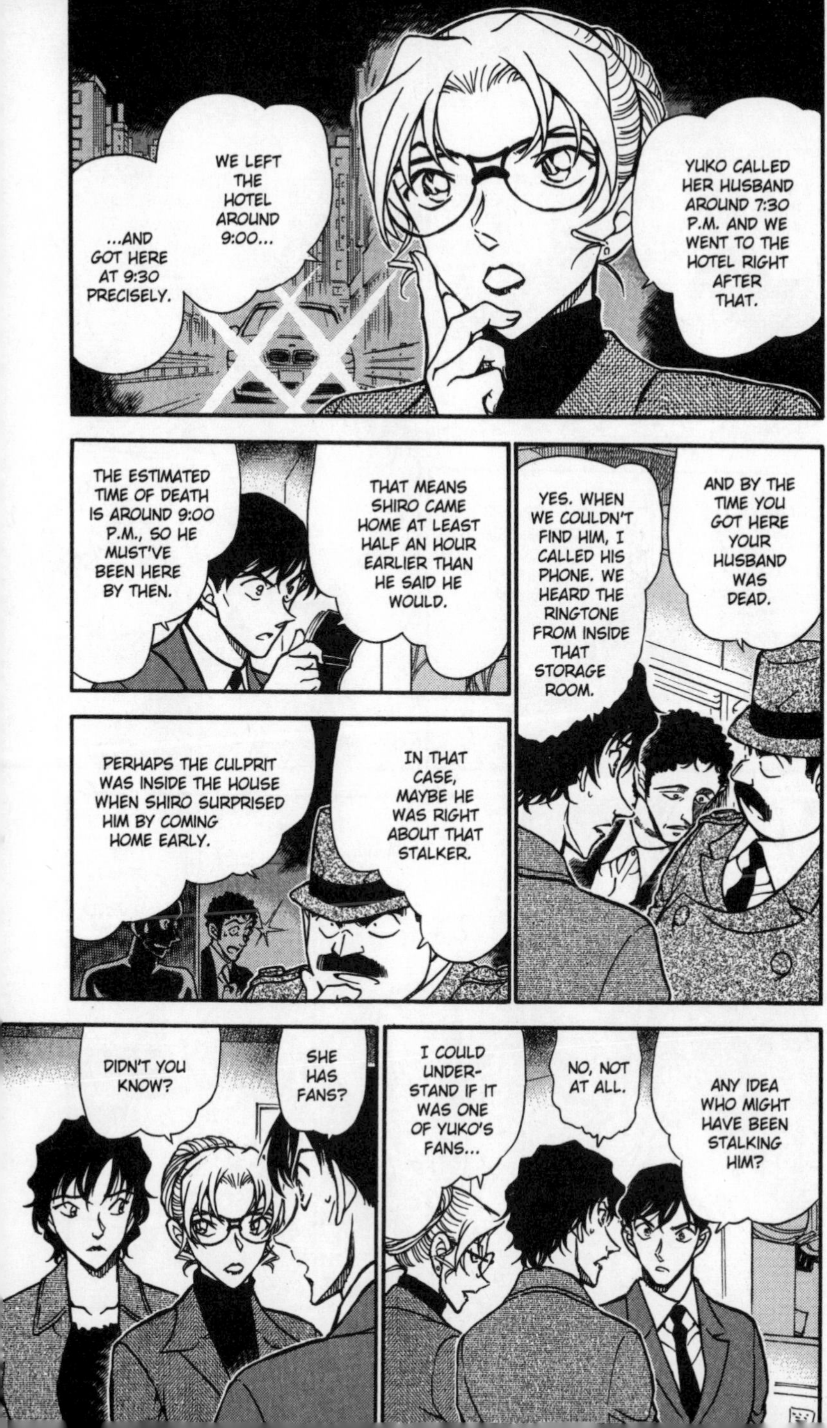
YUKO CALLED HER HUSBAND AROUND 7:30 P.M. AND WE WENT TO THE HOTEL RIGHT AFTER THAT.
WE LEFT THE HOTEL AROUND 9:00...
...AND GOT HERE AT 9:30 PRECISELY.
AND BY THE TIME YOU GOT HERE YOUR HUSBAND WAS DEAD.
YES. WHEN WE COULDN'T FIND HIM, I CALLED HIS PHONE. WE HEARD THE RINGTONE FROM INSIDE THAT STORAGE ROOM.
THAT MEANS SHIRO CAME HOME AT LEAST HALF AN HOUR EARLIER THAN HE SAID HE WOULD.
THE ESTIMATED TIME OF DEATH IS AROUND 9:00 P.M., SO HE MUST'VE BEEN HERE BY THEN.
IN THAT CASE, MAYBE HE WAS RIGHT ABOUT THAT STALKER.
PERHAPS THE CULPRIT WAS INSIDE THE HOUSE WHEN SHIRO SURPRISED HIM BY COMING HOME EARLY.
ANY IDEA WHO MIGHT HAVE BEEN STALKING HIM?
NO, NOT AT ALL.
I COULD UNDER-STAND IF IT WAS ONE OF YUKO'S FANS...
SHE HAS FANS?
DIDN'T YOU KNOW?

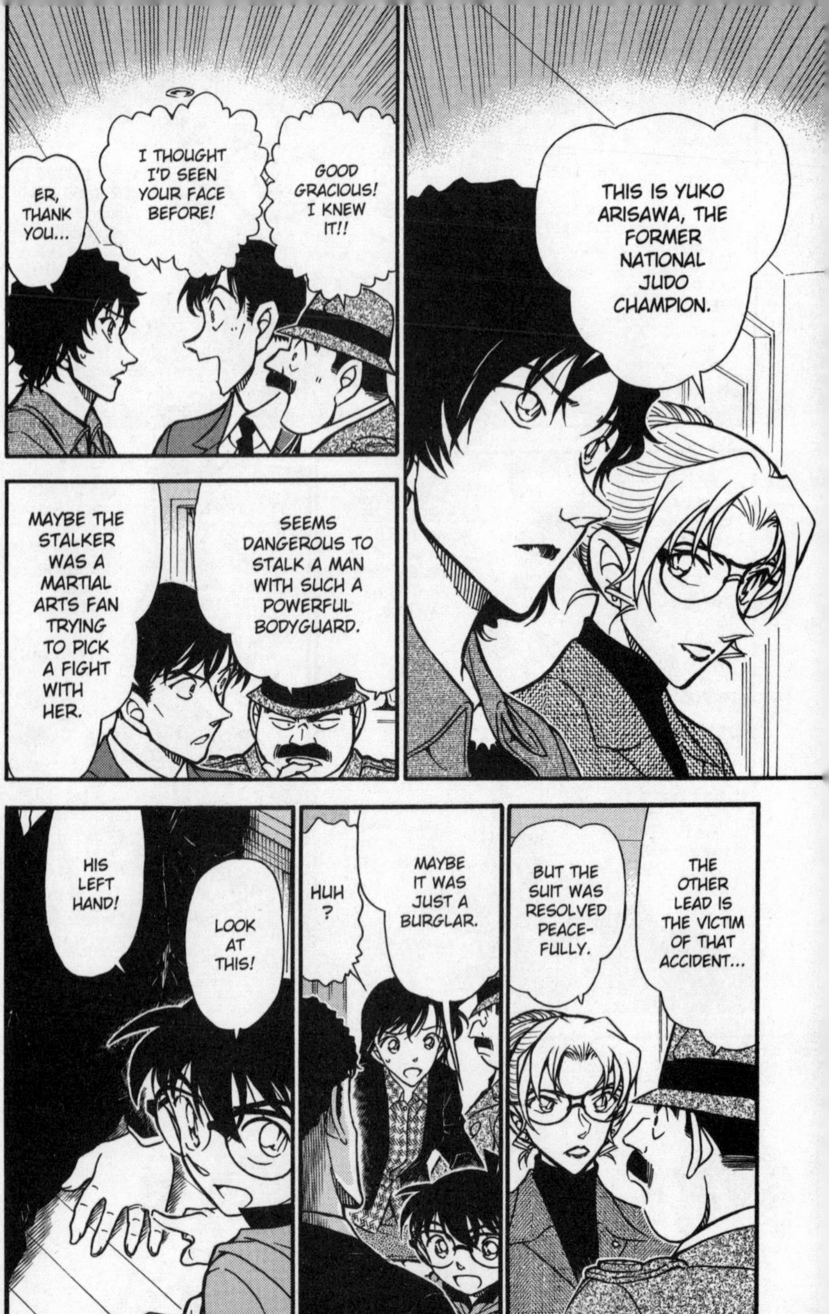
THIS IS YUKO ARISAWA, THE FORMER NATIONAL JUDO CHAMPION.
GOOD GRACIOUS! I KNEW IT!!
I THOUGHT I'D SEEN YOUR FACE BEFORE!
ER, THANK YOU...
SEEMS DANGEROUS TO STALK A MAN WITH SUCH A POWERFUL BODYGUARD.
MAYBE THE STALKER WAS A MARTIAL ARTS FAN TRYING TO PICK A FIGHT WITH HER.
THE OTHER LEAD IS THE VICTIM OF THAT ACCIDENT...
BUT THE SUIT WAS RESOLVED PEACE-FULLY.
MAYBE IT WAS JUST A BURGLAR.
HUH?
LOOK AT THIS!
HIS LEFT HAND!

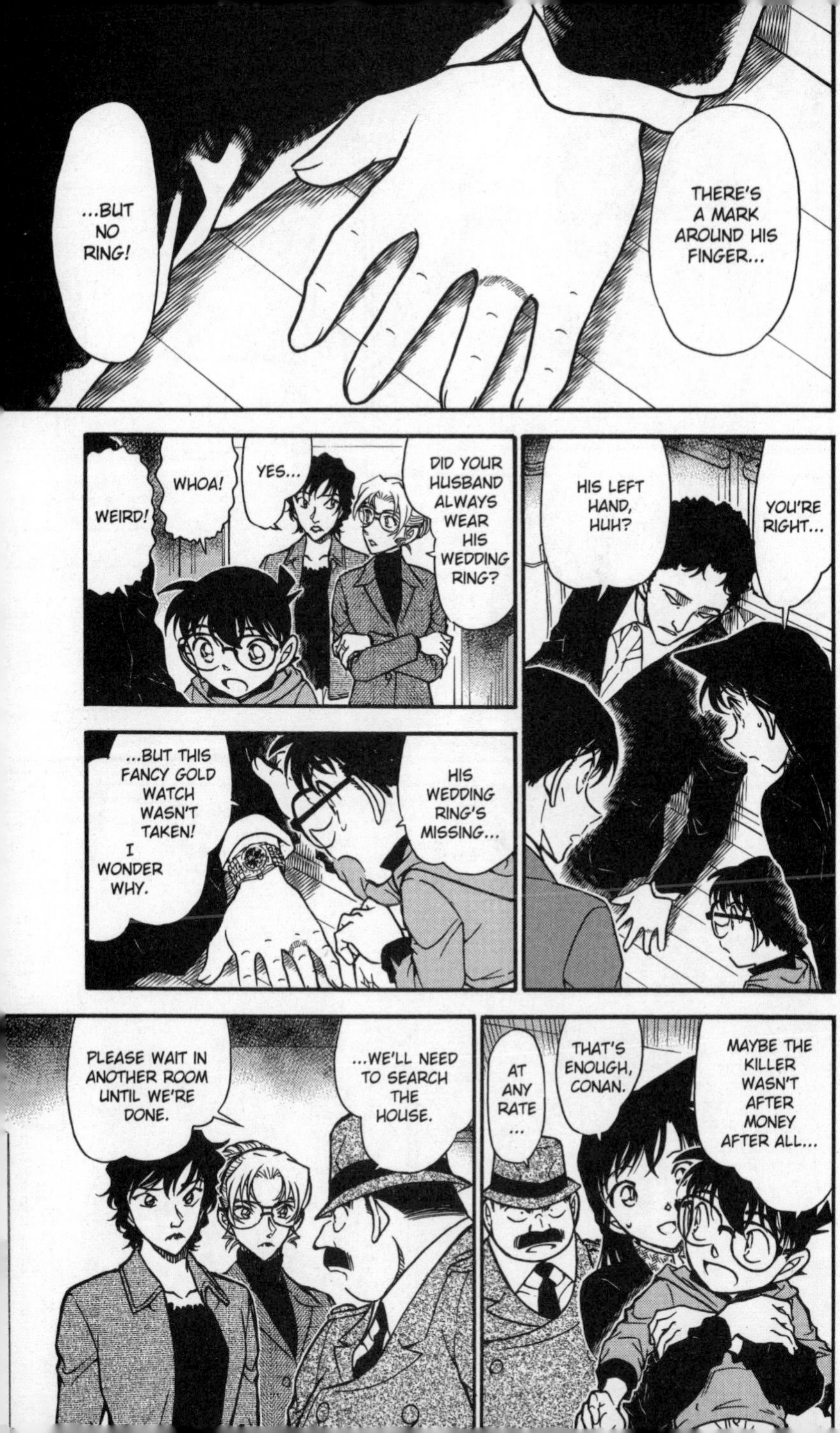
THERE'S A MARK AROUND HIS FINGER...
...BUT NO RING!
YOU'RE RIGHT...
HIS LEFT HAND, HUH?
DID YOUR HUSBAND ALWAYS WEAR HIS WEDDING RING?
YES...
WHOA!
WEIRD!
HIS WEDDING RING'S MISSING...
...BUT THIS FANCY GOLD WATCH WASN'T TAKEN!
I WONDER WHY.
MAYBE THE KILLER WASN'T AFTER MONEY AFTER ALL...
THAT'S ENOUGH, CONAN.
AT ANY RATE...
...WE'LL NEED TO SEARCH THE HOUSE.
PLEASE WAIT IN ANOTHER ROOM UNTIL WE'RE DONE.

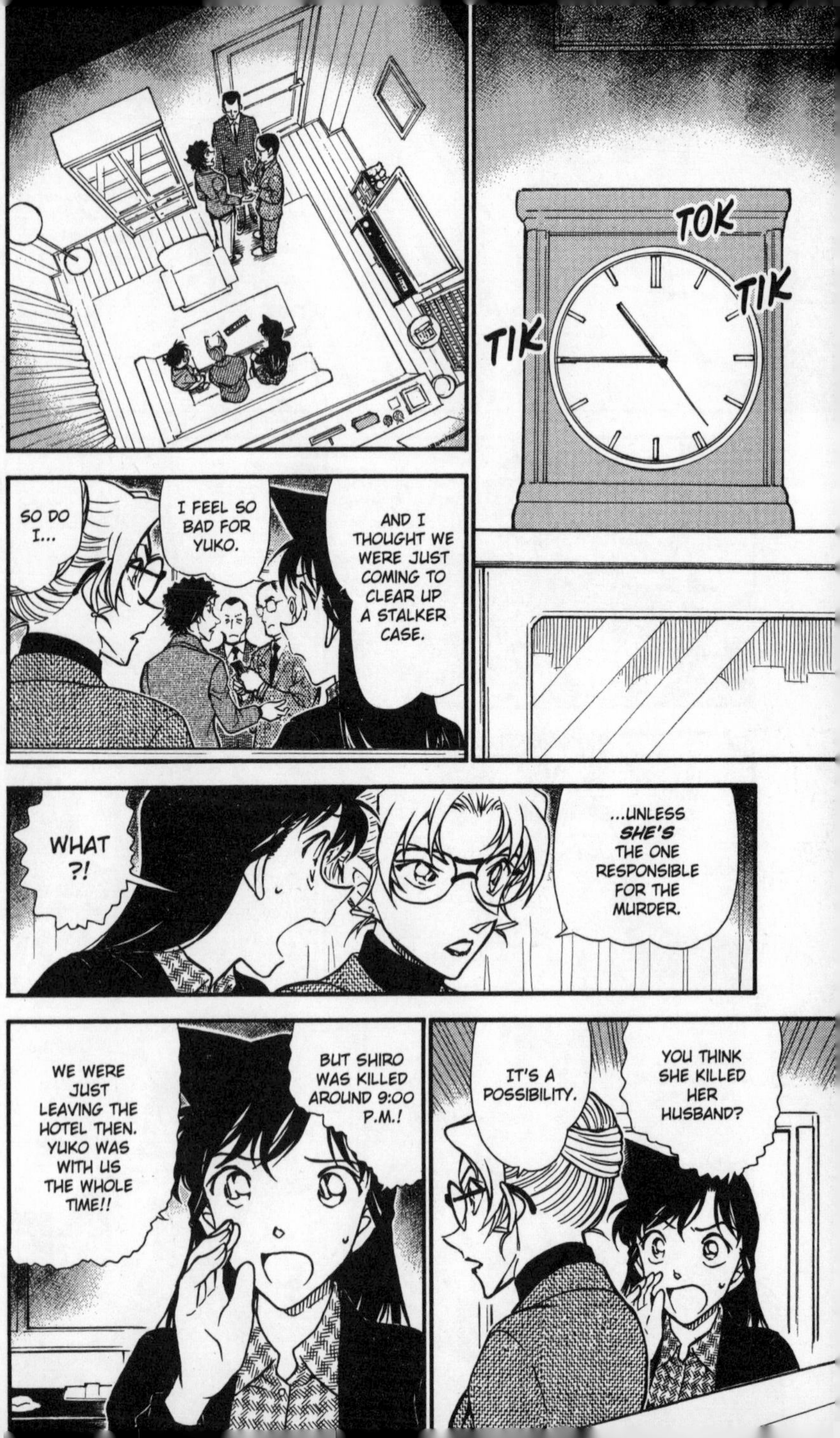
TOK
TIK
TIK
AND I THOUGHT WE WERE JUST COMING TO CLEAR UP A STALKER CASE.
I FEEL SO BAD FOR YUKO.
SO DO I...
...UNLESS *SHE'S* THE ONE RESPONSIBLE FOR THE MURDER.
WHAT ?!
YOU THINK SHE KILLED HER HUSBAND?
IT'S A POSSIBILITY.
BUT SHIRO WAS KILLED AROUND 9:00 P.M.!
WE WERE JUST LEAVING THE HOTEL THEN. YUKO WAS WITH US THE WHOLE TIME!!

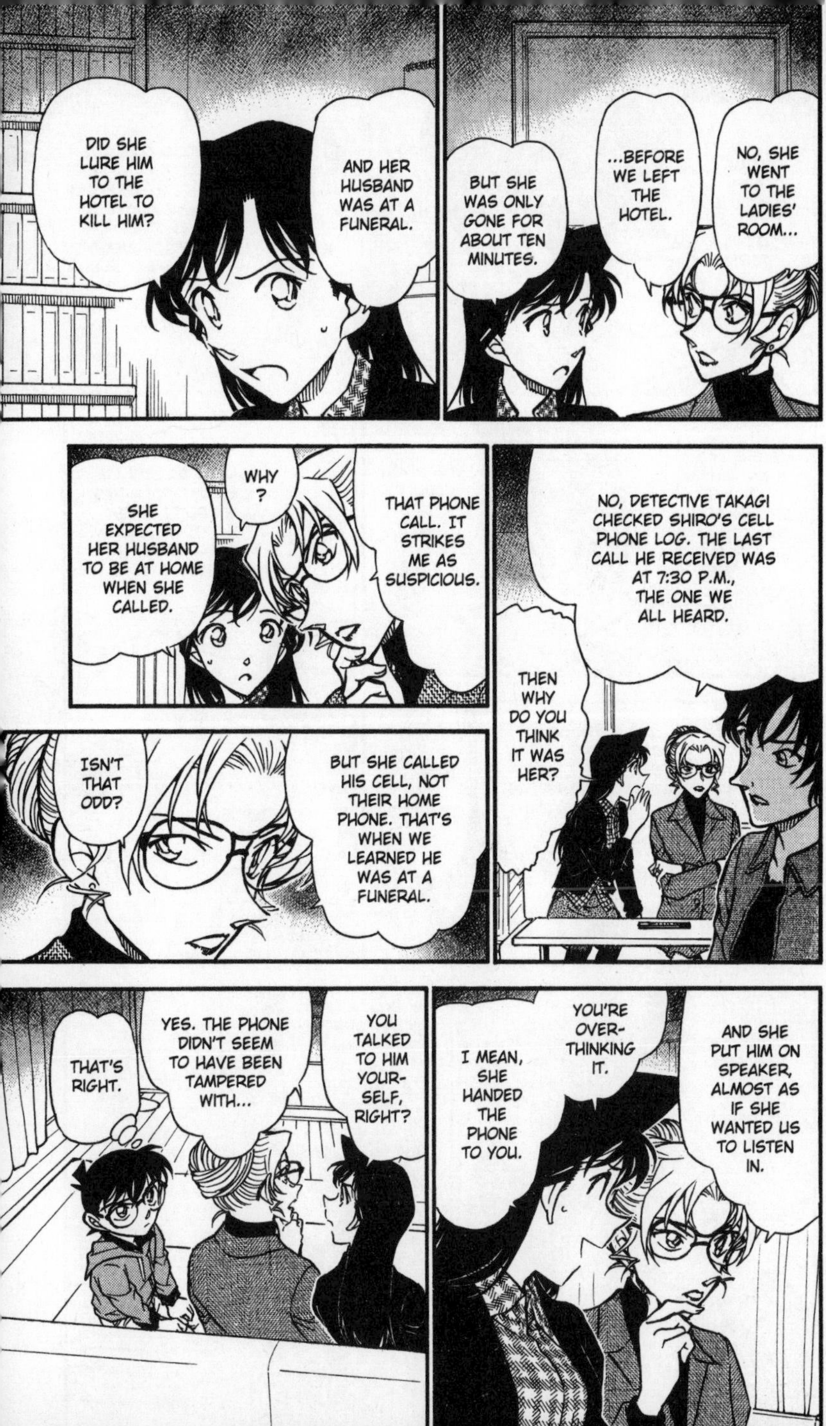
NO, SHE WENT TO THE LADIES' ROOM...
...BEFORE WE LEFT THE HOTEL.
BUT SHE WAS ONLY GONE FOR ABOUT TEN MINUTES.
AND HER HUSBAND WAS AT A FUNERAL.
DID SHE LURE HIM TO THE HOTEL TO KILL HIM?
NO, DETECTIVE TAKAGI CHECKED SHIRO'S CELL PHONE LOG. THE LAST CALL HE RECEIVED WAS AT 7:30 P.M., THE ONE WE ALL HEARD.
THEN WHY DO YOU THINK IT WAS HER?
THAT PHONE CALL. IT STRIKES ME AS SUSPICIOUS.
WHY?
SHE EXPECTED HER HUSBAND TO BE AT HOME WHEN SHE CALLED.
BUT SHE CALLED HIS CELL, NOT THEIR HOME PHONE. THAT'S WHEN WE LEARNED HE WAS AT A FUNERAL.
ISN'T THAT ODD?
AND SHE PUT HIM ON SPEAKER, ALMOST AS IF SHE WANTED US TO LISTEN IN.
YOU'RE OVER-THINKING IT.
I MEAN, SHE HANDED THE PHONE TO YOU.
YOU TALKED TO HIM YOURSELF, RIGHT?
YES. THE PHONE DIDN'T SEEM TO HAVE BEEN TAMPERED WITH...
THAT'S RIGHT.

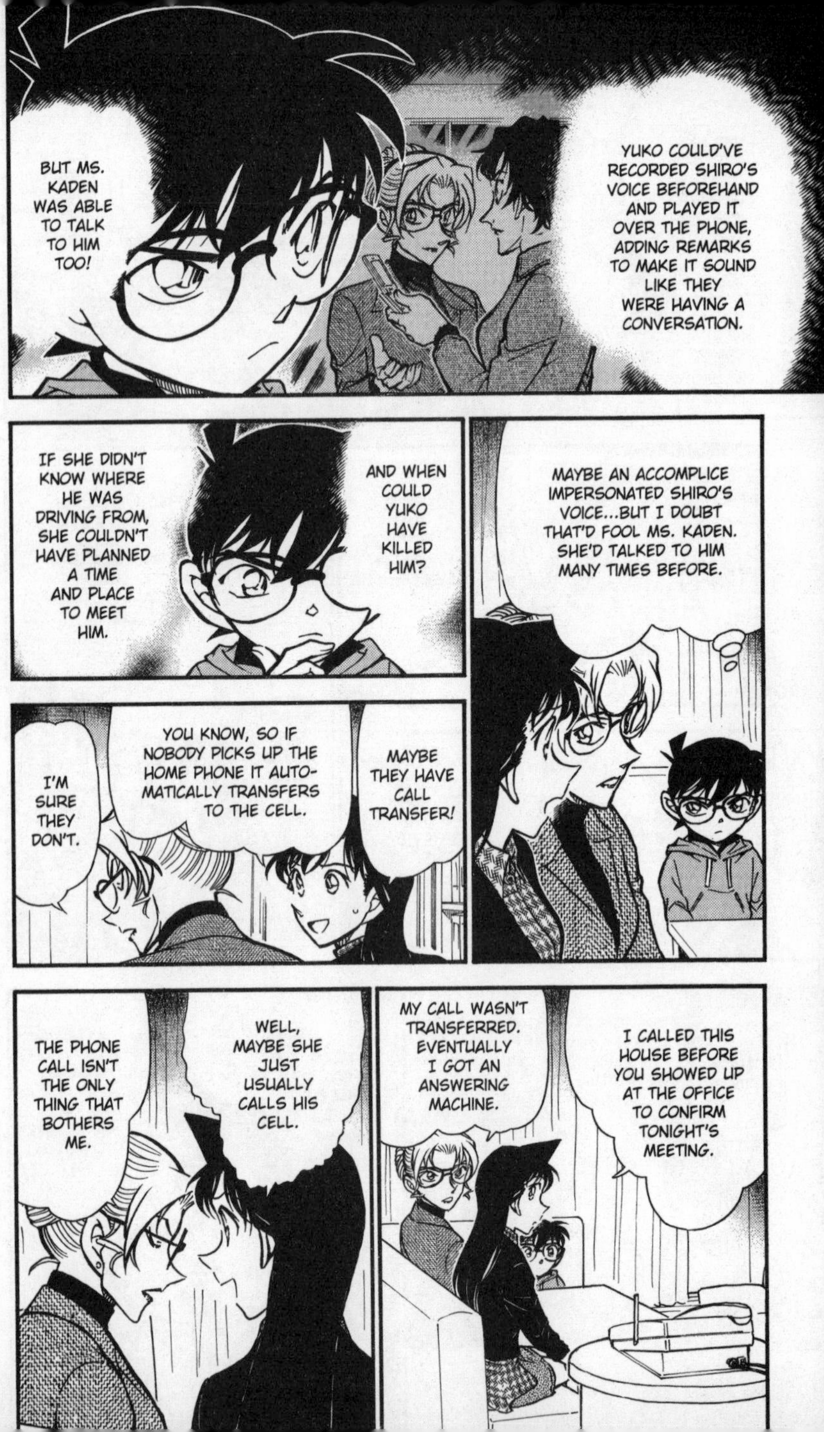
YUKO COULD'VE RECORDED SHIRO'S VOICE BEFOREHAND AND PLAYED IT OVER THE PHONE, ADDING REMARKS TO MAKE IT SOUND LIKE THEY WERE HAVING A CONVERSATION.
BUT MS. KADEN WAS ABLE TO TALK TO HIM TOO!
MAYBE AN ACCOMPLICE IMPERSONATED SHIRO'S VOICE...BUT I DOUBT THAT'D FOOL MS. KADEN. SHE'D TALKED TO HIM MANY TIMES BEFORE.
AND WHEN COULD YUKO HAVE KILLED HIM?
IF SHE DIDN'T KNOW WHERE HE WAS DRIVING FROM, SHE COULDN'T HAVE PLANNED A TIME AND PLACE TO MEET HIM.
MAYBE THEY HAVE CALL TRANSFER!
YOU KNOW, SO IF NOBODY PICKS UP THE HOME PHONE IT AUTO-MATICALLY TRANSFERS TO THE CELL.
I'M SURE THEY DON'T.
I CALLED THIS HOUSE BEFORE YOU SHOWED UP AT THE OFFICE TO CONFIRM TONIGHT'S MEETING.
MY CALL WASN'T TRANSFERRED. EVENTUALLY I GOT AN ANSWERING MACHINE.
WELL, MAYBE SHE JUST USUALLY CALLS HIS CELL.
THE PHONE CALL ISN'T THE ONLY THING THAT BOTHERS ME.

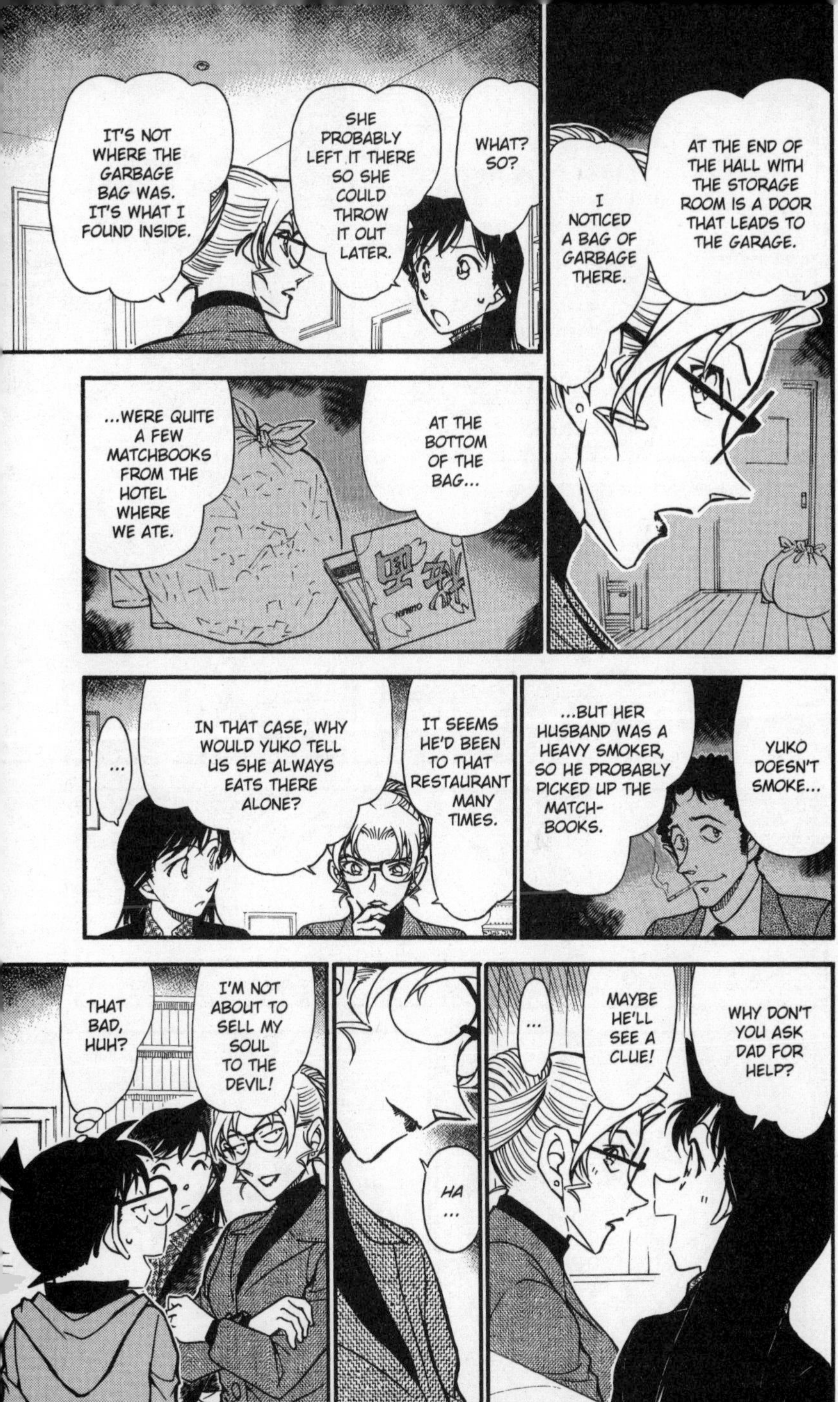
AT THE END OF THE HALL WITH THE STORAGE ROOM IS A DOOR THAT LEADS TO THE GARAGE.
I NOTICED A BAG OF GARBAGE THERE.
WHAT? SO?
SHE PROBABLY LEFT IT THERE SO SHE COULD THROW IT OUT LATER.
IT'S NOT WHERE THE GARBAGE BAG WAS. IT'S WHAT I FOUND INSIDE.
AT THE BOTTOM OF THE BAG...
...WERE QUITE A FEW MATCHBOOKS FROM THE HOTEL WHERE WE ATE.
YUKO DOESN'T SMOKE...
...BUT HER HUSBAND WAS A HEAVY SMOKER, SO HE PROBABLY PICKED UP THE MATCHBOOKS.
IT SEEMS HE'D BEEN TO THAT RESTAURANT MANY TIMES.
IN THAT CASE, WHY WOULD YUKO TELL US SHE ALWAYS EATS THERE ALONE?
...
WHY DON'T YOU ASK DAD FOR HELP?
MAYBE HE'LL SEE A CLUE!
...
HA ...
I'M NOT ABOUT TO SELL MY SOUL TO THE DEVIL!
THAT BAD, HUH?

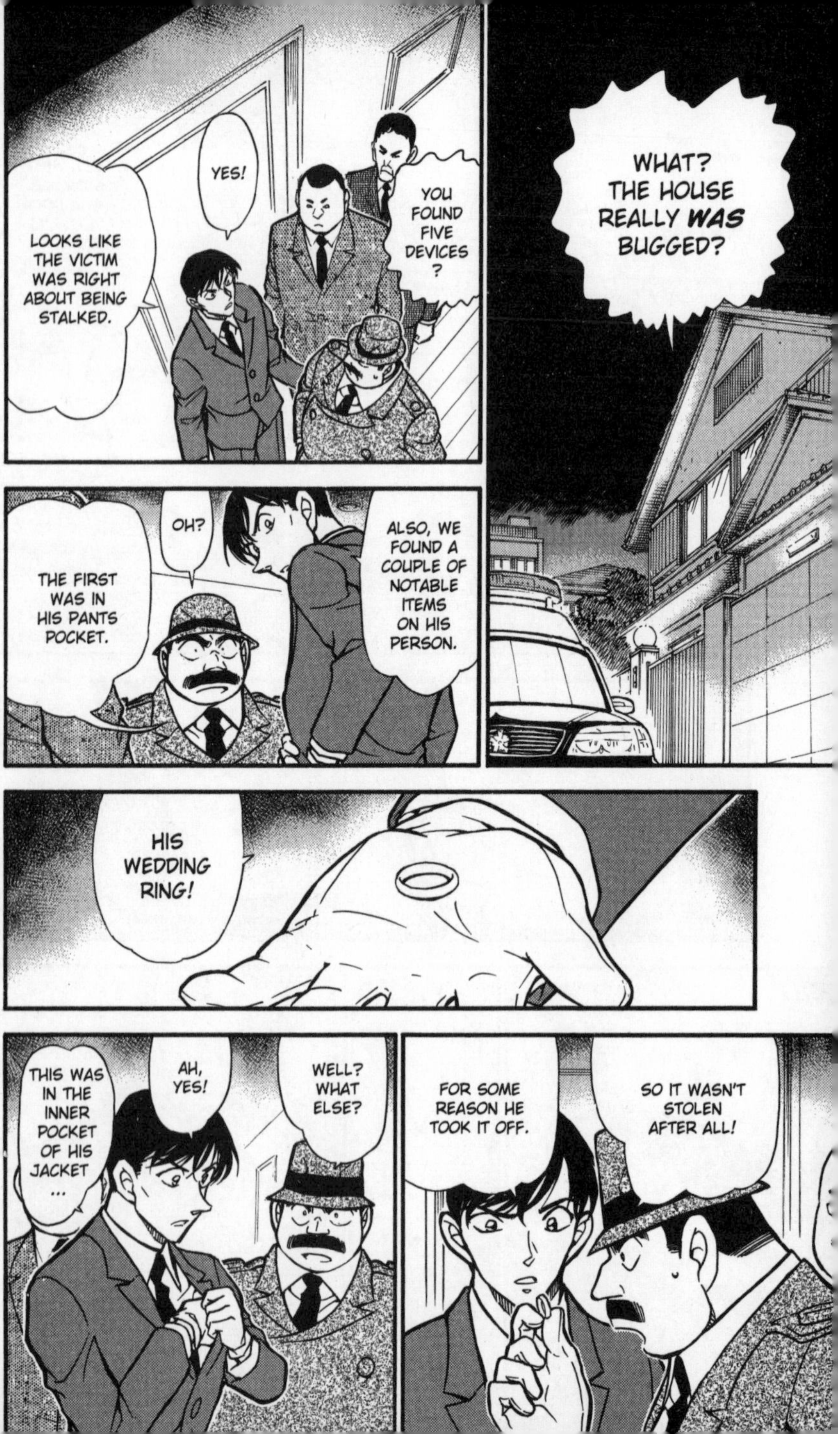
WHAT? THE HOUSE REALLY WAS BUGGED?
YOU FOUND FIVE DEVICES ?
YES!
LOOKS LIKE THE VICTIM WAS RIGHT ABOUT BEING STALKED.
ALSO, WE FOUND A COUPLE OF NOTABLE ITEMS ON HIS PERSON.
OH?
THE FIRST WAS IN HIS PANTS POCKET.
HIS WEDDING RING!
SO IT WASN'T STOLEN AFTER ALL!
FOR SOME REASON HE TOOK IT OFF.
WELL? WHAT ELSE?
AH, YES!
THIS WAS IN THE INNER POCKET OF HIS JACKET ...

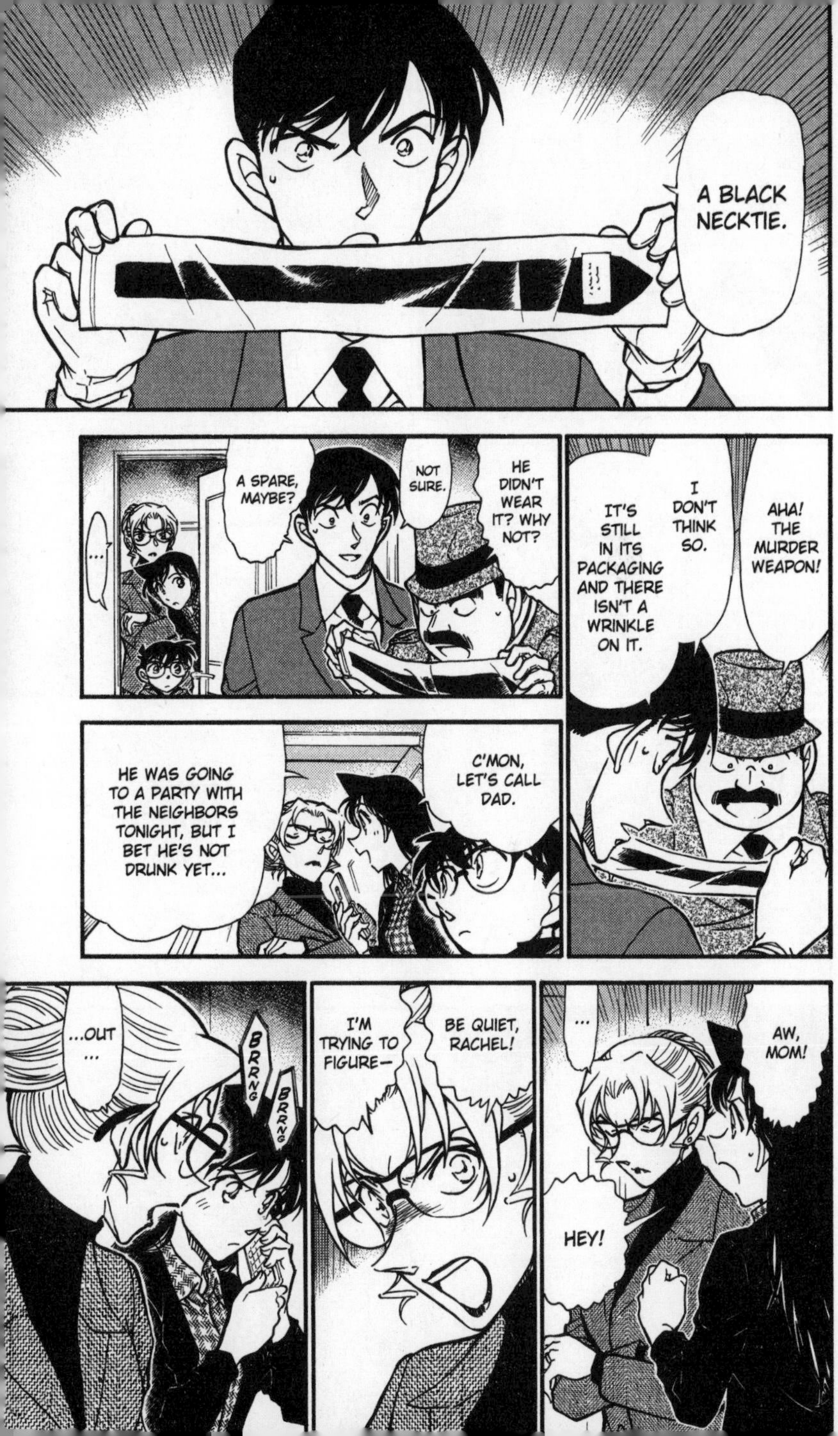
A BLACK NECKTIE.
AHA! THE MURDER WEAPON!
I DON'T THINK SO.
IT'S STILL IN ITS PACKAGING AND THERE ISN'T A WRINKLE ON IT.
HE DIDN'T WEAR IT? WHY NOT?
NOT SURE.
A SPARE, MAYBE?
...
C'MON, LET'S CALL DAD.
HE WAS GOING TO A PARTY WITH THE NEIGHBORS TONIGHT, BUT I BET HE'S NOT DRUNK YET...
AW, MOM!
...
HEY!
BE QUIET, RACHEL!
I'M TRYING TO FIGURE—
BRRNG
BRRNG
...OUT ...

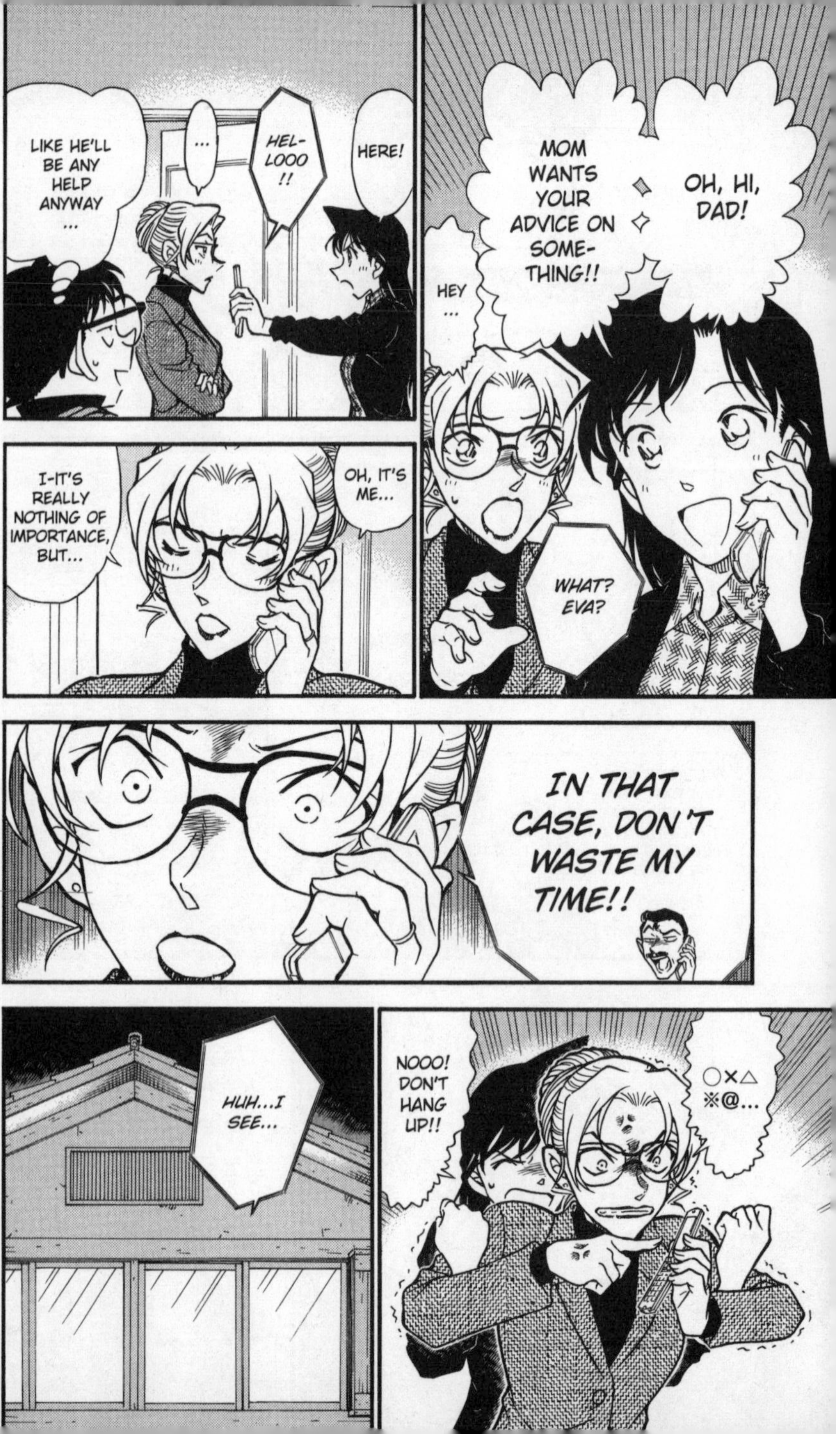
OH, HI, DAD!
MOM WANTS YOUR ADVICE ON SOMETHING!!
HEY ...
WHAT? EVA?
HERE!
HEL-LOOO !!
...
LIKE HE'LL BE ANY HELP ANYWAY ...
OH, IT'S ME...
I-IT'S REALLY NOTHING OF IMPORTANCE, BUT...
IN THAT CASE, DON'T WASTE MY TIME!!
○×△ ※@...
NOOO! DON'T HANG UP!!
HUH...I SEE...

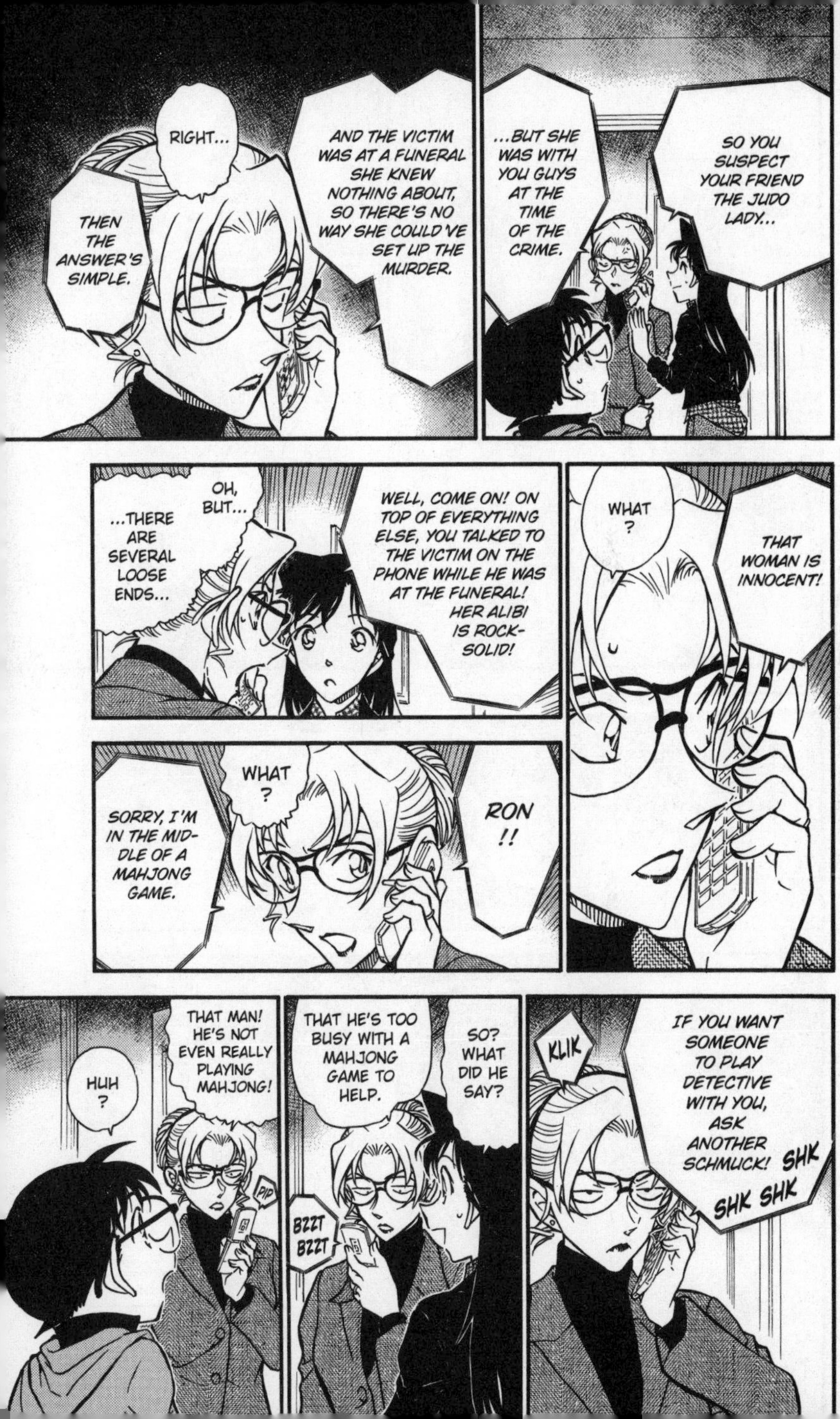
SO YOU SUSPECT YOUR FRIEND THE JUDO LADY...
...BUT SHE WAS WITH YOU GUYS AT THE TIME OF THE CRIME.
AND THE VICTIM WAS AT A FUNERAL SHE KNEW NOTHING ABOUT, SO THERE'S NO WAY SHE COULD'VE SET UP THE MURDER.
RIGHT...
THEN THE ANSWER'S SIMPLE.
WHAT?
THAT WOMAN IS INNOCENT!
WELL, COME ON! ON TOP OF EVERYTHING ELSE, YOU TALKED TO THE VICTIM ON THE PHONE WHILE HE WAS AT THE FUNERAL! HER ALIBI IS ROCK-SOLID!
OH, BUT...
...THERE ARE SEVERAL LOOSE ENDS...
RON!!
WHAT?
SORRY, I'M IN THE MIDDLE OF A MAHJONG GAME.
IF YOU WANT SOMEONE TO PLAY DETECTIVE WITH YOU, ASK ANOTHER SCHMUCK!
SHK SHK SHK
KLIK
SO? WHAT DID HE SAY?
THAT HE'S TOO BUSY WITH A MAHJONG GAME TO HELP.
BZZT BZZT
THAT MAN! HE'S NOT EVEN REALLY PLAYING MAHJONG!
PIP
HUH?

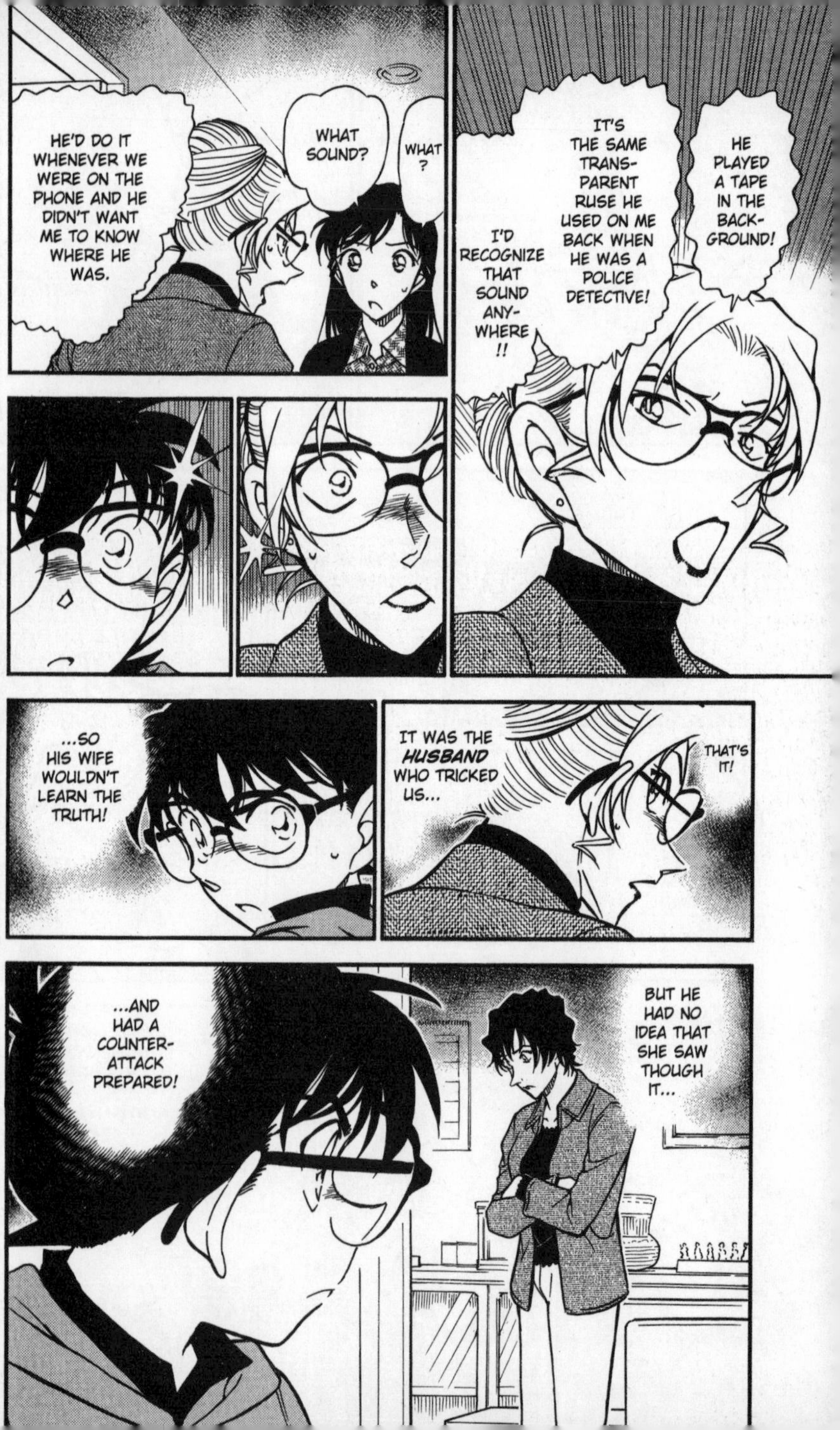
HE PLAYED A TAPE IN THE BACKGROUND!
IT'S THE SAME TRANSPARENT RUSE HE USED ON ME BACK WHEN HE WAS A POLICE DETECTIVE!
I'D RECOGNIZE THAT SOUND ANYWHERE !!
WHAT?
WHAT SOUND?
HE'D DO IT WHENEVER WE WERE ON THE PHONE AND HE DIDN'T WANT ME TO KNOW WHERE HE WAS.
THAT'S IT!
IT WAS THE *HUSBAND* WHO TRICKED US...
...SO HIS WIFE WOULDN'T LEARN THE TRUTH!
BUT HE HAD NO IDEA THAT SHE SAW THOUGH IT...
...AND HAD A COUNTER-ATTACK PREPARED!

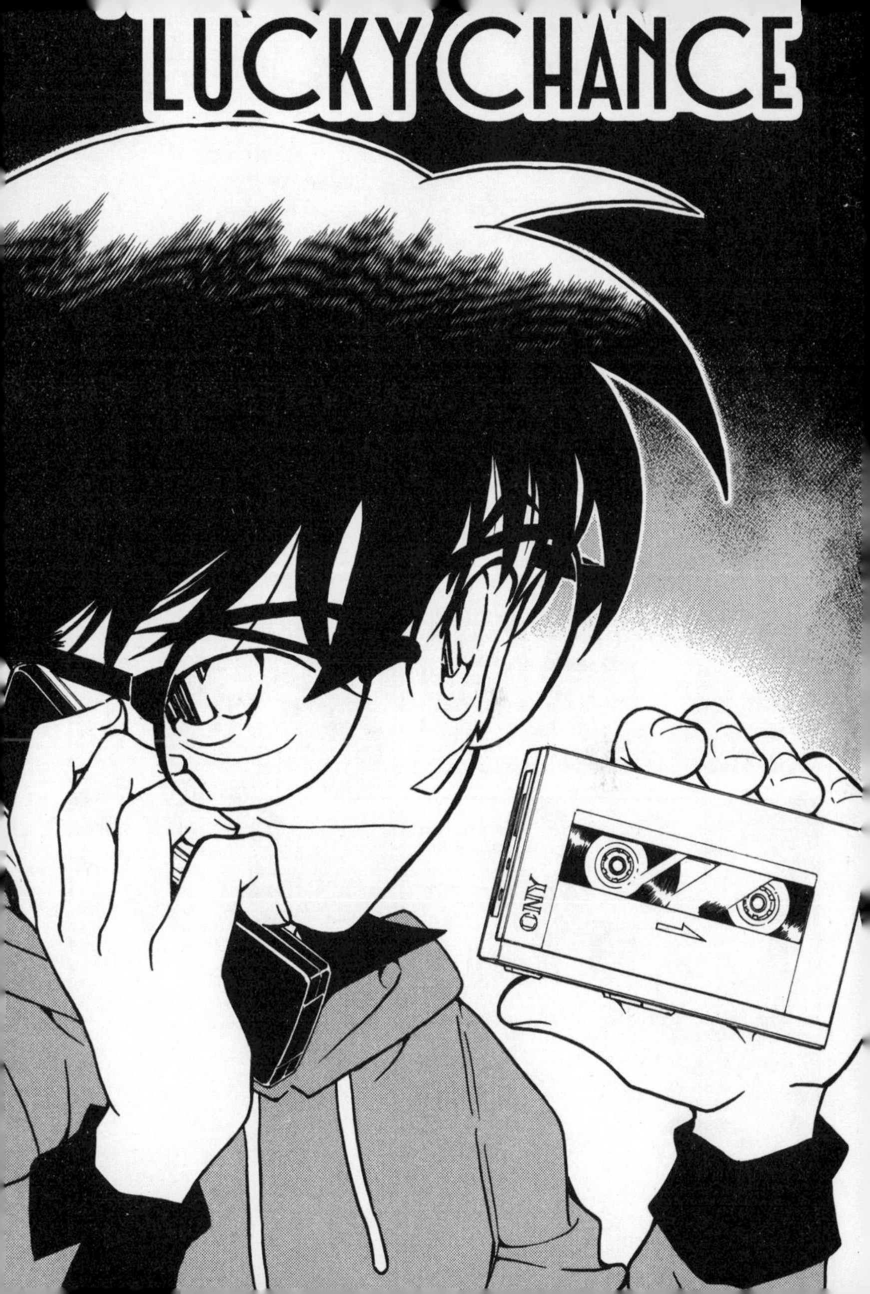
LUCKY CHANCE

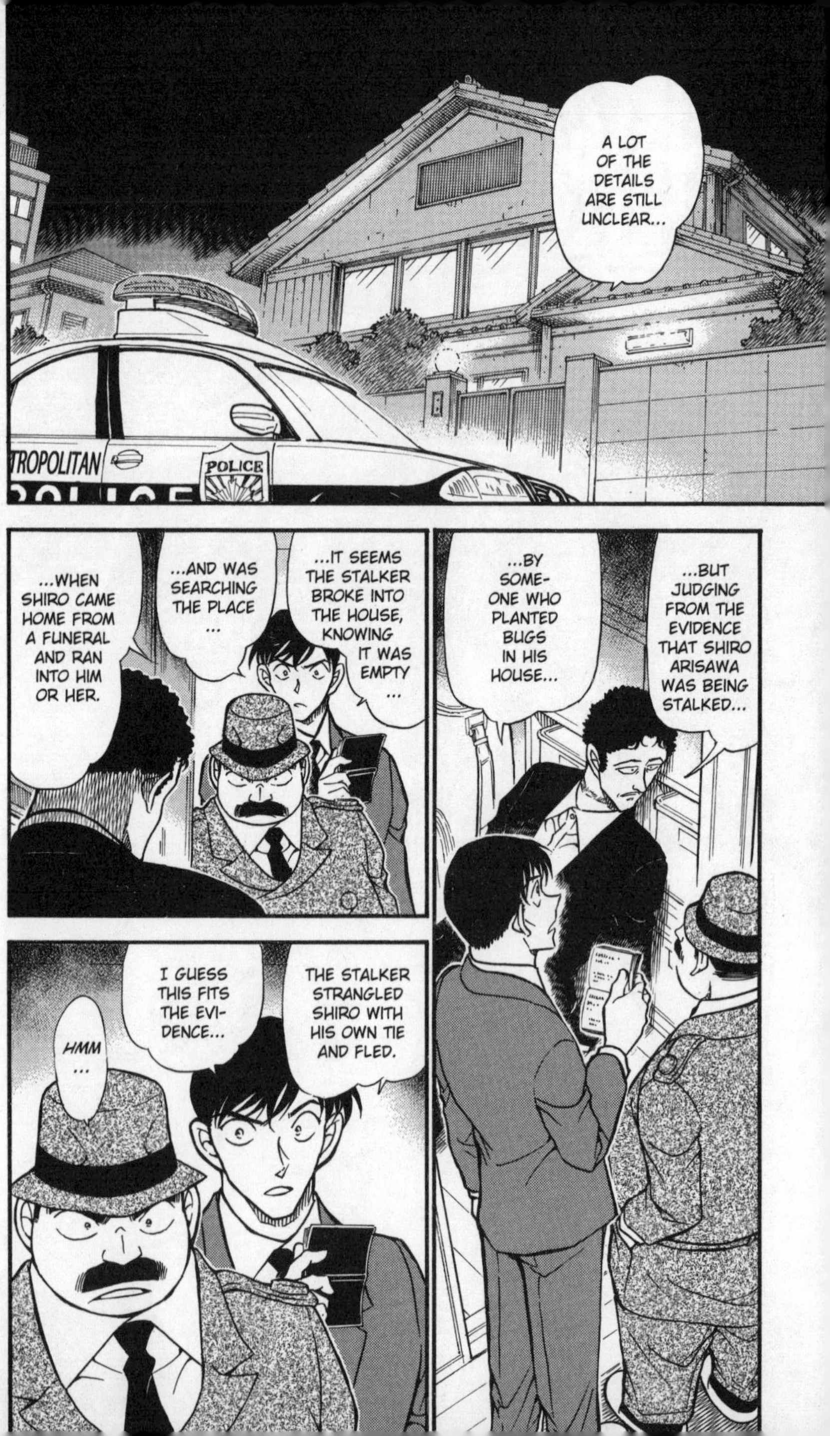
A LOT OF THE DETAILS ARE STILL UNCLEAR...
TROPOLITAN
POLICE
...BUT JUDGING FROM THE EVIDENCE THAT SHIRO ARISAWA WAS BEING STALKED...
...BY SOME-ONE WHO PLANTED BUGS IN HIS HOUSE...
...IT SEEMS THE STALKER BROKE INTO THE HOUSE, KNOWING IT WAS EMPTY...
...AND WAS SEARCHING THE PLACE...
...WHEN SHIRO CAME HOME FROM A FUNERAL AND RAN INTO HIM OR HER.
THE STALKER STRANGLED SHIRO WITH HIS OWN TIE AND FLED.
I GUESS THIS FITS THE EVI-DENCE...
HMM...

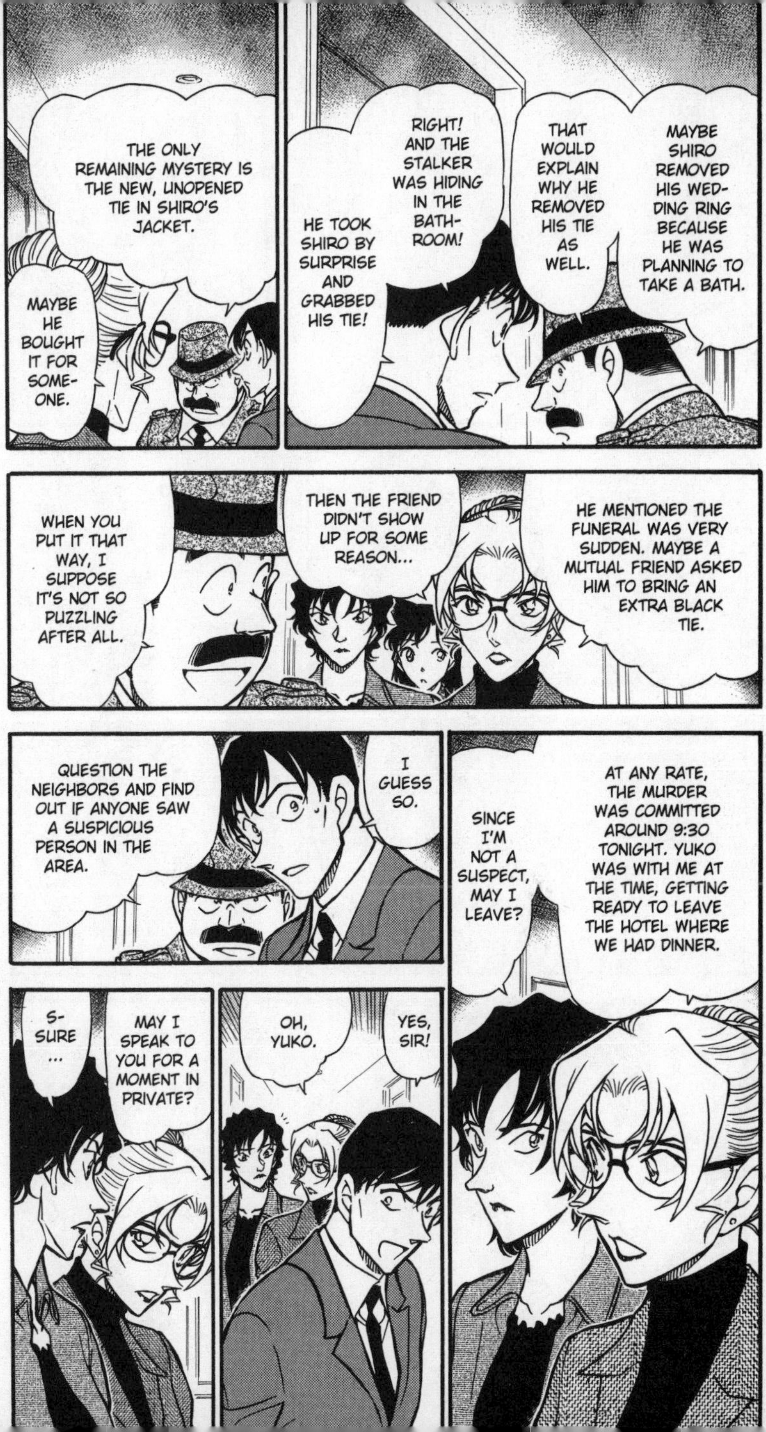
MAYBE SHIRO REMOVED HIS WED-DING RING BECAUSE HE WAS PLANNING TO TAKE A BATH.
THAT WOULD EXPLAIN WHY HE REMOVED HIS TIE AS WELL.
RIGHT! AND THE STALKER WAS HIDING IN THE BATH-ROOM!
HE TOOK SHIRO BY SURPRISE AND GRABBED HIS TIE!
THE ONLY REMAINING MYSTERY IS THE NEW, UNOPENED TIE IN SHIRO'S JACKET.
MAYBE HE BOUGHT IT FOR SOME-ONE.
HE MENTIONED THE FUNERAL WAS VERY SUDDEN. MAYBE A MUTUAL FRIEND ASKED HIM TO BRING AN EXTRA BLACK TIE.
THEN THE FRIEND DIDN'T SHOW UP FOR SOME REASON...
WHEN YOU PUT IT THAT WAY, I SUPPOSE IT'S NOT SO PUZZLING AFTER ALL.
AT ANY RATE, THE MURDER WAS COMMITTED AROUND 9:30 TONIGHT. YUKO WAS WITH ME AT THE TIME, GETTING READY TO LEAVE THE HOTEL WHERE WE HAD DINNER.
SINCE I'M NOT A SUSPECT, MAY I LEAVE?
I GUESS SO.
QUESTION THE NEIGHBORS AND FIND OUT IF ANYONE SAW A SUSPICIOUS PERSON IN THE AREA.
YES, SIR!
OH, YUKO.
MAY I SPEAK TO YOU FOR A MOMENT IN PRIVATE?
S-SURE...

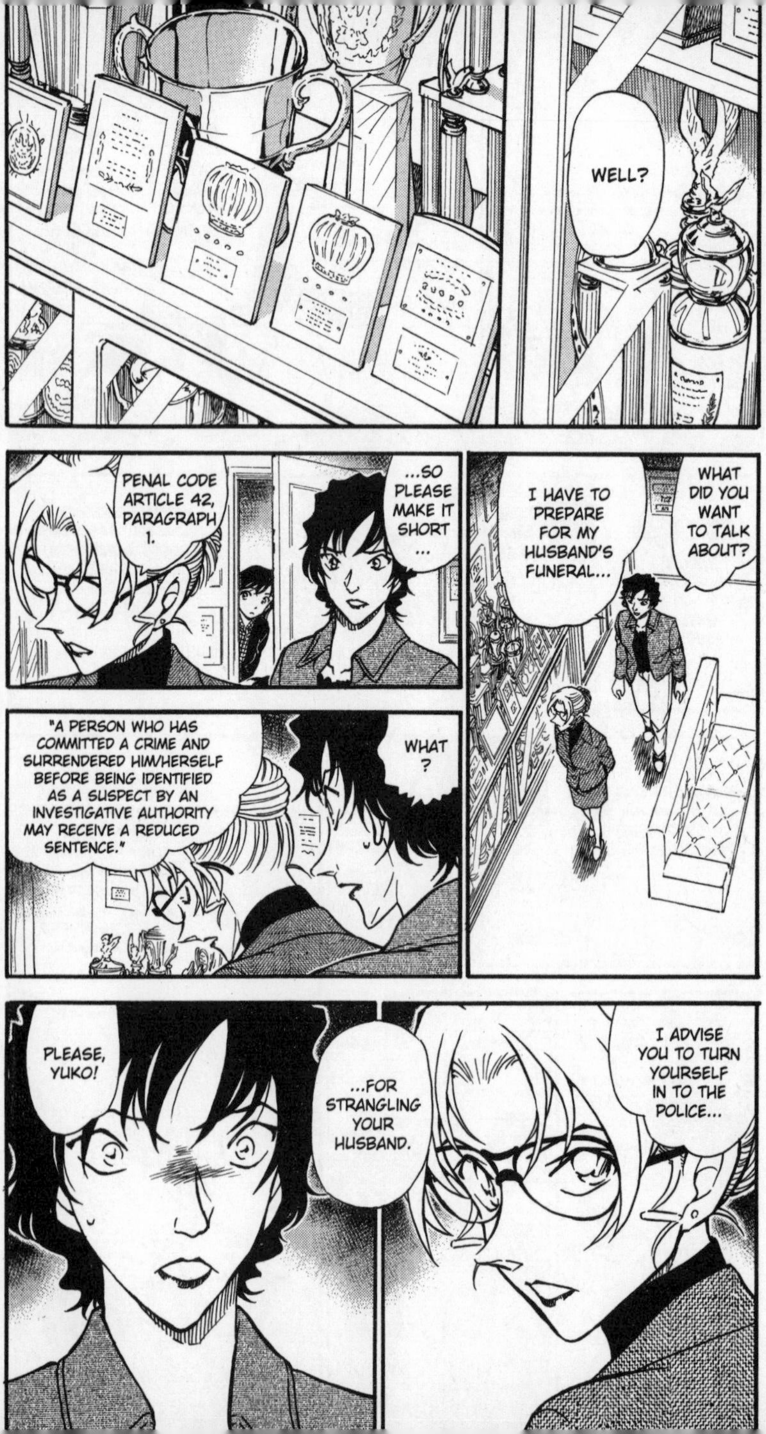
WELL?
WHAT DID YOU WANT TO TALK ABOUT?
I HAVE TO PREPARE FOR MY HUSBAND'S FUNERAL...
...SO PLEASE MAKE IT SHORT ...
PENAL CODE ARTICLE 42, PARAGRAPH 1.
WHAT ?
"A PERSON WHO HAS COMMITTED A CRIME AND SURRENDERED HIM/HERSELF BEFORE BEING IDENTIFIED AS A SUSPECT BY AN INVESTIGATIVE AUTHORITY MAY RECEIVE A REDUCED SENTENCE."
I ADVISE YOU TO TURN YOURSELF IN TO THE POLICE...
...FOR STRANGLING YOUR HUSBAND.
PLEASE, YUKO!

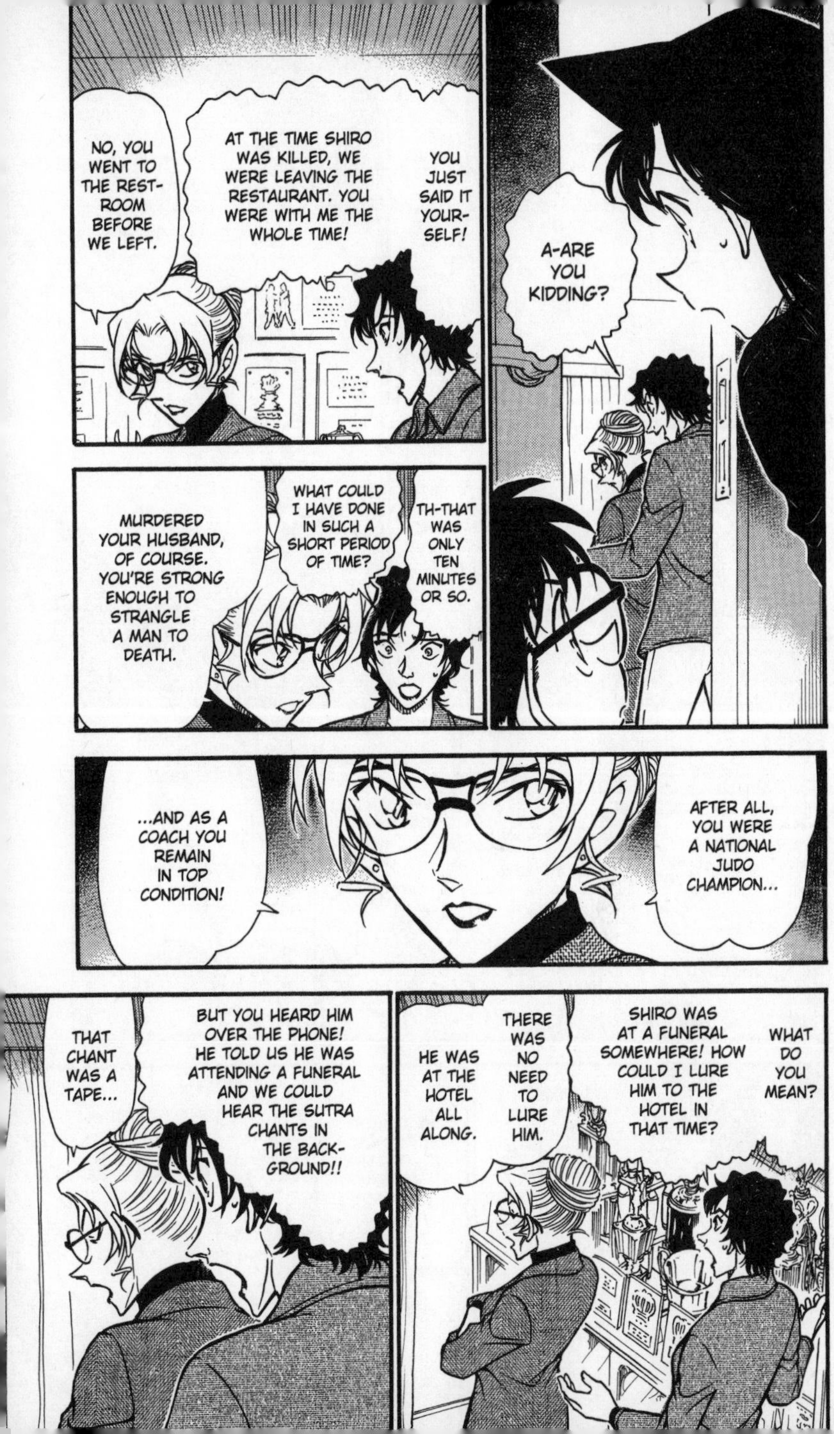
A-ARE YOU KIDDING?
YOU JUST SAID IT YOURSELF!
AT THE TIME SHIRO WAS KILLED, WE WERE LEAVING THE RESTAURANT. YOU WERE WITH ME THE WHOLE TIME!
NO, YOU WENT TO THE REST-ROOM BEFORE WE LEFT.
TH-THAT WAS ONLY TEN MINUTES OR SO.
WHAT COULD I HAVE DONE IN SUCH A SHORT PERIOD OF TIME?
MURDERED YOUR HUSBAND, OF COURSE. YOU'RE STRONG ENOUGH TO STRANGLE A MAN TO DEATH.
AFTER ALL, YOU WERE A NATIONAL JUDO CHAMPION...
...AND AS A COACH YOU REMAIN IN TOP CONDITION!
WHAT DO YOU MEAN?
SHIRO WAS AT A FUNERAL SOMEWHERE! HOW COULD I LURE HIM TO THE HOTEL IN THAT TIME?
THERE WAS NO NEED TO LURE HIM.
HE WAS AT THE HOTEL ALL ALONG.
BUT YOU HEARD HIM OVER THE PHONE! HE TOLD US HE WAS ATTENDING A FUNERAL AND WE COULD HEAR THE SUTRA CHANTS IN THE BACK-GROUND!!
THAT CHANT WAS A TAPE...

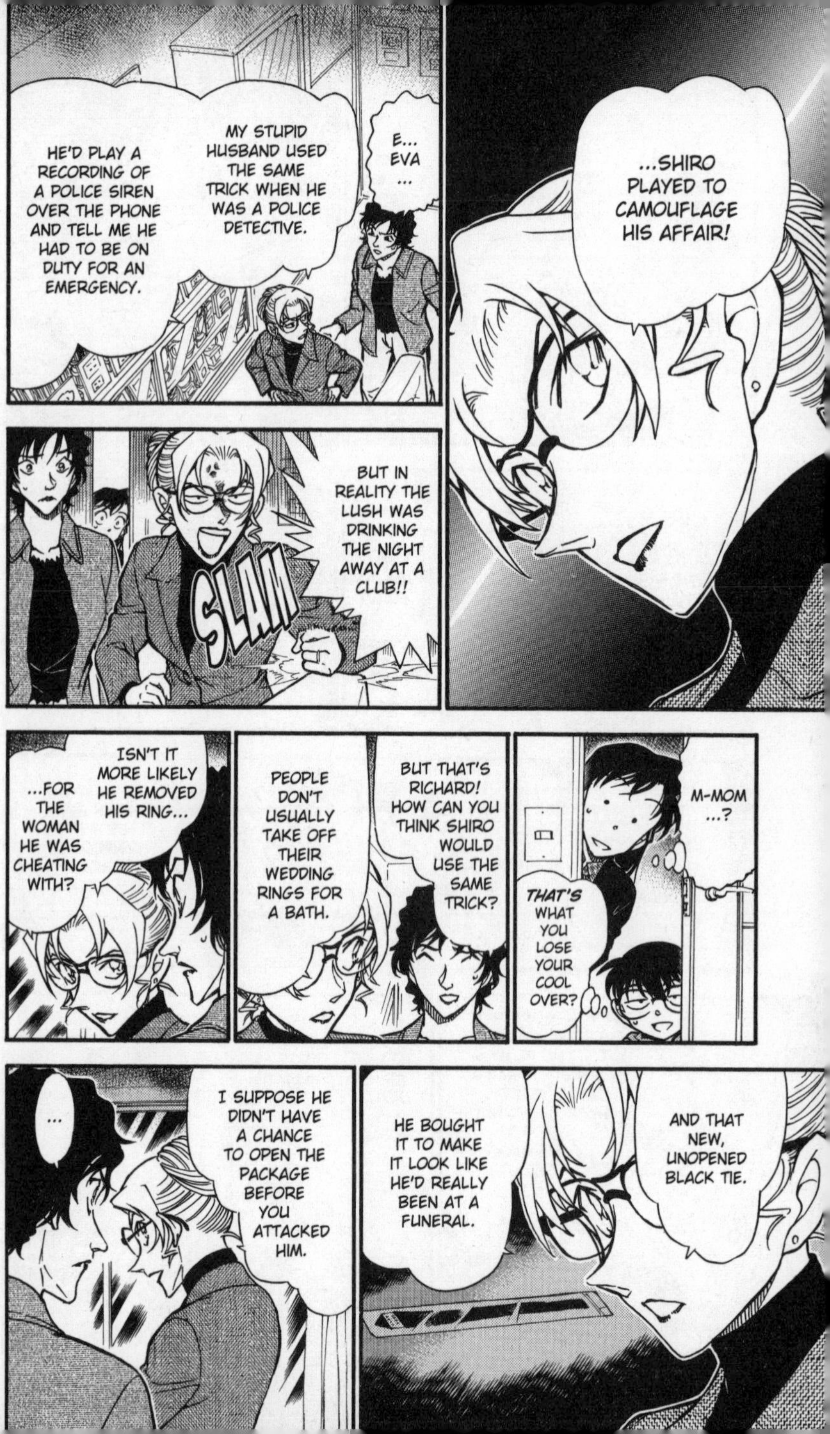
...SHIRO PLAYED TO CAMOUFLAGE HIS AFFAIR!
E... EVA ...
MY STUPID HUSBAND USED THE SAME TRICK WHEN HE WAS A POLICE DETECTIVE.
HE'D PLAY A RECORDING OF A POLICE SIREN OVER THE PHONE AND TELL ME HE HAD TO BE ON DUTY FOR AN EMERGENCY.
BUT IN REALITY THE LUSH WAS DRINKING THE NIGHT AWAY AT A CLUB!!
SLAM
M-MOM ...?
THAT'S WHAT YOU LOSE YOUR COOL OVER?
BUT THAT'S RICHARD! HOW CAN YOU THINK SHIRO WOULD USE THE SAME TRICK?
PEOPLE DON'T USUALLY TAKE OFF THEIR WEDDING RINGS FOR A BATH.
ISN'T IT MORE LIKELY HE REMOVED HIS RING...
...FOR THE WOMAN HE WAS CHEATING WITH?
AND THAT NEW, UNOPENED BLACK TIE.
HE BOUGHT IT TO MAKE IT LOOK LIKE HE'D REALLY BEEN AT A FUNERAL.
I SUPPOSE HE DIDN'T HAVE A CHANCE TO OPEN THE PACKAGE BEFORE YOU ATTACKED HIM.
...

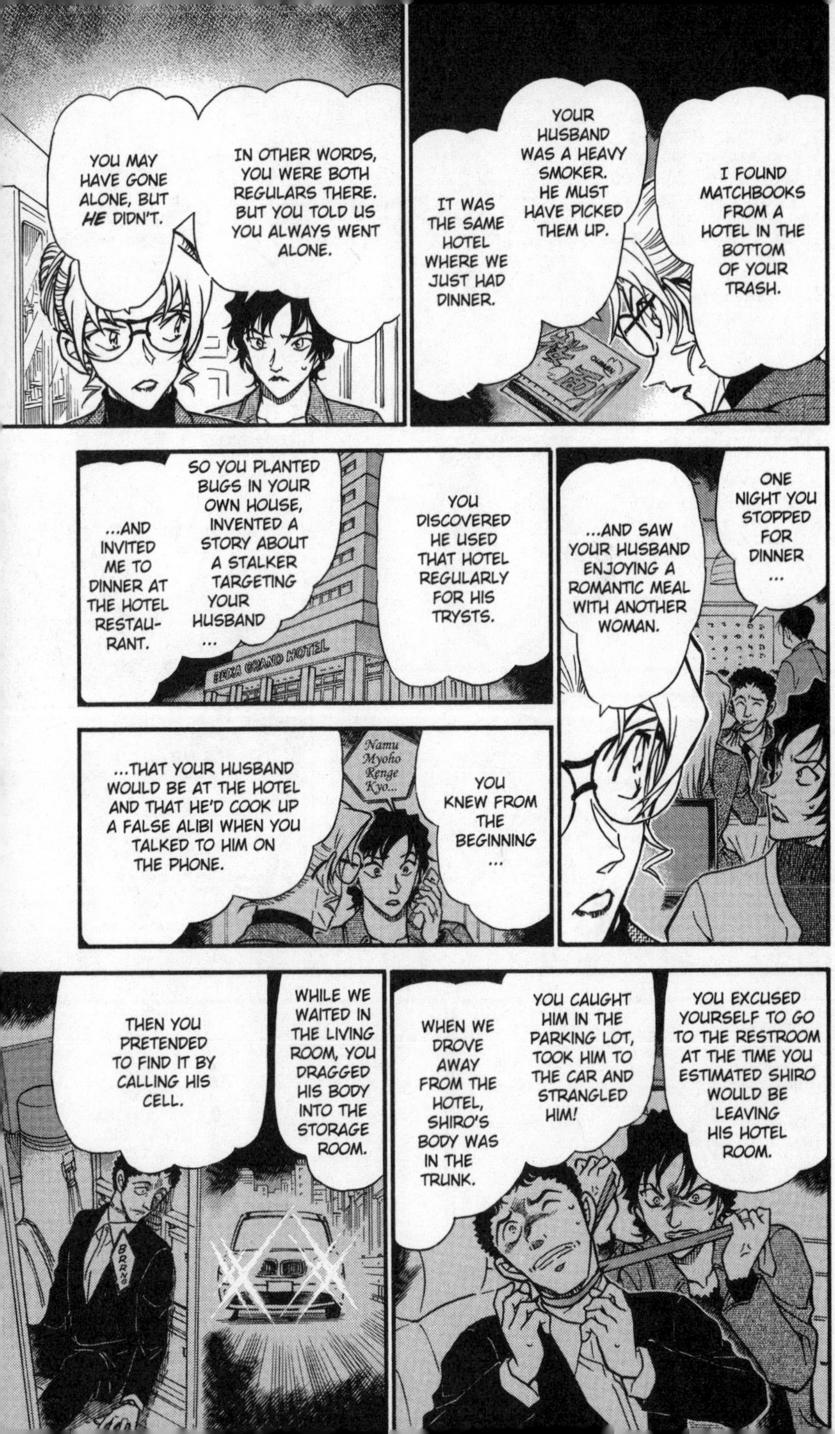
I FOUND MATCHBOOKS FROM A HOTEL IN THE BOTTOM OF YOUR TRASH.
YOUR HUSBAND WAS A HEAVY SMOKER. HE MUST HAVE PICKED THEM UP.
IT WAS THE SAME HOTEL WHERE WE JUST HAD DINNER.
IN OTHER WORDS, YOU WERE BOTH REGULARS THERE. BUT YOU TOLD US YOU ALWAYS WENT ALONE.
YOU MAY HAVE GONE ALONE, BUT ***HE*** DIDN'T.
ONE NIGHT YOU STOPPED FOR DINNER...
...AND SAW YOUR HUSBAND ENJOYING A ROMANTIC MEAL WITH ANOTHER WOMAN.
YOU DISCOVERED HE USED THAT HOTEL REGULARLY FOR HIS TRYSTS.
SO YOU PLANTED BUGS IN YOUR OWN HOUSE, INVENTED A STORY ABOUT A STALKER TARGETING YOUR HUSBAND...
...AND INVITED ME TO DINNER AT THE HOTEL RESTAU-RANT.
YOU KNEW FROM THE BEGINNING...
Namu Myoho Renge Kyo...
...THAT YOUR HUSBAND WOULD BE AT THE HOTEL AND THAT HE'D COOK UP A FALSE ALIBI WHEN YOU TALKED TO HIM ON THE PHONE.
YOU EXCUSED YOURSELF TO GO TO THE RESTROOM AT THE TIME YOU ESTIMATED SHIRO WOULD BE LEAVING HIS HOTEL ROOM.
YOU CAUGHT HIM IN THE PARKING LOT, TOOK HIM TO THE CAR AND STRANGLED HIM!
WHEN WE DROVE AWAY FROM THE HOTEL, SHIRO'S BODY WAS IN THE TRUNK.
WHILE WE WAITED IN THE LIVING ROOM, YOU DRAGGED HIS BODY INTO THE STORAGE ROOM.
THEN YOU PRETENDED TO FIND IT BY CALLING HIS CELL.

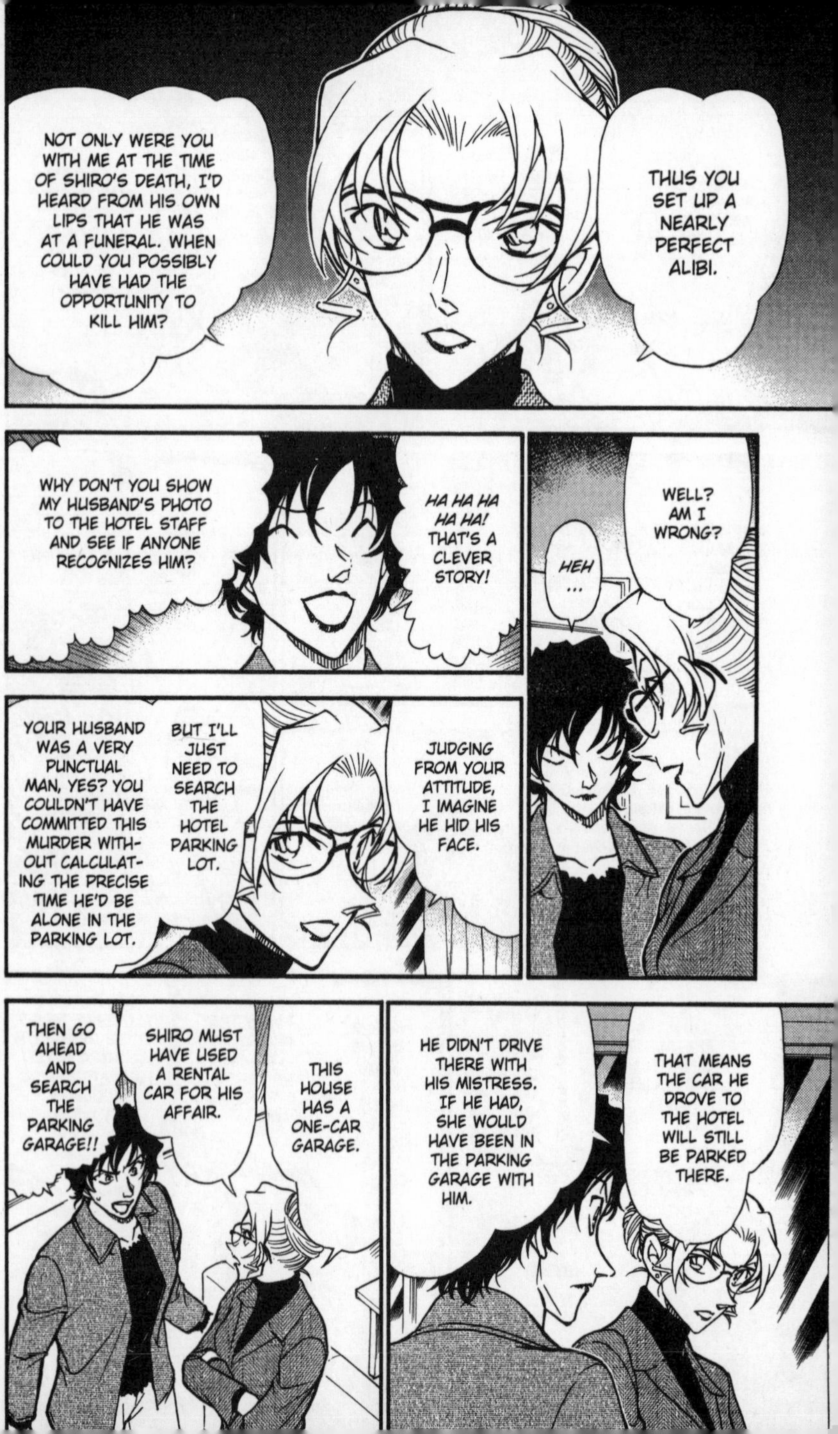
THUS YOU SET UP A NEARLY PERFECT ALIBI.
NOT ONLY WERE YOU WITH ME AT THE TIME OF SHIRO'S DEATH, I'D HEARD FROM HIS OWN LIPS THAT HE WAS AT A FUNERAL. WHEN COULD YOU POSSIBLY HAVE HAD THE OPPORTUNITY TO KILL HIM?
WELL? AM I WRONG?
HEH ...
HA HA HA HA HA! THAT'S A CLEVER STORY!
WHY DON'T YOU SHOW MY HUSBAND'S PHOTO TO THE HOTEL STAFF AND SEE IF ANYONE RECOGNIZES HIM?
JUDGING FROM YOUR ATTITUDE, I IMAGINE HE HID HIS FACE.
BUT I'LL JUST NEED TO SEARCH THE HOTEL PARKING LOT.
YOUR HUSBAND WAS A VERY PUNCTUAL MAN, YES? YOU COULDN'T HAVE COMMITTED THIS MURDER WITHOUT CALCULATING THE PRECISE TIME HE'D BE ALONE IN THE PARKING LOT.
THAT MEANS THE CAR HE DROVE TO THE HOTEL WILL STILL BE PARKED THERE.
HE DIDN'T DRIVE THERE WITH HIS MISTRESS. IF HE HAD, SHE WOULD HAVE BEEN IN THE PARKING GARAGE WITH HIM.
THIS HOUSE HAS A ONE-CAR GARAGE.
SHIRO MUST HAVE USED A RENTAL CAR FOR HIS AFFAIR.
THEN GO AHEAD AND SEARCH THE PARKING GARAGE!!

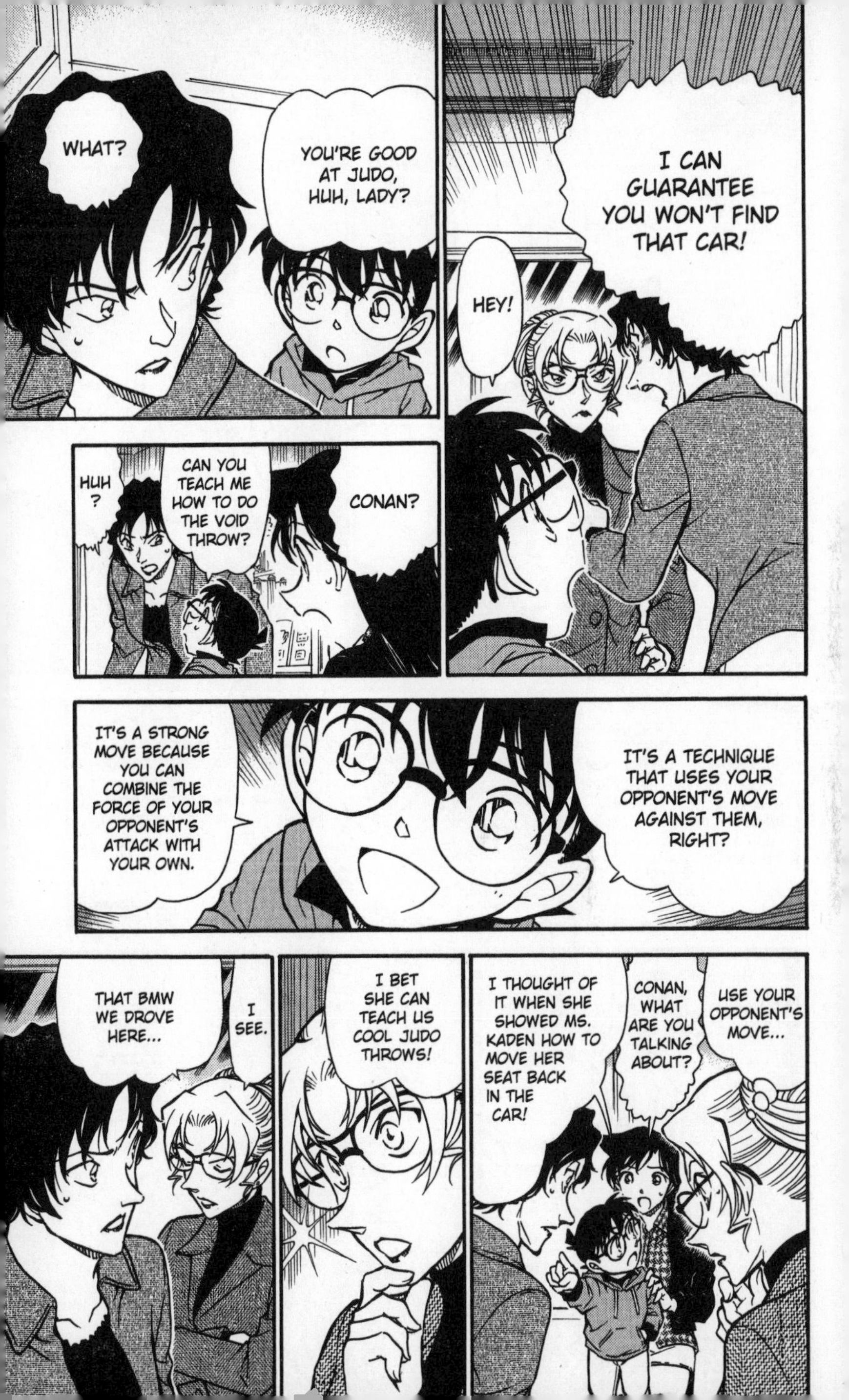
I CAN GUARANTEE YOU WON'T FIND THAT CAR!
HEY!
YOU'RE GOOD AT JUDO, HUH, LADY?
WHAT?
CONAN?
CAN YOU TEACH ME HOW TO DO THE VOID THROW?
HUH?
IT'S A TECHNIQUE THAT USES YOUR OPPONENT'S MOVE AGAINST THEM, RIGHT?
IT'S A STRONG MOVE BECAUSE YOU CAN COMBINE THE FORCE OF YOUR OPPONENT'S ATTACK WITH YOUR OWN.
USE YOUR OPPONENT'S MOVE...
CONAN, WHAT ARE YOU TALKING ABOUT?
I THOUGHT OF IT WHEN SHE SHOWED MS. KADEN HOW TO MOVE HER SEAT BACK IN THE CAR!
I BET SHE CAN TEACH US COOL JUDO THROWS!
I SEE.
THAT BMW WE DROVE HERE...

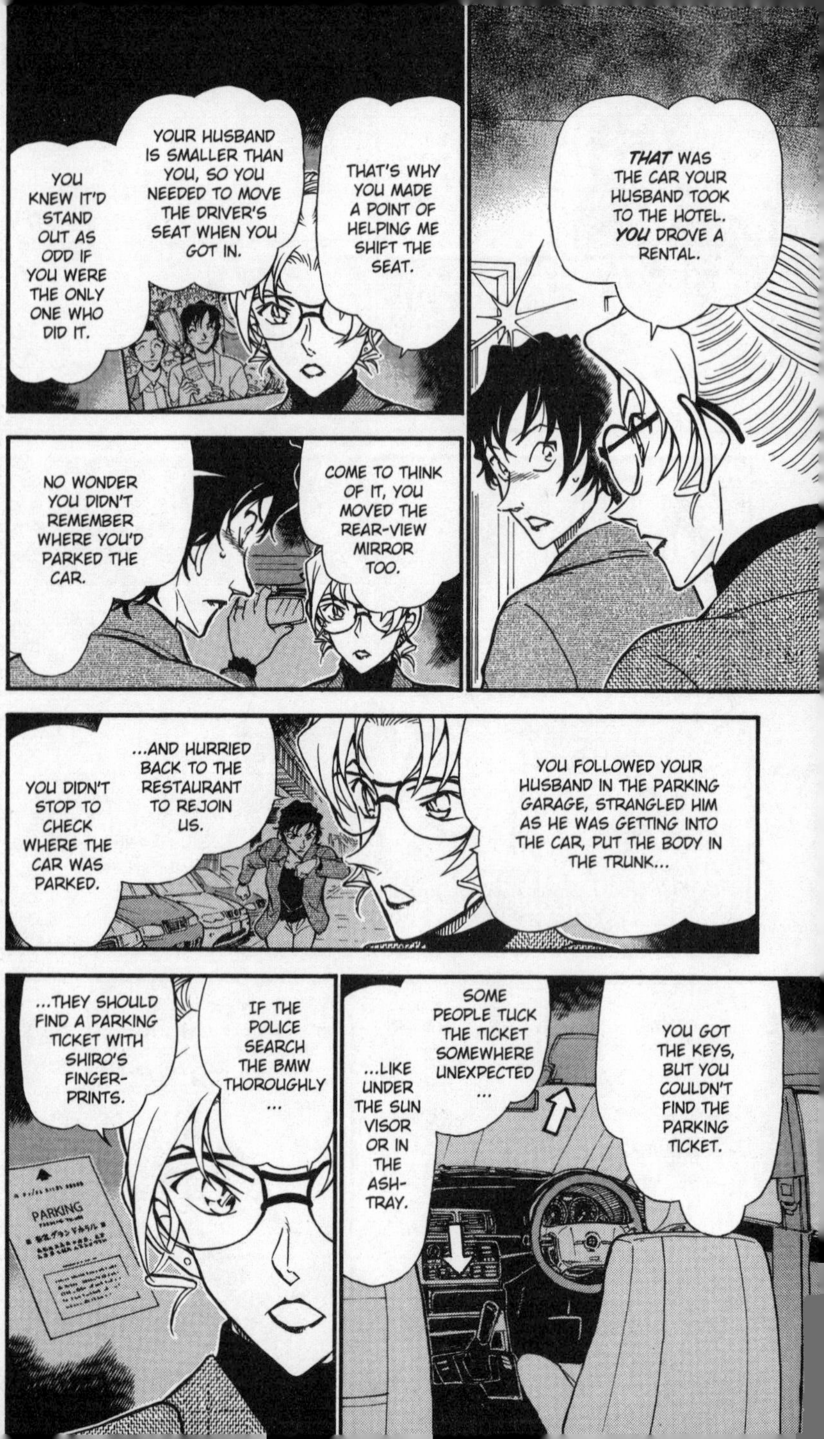
THAT WAS THE CAR YOUR HUSBAND TOOK TO THE HOTEL. YOU DROVE A RENTAL.
THAT'S WHY YOU MADE A POINT OF HELPING ME SHIFT THE SEAT.
YOUR HUSBAND IS SMALLER THAN YOU, SO YOU NEEDED TO MOVE THE DRIVER'S SEAT WHEN YOU GOT IN.
YOU KNEW IT'D STAND OUT AS ODD IF YOU WERE THE ONLY ONE WHO DID IT.
COME TO THINK OF IT, YOU MOVED THE REAR-VIEW MIRROR TOO.
NO WONDER YOU DIDN'T REMEMBER WHERE YOU'D PARKED THE CAR.
YOU FOLLOWED YOUR HUSBAND IN THE PARKING GARAGE, STRANGLED HIM AS HE WAS GETTING INTO THE CAR, PUT THE BODY IN THE TRUNK...
...AND HURRIED BACK TO THE RESTAURANT TO REJOIN US.
YOU DIDN'T STOP TO CHECK WHERE THE CAR WAS PARKED.
YOU GOT THE KEYS, BUT YOU COULDN'T FIND THE PARKING TICKET.
SOME PEOPLE TUCK THE TICKET SOMEWHERE UNEXPECTED...
...LIKE UNDER THE SUN VISOR OR IN THE ASHTRAY.
IF THE POLICE SEARCH THE BMW THOROUGHLY...
...THEY SHOULD FIND A PARKING TICKET WITH SHIRO'S FINGERPRINTS.
PARKING

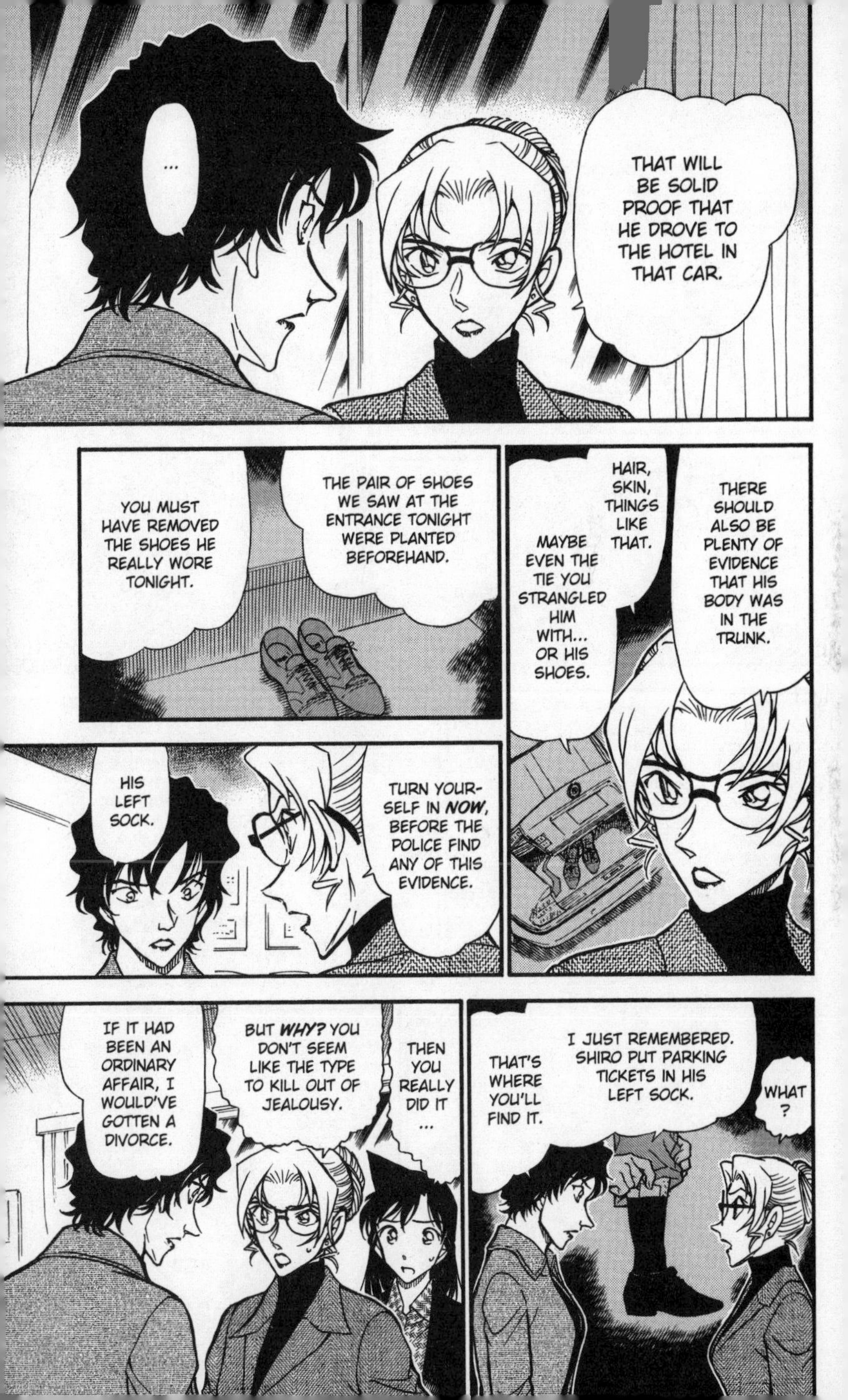
THAT WILL BE SOLID PROOF THAT HE DROVE TO THE HOTEL IN THAT CAR.
...
THERE SHOULD ALSO BE PLENTY OF EVIDENCE THAT HIS BODY WAS IN THE TRUNK.
HAIR, SKIN, THINGS LIKE THAT.
MAYBE EVEN THE TIE YOU STRANGLED HIM WITH... OR HIS SHOES.
THE PAIR OF SHOES WE SAW AT THE ENTRANCE TONIGHT WERE PLANTED BEFOREHAND.
YOU MUST HAVE REMOVED THE SHOES HE REALLY WORE TONIGHT.
TURN YOURSELF IN *NOW*, BEFORE THE POLICE FIND ANY OF THIS EVIDENCE.
HIS LEFT SOCK.
WHAT?
I JUST REMEMBERED. SHIRO PUT PARKING TICKETS IN HIS LEFT SOCK.
THAT'S WHERE YOU'LL FIND IT.
THEN YOU REALLY DID IT ...
BUT *WHY?* YOU DON'T SEEM LIKE THE TYPE TO KILL OUT OF JEALOUSY.
IF IT HAD BEEN AN ORDINARY AFFAIR, I WOULD'VE GOTTEN A DIVORCE.

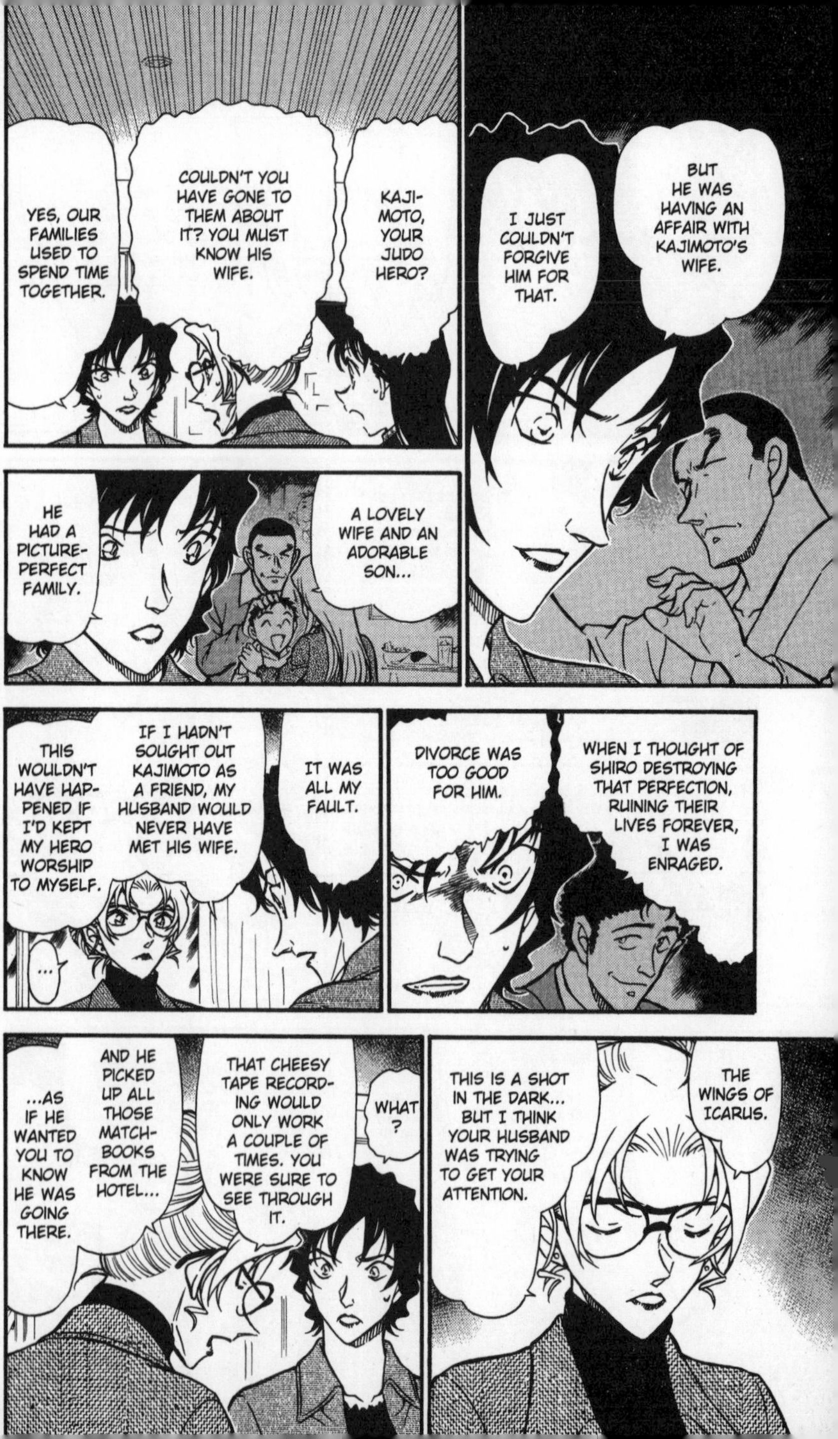
KAJI-MOTO, YOUR JUDO HERO?
COULDN'T YOU HAVE GONE TO THEM ABOUT IT? YOU MUST KNOW HIS WIFE.
YES, OUR FAMILIES USED TO SPEND TIME TOGETHER.
A LOVELY WIFE AND AN ADORABLE SON...
HE HAD A PICTURE-PERFECT FAMILY.
BUT HE WAS HAVING AN AFFAIR WITH KAJIMOTO'S WIFE.
I JUST COULDN'T FORGIVE HIM FOR THAT.
WHEN I THOUGHT OF SHIRO DESTROYING THAT PERFECTION, RUINING THEIR LIVES FOREVER, I WAS ENRAGED.
DIVORCE WAS TOO GOOD FOR HIM.
IT WAS ALL MY FAULT.
IF I HADN'T SOUGHT OUT KAJIMOTO AS A FRIEND, MY HUSBAND WOULD NEVER HAVE MET HIS WIFE.
THIS WOULDN'T HAVE HAP-PENED IF I'D KEPT MY HERO WORSHIP TO MYSELF.
...
THE WINGS OF ICARUS.
THIS IS A SHOT IN THE DARK... BUT I THINK YOUR HUSBAND WAS TRYING TO GET YOUR ATTENTION.
WHAT?
THAT CHEESY TAPE RECORD-ING WOULD ONLY WORK A COUPLE OF TIMES. YOU WERE SURE TO SEE THROUGH IT.
AND HE PICKED UP ALL THOSE MATCH-BOOKS FROM THE HOTEL...
...AS IF HE WANTED YOU TO KNOW HE WAS GOING THERE.

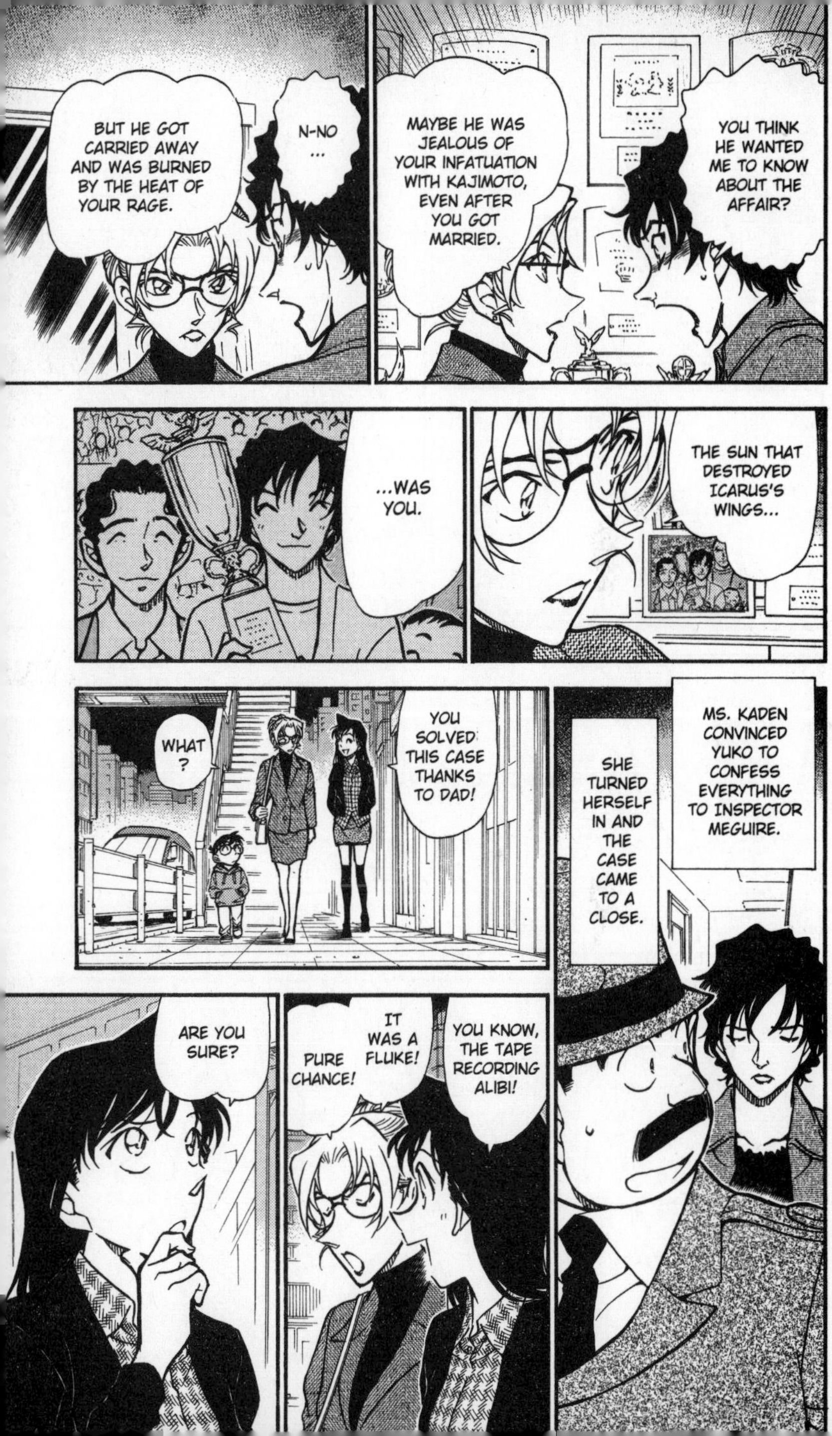
YOU THINK HE WANTED ME TO KNOW ABOUT THE AFFAIR?
MAYBE HE WAS JEALOUS OF YOUR INFATUATION WITH KAJIMOTO, EVEN AFTER YOU GOT MARRIED.
N-NO ...
BUT HE GOT CARRIED AWAY AND WAS BURNED BY THE HEAT OF YOUR RAGE.
THE SUN THAT DESTROYED ICARUS'S WINGS...
...WAS YOU.
MS. KADEN CONVINCED YUKO TO CONFESS EVERYTHING TO INSPECTOR MEGUIRE.
SHE TURNED HERSELF IN AND THE CASE CAME TO A CLOSE.
YOU SOLVED THIS CASE THANKS TO DAD!
WHAT?
YOU KNOW, THE TAPE RECORDING ALIBI!
IT WAS A FLUKE!
PURE CHANCE!
ARE YOU SURE?

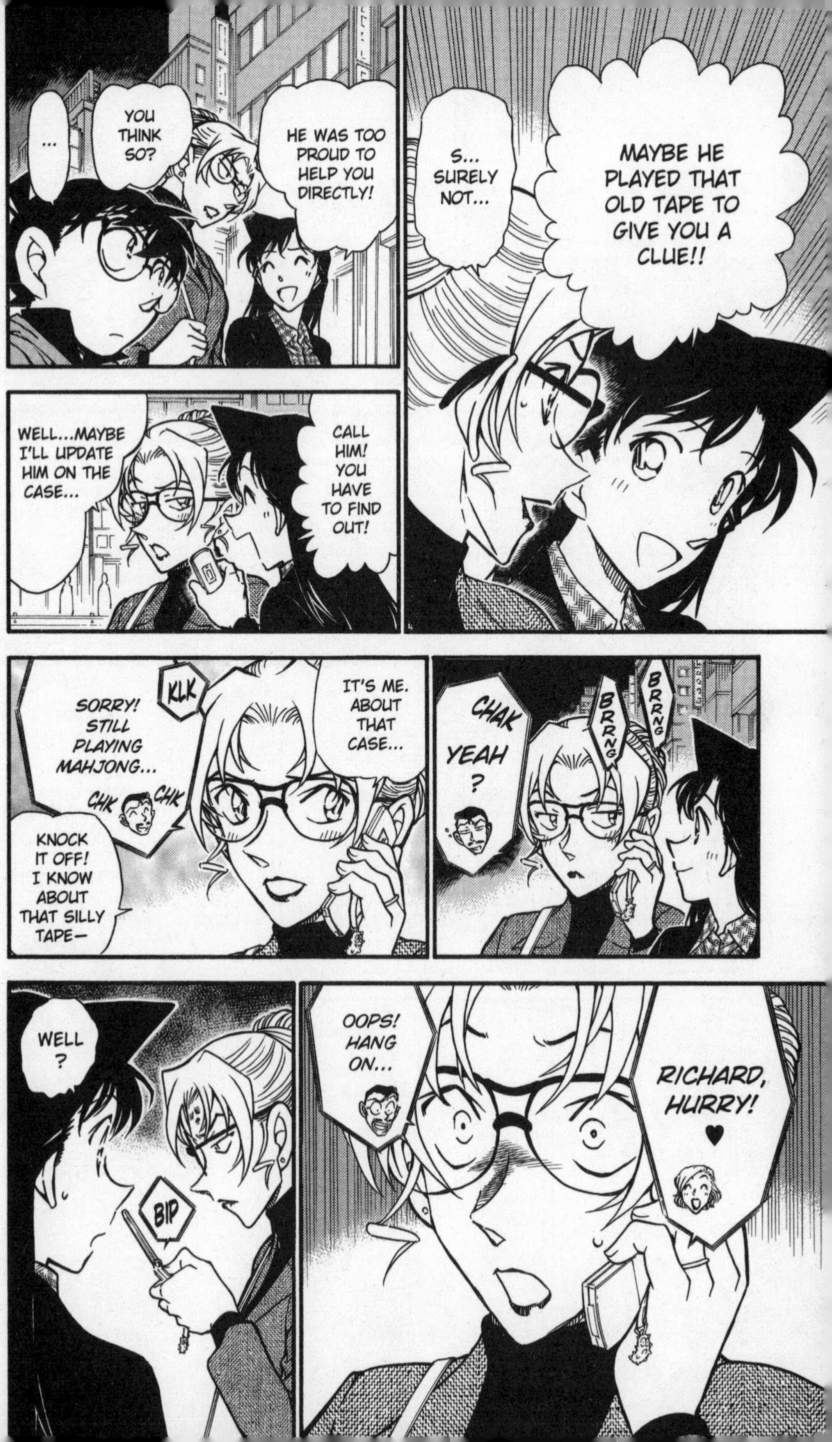
MAYBE HE PLAYED THAT OLD TAPE TO GIVE YOU A CLUE!!
S... SURELY NOT...
HE WAS TOO PROUD TO HELP YOU DIRECTLY!
YOU THINK SO?
...
CALL HIM! YOU HAVE TO FIND OUT!
WELL...MAYBE I'LL UPDATE HIM ON THE CASE...
BRRNG
BRRNG
CHAK
YEAH ?
IT'S ME. ABOUT THAT CASE...
KLK
SORRY! STILL PLAYING MAHJONG...
CHK CHK
KNOCK IT OFF! I KNOW ABOUT THAT SILLY TAPE—
RICHARD, HURRY! ♥
OOPS! HANG ON...
WELL ?
BIP

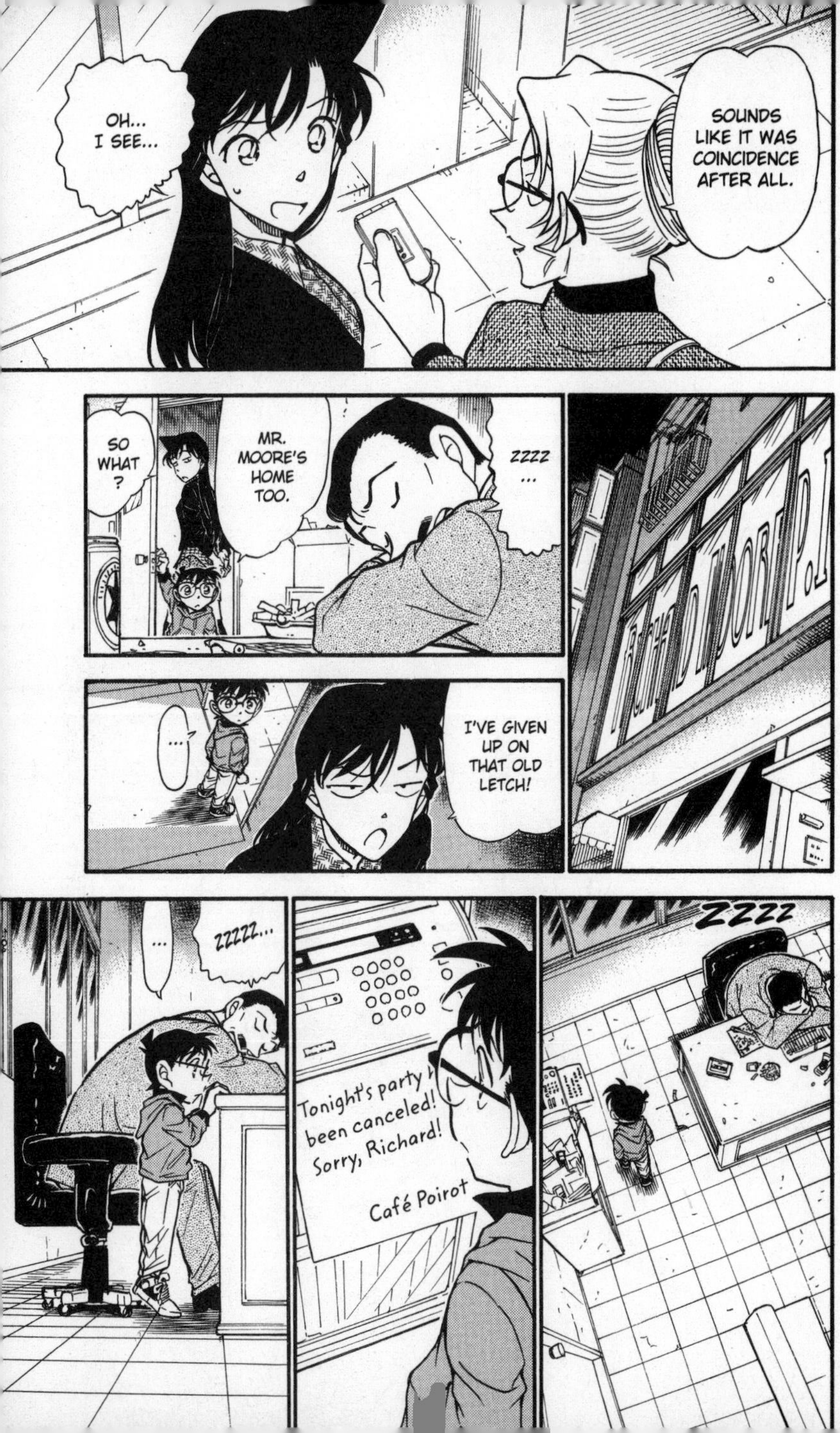
SOUNDS LIKE IT WAS COINCIDENCE AFTER ALL.
OH... I SEE...
ZZZZ ...
MR. MOORE'S HOME TOO.
SO WHAT ?
I'VE GIVEN UP ON THAT OLD LETCH!
...
ZZZZ
Tonight's party
been canceled!
Sorry, Richard!
Café Poirot
ZZZZZ...
...

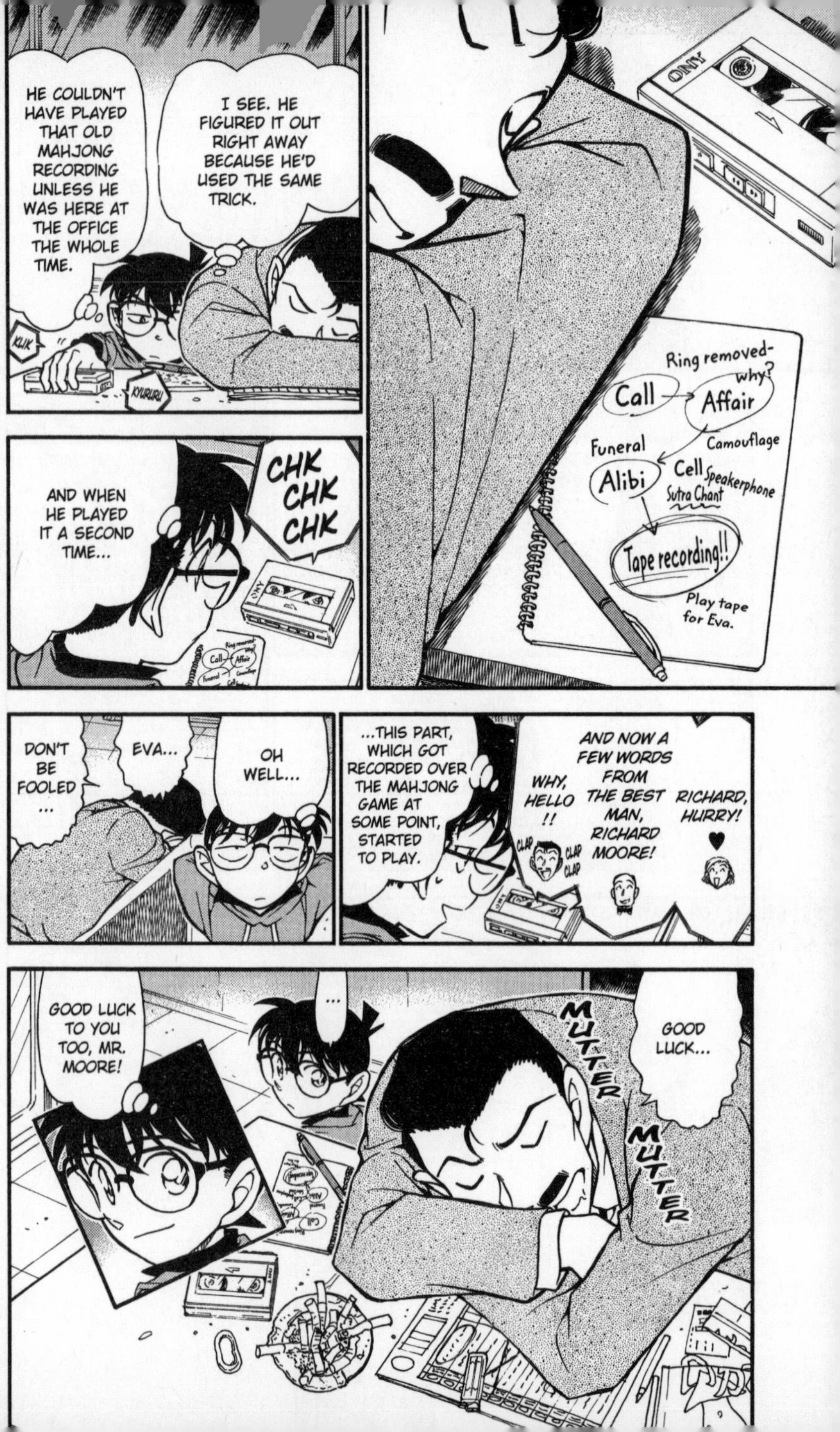
Ring removed-why?
Call
Affair
Camouflage
Funeral
Alibi
Cell
Speakerphone
Sutra Chant
Tape recording!!
Play tape for Eva.
I SEE. HE FIGURED IT OUT RIGHT AWAY BECAUSE HE'D USED THE SAME TRICK.
HE COULDN'T HAVE PLAYED THAT OLD MAHJONG RECORDING UNLESS HE WAS HERE AT THE OFFICE THE WHOLE TIME.
KLIK
KYURURU
CHK CHK CHK
AND WHEN HE PLAYED IT A SECOND TIME...
RICHARD, HURRY!
AND NOW A FEW WORDS FROM THE BEST MAN, RICHARD MOORE!
WHY, HELLO!!
CLAP CLAP CLAP
...THIS PART, WHICH GOT RECORDED OVER THE MAHJONG GAME AT SOME POINT, STARTED TO PLAY.
OH WELL...
EVA...
DON'T BE FOOLED...
GOOD LUCK...
MUTTER
MUTTER
...
GOOD LUCK TO YOU TOO, MR. MOORE!

FILE 5: VILLAGE OF HATRED

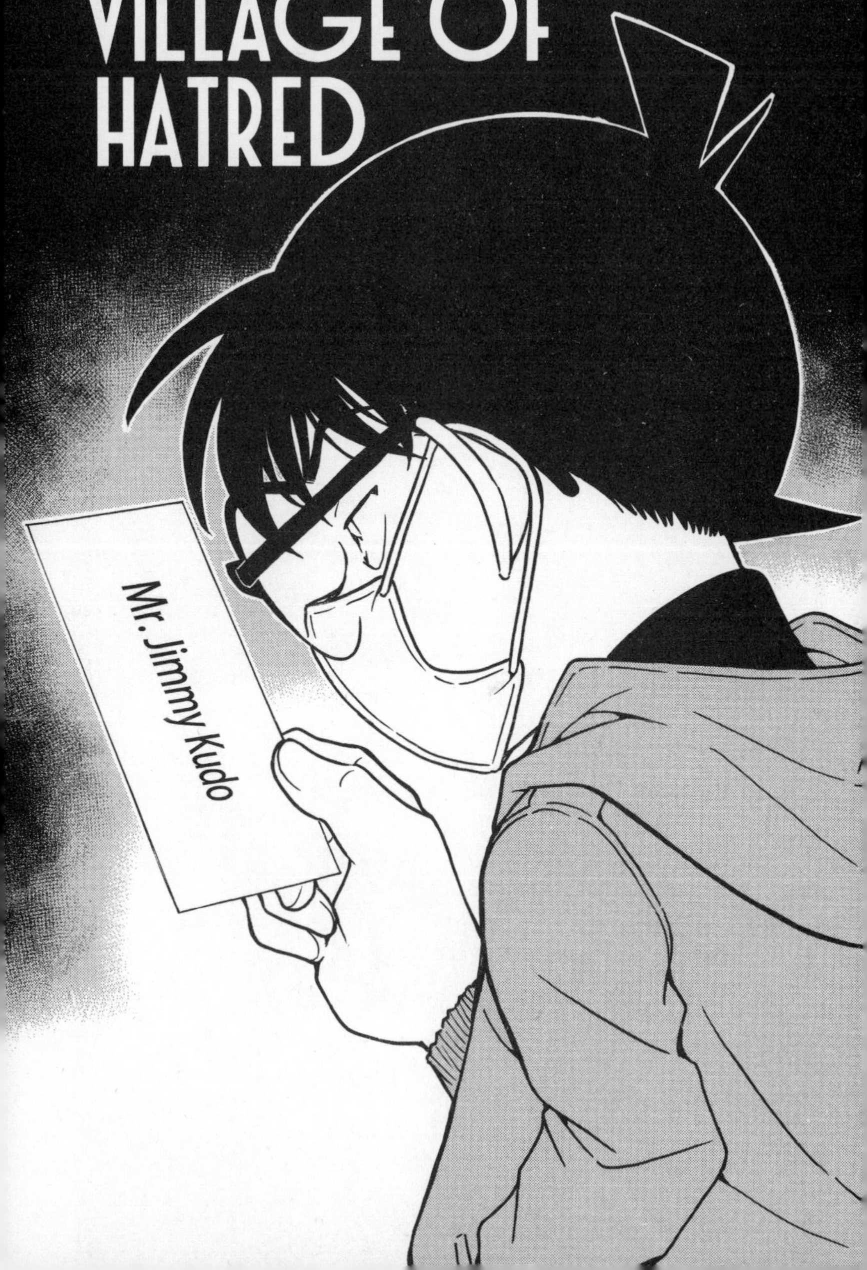
Mr. Jimmy Kudo

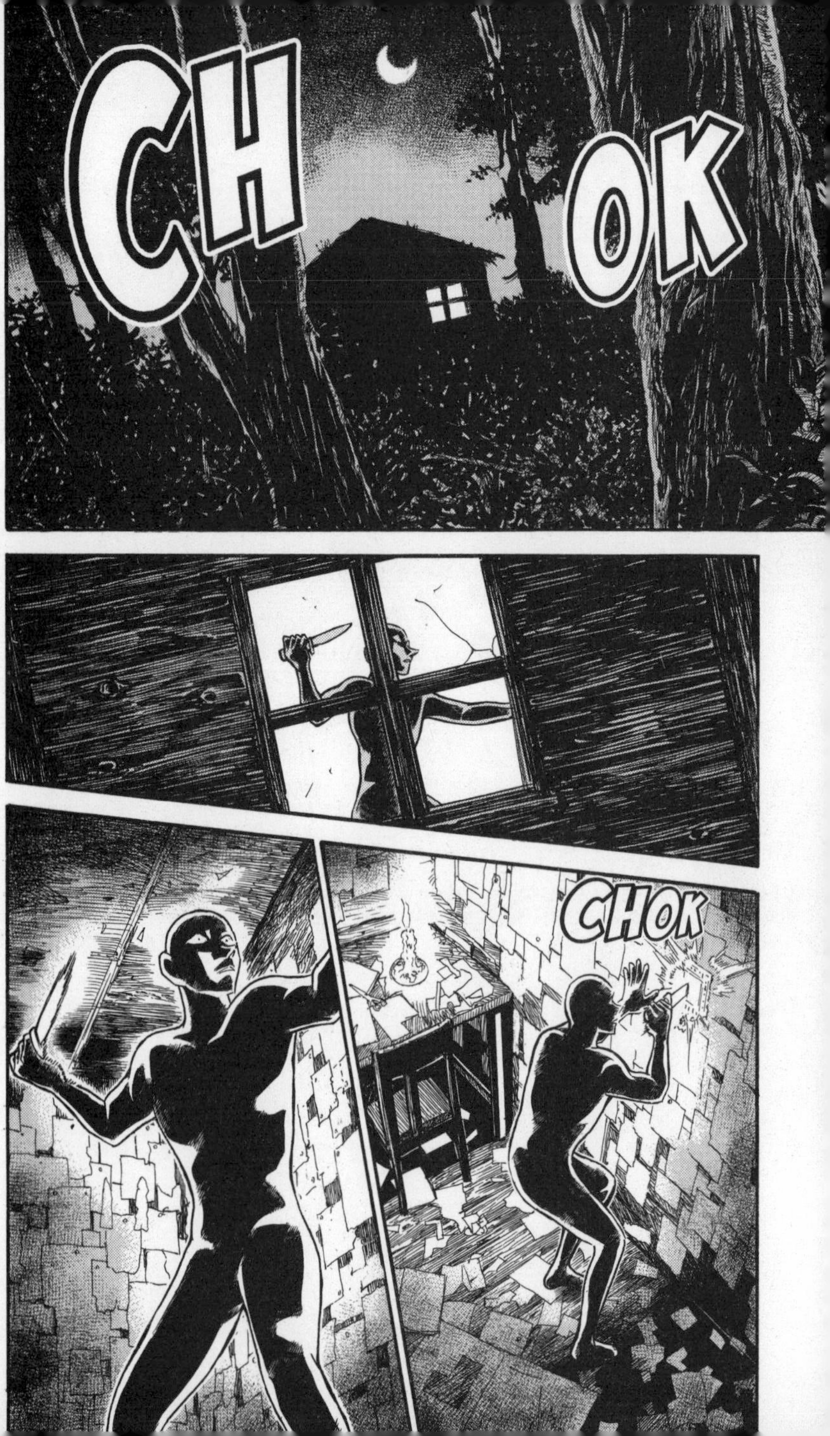
CH OK
CHOK

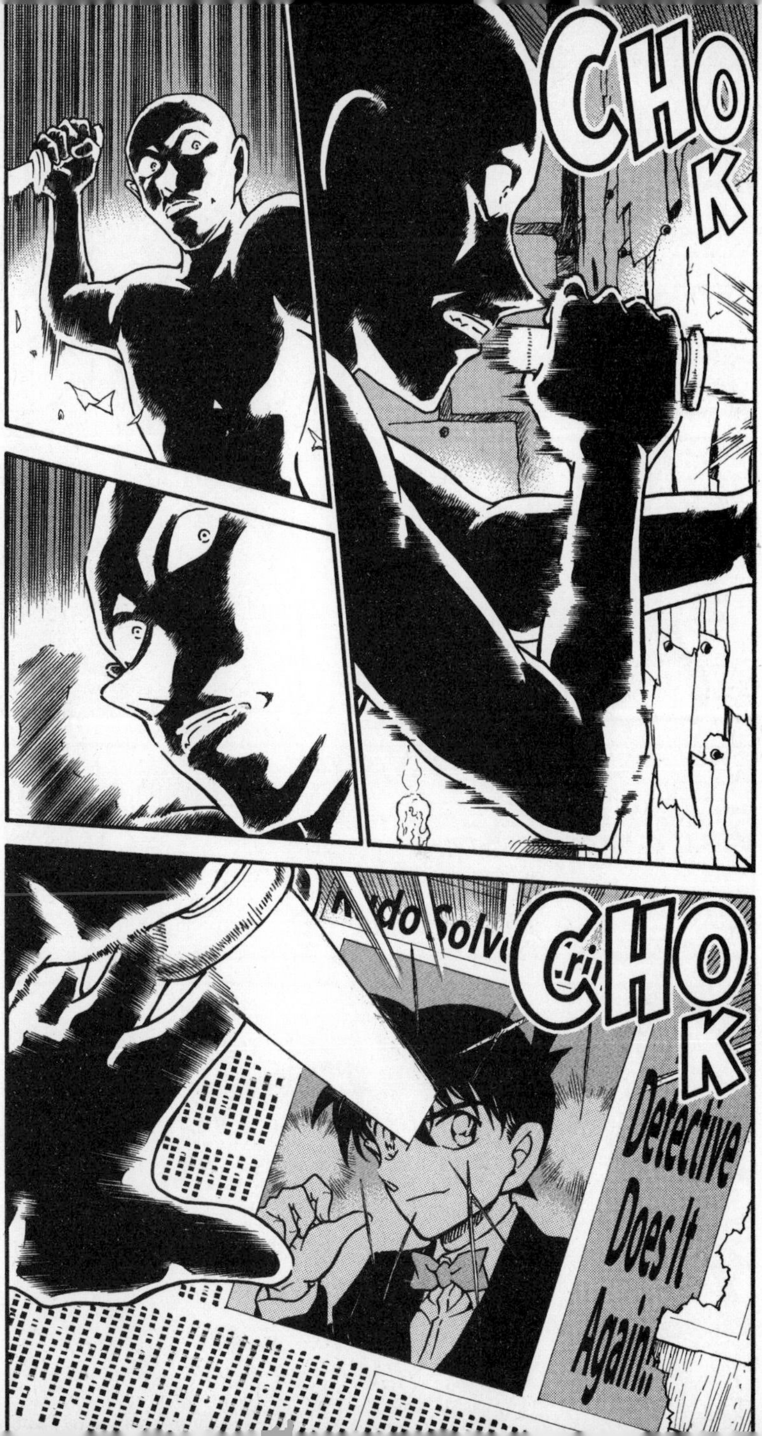
CHOK
CHOK
Detective Does It Again!!

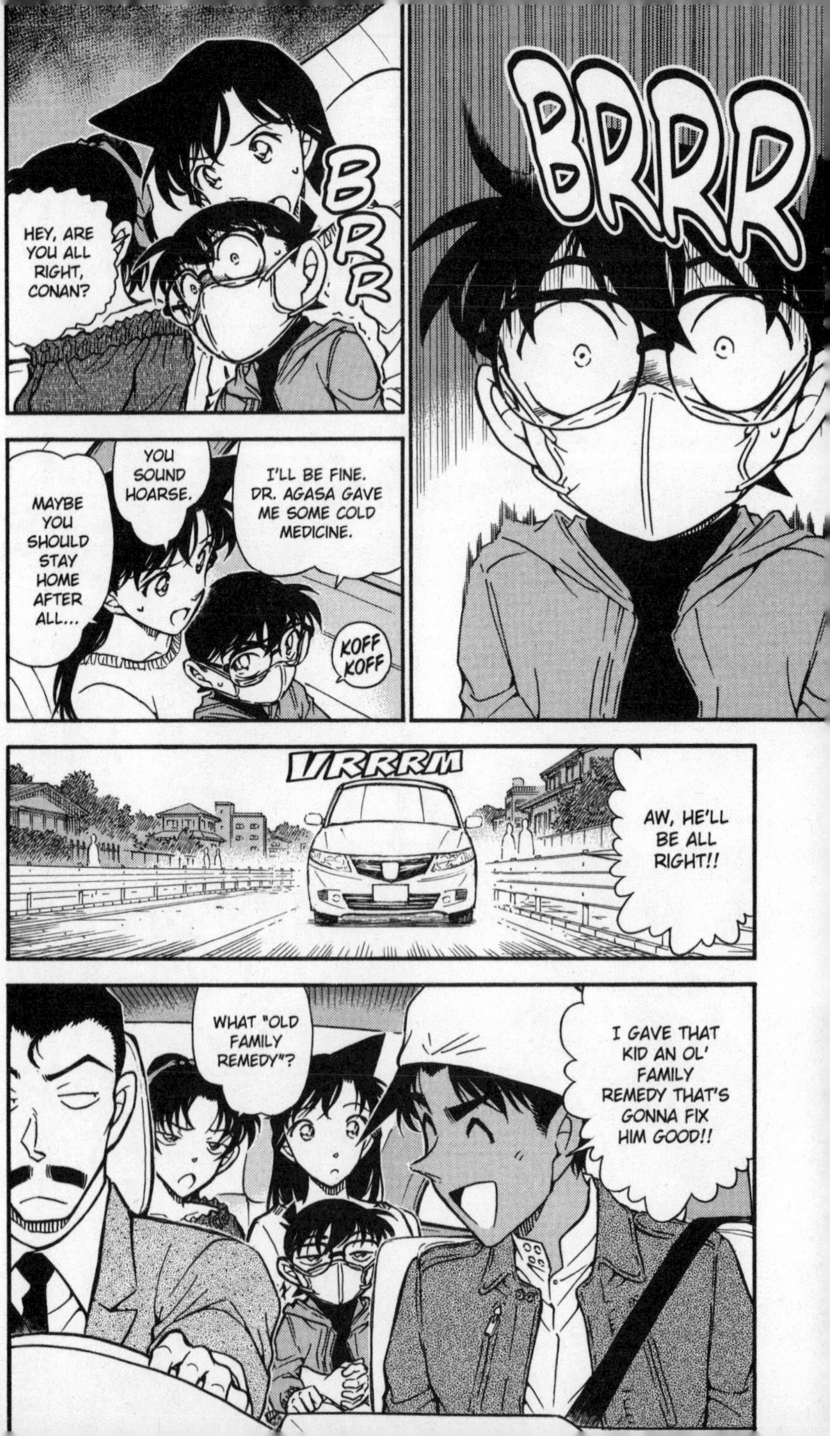
BRRRR
HEY, ARE YOU ALL RIGHT, CONAN?
BRR
I'LL BE FINE. DR. AGASA GAVE ME SOME COLD MEDICINE.
KOFF KOFF
YOU SOUND HOARSE.
MAYBE YOU SHOULD STAY HOME AFTER ALL...
AW, HE'LL BE ALL RIGHT!!
VRRRM
I GAVE THAT KID AN OL' FAMILY REMEDY THAT'S GONNA FIX HIM GOOD!!
WHAT "OLD FAMILY REMEDY"?

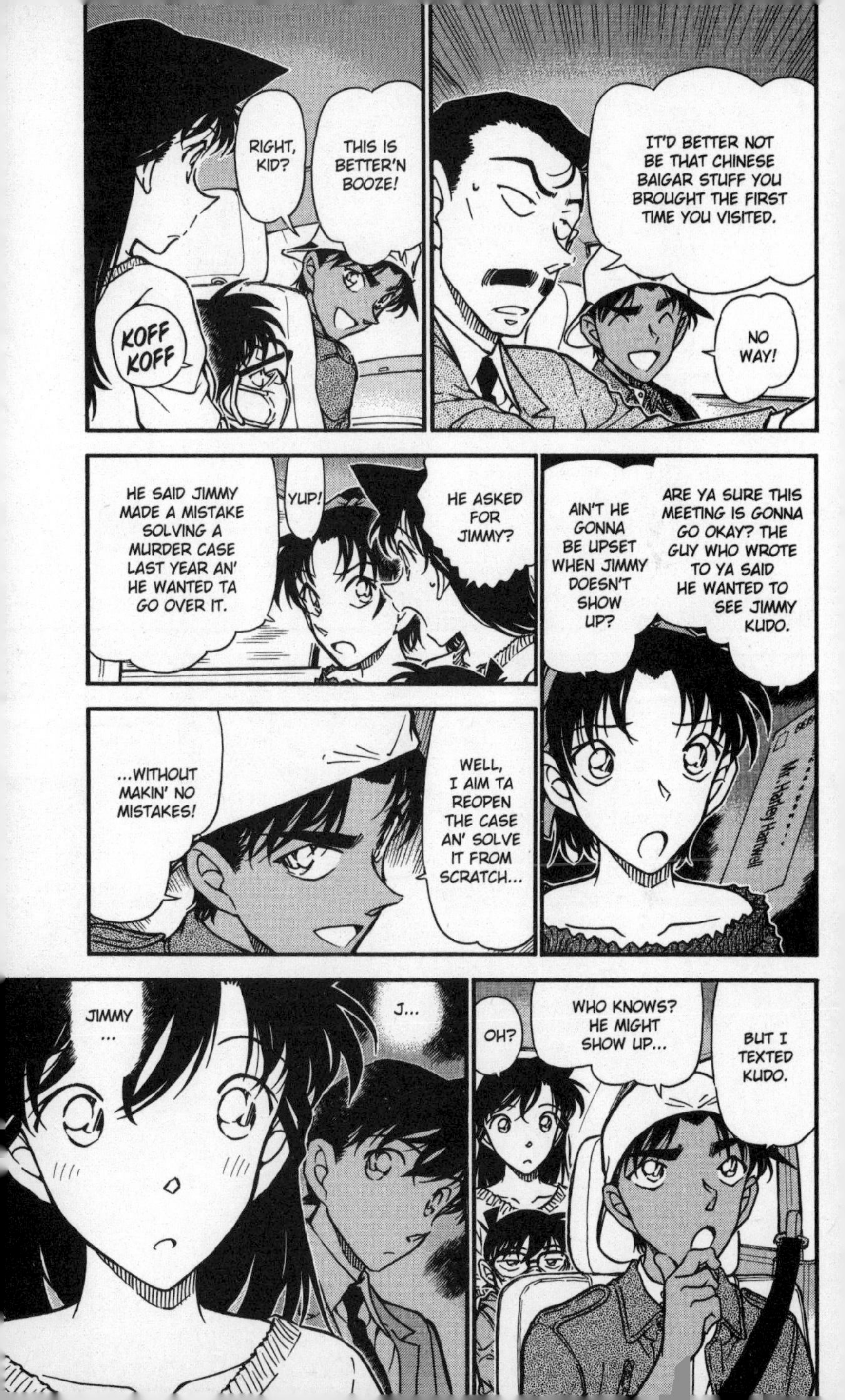
IT'D BETTER NOT BE THAT CHINESE BAIGAR STUFF YOU BROUGHT THE FIRST TIME YOU VISITED.
NO WAY!
THIS IS BETTER'N BOOZE!
RIGHT, KID?
KOFF KOFF
ARE YA SURE THIS MEETING IS GONNA GO OKAY? THE GUY WHO WROTE TO YA SAID HE WANTED TO SEE JIMMY KUDO.
AIN'T HE GONNA BE UPSET WHEN JIMMY DOESN'T SHOW UP?
Mr. Harley Hartwell
HE ASKED FOR JIMMY?
YUP!
HE SAID JIMMY MADE A MISTAKE SOLVING A MURDER CASE LAST YEAR AN' HE WANTED TA GO OVER IT.
WELL, I AIM TA REOPEN THE CASE AN' SOLVE IT FROM SCRATCH...
...WITHOUT MAKIN' NO MISTAKES!
BUT I TEXTED KUDO.
WHO KNOWS? HE MIGHT SHOW UP...
OH?
J...
JIMMY ...

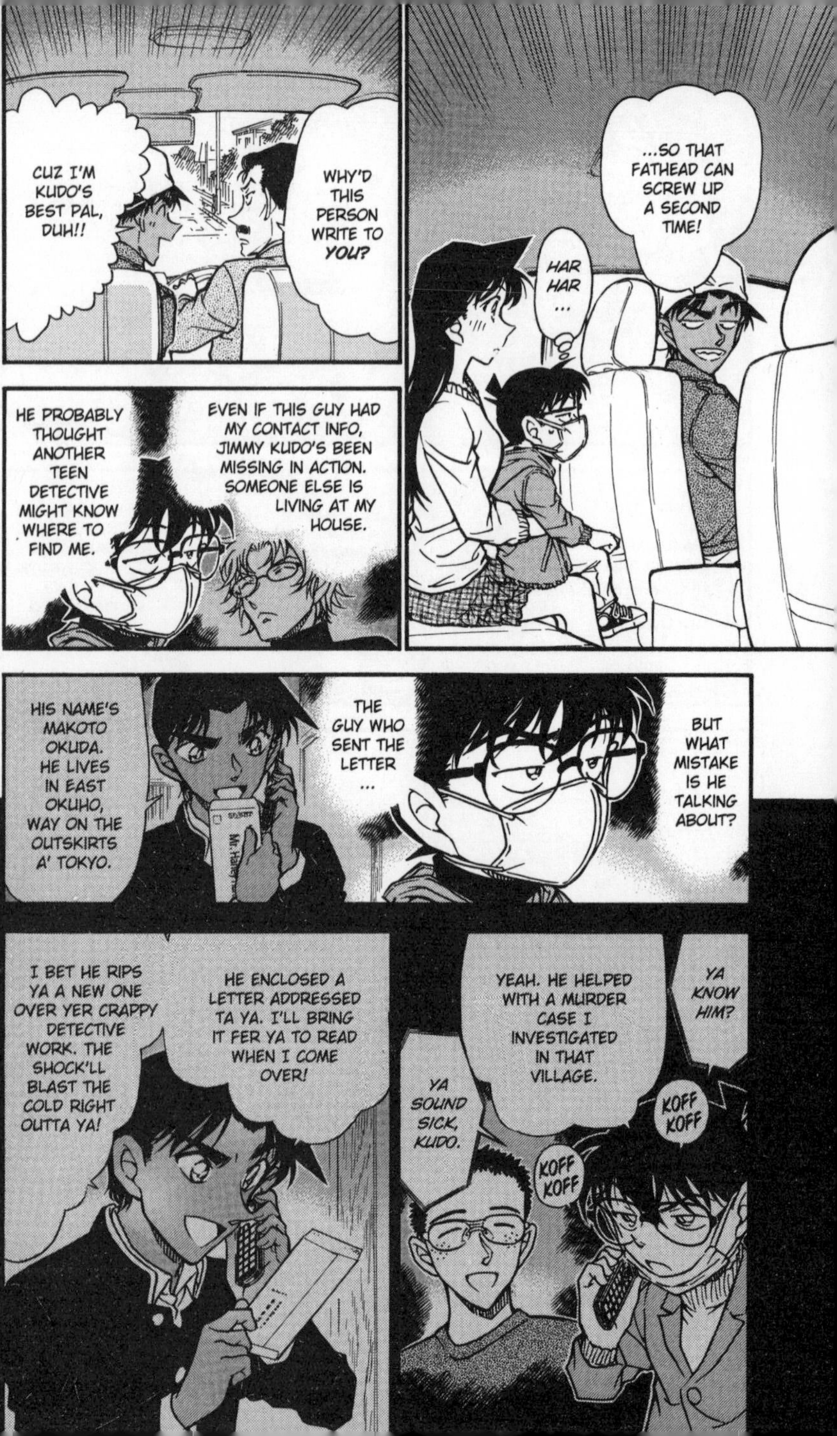
...SO THAT FATHEAD CAN SCREW UP A SECOND TIME!
HAR HAR ...
WHY'D THIS PERSON WRITE TO *YOU?*
CUZ I'M KUDO'S BEST PAL, DUH!!
EVEN IF THIS GUY HAD MY CONTACT INFO, JIMMY KUDO'S BEEN MISSING IN ACTION. SOMEONE ELSE IS LIVING AT MY HOUSE.
HE PROBABLY THOUGHT ANOTHER TEEN DETECTIVE MIGHT KNOW WHERE TO FIND ME.
BUT WHAT MISTAKE IS HE TALKING ABOUT?
THE GUY WHO SENT THE LETTER ...
HIS NAME'S MAKOTO OKUDA. HE LIVES IN EAST OKUHO, WAY ON THE OUTSKIRTS A' TOKYO.
YA KNOW HIM?
YEAH. HE HELPED WITH A MURDER CASE I INVESTIGATED IN THAT VILLAGE.
KOFF KOFF
YA SOUND SICK, KUDO.
KOFF KOFF
HE ENCLOSED A LETTER ADDRESSED TA YA. I'LL BRING IT FER YA TO READ WHEN I COME OVER!
I BET HE RIPS YA A NEW ONE OVER YER CRAPPY DETECTIVE WORK. THE SHOCK'LL BLAST THE COLD RIGHT OUTTA YA!

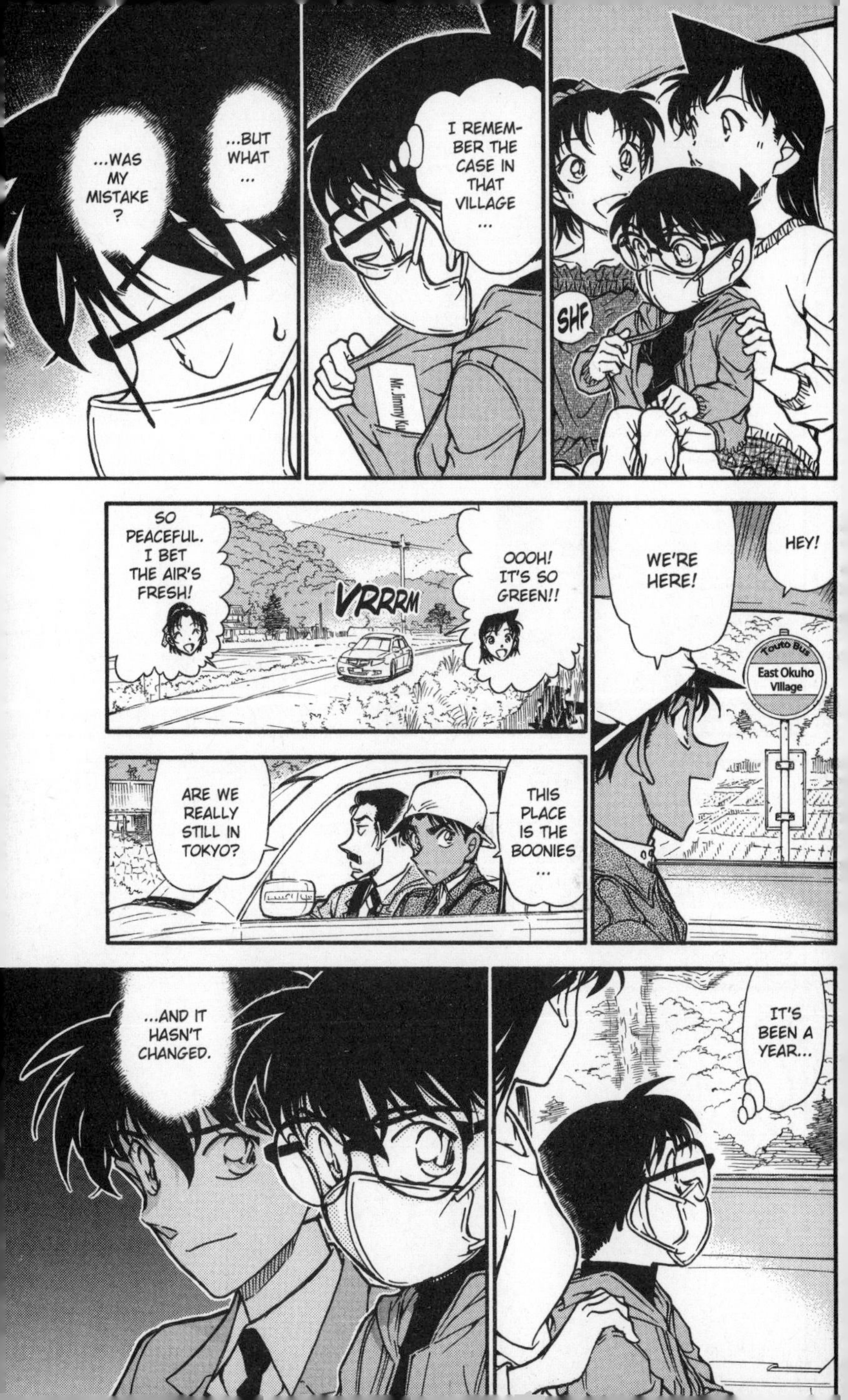
SHF
I REMEMBER THE CASE IN THAT VILLAGE ...
...BUT WHAT ...
...WAS MY MISTAKE ?
HEY!
WE'RE HERE!
Touto Bus
East Okuho Village
OOOH! IT'S SO GREEN!!
VRRRM
SO PEACEFUL. I BET THE AIR'S FRESH!
THIS PLACE IS THE BOONIES ...
ARE WE REALLY STILL IN TOKYO?
IT'S BEEN A YEAR...
...AND IT HASN'T CHANGED.

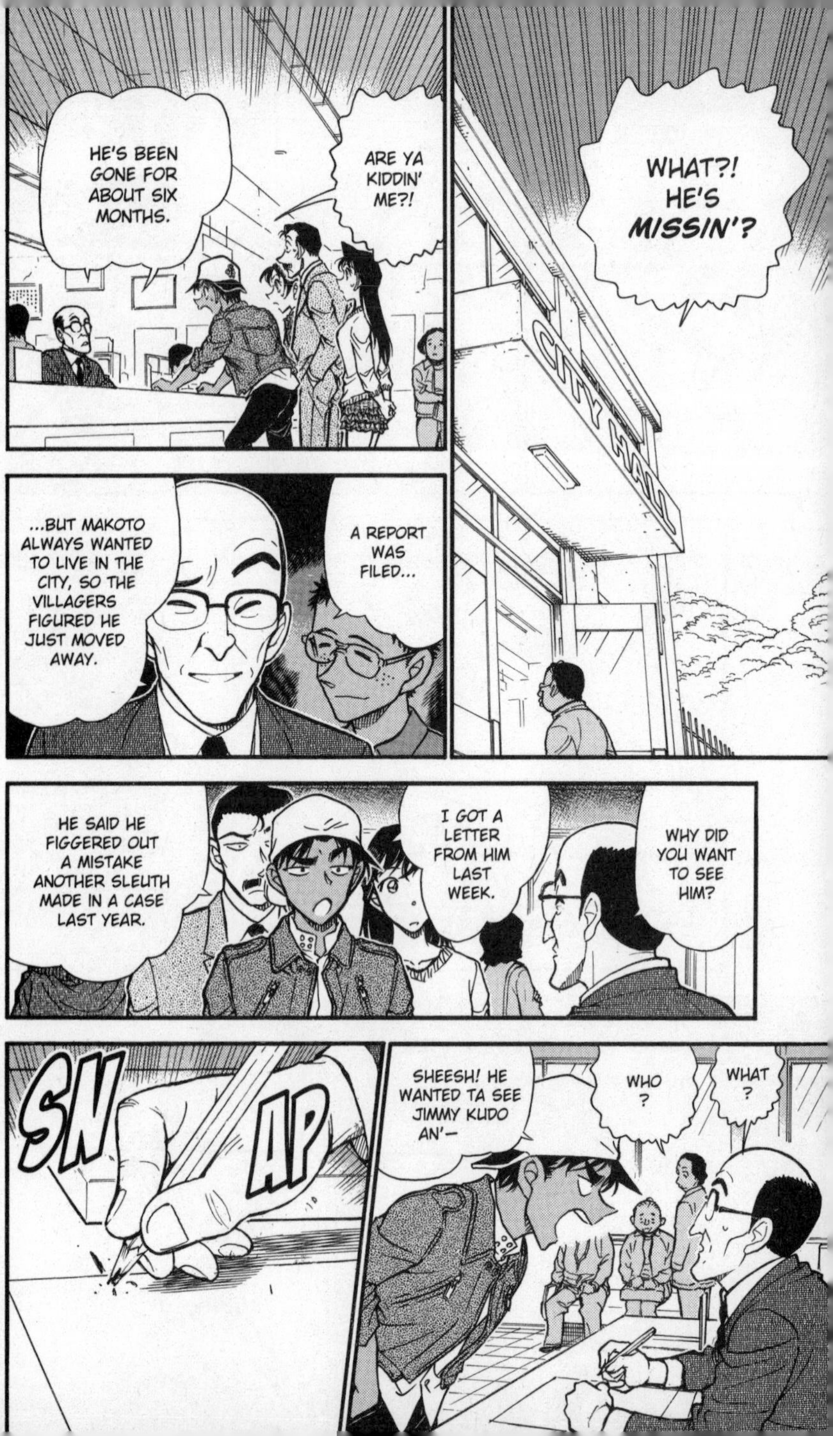
WHAT?! HE'S *MISSIN'*?
ARE YA KIDDIN' ME?!
HE'S BEEN GONE FOR ABOUT SIX MONTHS.
CITY HALL
A REPORT WAS FILED...
...BUT MAKOTO ALWAYS WANTED TO LIVE IN THE CITY, SO THE VILLAGERS FIGURED HE JUST MOVED AWAY.
WHY DID YOU WANT TO SEE HIM?
I GOT A LETTER FROM HIM LAST WEEK.
HE SAID HE FIGGERED OUT A MISTAKE ANOTHER SLEUTH MADE IN A CASE LAST YEAR.
WHAT ?
WHO ?
SHEESH! HE WANTED TA SEE JIMMY KUDO AN'—
SNAP

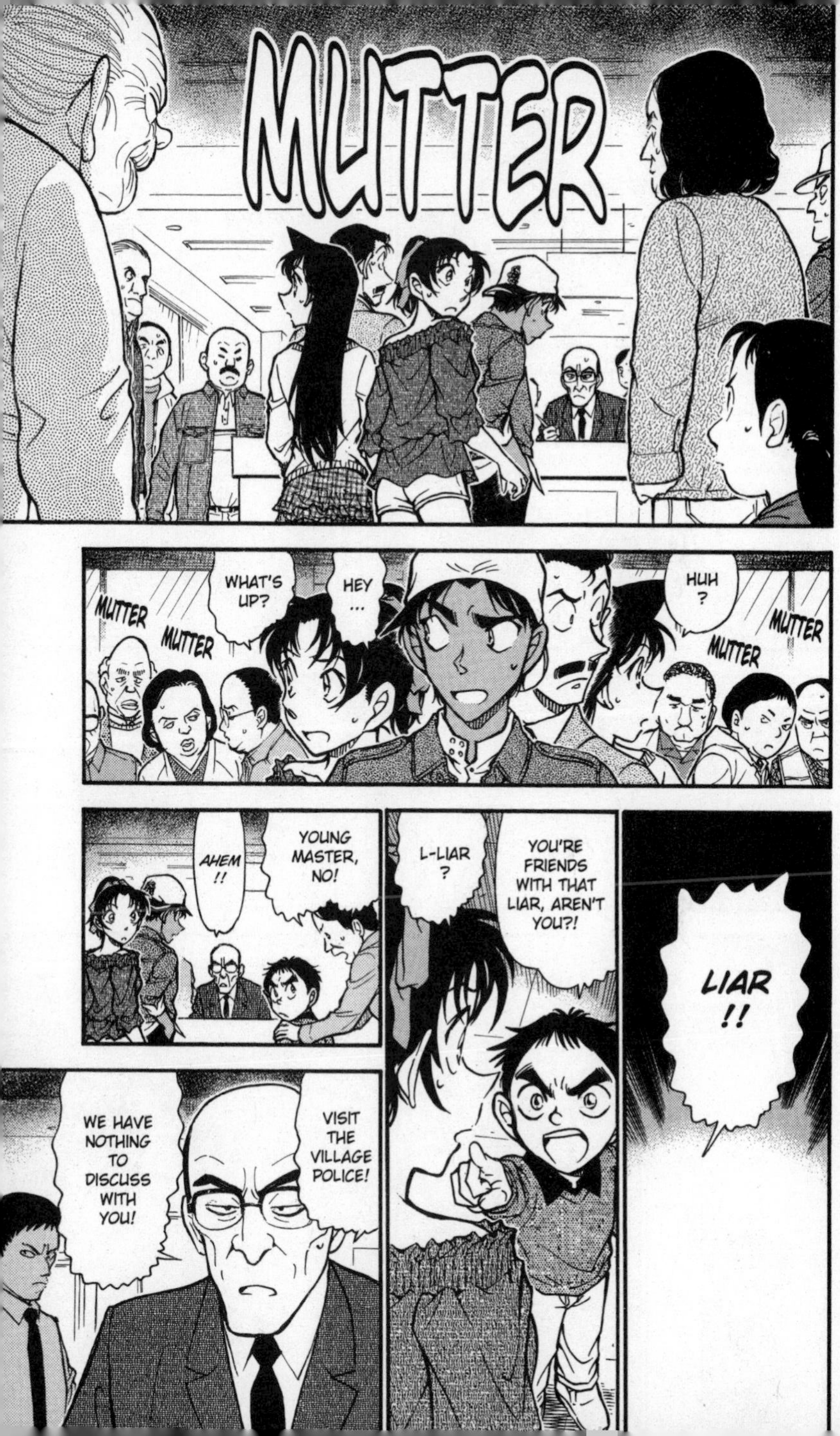
MUTTER
MUTTER
MUTTER
HUH ?
HEY ...
WHAT'S UP?
MUTTER
MUTTER
LIAR !!
YOU'RE FRIENDS WITH THAT LIAR, AREN'T YOU?!
L-LIAR ?
YOUNG MASTER, NO!
AHEM !!
VISIT THE VILLAGE POLICE!
WE HAVE NOTHING TO DISCUSS WITH YOU!

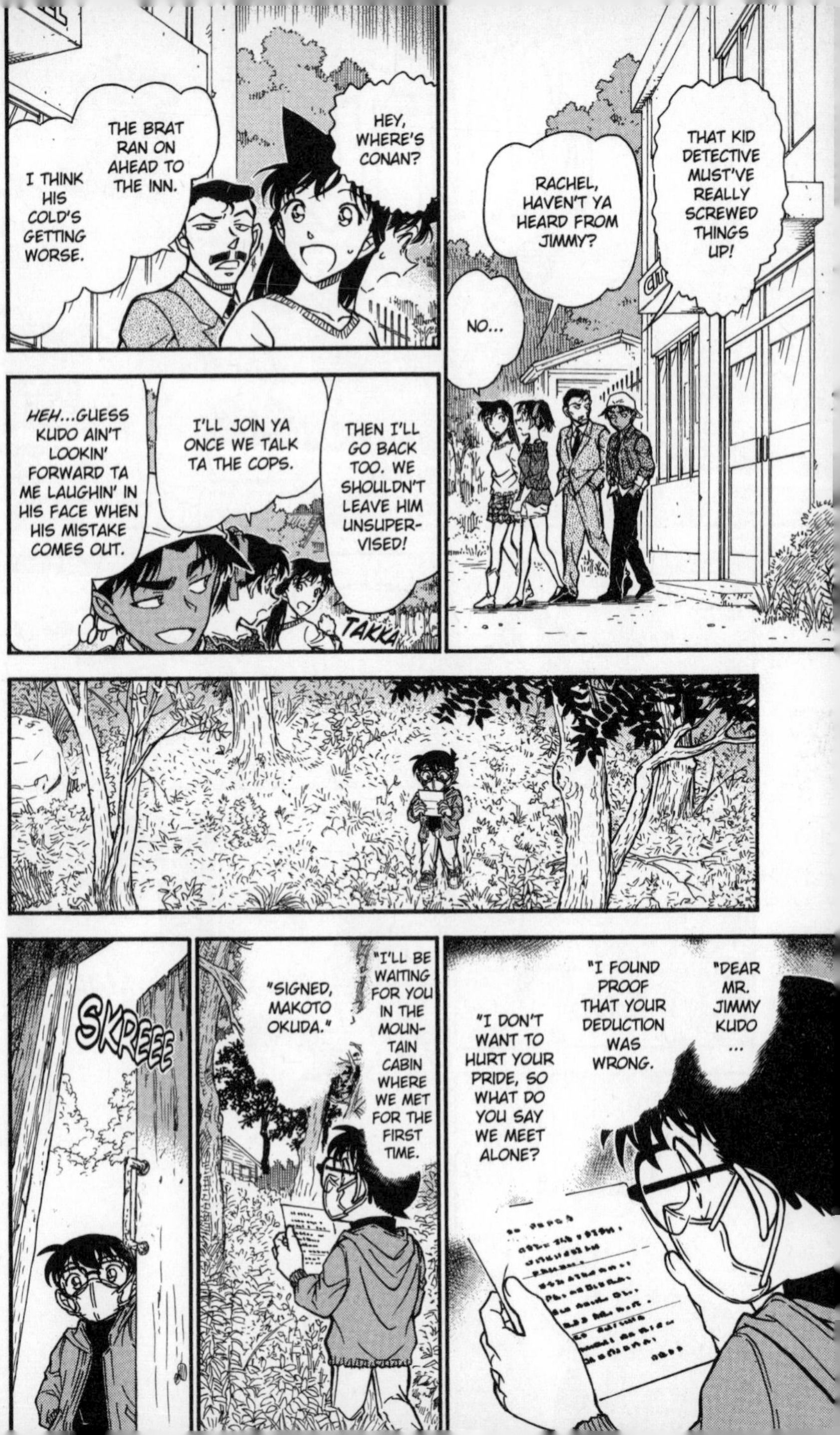
THAT KID DETECTIVE MUST'VE REALLY SCREWED THINGS UP!
RACHEL, HAVEN'T YA HEARD FROM JIMMY?
NO...
HEY, WHERE'S CONAN?
THE BRAT RAN ON AHEAD TO THE INN.
I THINK HIS COLD'S GETTING WORSE.
THEN I'LL GO BACK TOO. WE SHOULDN'T LEAVE HIM UNSUPER-VISED!
I'LL JOIN YA ONCE WE TALK TA THE COPS.
HEH...GUESS KUDO AIN'T LOOKIN' FORWARD TA ME LAUGHIN' IN HIS FACE WHEN HIS MISTAKE COMES OUT.
TAKKA
"DEAR MR. JIMMY KUDO ...
"I FOUND PROOF THAT YOUR DEDUCTION WAS WRONG.
"I DON'T WANT TO HURT YOUR PRIDE, SO WHAT DO YOU SAY WE MEET ALONE?
"I'LL BE WAITING FOR YOU IN THE MOUN-TAIN CABIN WHERE WE MET FOR THE FIRST TIME.
"SIGNED, MAKOTO OKUDA."
SKREEEE

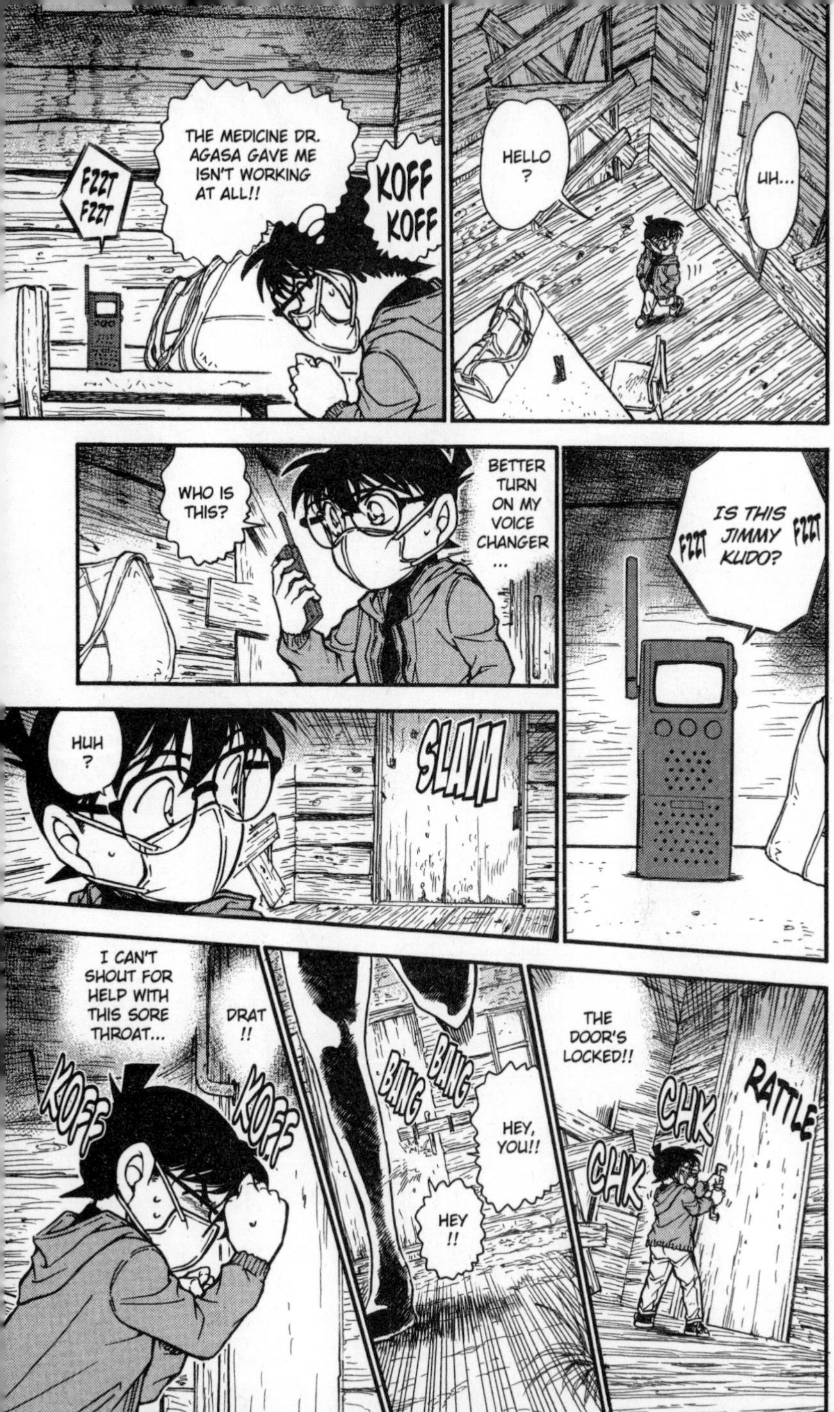
UH...
HELLO ?
KOFF KOFF
THE MEDICINE DR. AGASA GAVE ME ISN'T WORKING AT ALL!!
FZZT FZZT
FZZT
IS THIS JIMMY KUDO?
FZZT
BETTER TURN ON MY VOICE CHANGER...
WHO IS THIS?
SLAM
HUH ?
RATTLE
CHK
THE DOOR'S LOCKED!!
CHK
BANG BANG
HEY, YOU!!
HEY !!
DRAT !!
I CAN'T SHOUT FOR HELP WITH THIS SORE THROAT...
KOFF
KOFF

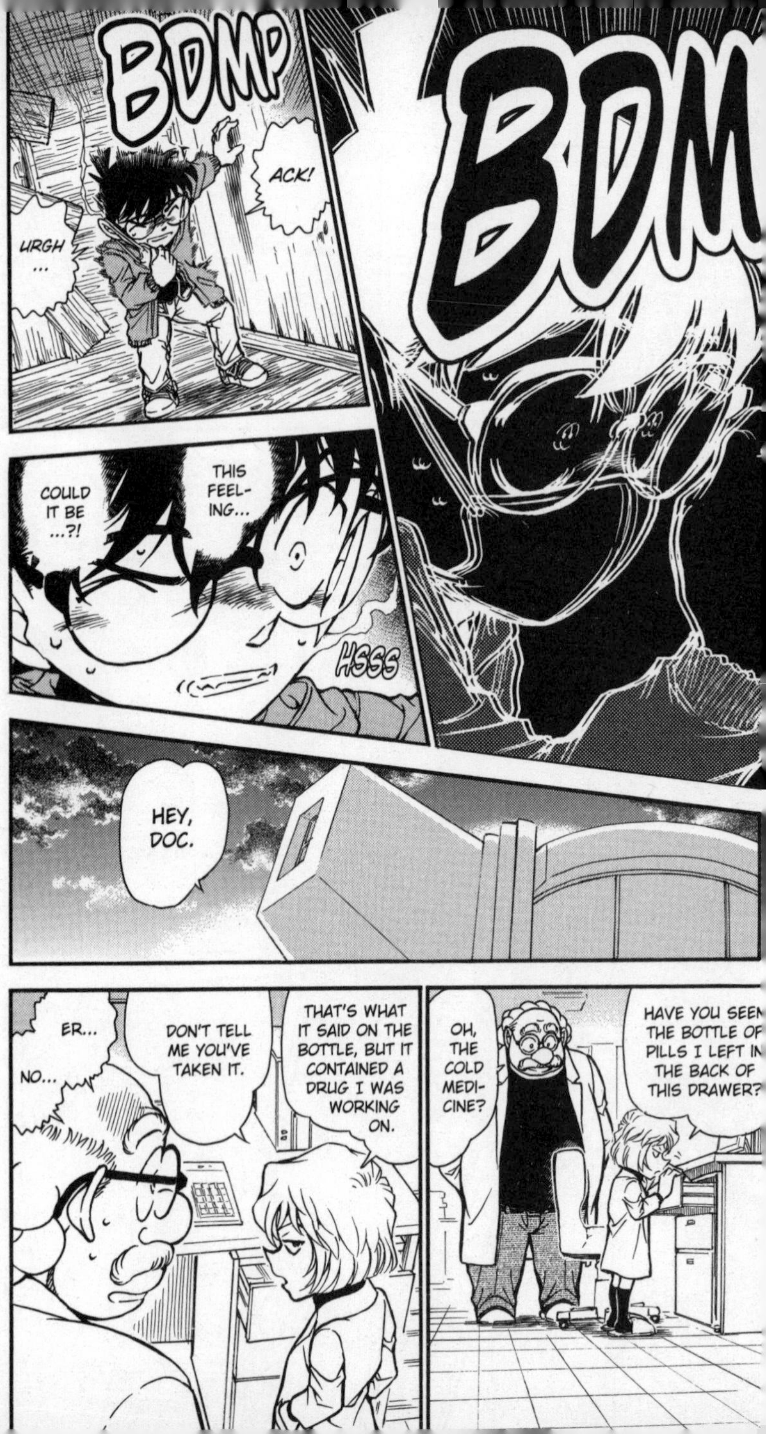
BDM
BDMP
ACK!
URGH ...
THIS FEEL-ING...
COULD IT BE ...?!
HSSS
HEY, DOC.
HAVE YOU SEEN THE BOTTLE OF PILLS I LEFT IN THE BACK OF THIS DRAWER?
OH, THE COLD MEDI-CINE?
THAT'S WHAT IT SAID ON THE BOTTLE, BUT IT CONTAINED A DRUG I WAS WORKING ON.
DON'T TELL ME YOU'VE TAKEN IT.
ER...
NO...

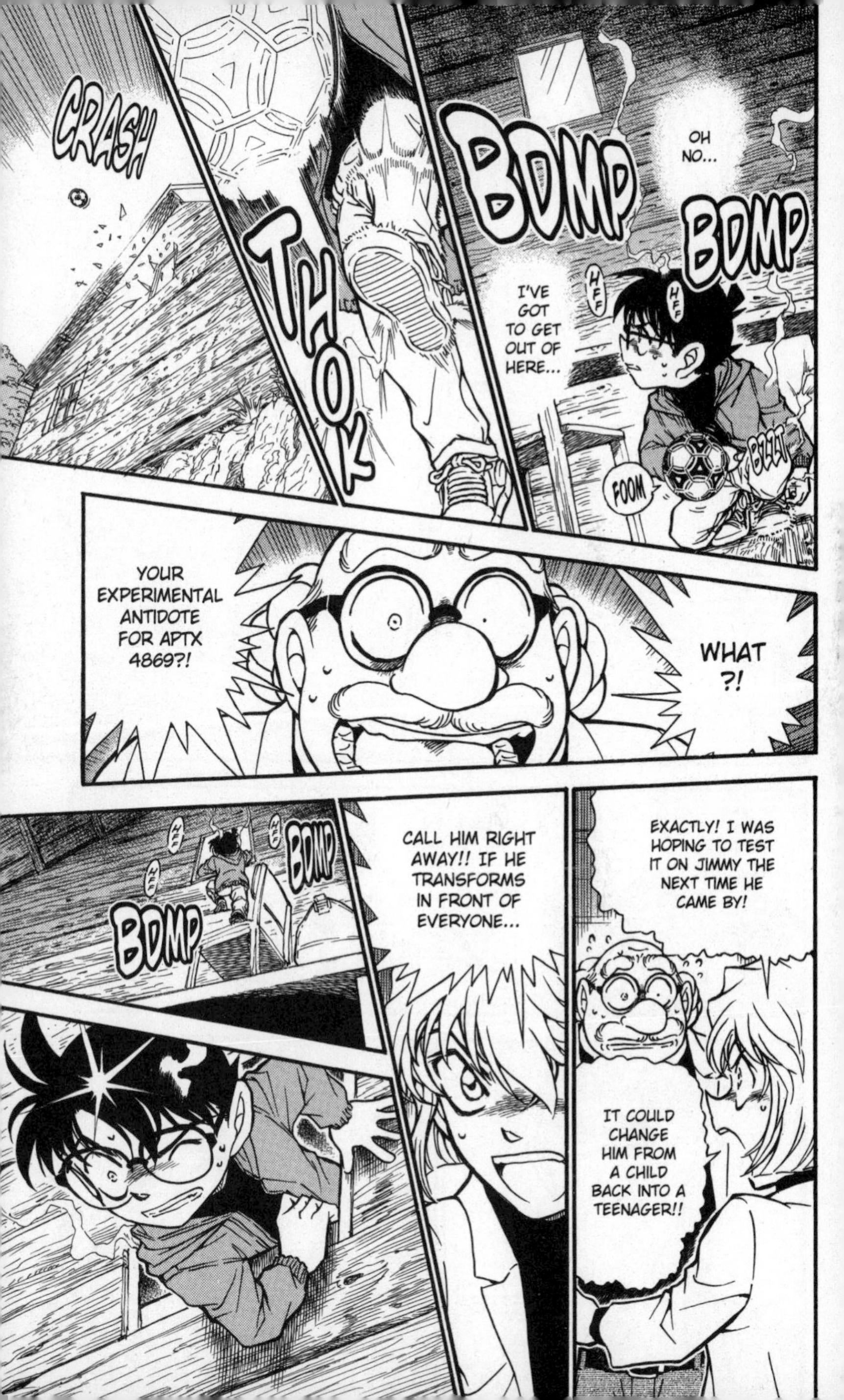
BDMP
OH NO...
BDMP
HFF
HFF
I'VE GOT TO GET OUT OF HERE...
BZZT
FOOM
THOK
CRASH
WHAT ?!
YOUR EXPERIMENTAL ANTIDOTE FOR APTX 4869?!
EXACTLY! I WAS HOPING TO TEST IT ON JIMMY THE NEXT TIME HE CAME BY!
IT COULD CHANGE HIM FROM A CHILD BACK INTO A TEENAGER!!
CALL HIM RIGHT AWAY!! IF HE TRANSFORMS IN FRONT OF EVERYONE...
BDMP
HFF
HFF
BDMP

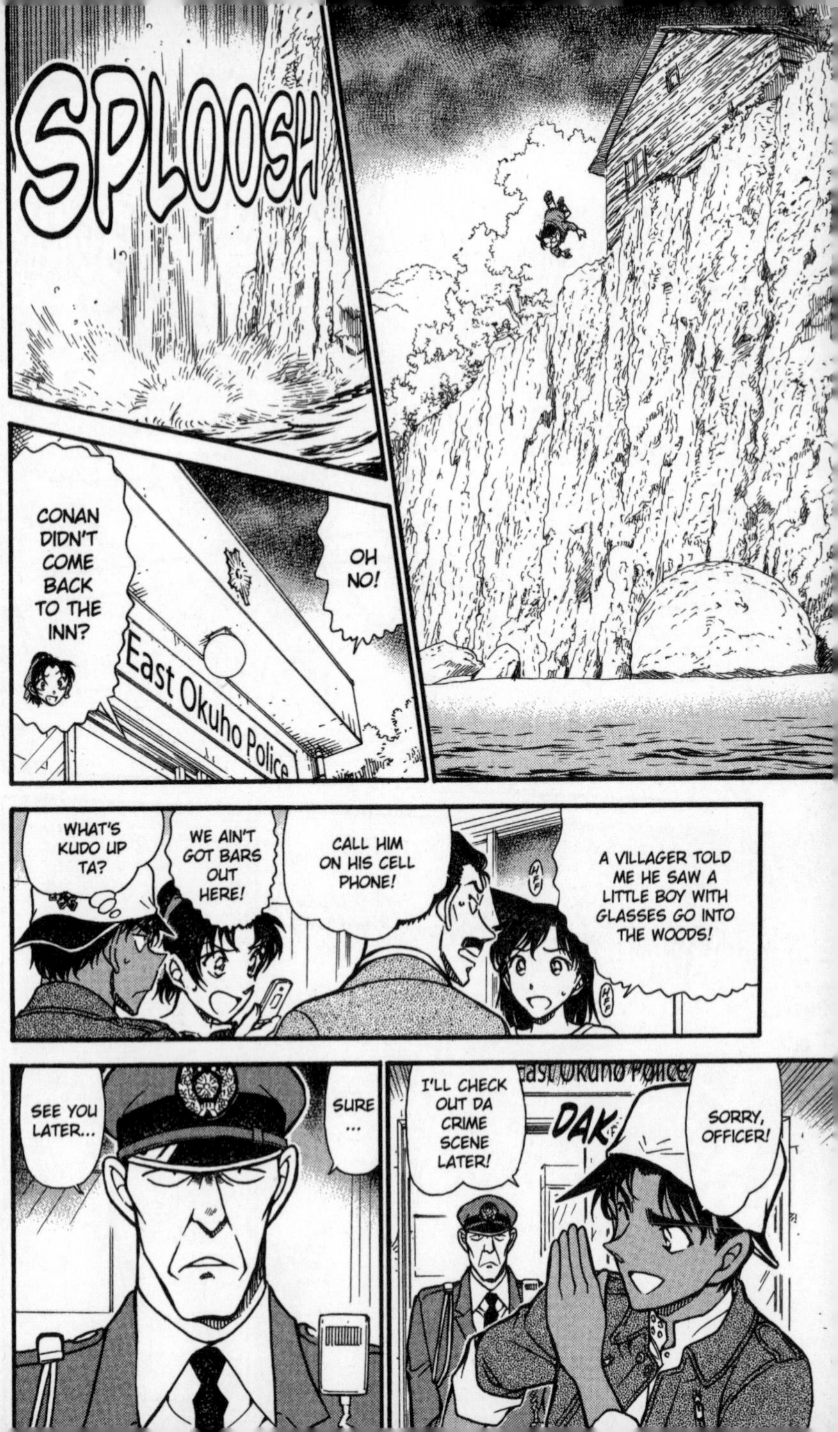
SPLOOSH
OH NO!
CONAN DIDN'T COME BACK TO THE INN?
East Okuho Police
A VILLAGER TOLD ME HE SAW A LITTLE BOY WITH GLASSES GO INTO THE WOODS!
CALL HIM ON HIS CELL PHONE!
WE AIN'T GOT BARS OUT HERE!
WHAT'S KUDO UP TA?
SORRY, OFFICER!
DAK
I'LL CHECK OUT DA CRIME SCENE LATER!
SURE ...
SEE YOU LATER...

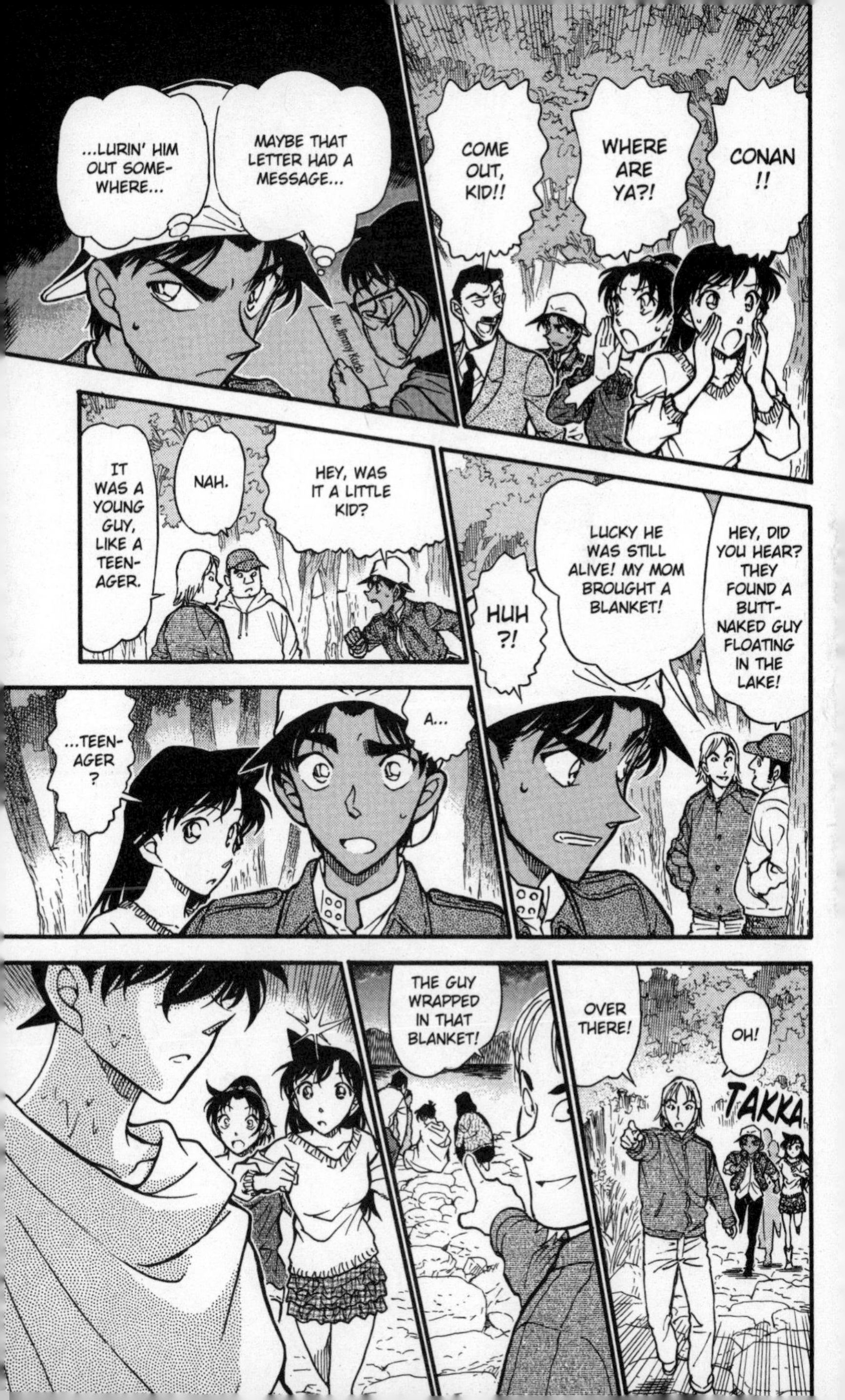
CONAN!!
WHERE ARE YA?!
COME OUT, KID!!
MAYBE THAT LETTER HAD A MESSAGE...
...LURIN' HIM OUT SOMEWHERE...
Mr. Jimmy Kudo
HEY, DID YOU HEAR? THEY FOUND A BUTT-NAKED GUY FLOATING IN THE LAKE!
LUCKY HE WAS STILL ALIVE! MY MOM BROUGHT A BLANKET!
HUH?!
HEY, WAS IT A LITTLE KID?
NAH.
IT WAS A YOUNG GUY, LIKE A TEENAGER.
A...
...TEENAGER?
OH!
TAKKA
OVER THERE!
THE GUY WRAPPED IN THAT BLANKET!

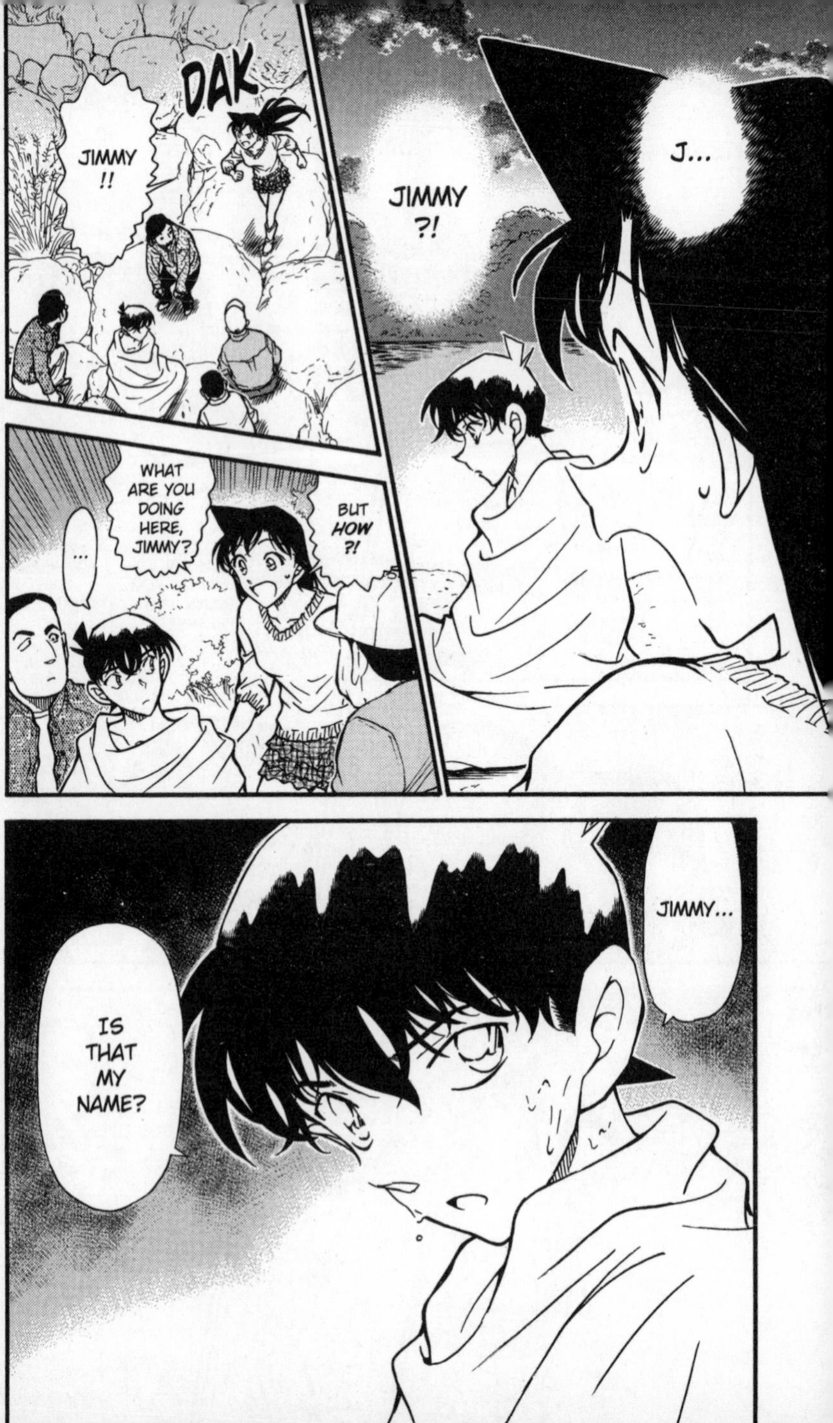
J...
JIMMY ?!
DAK
JIMMY !!
BUT HOW ?!
WHAT ARE YOU DOING HERE, JIMMY?
...
JIMMY...
IS THAT MY NAME?

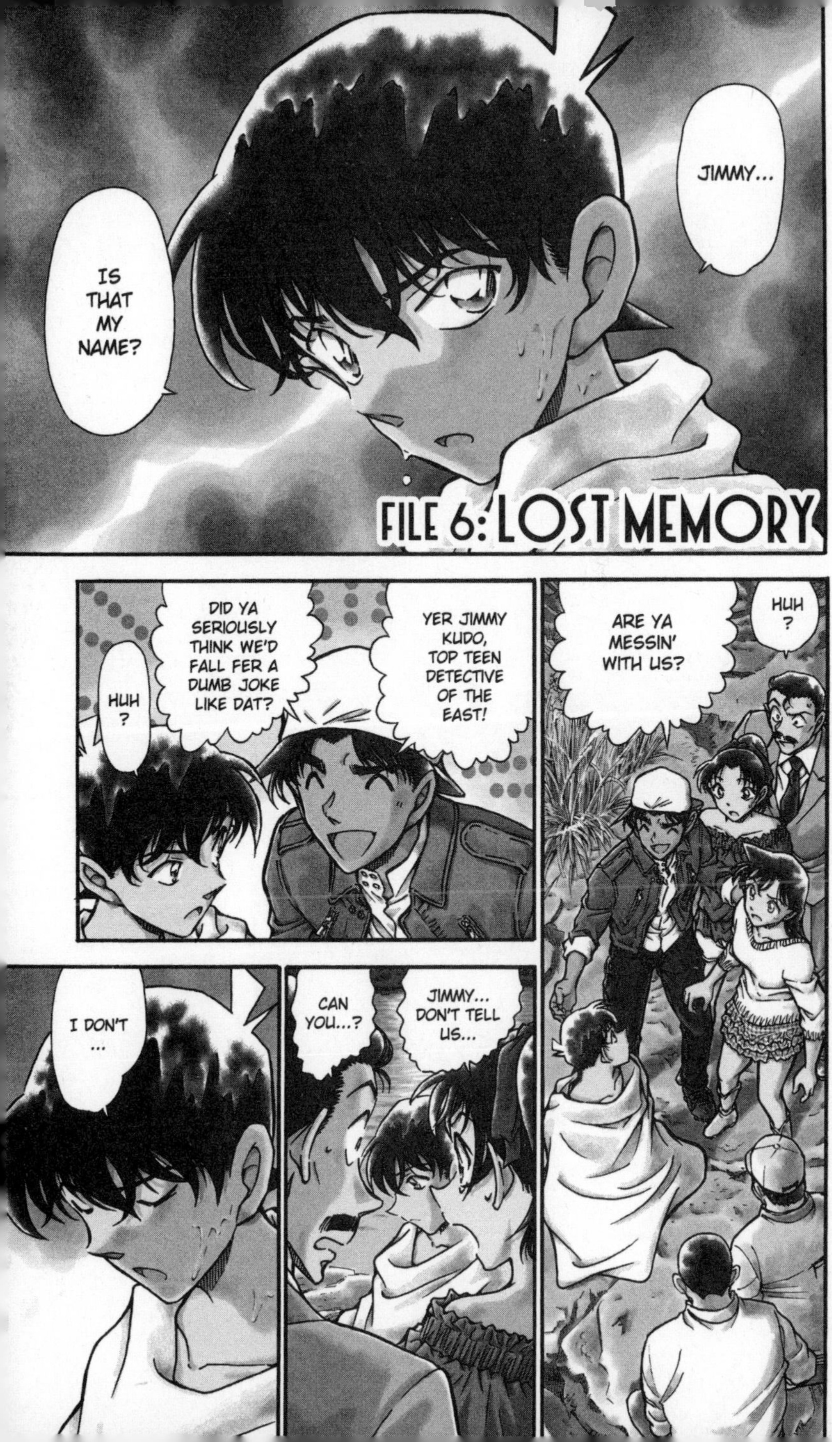
JIMMY...
IS THAT MY NAME?
FILE 6: LOST MEMORY
HUH?
ARE YA MESSIN' WITH US?
YER JIMMY KUDO, TOP TEEN DETECTIVE OF THE EAST!
DID YA SERIOUSLY THINK WE'D FALL FER A DUMB JOKE LIKE DAT?
HUH?
JIMMY... DON'T TELL US...
CAN YOU...?
I DON'T ...

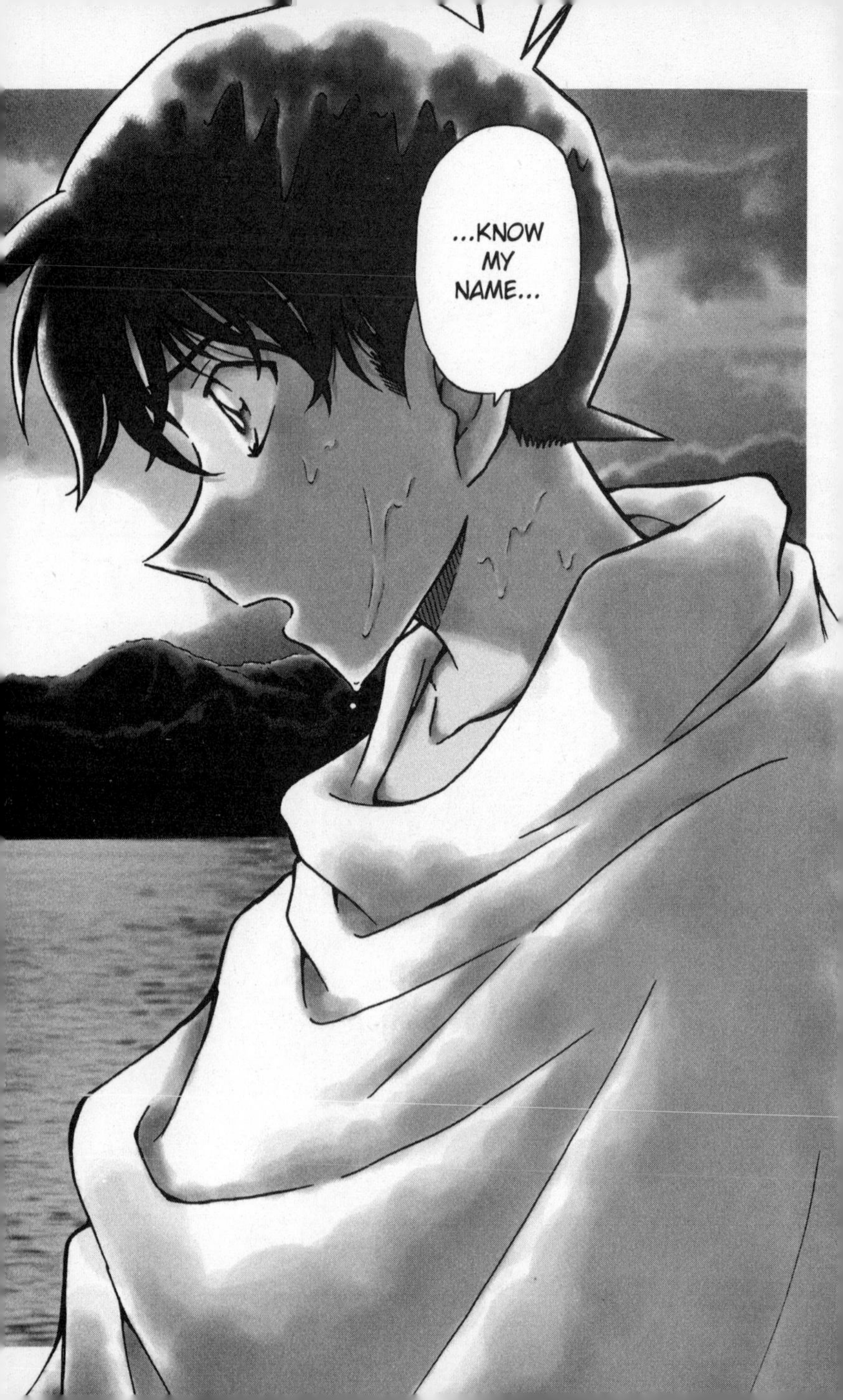
...KNOW MY NAME...

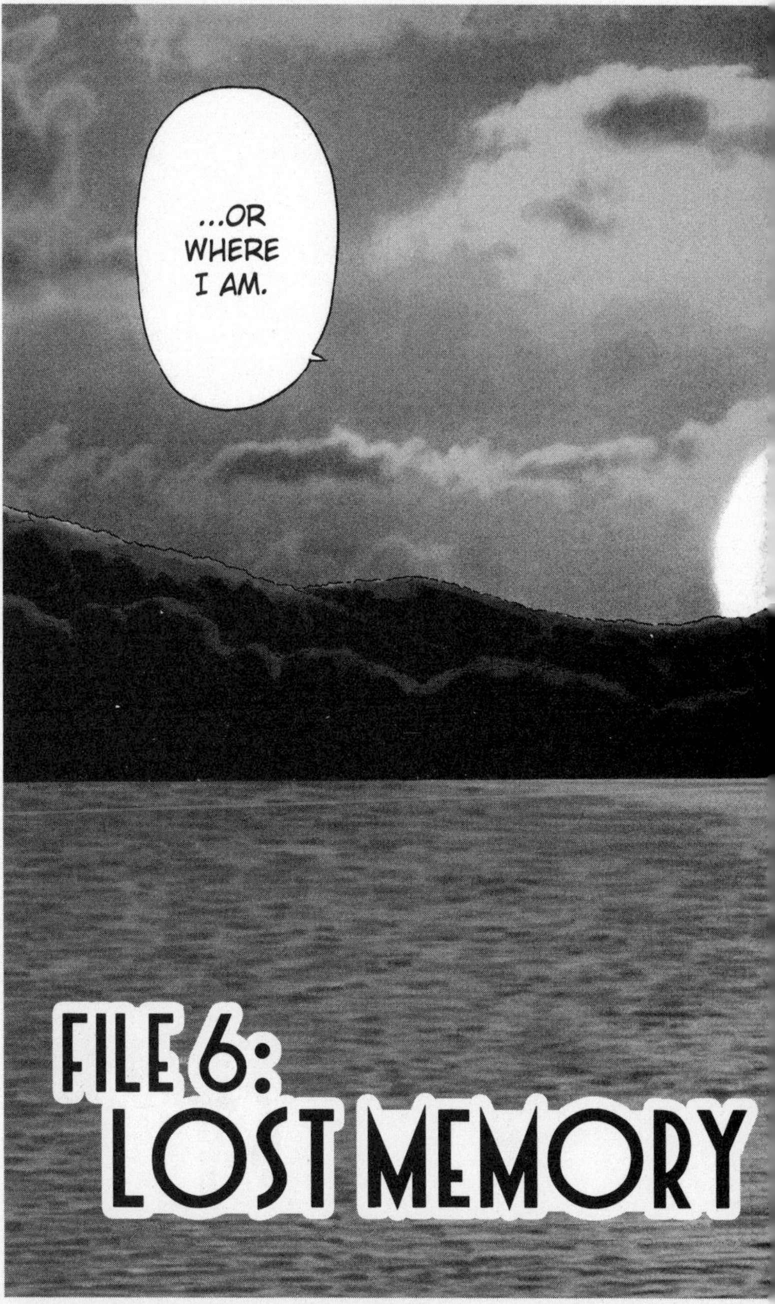
...OR WHERE I AM.
FILE 6:
LOST MEMORY

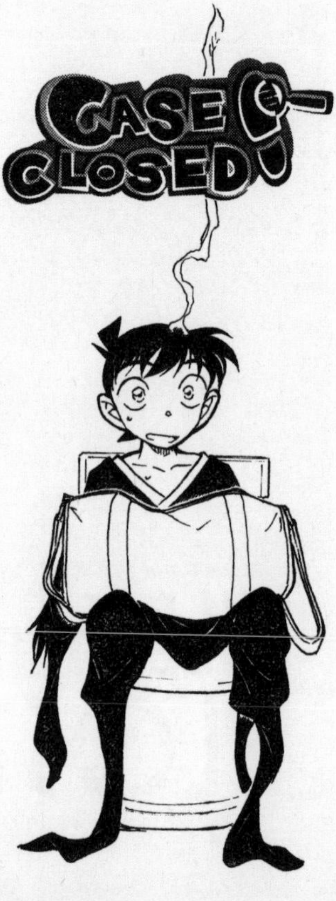
CASE CLOSED

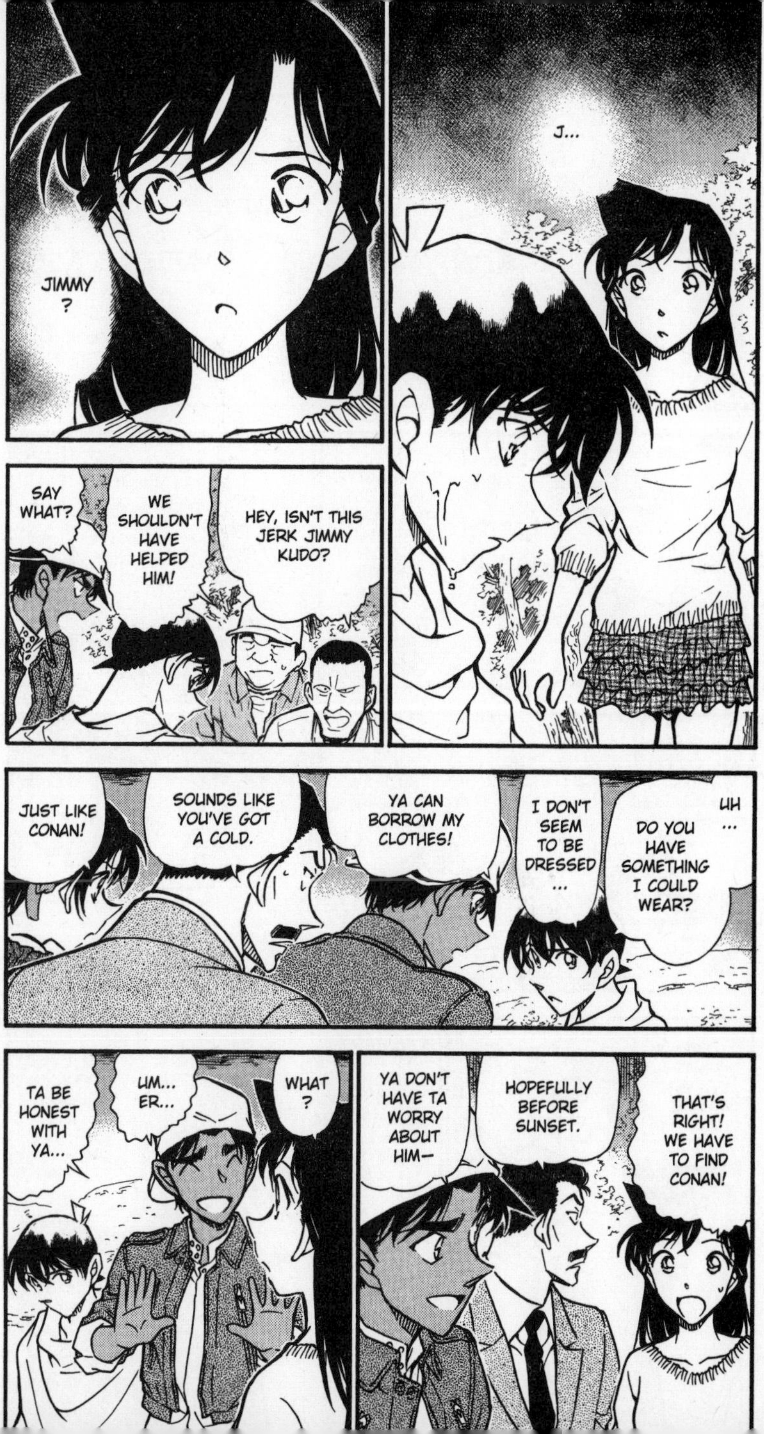
J...
JIMMY ?
HEY, ISN'T THIS JERK JIMMY KUDO?
WE SHOULDN'T HAVE HELPED HIM!
SAY WHAT?
UH ...
DO YOU HAVE SOMETHING I COULD WEAR?
I DON'T SEEM TO BE DRESSED ...
YA CAN BORROW MY CLOTHES!
SOUNDS LIKE YOU'VE GOT A COLD.
JUST LIKE CONAN!
THAT'S RIGHT! WE HAVE TO FIND CONAN!
HOPEFULLY BEFORE SUNSET.
YA DON'T HAVE TA WORRY ABOUT HIM—
WHAT ?
UM... ER...
TA BE HONEST WITH YA...

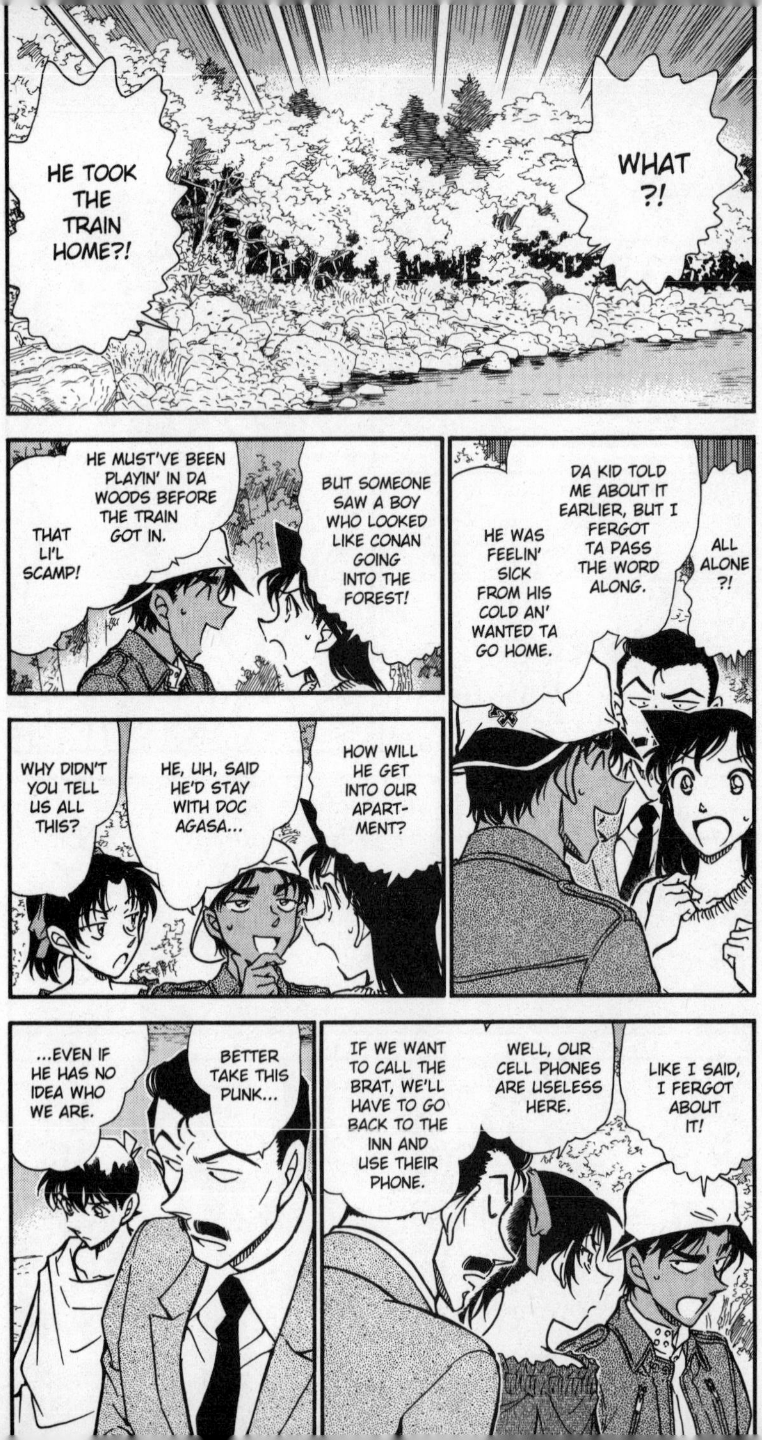
WHAT ?!
HE TOOK THE TRAIN HOME?!
ALL ALONE ?!
DA KID TOLD ME ABOUT IT EARLIER, BUT I FERGOT TA PASS THE WORD ALONG.
HE WAS FEELIN' SICK FROM HIS COLD AN' WANTED TA GO HOME.
BUT SOMEONE SAW A BOY WHO LOOKED LIKE CONAN GOING INTO THE FOREST!
HE MUST'VE BEEN PLAYIN' IN DA WOODS BEFORE THE TRAIN GOT IN.
THAT LI'L SCAMP!
HOW WILL HE GET INTO OUR APART-MENT?
HE, UH, SAID HE'D STAY WITH DOC AGASA...
WHY DIDN'T YOU TELL US ALL THIS?
LIKE I SAID, I FERGOT ABOUT IT!
WELL, OUR CELL PHONES ARE USELESS HERE.
IF WE WANT TO CALL THE BRAT, WE'LL HAVE TO GO BACK TO THE INN AND USE THEIR PHONE.
BETTER TAKE THIS PUNK...
...EVEN IF HE HAS NO IDEA WHO WE ARE.

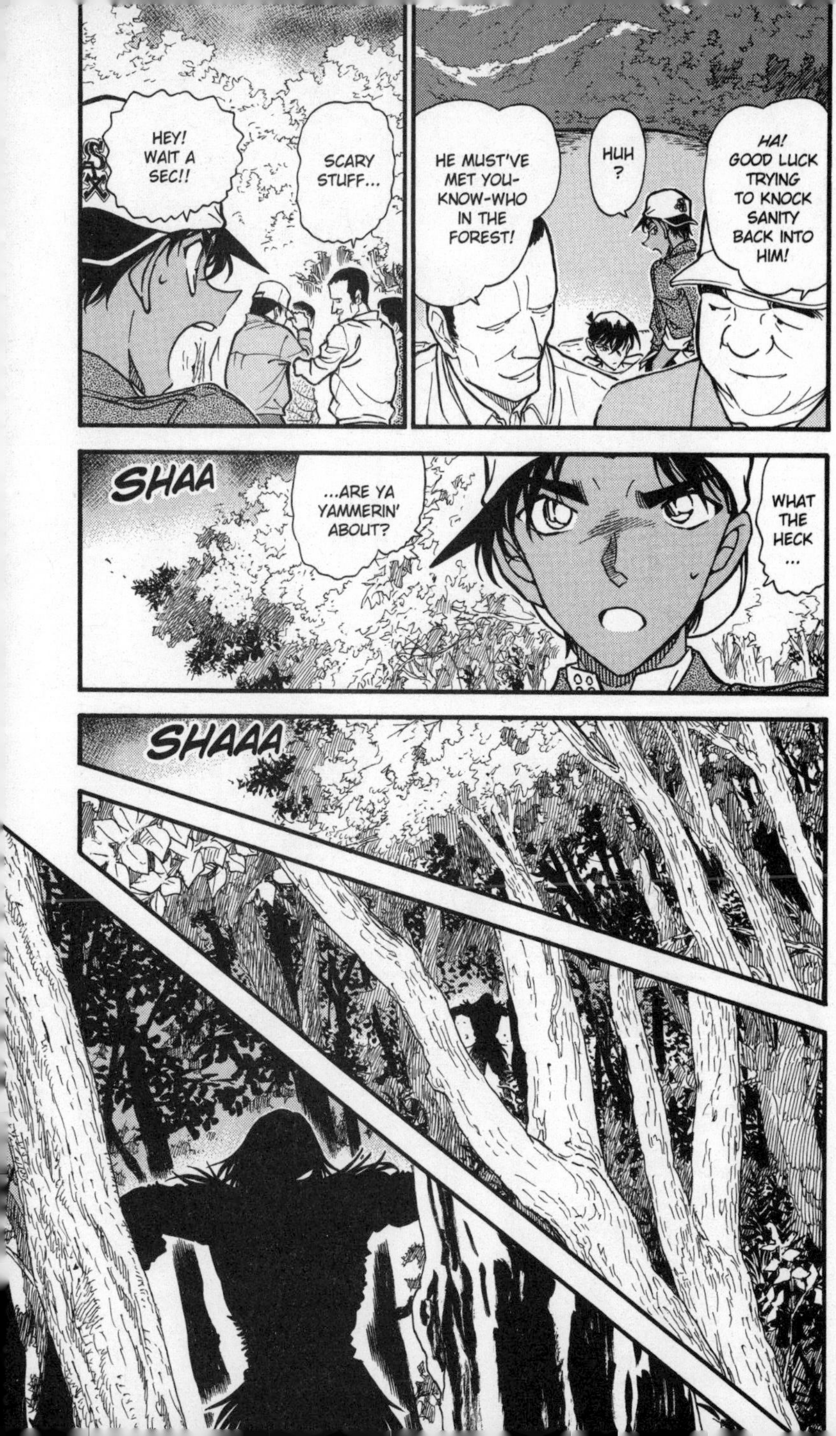
HA! GOOD LUCK TRYING TO KNOCK SANITY BACK INTO HIM!
HUH?
HE MUST'VE MET YOU-KNOW-WHO IN THE FOREST!
SCARY STUFF...
HEY! WAIT A SEC!!
WHAT THE HECK ...
...ARE YA YAMMERIN' ABOUT?
SHAA
SHAAA

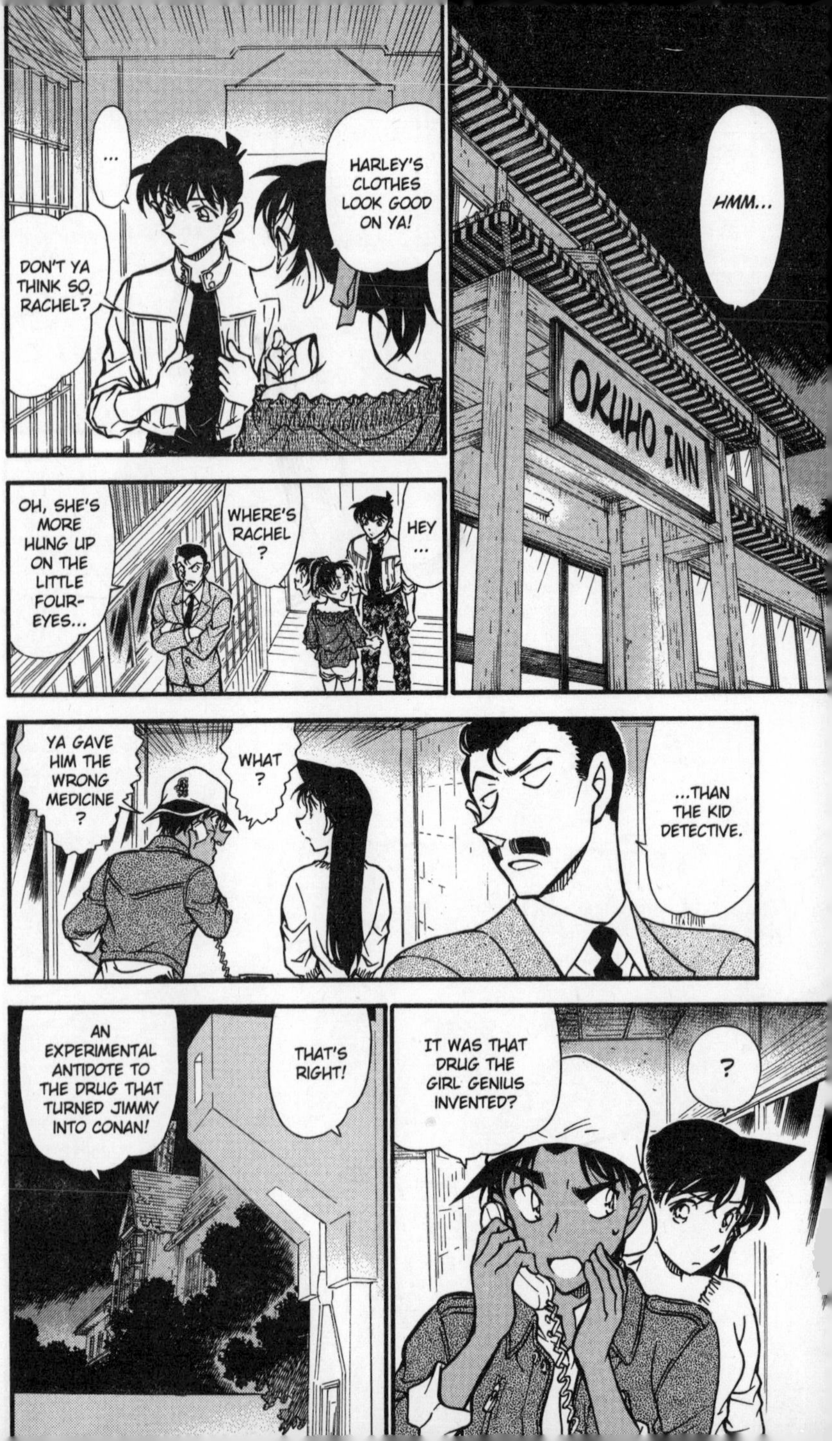
HMM...
OKUHO INN
HARLEY'S CLOTHES LOOK GOOD ON YA!
...
DON'T YA THINK SO, RACHEL?
HEY ...
WHERE'S RACHEL ?
OH, SHE'S MORE HUNG UP ON THE LITTLE FOUR-EYES...
...THAN THE KID DETECTIVE.
WHAT ?
YA GAVE HIM THE WRONG MEDICINE ?
?
IT WAS THAT DRUG THE GIRL GENIUS INVENTED?
THAT'S RIGHT!
AN EXPERIMENTAL ANTIDOTE TO THE DRUG THAT TURNED JIMMY INTO CONAN!

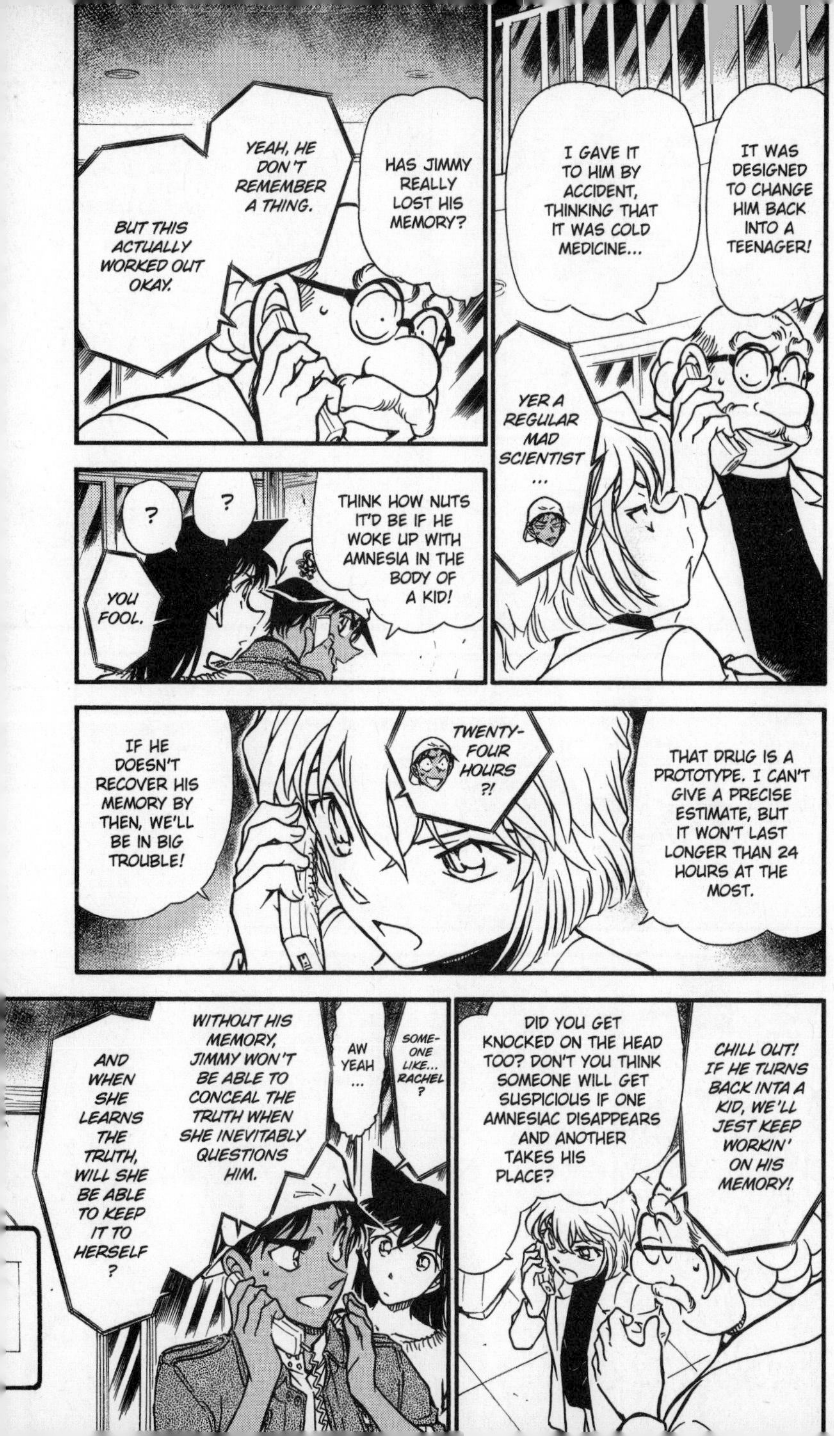
IT WAS DESIGNED TO CHANGE HIM BACK INTO A TEENAGER!
I GAVE IT TO HIM BY ACCIDENT, THINKING THAT IT WAS COLD MEDICINE...
YER A REGULAR MAD SCIENTIST ...
HAS JIMMY REALLY LOST HIS MEMORY?
YEAH, HE DON'T REMEMBER A THING.
BUT THIS ACTUALLY WORKED OUT OKAY.
THINK HOW NUTS IT'D BE IF HE WOKE UP WITH AMNESIA IN THE BODY OF A KID!
?
?
YOU FOOL.
THAT DRUG IS A PROTOTYPE. I CAN'T GIVE A PRECISE ESTIMATE, BUT IT WON'T LAST LONGER THAN 24 HOURS AT THE MOST.
TWENTY-FOUR HOURS ?!
IF HE DOESN'T RECOVER HIS MEMORY BY THEN, WE'LL BE IN BIG TROUBLE!
CHILL OUT! IF HE TURNS BACK INTA A KID, WE'LL JEST KEEP WORKIN' ON HIS MEMORY!
DID YOU GET KNOCKED ON THE HEAD TOO? DON'T YOU THINK SOMEONE WILL GET SUSPICIOUS IF ONE AMNESIAC DISAPPEARS AND ANOTHER TAKES HIS PLACE?
SOME-ONE LIKE... RACHEL ?
AW YEAH ...
WITHOUT HIS MEMORY, JIMMY WON'T BE ABLE TO CONCEAL THE TRUTH WHEN SHE INEVITABLY QUESTIONS HIM.
AND WHEN SHE LEARNS THE TRUTH, WILL SHE BE ABLE TO KEEP IT TO HERSELF ?

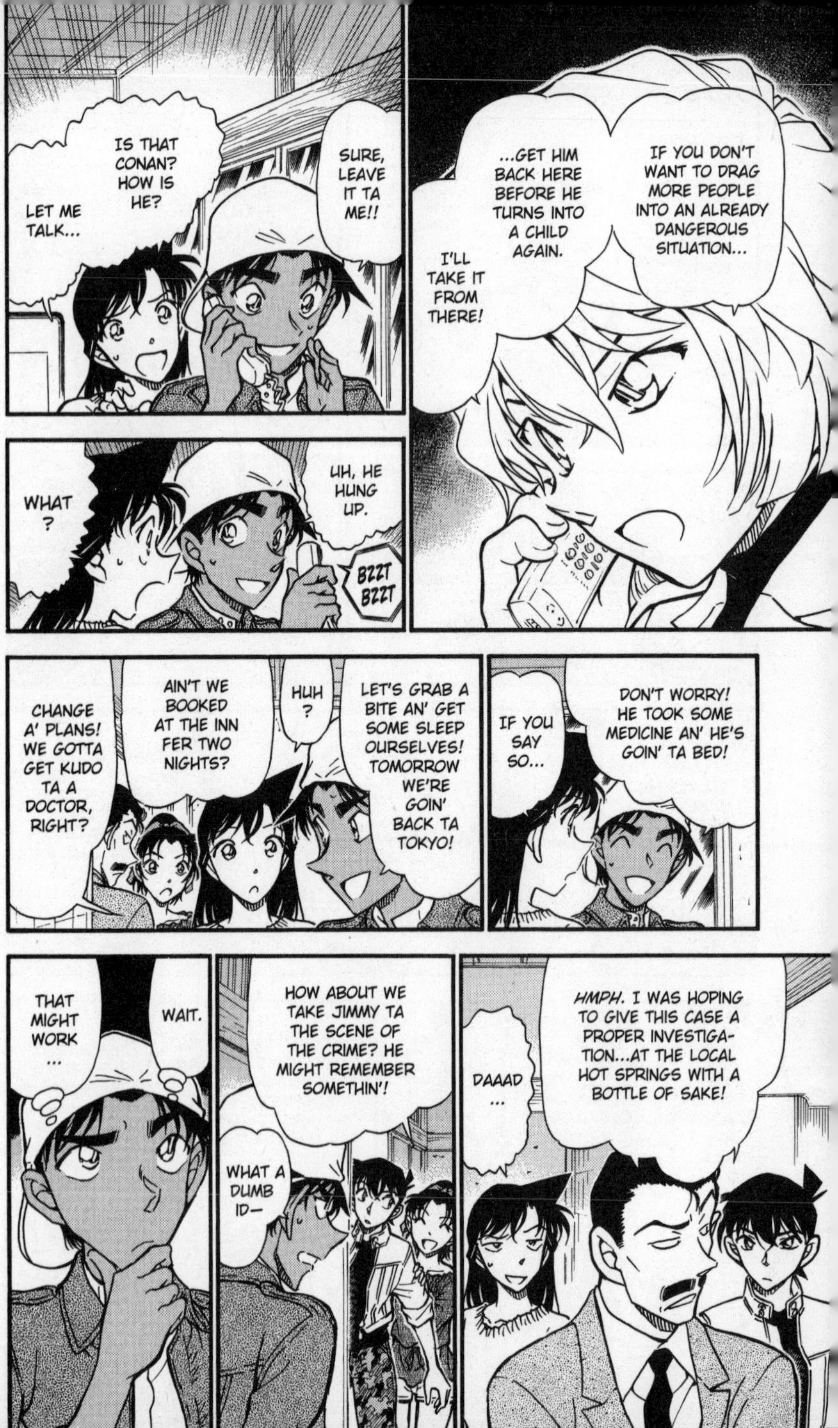
IF YOU DON'T WANT TO DRAG MORE PEOPLE INTO AN ALREADY DANGEROUS SITUATION...
...GET HIM BACK HERE BEFORE HE TURNS INTO A CHILD AGAIN.
I'LL TAKE IT FROM THERE!
SURE, LEAVE IT TA ME!!
IS THAT CONAN? HOW IS HE?
LET ME TALK...
UH, HE HUNG UP.
BZZT BZZT
WHAT ?
DON'T WORRY! HE TOOK SOME MEDICINE AN' HE'S GOIN' TA BED!
IF YOU SAY SO...
LET'S GRAB A BITE AN' GET SOME SLEEP OURSELVES! TOMORROW WE'RE GOIN' BACK TA TOKYO!
HUH ?
AIN'T WE BOOKED AT THE INN FER TWO NIGHTS?
CHANGE A' PLANS! WE GOTTA GET KUDO TA A DOCTOR, RIGHT?
HMPH. I WAS HOPING TO GIVE THIS CASE A PROPER INVESTIGA-TION...AT THE LOCAL HOT SPRINGS WITH A BOTTLE OF SAKE!
DAAAD ...
HOW ABOUT WE TAKE JIMMY TA THE SCENE OF THE CRIME? HE MIGHT REMEMBER SOMETHIN'!
WHAT A DUMB ID—
WAIT.
THAT MIGHT WORK ...

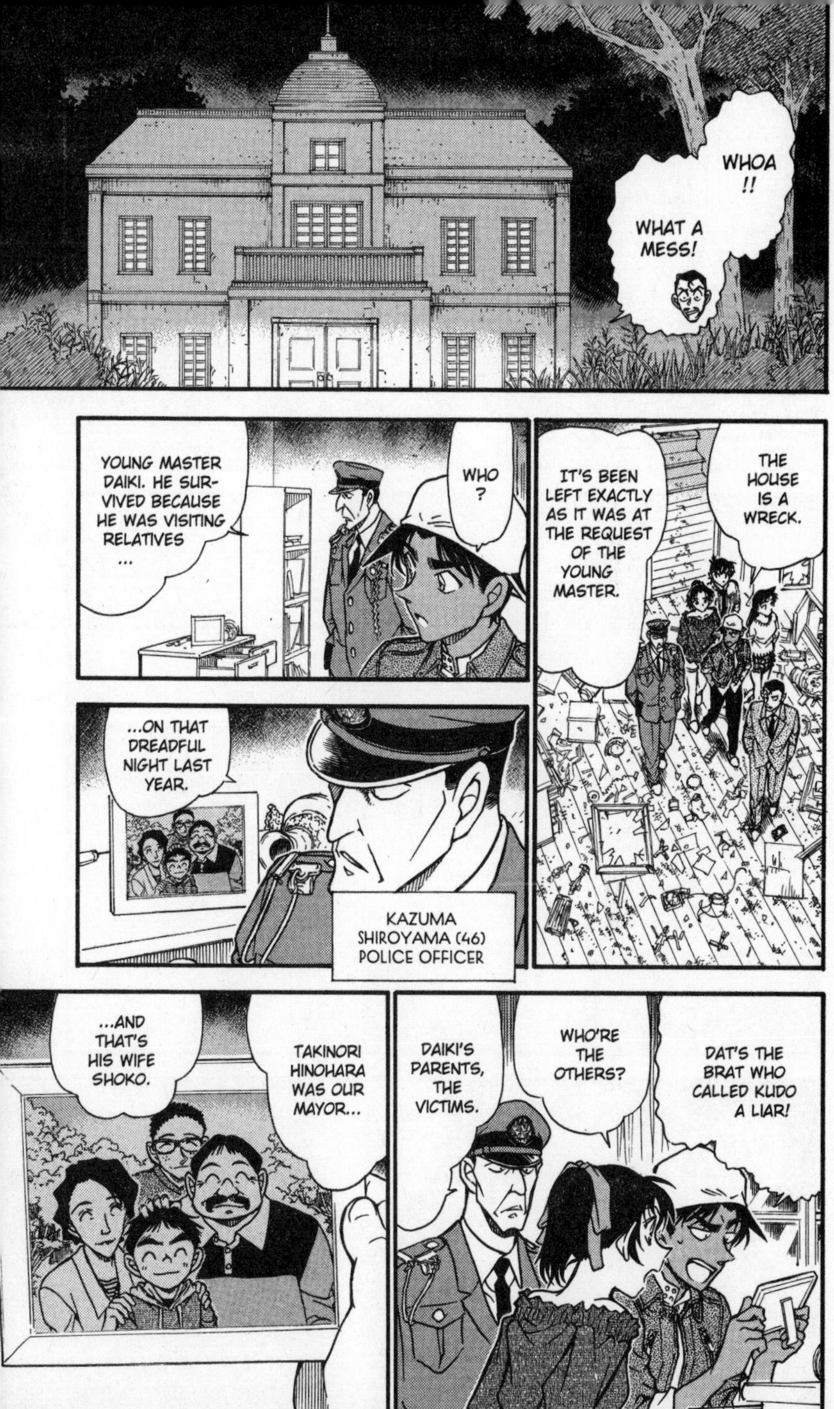
WHOA!!
WHAT A MESS!
THE HOUSE IS A WRECK.
IT'S BEEN LEFT EXACTLY AS IT WAS AT THE REQUEST OF THE YOUNG MASTER.
WHO?
YOUNG MASTER DAIKI. HE SURVIVED BECAUSE HE WAS VISITING RELATIVES ...
...ON THAT DREADFUL NIGHT LAST YEAR.
KAZUMA SHIROYAMA (46) POLICE OFFICER
DAT'S THE BRAT WHO CALLED KUDO A LIAR!
WHO'RE THE OTHERS?
DAIKI'S PARENTS, THE VICTIMS.
TAKINORI HINOHARA WAS OUR MAYOR...
...AND THAT'S HIS WIFE SHOKO.

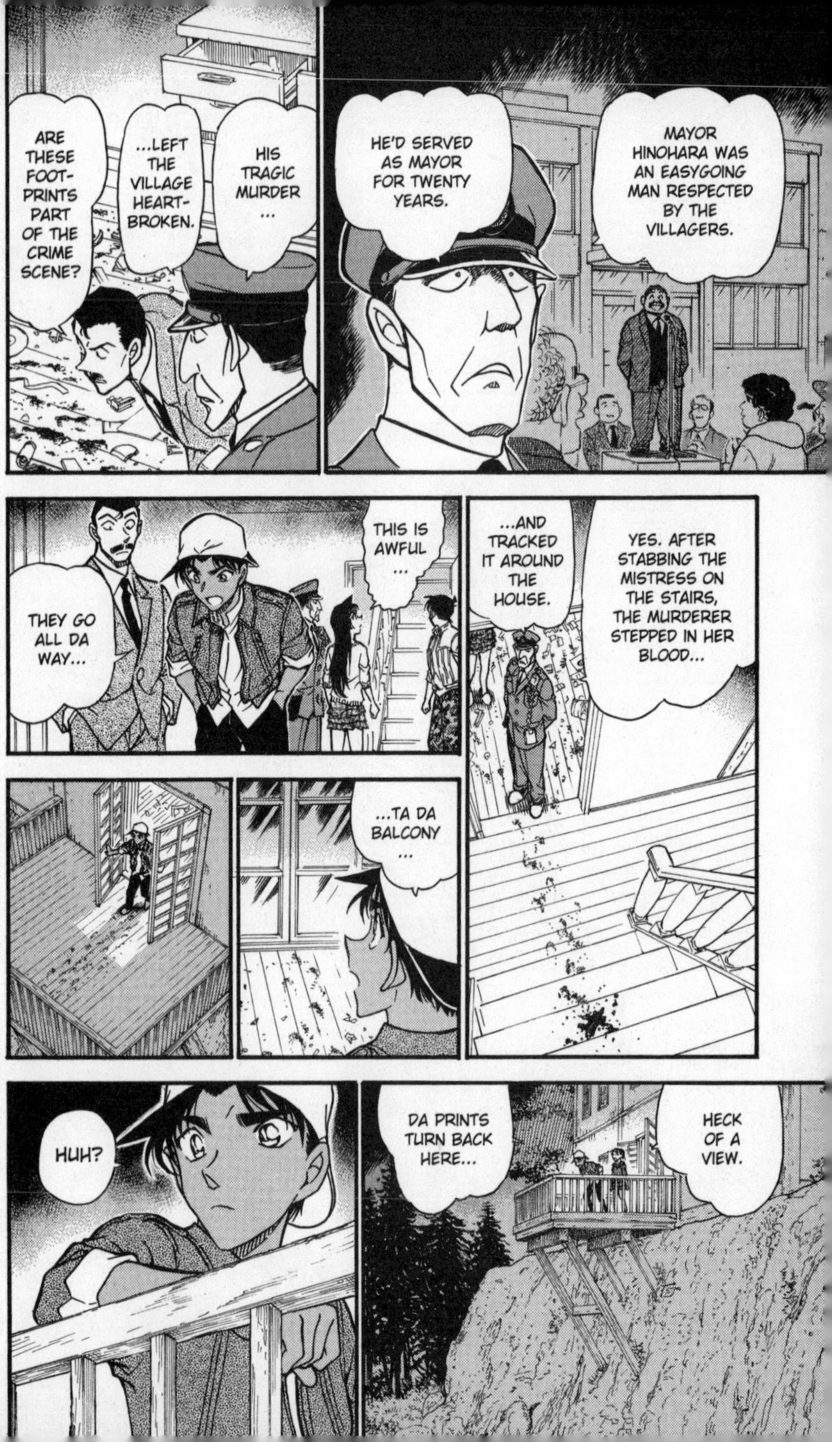
MAYOR HINOHARA WAS AN EASYGOING MAN RESPECTED BY THE VILLAGERS.
HE'D SERVED AS MAYOR FOR TWENTY YEARS.
HIS TRAGIC MURDER ...
...LEFT THE VILLAGE HEART-BROKEN.
ARE THESE FOOT-PRINTS PART OF THE CRIME SCENE?
YES. AFTER STABBING THE MISTRESS ON THE STAIRS, THE MURDERER STEPPED IN HER BLOOD...
...AND TRACKED IT AROUND THE HOUSE.
THIS IS AWFUL ...
THEY GO ALL DA WAY...
...TA DA BALCONY ...
HECK OF A VIEW.
DA PRINTS TURN BACK HERE...
HUH?

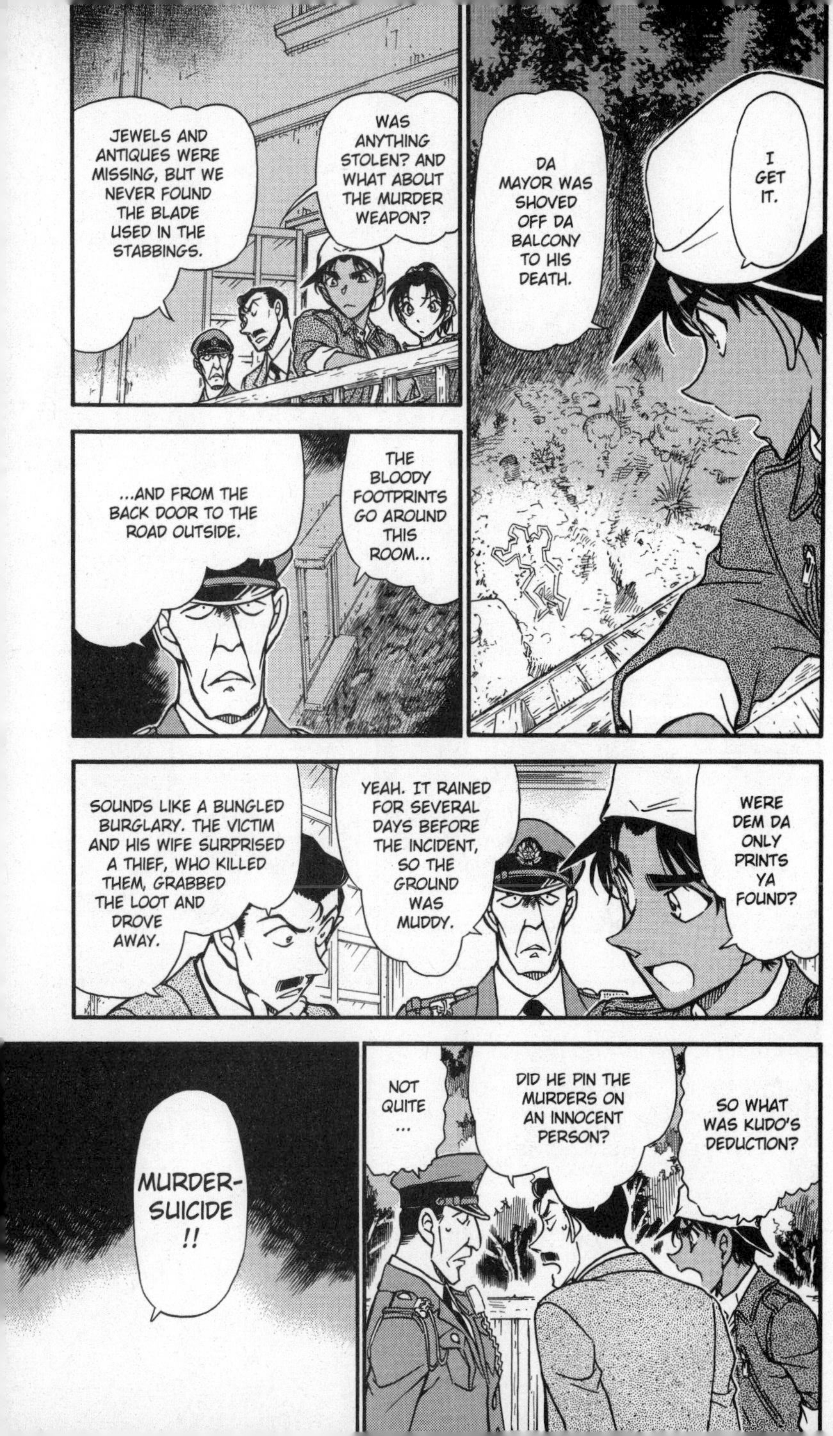
I GET IT.
DA MAYOR WAS SHOVED OFF DA BALCONY TO HIS DEATH.
WAS ANYTHING STOLEN? AND WHAT ABOUT THE MURDER WEAPON?
JEWELS AND ANTIQUES WERE MISSING, BUT WE NEVER FOUND THE BLADE USED IN THE STABBINGS.
THE BLOODY FOOTPRINTS GO AROUND THIS ROOM...
...AND FROM THE BACK DOOR TO THE ROAD OUTSIDE.
WERE DEM DA ONLY PRINTS YA FOUND?
YEAH. IT RAINED FOR SEVERAL DAYS BEFORE THE INCIDENT, SO THE GROUND WAS MUDDY.
SOUNDS LIKE A BUNGLED BURGLARY. THE VICTIM AND HIS WIFE SURPRISED A THIEF, WHO KILLED THEM, GRABBED THE LOOT AND DROVE AWAY.
SO WHAT WAS KUDO'S DEDUCTION?
DID HE PIN THE MURDERS ON AN INNOCENT PERSON?
NOT QUITE ...
MURDER-SUICIDE !!

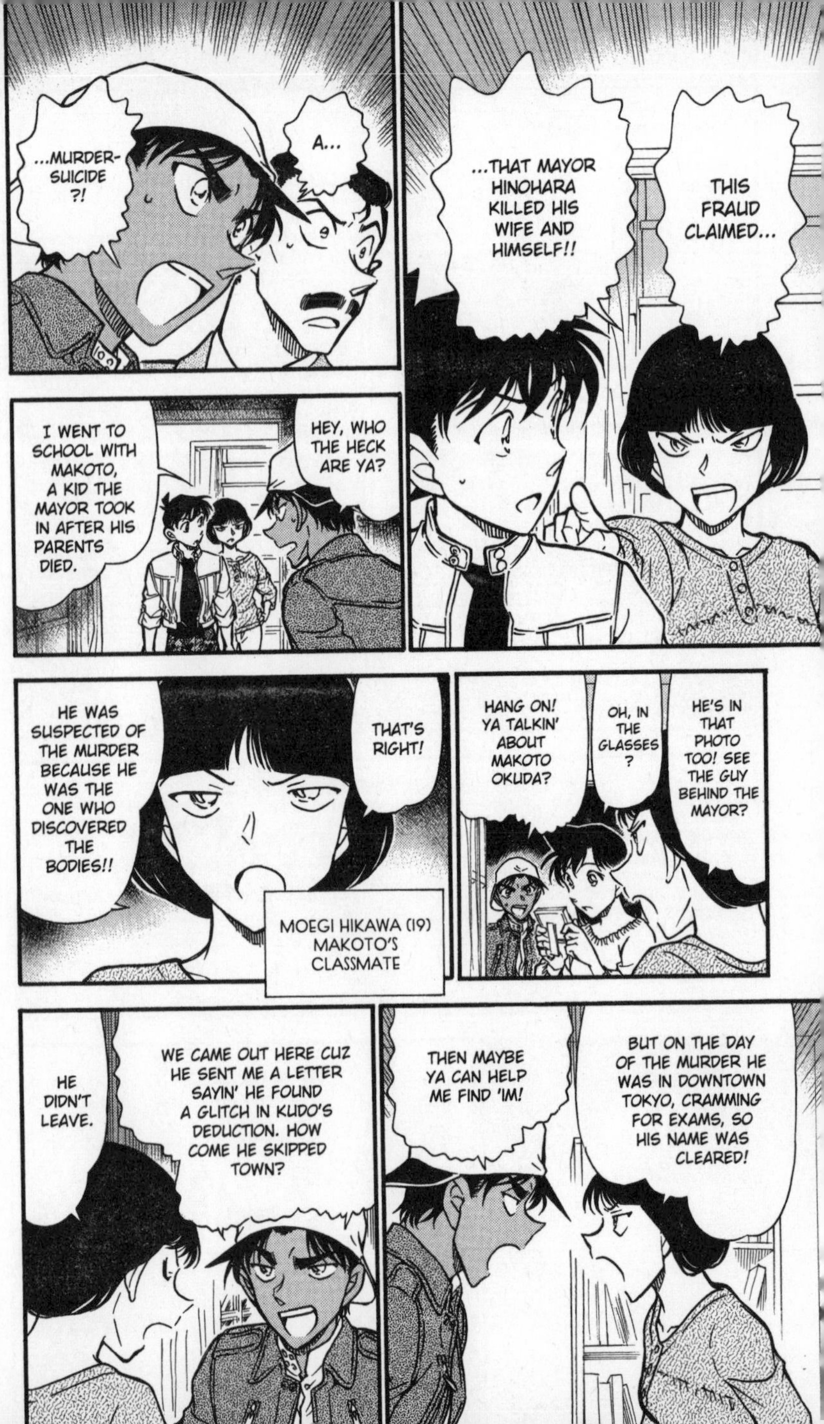
THIS FRAUD CLAIMED...
...THAT MAYOR HINOHARA KILLED HIS WIFE AND HIMSELF!!
A...
...MURDER-SUICIDE?!
HEY, WHO THE HECK ARE YA?
I WENT TO SCHOOL WITH MAKOTO, A KID THE MAYOR TOOK IN AFTER HIS PARENTS DIED.
HE'S IN THAT PHOTO TOO! SEE THE GUY BEHIND THE MAYOR?
OH, IN THE GLASSES?
HANG ON! YA TALKIN' ABOUT MAKOTO OKUDA?
THAT'S RIGHT!
HE WAS SUSPECTED OF THE MURDER BECAUSE HE WAS THE ONE WHO DISCOVERED THE BODIES!!
MOEGI HIKAWA (19) MAKOTO'S CLASSMATE
BUT ON THE DAY OF THE MURDER HE WAS IN DOWNTOWN TOKYO, CRAMMING FOR EXAMS, SO HIS NAME WAS CLEARED!
THEN MAYBE YA CAN HELP ME FIND 'IM!
WE CAME OUT HERE CUZ HE SENT ME A LETTER SAYIN' HE FOUND A GLITCH IN KUDO'S DEDUCTION. HOW COME HE SKIPPED TOWN?
HE DIDN'T LEAVE.

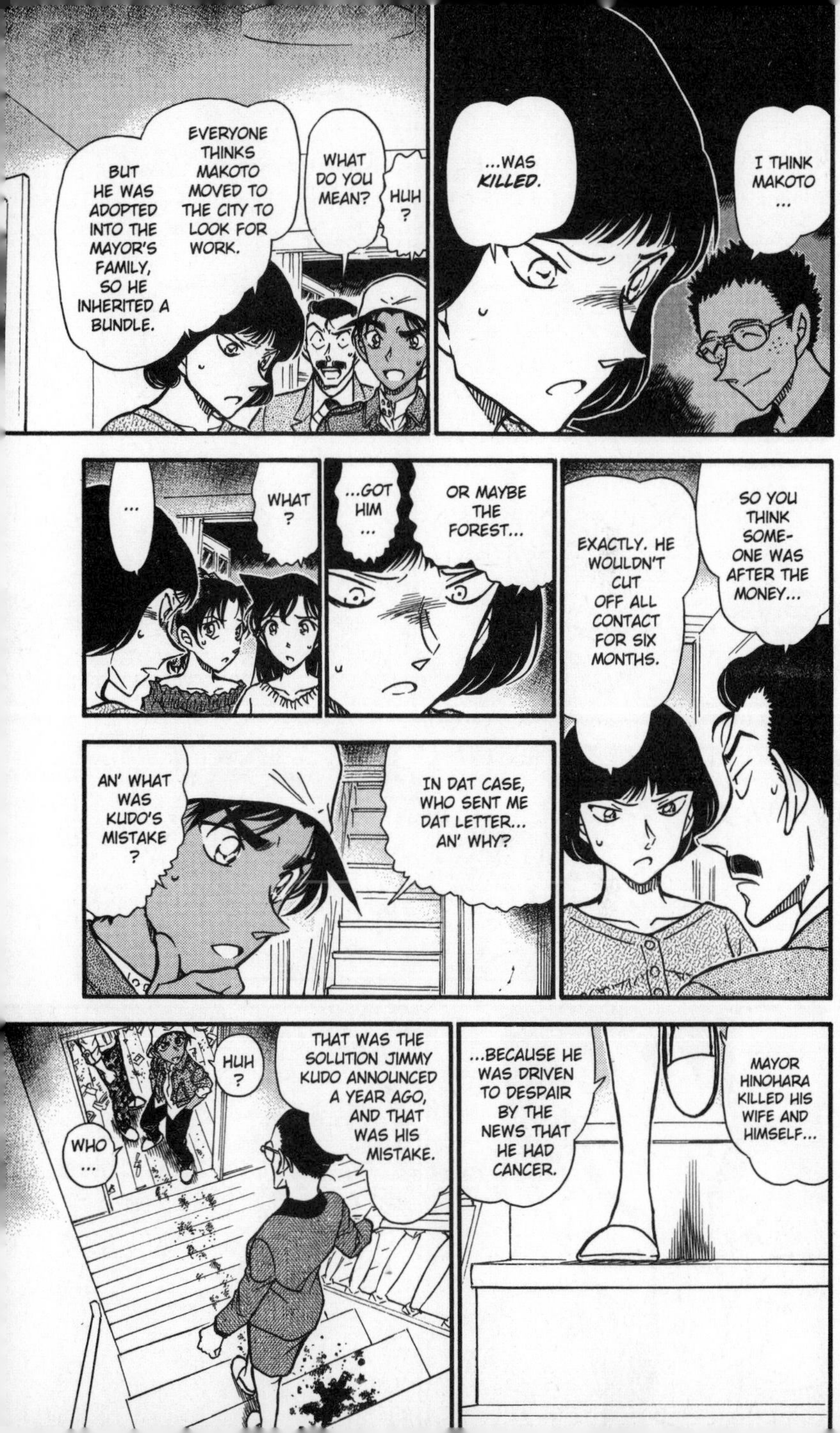
I THINK MAKOTO ...
...WAS *KILLED*.
HUH ?
WHAT DO YOU MEAN?
EVERYONE THINKS MAKOTO MOVED TO THE CITY TO LOOK FOR WORK.
BUT HE WAS ADOPTED INTO THE MAYOR'S FAMILY, SO HE INHERITED A BUNDLE.
SO YOU THINK SOME-ONE WAS AFTER THE MONEY...
EXACTLY. HE WOULDN'T CUT OFF ALL CONTACT FOR SIX MONTHS.
OR MAYBE THE FOREST...
...GOT HIM ...
WHAT ?
...
IN DAT CASE, WHO SENT ME DAT LETTER... AN' WHY?
AN' WHAT WAS KUDO'S MISTAKE ?
MAYOR HINOHARA KILLED HIS WIFE AND HIMSELF...
...BECAUSE HE WAS DRIVEN TO DESPAIR BY THE NEWS THAT HE HAD CANCER.
THAT WAS THE SOLUTION JIMMY KUDO ANNOUNCED A YEAR AGO, AND THAT WAS HIS MISTAKE.
HUH ?
WHO ...

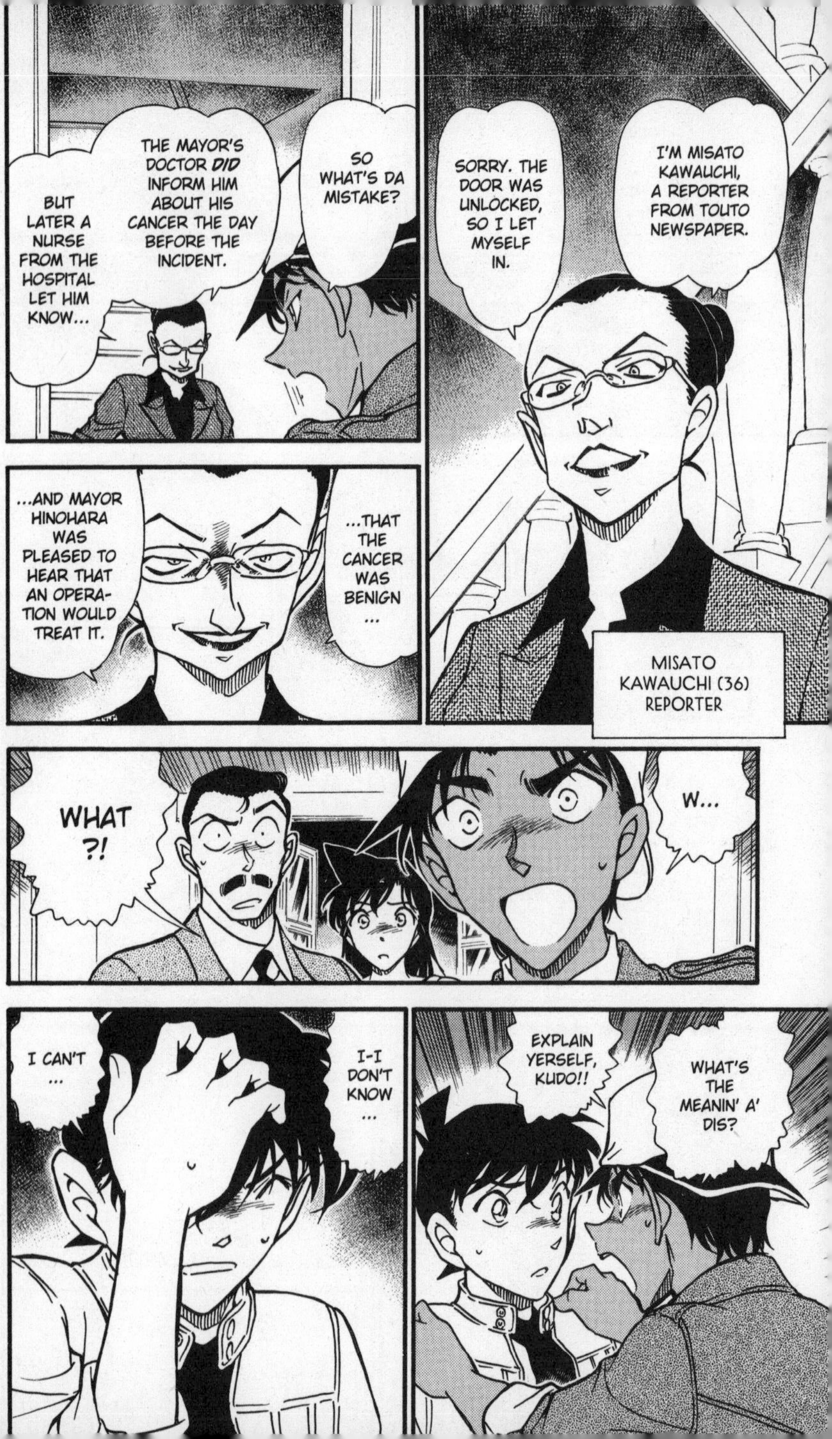
I'M MISATO KAWAUCHI, A REPORTER FROM TOUTO NEWSPAPER.
SORRY. THE DOOR WAS UNLOCKED, SO I LET MYSELF IN.
MISATO KAWAUCHI (36) REPORTER
SO WHAT'S DA MISTAKE?
THE MAYOR'S DOCTOR *DID* INFORM HIM ABOUT HIS CANCER THE DAY BEFORE THE INCIDENT.
BUT LATER A NURSE FROM THE HOSPITAL LET HIM KNOW...
...THAT THE CANCER WAS BENIGN ...
...AND MAYOR HINOHARA WAS PLEASED TO HEAR THAT AN OPERA-TION WOULD TREAT IT.
W...
WHAT ?!
WHAT'S THE MEANIN' A' DIS?
EXPLAIN YERSELF, KUDO!!
I-I DON'T KNOW ...
I CAN'T ...

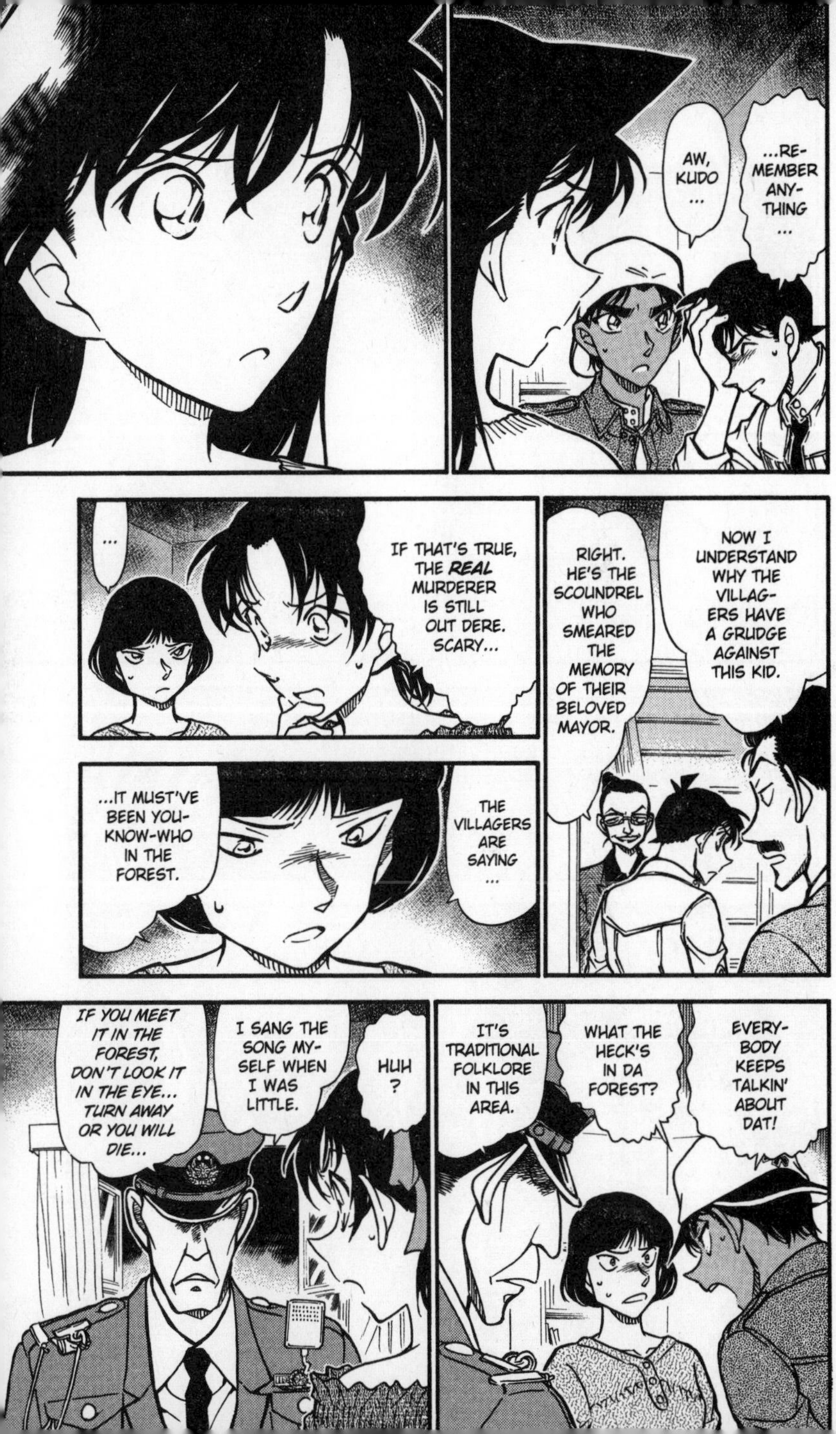
...RE-MEMBER ANY-THING ...
AW, KUDO ...
NOW I UNDERSTAND WHY THE VILLAG-ERS HAVE A GRUDGE AGAINST THIS KID.
RIGHT. HE'S THE SCOUNDREL WHO SMEARED THE MEMORY OF THEIR BELOVED MAYOR.
IF THAT'S TRUE, THE *REAL* MURDERER IS STILL OUT DERE. SCARY...
...
THE VILLAGERS ARE SAYING ...
...IT MUST'VE BEEN YOU-KNOW-WHO IN THE FOREST.
EVERY-BODY KEEPS TALKIN' ABOUT DAT!
WHAT THE HECK'S IN DA FOREST?
IT'S TRADITIONAL FOLKLORE IN THIS AREA.
HUH ?
I SANG THE SONG MY-SELF WHEN I WAS LITTLE.
IF YOU MEET IT IN THE FOREST, DON'T LOOK IT IN THE EYE... TURN AWAY OR YOU WILL DIE...

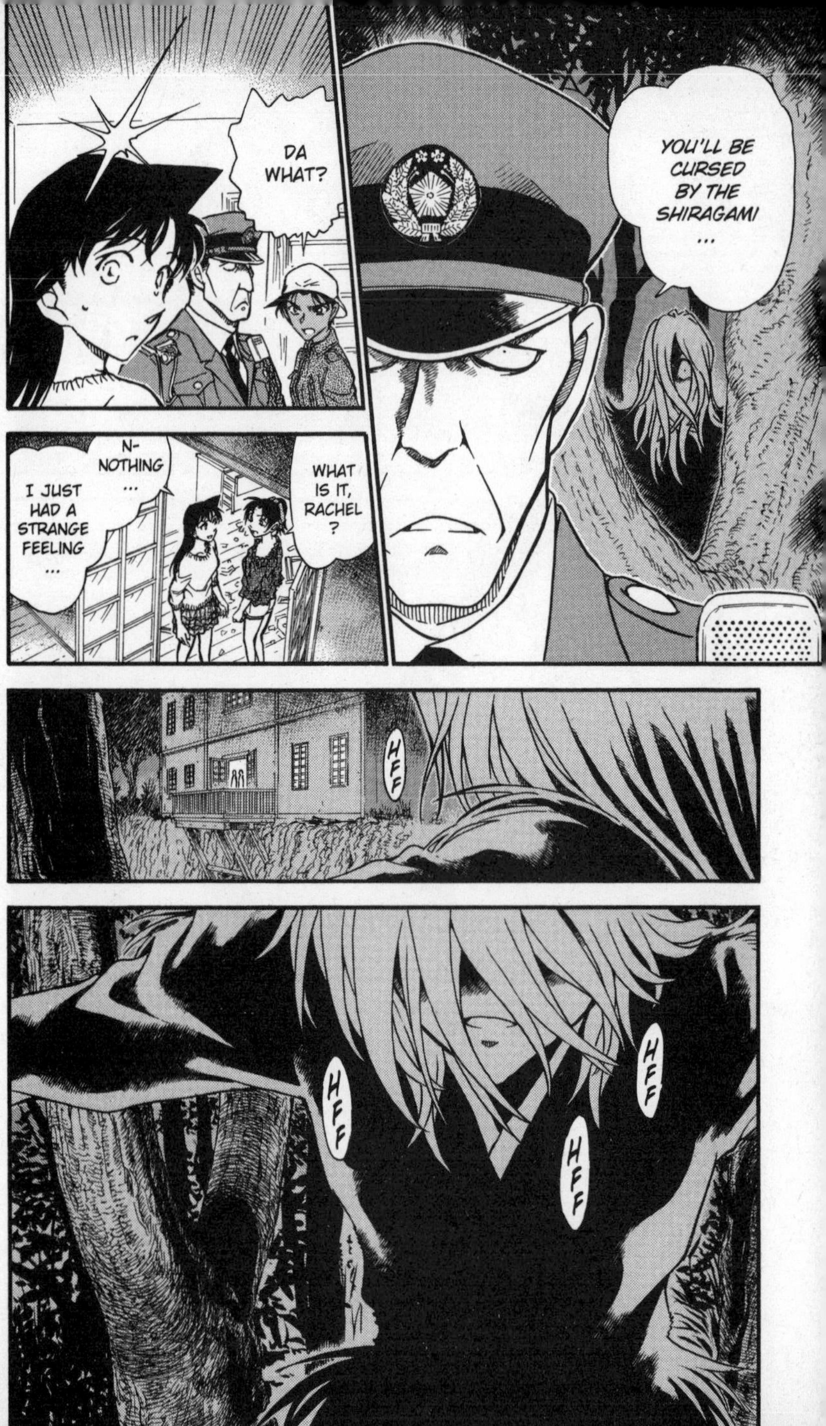
YOU'LL BE CURSED BY THE SHIRAGAMI ...
DA WHAT?
WHAT IS IT, RACHEL?
N- NOTHING ...
I JUST HAD A STRANGE FEELING ...
HFF
HFF
HFF
HFF

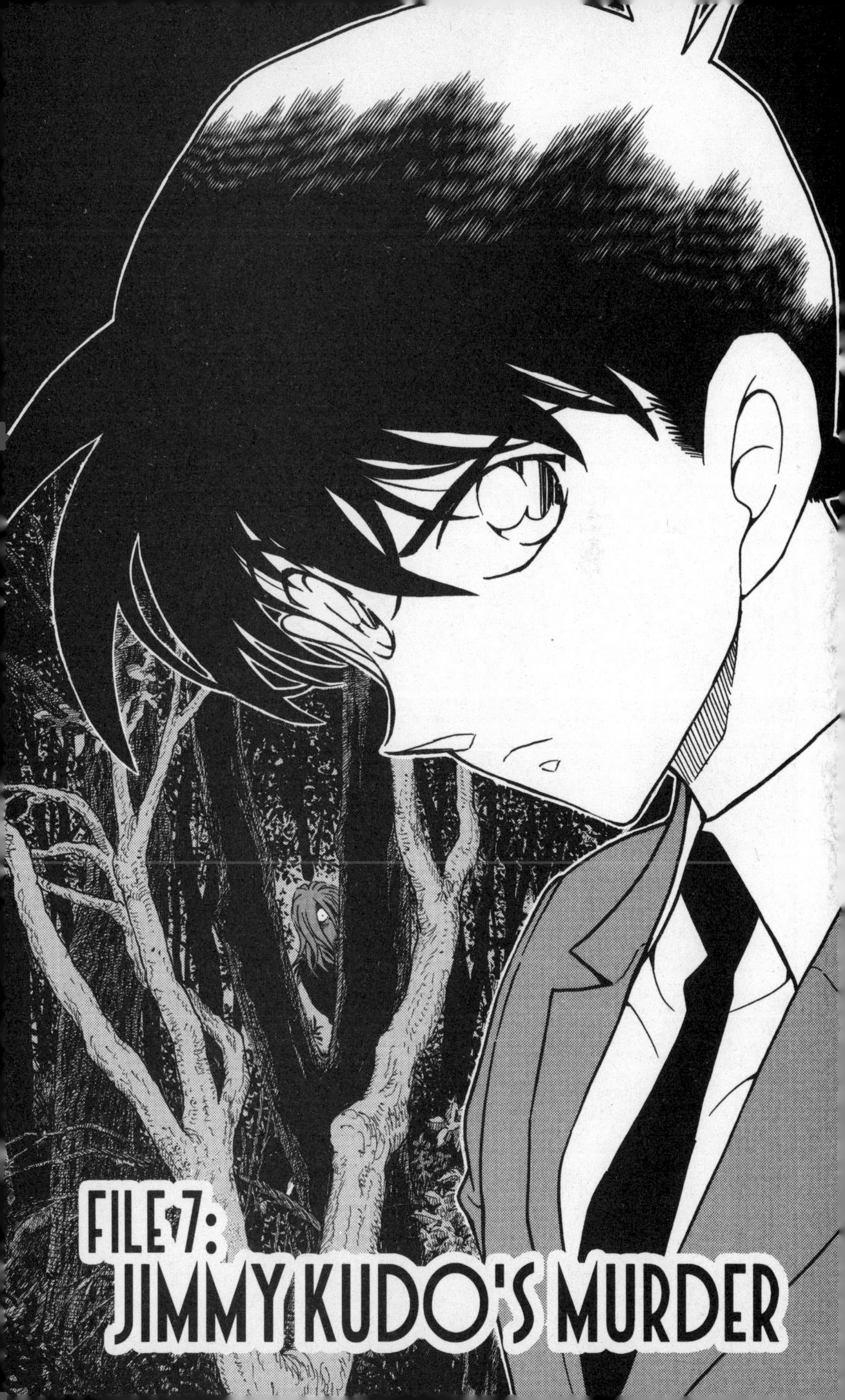
FILE 7:
JIMMY KUDO'S MURDER

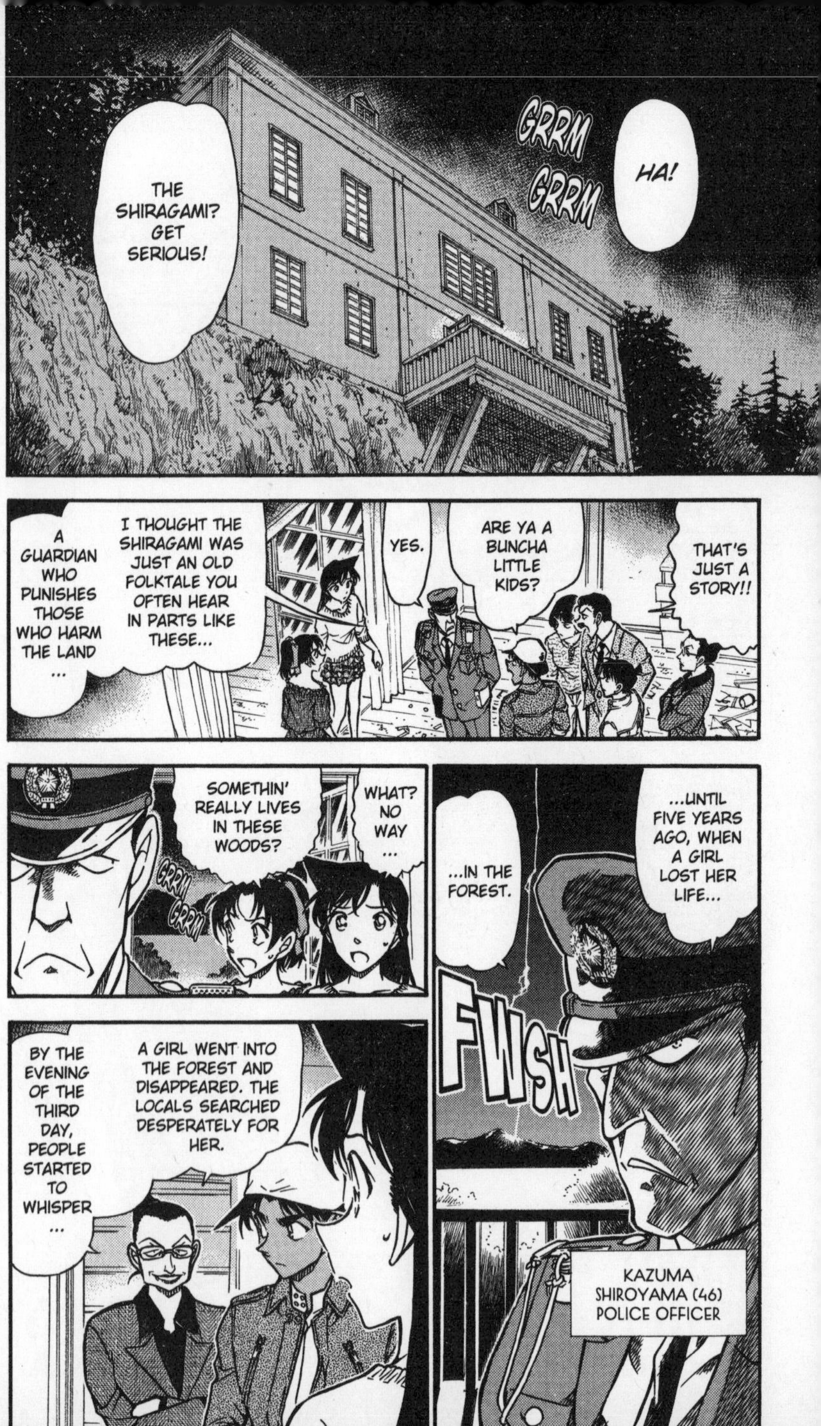
HA!
GRRM GRRM
THE SHIRAGAMI? GET SERIOUS!
THAT'S JUST A STORY!!
ARE YA A BUNCHA LITTLE KIDS?
YES.
I THOUGHT THE SHIRAGAMI WAS JUST AN OLD FOLKTALE YOU OFTEN HEAR IN PARTS LIKE THESE...
A GUARDIAN WHO PUNISHES THOSE WHO HARM THE LAND...
...UNTIL FIVE YEARS AGO, WHEN A GIRL LOST HER LIFE...
...IN THE FOREST.
FWSH
KAZUMA SHIROYAMA (46) POLICE OFFICER
WHAT? NO WAY...
SOMETHIN' REALLY LIVES IN THESE WOODS?
GRRM GRRM
A GIRL WENT INTO THE FOREST AND DISAPPEARED. THE LOCALS SEARCHED DESPERATELY FOR HER.
BY THE EVENING OF THE THIRD DAY, PEOPLE STARTED TO WHISPER...

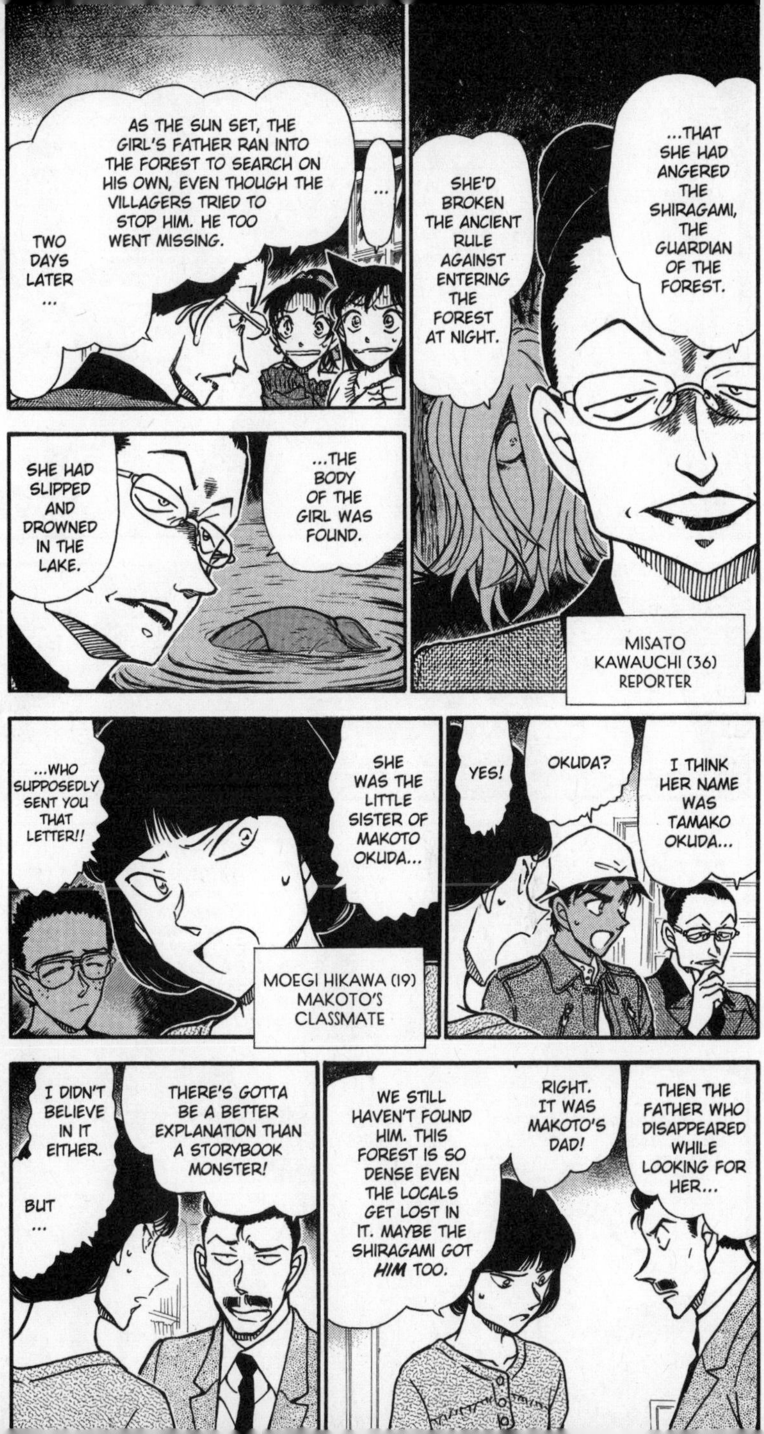
...THAT SHE HAD ANGERED THE SHIRAGAMI, THE GUARDIAN OF THE FOREST.
SHE'D BROKEN THE ANCIENT RULE AGAINST ENTERING THE FOREST AT NIGHT.
MISATO KAWAUCHI (36) REPORTER
AS THE SUN SET, THE GIRL'S FATHER RAN INTO THE FOREST TO SEARCH ON HIS OWN, EVEN THOUGH THE VILLAGERS TRIED TO STOP HIM. HE TOO WENT MISSING.
...
TWO DAYS LATER ...
...THE BODY OF THE GIRL WAS FOUND.
SHE HAD SLIPPED AND DROWNED IN THE LAKE.
I THINK HER NAME WAS TAMAKO OKUDA...
OKUDA?
YES!
SHE WAS THE LITTLE SISTER OF MAKOTO OKUDA...
...WHO SUPPOSEDLY SENT YOU THAT LETTER!!
MOEGI HIKAWA (19) MAKOTO'S CLASSMATE
THEN THE FATHER WHO DISAPPEARED WHILE LOOKING FOR HER...
RIGHT. IT WAS MAKOTO'S DAD!
WE STILL HAVEN'T FOUND HIM. THIS FOREST IS SO DENSE EVEN THE LOCALS GET LOST IN IT. MAYBE THE SHIRAGAMI GOT *HIM* TOO.
THERE'S GOTTA BE A BETTER EXPLANATION THAN A STORYBOOK MONSTER!
I DIDN'T BELIEVE IN IT EITHER.
BUT ...

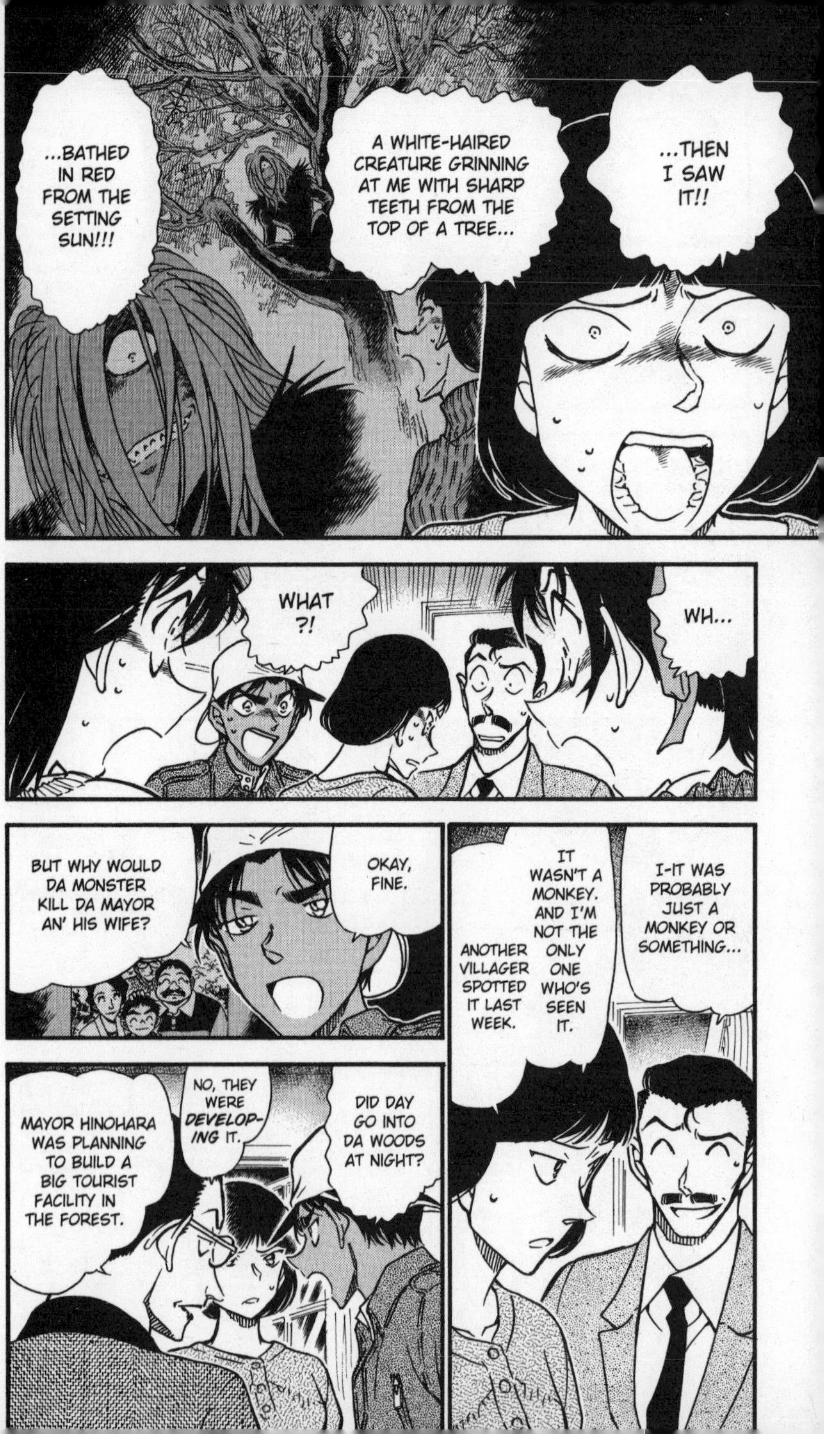
...THEN I SAW IT!!
A WHITE-HAIRED CREATURE GRINNING AT ME WITH SHARP TEETH FROM THE TOP OF A TREE...
...BATHED IN RED FROM THE SETTING SUN!!!
WH...
WHAT ?!
I-IT WAS PROBABLY JUST A MONKEY OR SOMETHING...
IT WASN'T A MONKEY. AND I'M NOT THE ONLY ONE WHO'S SEEN IT.
ANOTHER VILLAGER SPOTTED IT LAST WEEK.
OKAY, FINE.
BUT WHY WOULD DA MONSTER KILL DA MAYOR AN' HIS WIFE?
DID DAY GO INTO DA WOODS AT NIGHT?
NO, THEY WERE DEVELOPING IT.
MAYOR HINOHARA WAS PLANNING TO BUILD A BIG TOURIST FACILITY IN THE FOREST.

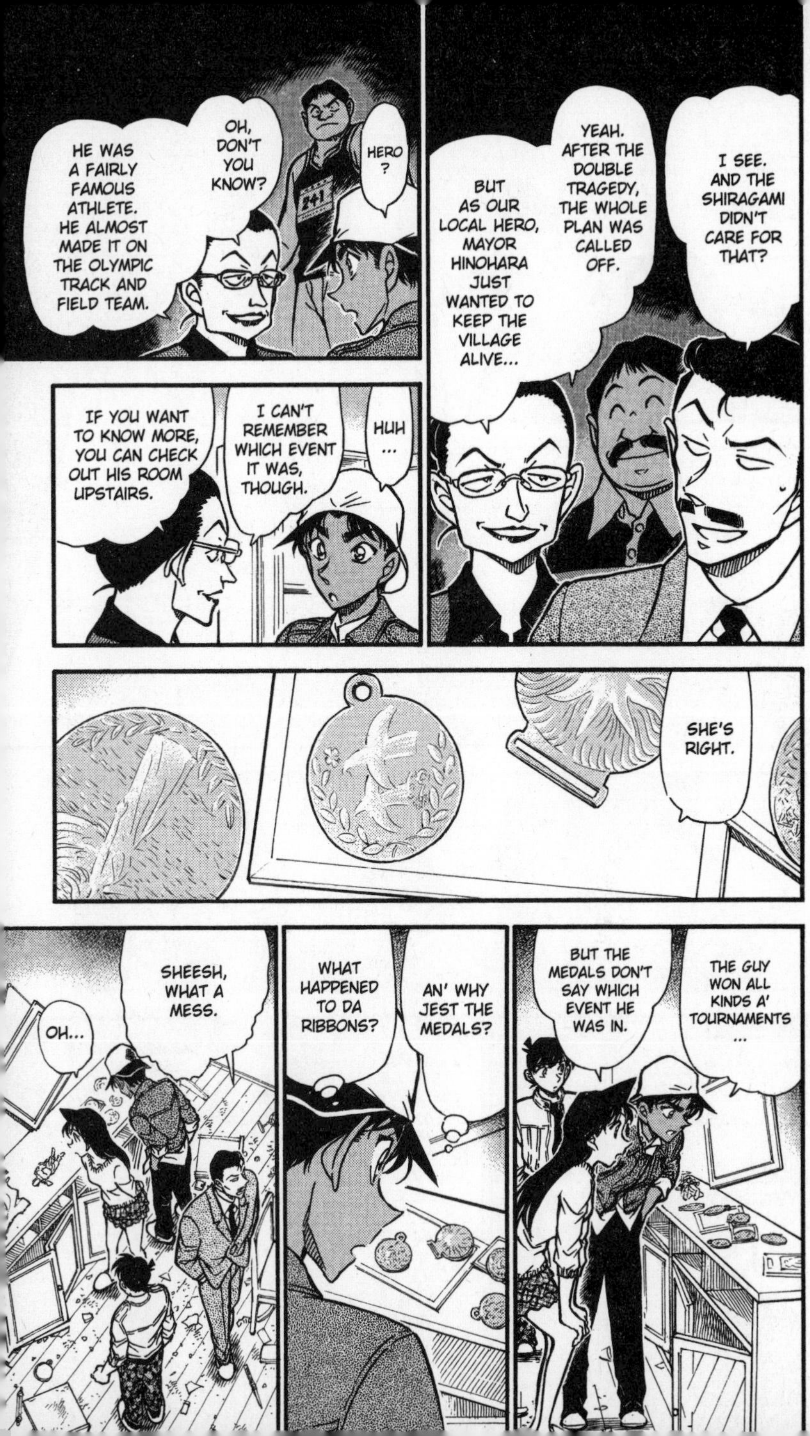
I SEE. AND THE SHIRAGAMI DIDN'T CARE FOR THAT?
YEAH. AFTER THE DOUBLE TRAGEDY, THE WHOLE PLAN WAS CALLED OFF.
BUT AS OUR LOCAL HERO, MAYOR HINOHARA JUST WANTED TO KEEP THE VILLAGE ALIVE...
HERO?
OH, DON'T YOU KNOW?
HE WAS A FAIRLY FAMOUS ATHLETE. HE ALMOST MADE IT ON THE OLYMPIC TRACK AND FIELD TEAM.
HUH...
I CAN'T REMEMBER WHICH EVENT IT WAS, THOUGH.
IF YOU WANT TO KNOW MORE, YOU CAN CHECK OUT HIS ROOM UPSTAIRS.
SHE'S RIGHT.
THE GUY WON ALL KINDS A' TOURNAMENTS...
BUT THE MEDALS DON'T SAY WHICH EVENT HE WAS IN.
AN' WHY JEST THE MEDALS?
WHAT HAPPENED TO DA RIBBONS?
SHEESH, WHAT A MESS.
OH...

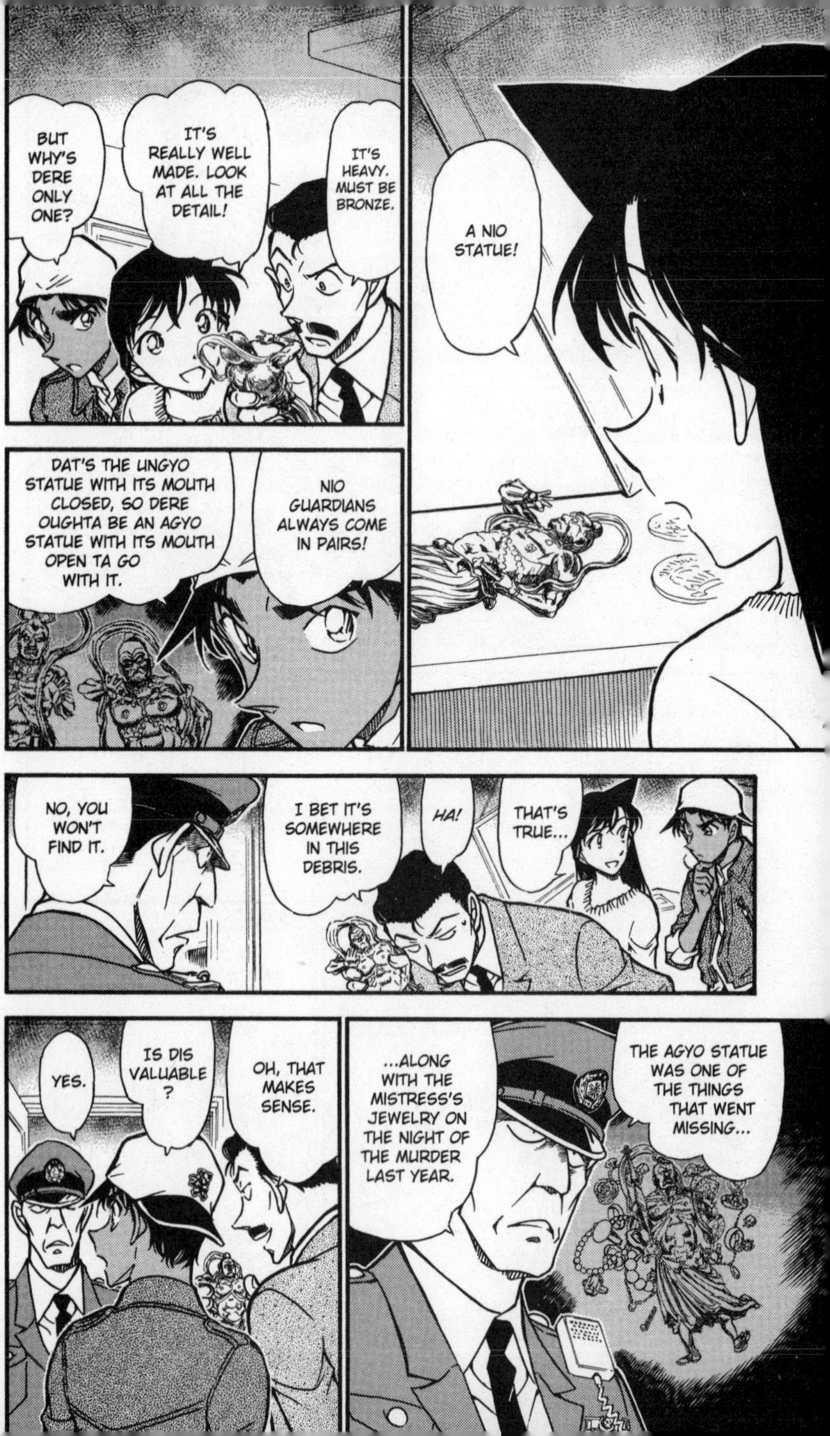
A NIO STATUE!
IT'S HEAVY. MUST BE BRONZE.
IT'S REALLY WELL MADE. LOOK AT ALL THE DETAIL!
BUT WHY'S DERE ONLY ONE?
NIO GUARDIANS ALWAYS COME IN PAIRS!
DAT'S THE UNGYO STATUE WITH ITS MOUTH CLOSED, SO DERE OUGHTA BE AN AGYO STATUE WITH ITS MOUTH OPEN TA GO WITH IT.
THAT'S TRUE...
HA!
I BET IT'S SOMEWHERE IN THIS DEBRIS.
NO, YOU WON'T FIND IT.
THE AGYO STATUE WAS ONE OF THE THINGS THAT WENT MISSING...
...ALONG WITH THE MISTRESS'S JEWELRY ON THE NIGHT OF THE MURDER LAST YEAR.
OH, THAT MAKES SENSE.
IS DIS VALUABLE?
YES.

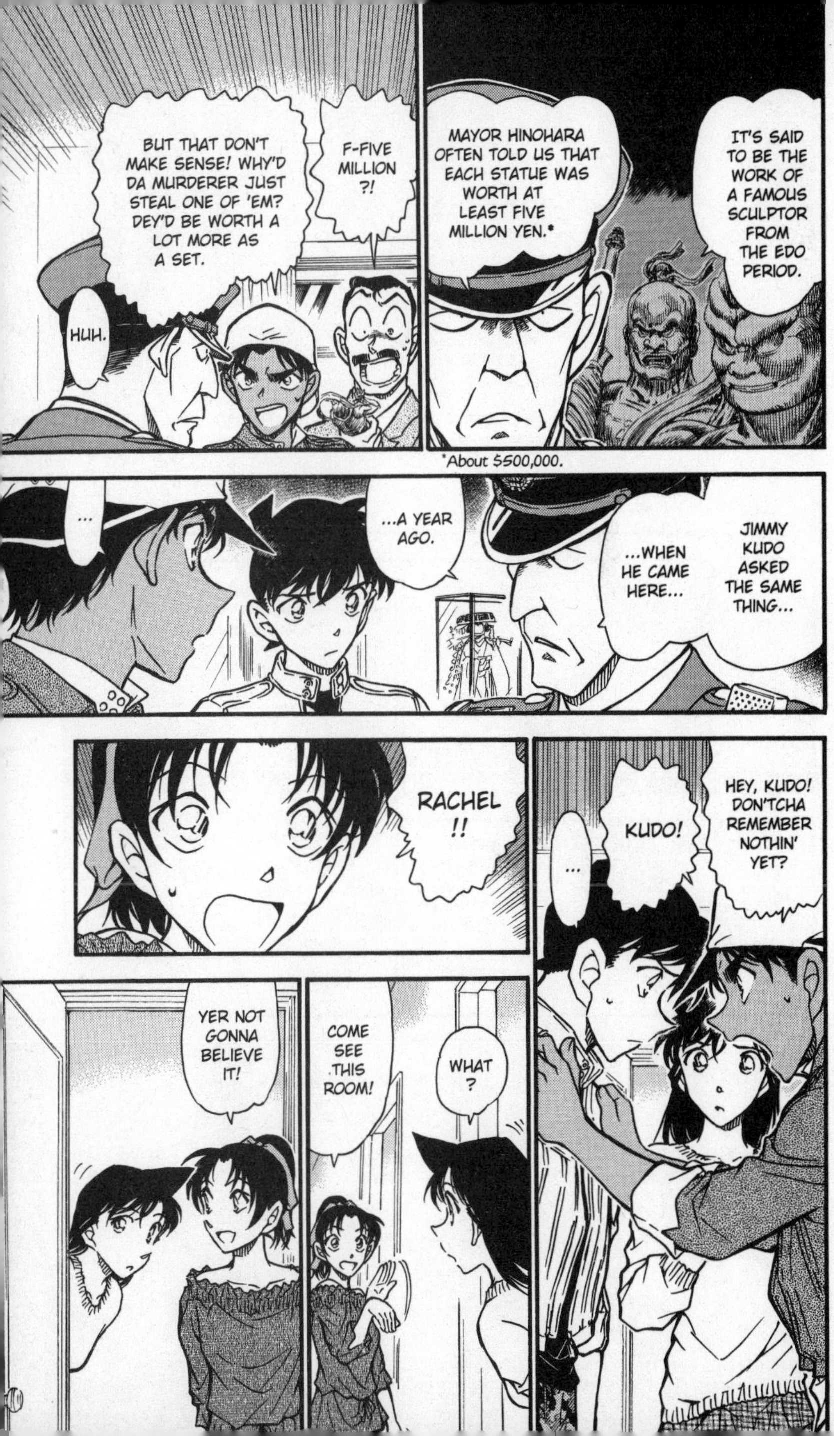
IT'S SAID TO BE THE WORK OF A FAMOUS SCULPTOR FROM THE EDO PERIOD.
MAYOR HINOHARA OFTEN TOLD US THAT EACH STATUE WAS WORTH AT LEAST FIVE MILLION YEN.*
F-FIVE MILLION ?!
BUT THAT DON'T MAKE SENSE! WHY'D DA MURDERER JUST STEAL ONE OF 'EM? DEY'D BE WORTH A LOT MORE AS A SET.
HUH.
JIMMY KUDO ASKED THE SAME THING...
...WHEN HE CAME HERE...
...A YEAR AGO.
...
HEY, KUDO! DON'TCHA REMEMBER NOTHIN' YET?
KUDO!
...
RACHEL !!
WHAT ?
COME SEE THIS ROOM!
YER NOT GONNA BELIEVE IT!

*About $500,000.

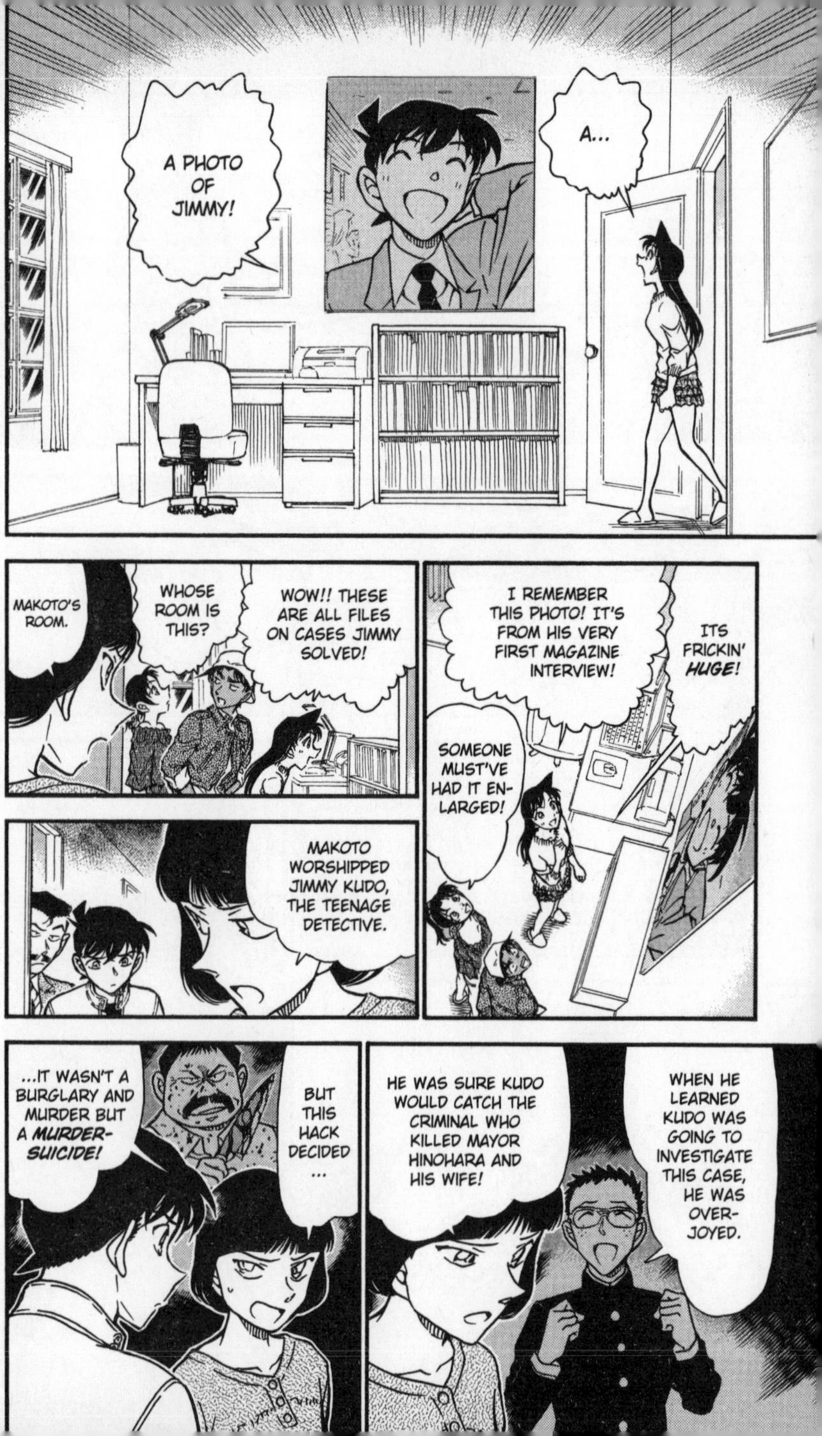

A...
A PHOTO OF JIMMY!
ITS FRICKIN' *HUGE!*
I REMEMBER THIS PHOTO! IT'S FROM HIS VERY FIRST MAGAZINE INTERVIEW!
SOMEONE MUST'VE HAD IT EN-LARGED!
WOW!! THESE ARE ALL FILES ON CASES JIMMY SOLVED!
WHOSE ROOM IS THIS?
MAKOTO'S ROOM.
MAKOTO WORSHIPPED JIMMY KUDO, THE TEENAGE DETECTIVE.
WHEN HE LEARNED KUDO WAS GOING TO INVESTIGATE THIS CASE, HE WAS OVER-JOYED.
HE WAS SURE KUDO WOULD CATCH THE CRIMINAL WHO KILLED MAYOR HINOHARA AND HIS WIFE!
BUT THIS HACK DECIDED...
...IT WASN'T A BURGLARY AND MURDER BUT A *MURDER-SUICIDE!*

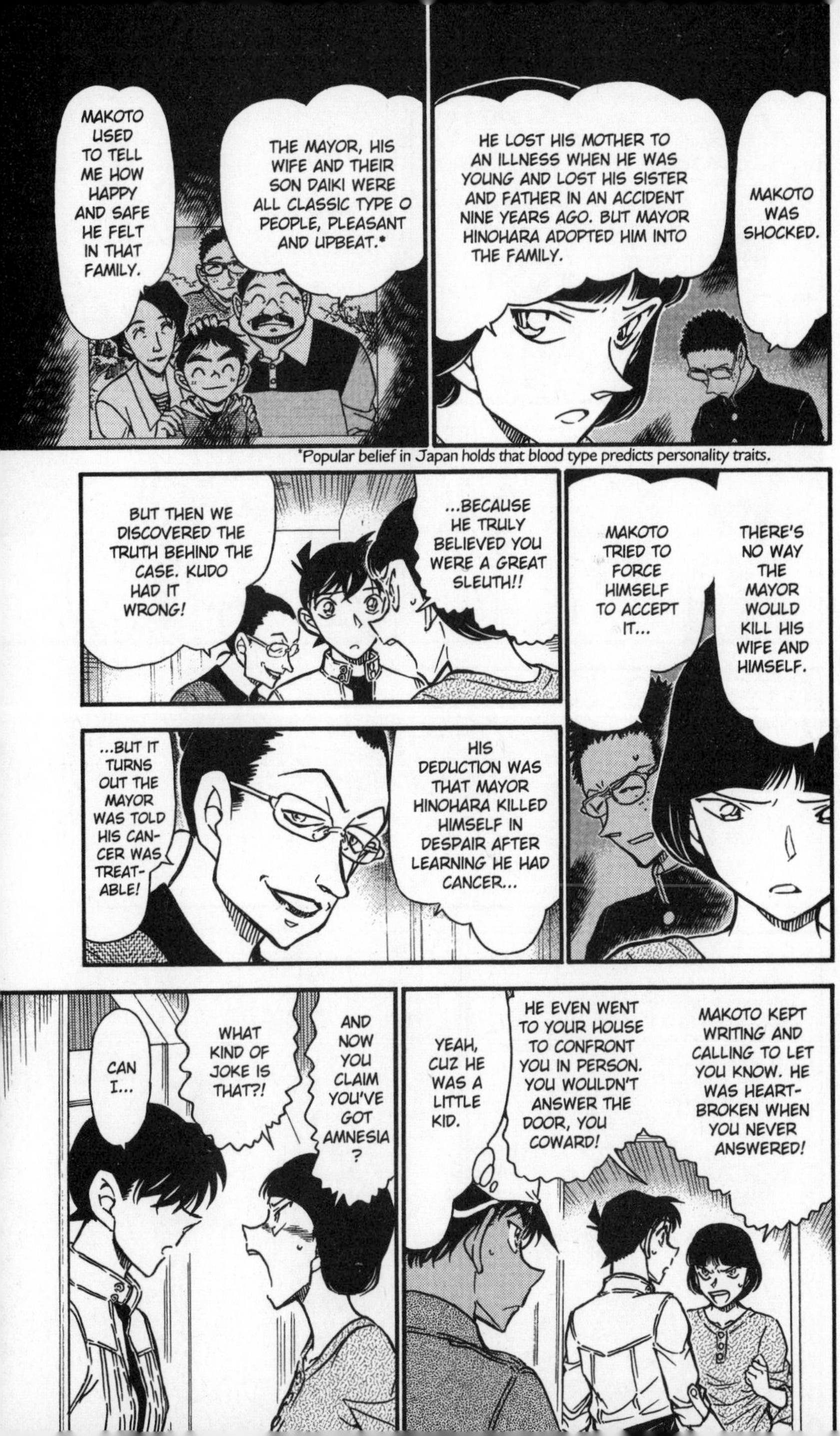
MAKOTO WAS SHOCKED.
HE LOST HIS MOTHER TO AN ILLNESS WHEN HE WAS YOUNG AND LOST HIS SISTER AND FATHER IN AN ACCIDENT NINE YEARS AGO. BUT MAYOR HINOHARA ADOPTED HIM INTO THE FAMILY.
THE MAYOR, HIS WIFE AND THEIR SON DAIKI WERE ALL CLASSIC TYPE O PEOPLE, PLEASANT AND UPBEAT.*
MAKOTO USED TO TELL ME HOW HAPPY AND SAFE HE FELT IN THAT FAMILY.
THERE'S NO WAY THE MAYOR WOULD KILL HIS WIFE AND HIMSELF.
MAKOTO TRIED TO FORCE HIMSELF TO ACCEPT IT...
...BECAUSE HE TRULY BELIEVED YOU WERE A GREAT SLEUTH!!
BUT THEN WE DISCOVERED THE TRUTH BEHIND THE CASE. KUDO HAD IT WRONG!
HIS DEDUCTION WAS THAT MAYOR HINOHARA KILLED HIMSELF IN DESPAIR AFTER LEARNING HE HAD CANCER...
...BUT IT TURNS OUT THE MAYOR WAS TOLD HIS CANCER WAS TREATABLE!
MAKOTO KEPT WRITING AND CALLING TO LET YOU KNOW. HE WAS HEARTBROKEN WHEN YOU NEVER ANSWERED!
HE EVEN WENT TO YOUR HOUSE TO CONFRONT YOU IN PERSON. YOU WOULDN'T ANSWER THE DOOR, YOU COWARD!
YEAH, CUZ HE WAS A LITTLE KID.
AND NOW YOU CLAIM YOU'VE GOT AMNESIA?
WHAT KIND OF JOKE IS THAT?!
CAN I...

*Popular belief in Japan holds that blood type predicts personality traits.

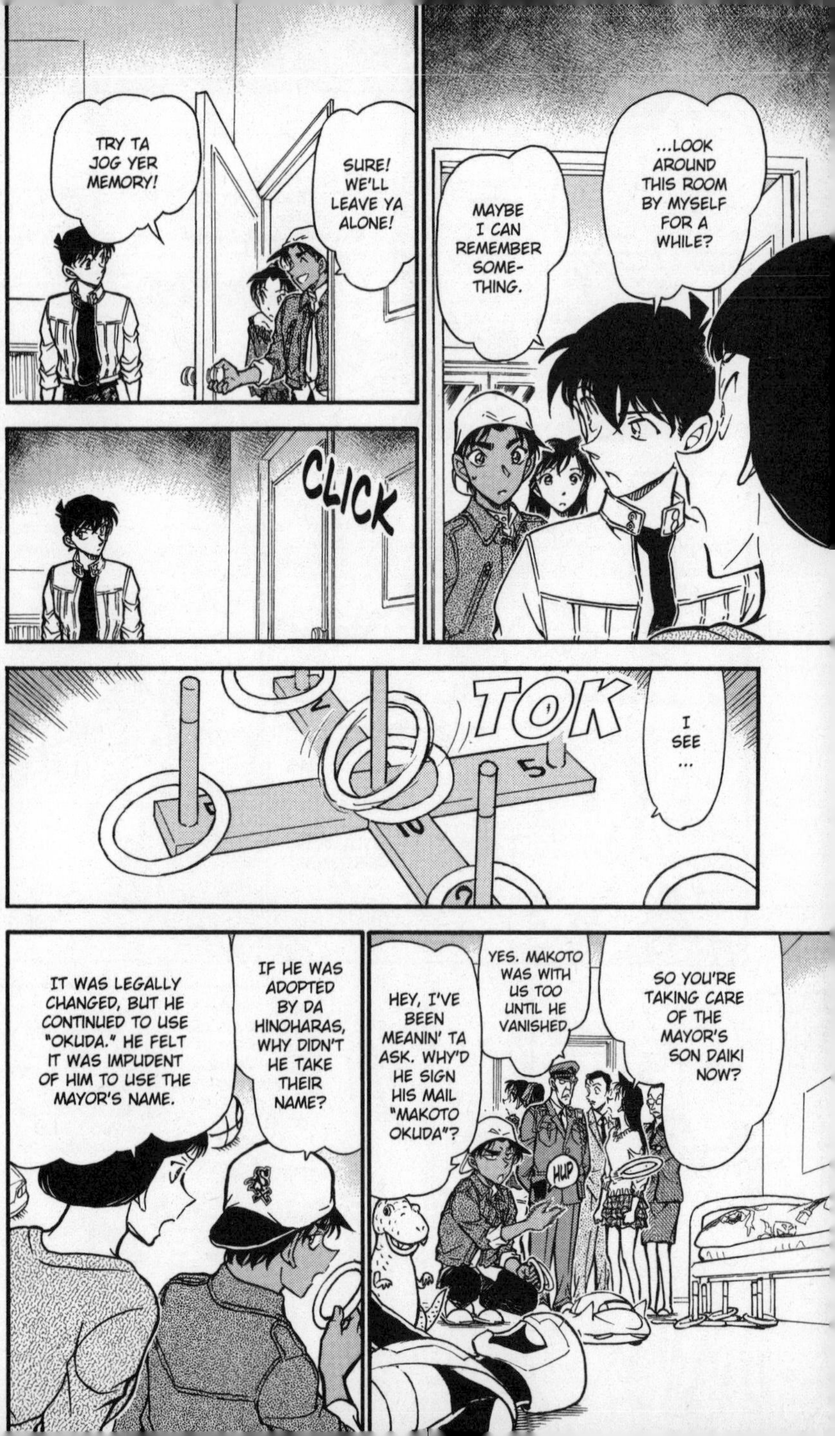
...LOOK AROUND THIS ROOM BY MYSELF FOR A WHILE?
MAYBE I CAN REMEMBER SOME-THING.
SURE! WE'LL LEAVE YA ALONE!
TRY TA JOG YER MEMORY!
CLICK
I SEE...
TOK
SO YOU'RE TAKING CARE OF THE MAYOR'S SON DAIKI NOW?
YES. MAKOTO WAS WITH US TOO UNTIL HE VANISHED.
HEY, I'VE BEEN MEANIN' TA ASK. WHY'D HE SIGN HIS MAIL "MAKOTO OKUDA"?
HUP
IF HE WAS ADOPTED BY DA HINOHARAS, WHY DIDN'T HE TAKE THEIR NAME?
IT WAS LEGALLY CHANGED, BUT HE CONTINUED TO USE "OKUDA." HE FELT IT WAS IMPUDENT OF HIM TO USE THE MAYOR'S NAME.

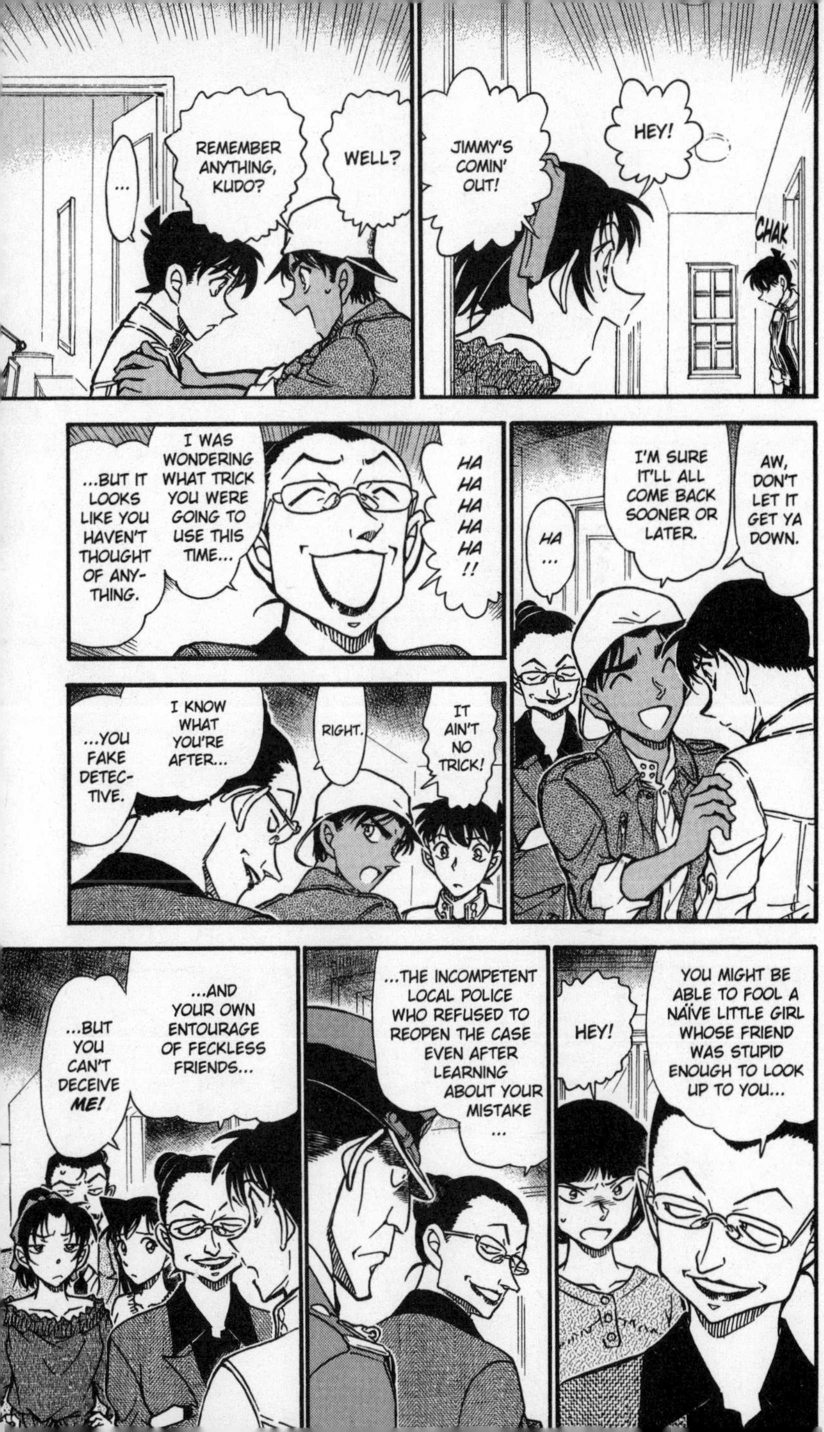
HEY!
CHAK
JIMMY'S COMIN' OUT!
WELL?
REMEMBER ANYTHING, KUDO?
...
AW, DON'T LET IT GET YA DOWN.
I'M SURE IT'LL ALL COME BACK SOONER OR LATER.
HA ...
HA HA HA HA HA !!
I WAS WONDERING WHAT TRICK YOU WERE GOING TO USE THIS TIME...
...BUT IT LOOKS LIKE YOU HAVEN'T THOUGHT OF ANY-THING.
IT AIN'T NO TRICK!
RIGHT.
I KNOW WHAT YOU'RE AFTER...
...YOU FAKE DETEC-TIVE.
YOU MIGHT BE ABLE TO FOOL A NAÏVE LITTLE GIRL WHOSE FRIEND WAS STUPID ENOUGH TO LOOK UP TO YOU...
HEY!
...THE INCOMPETENT LOCAL POLICE WHO REFUSED TO REOPEN THE CASE EVEN AFTER LEARNING ABOUT YOUR MISTAKE ...
...AND YOUR OWN ENTOURAGE OF FECKLESS FRIENDS...
...BUT YOU CAN'T DECEIVE ME!

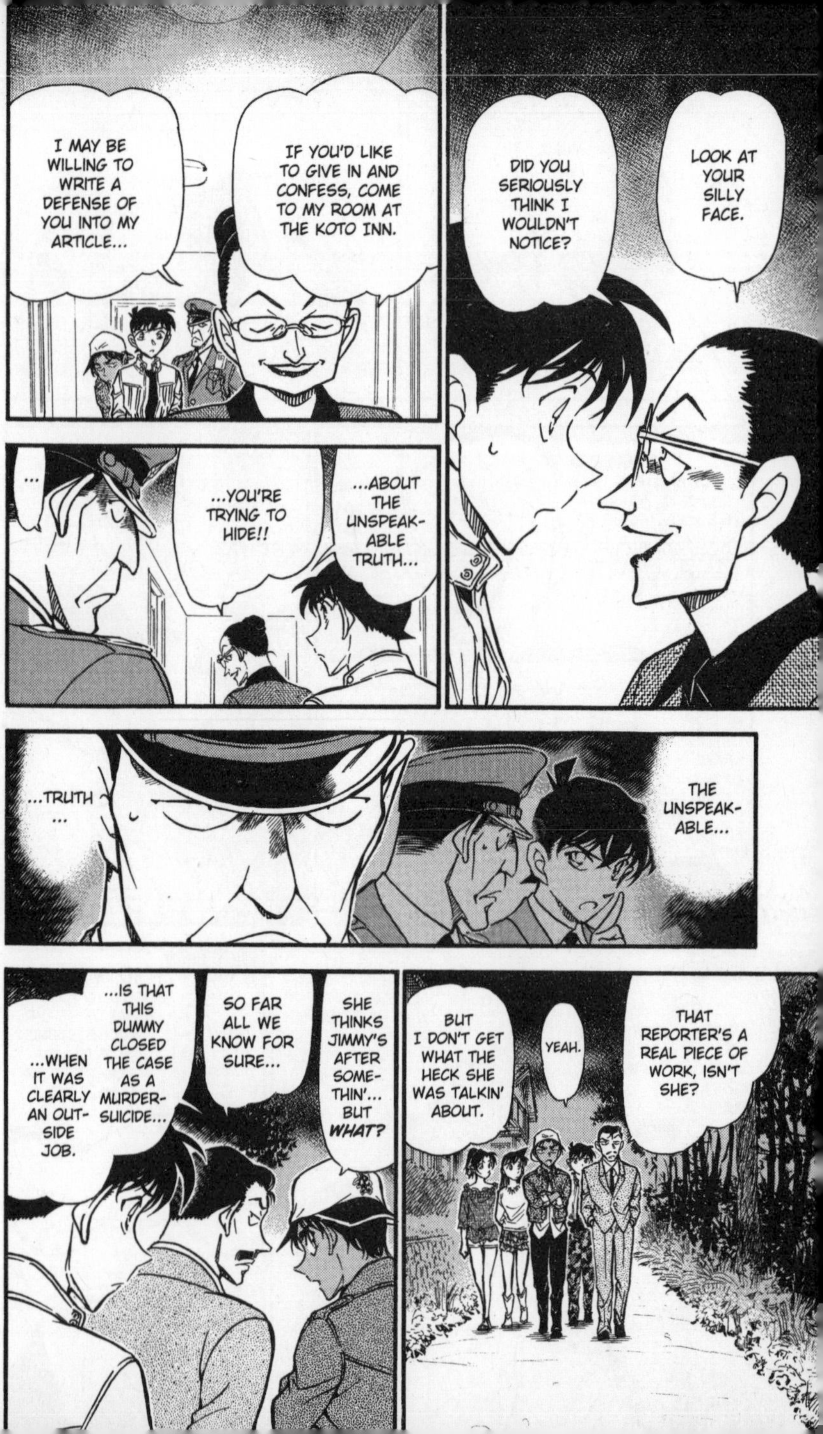
LOOK AT YOUR SILLY FACE.
DID YOU SERIOUSLY THINK I WOULDN'T NOTICE?
IF YOU'D LIKE TO GIVE IN AND CONFESS, COME TO MY ROOM AT THE KOTO INN.
I MAY BE WILLING TO WRITE A DEFENSE OF YOU INTO MY ARTICLE...
...ABOUT THE UNSPEAK-ABLE TRUTH...
...YOU'RE TRYING TO HIDE!!
...
THE UNSPEAK-ABLE...
...TRUTH ...
THAT REPORTER'S A REAL PIECE OF WORK, ISN'T SHE?
YEAH.
BUT I DON'T GET WHAT THE HECK SHE WAS TALKIN' ABOUT.
SHE THINKS JIMMY'S AFTER SOME-THIN'... BUT *WHAT?*
SO FAR ALL WE KNOW FOR SURE...
...IS THAT THIS DUMMY CLOSED THE CASE AS A MURDER-SUICIDE...
...WHEN IT WAS CLEARLY AN OUT-SIDE JOB.

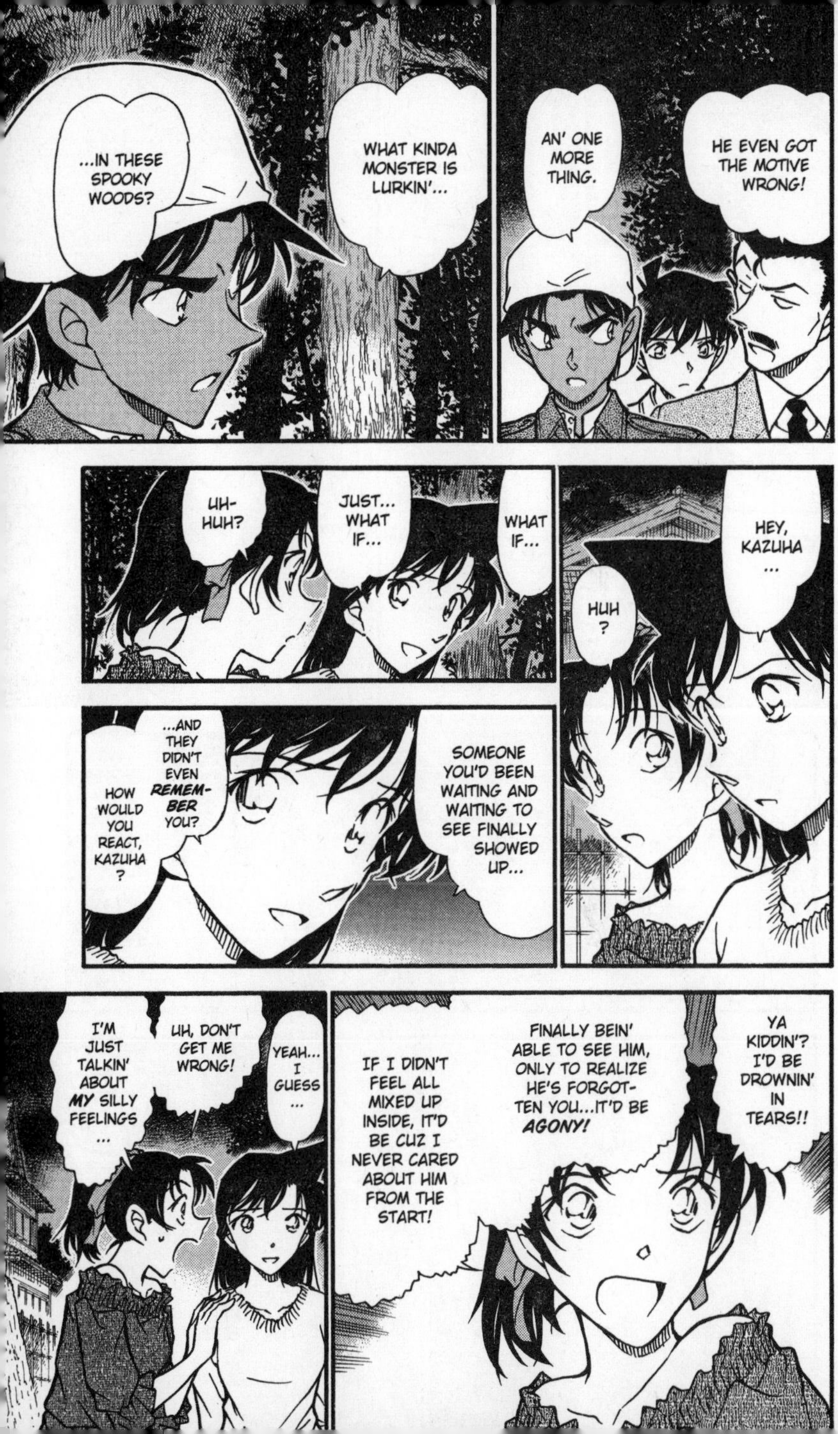
HE EVEN GOT THE MOTIVE WRONG!
AN' ONE MORE THING.
WHAT KINDA MONSTER IS LURKIN'...
...IN THESE SPOOKY WOODS?
HEY, KAZUHA ...
HUH ?
WHAT IF...
JUST... WHAT IF...
UH-HUH?
SOMEONE YOU'D BEEN WAITING AND WAITING TO SEE FINALLY SHOWED UP...
...AND THEY DIDN'T EVEN *REMEMBER* YOU?
HOW WOULD YOU REACT, KAZUHA ?
YA KIDDIN'? I'D BE DROWNIN' IN TEARS!!
FINALLY BEIN' ABLE TO SEE HIM, ONLY TO REALIZE HE'S FORGOTTEN YOU...IT'D BE *AGONY!*
IF I DIDN'T FEEL ALL MIXED UP INSIDE, IT'D BE CUZ I NEVER CARED ABOUT HIM FROM THE START!
YEAH... I GUESS ...
UH, DON'T GET ME WRONG!
I'M JUST TALKIN' ABOUT *MY* SILLY FEELINGS ...

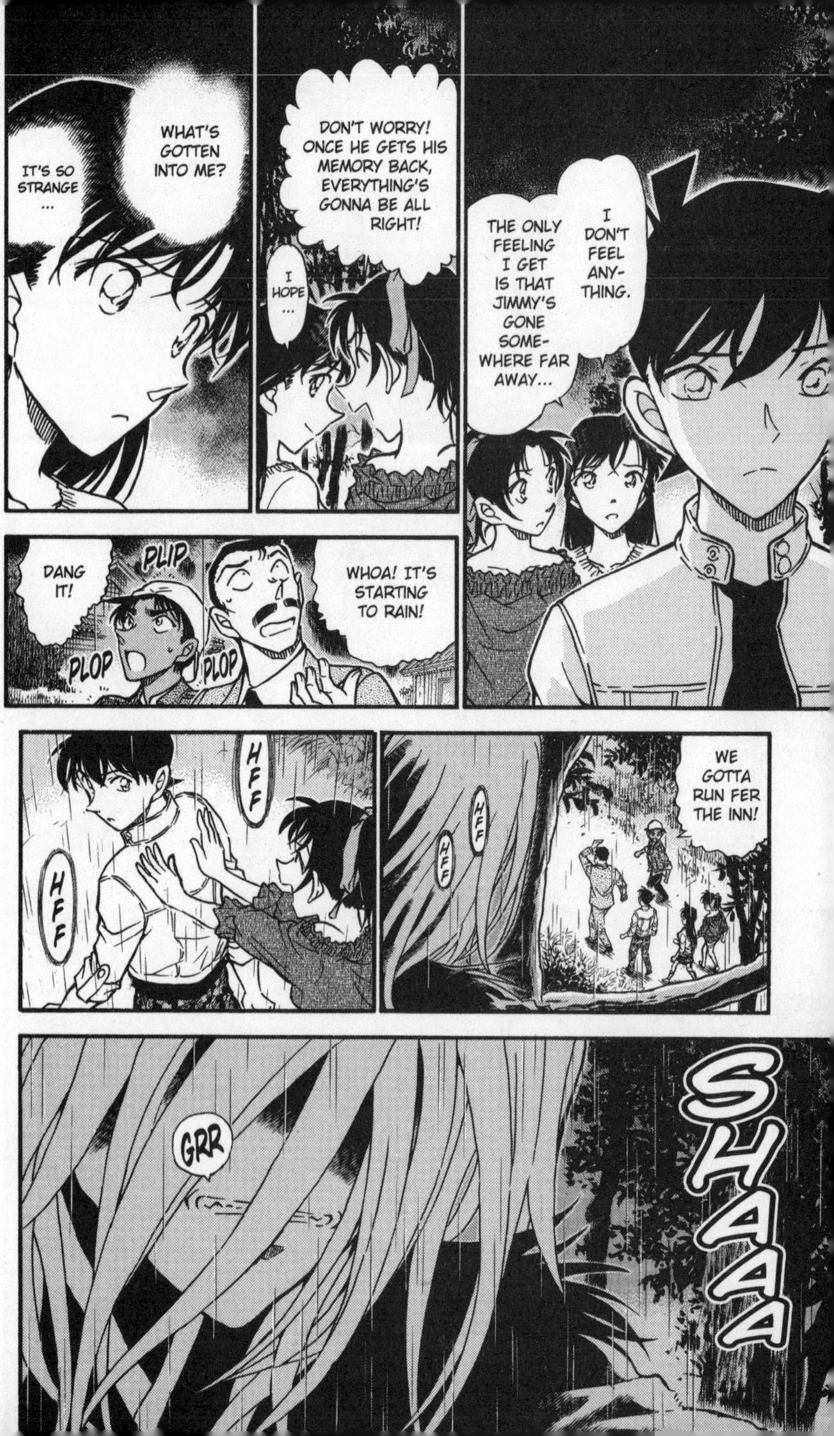
I DON'T FEEL ANY-THING.
THE ONLY FEELING I GET IS THAT JIMMY'S GONE SOME-WHERE FAR AWAY...
DON'T WORRY! ONCE HE GETS HIS MEMORY BACK, EVERYTHING'S GONNA BE ALL RIGHT!
I HOPE...
WHAT'S GOTTEN INTO ME?
IT'S SO STRANGE...
WHOA! IT'S STARTING TO RAIN!
PLIP
PLOP
PLOP
DANG IT!
WE GOTTA RUN FER THE INN!
HFF
HFF
HFF
HFF
SHAAA
GRR

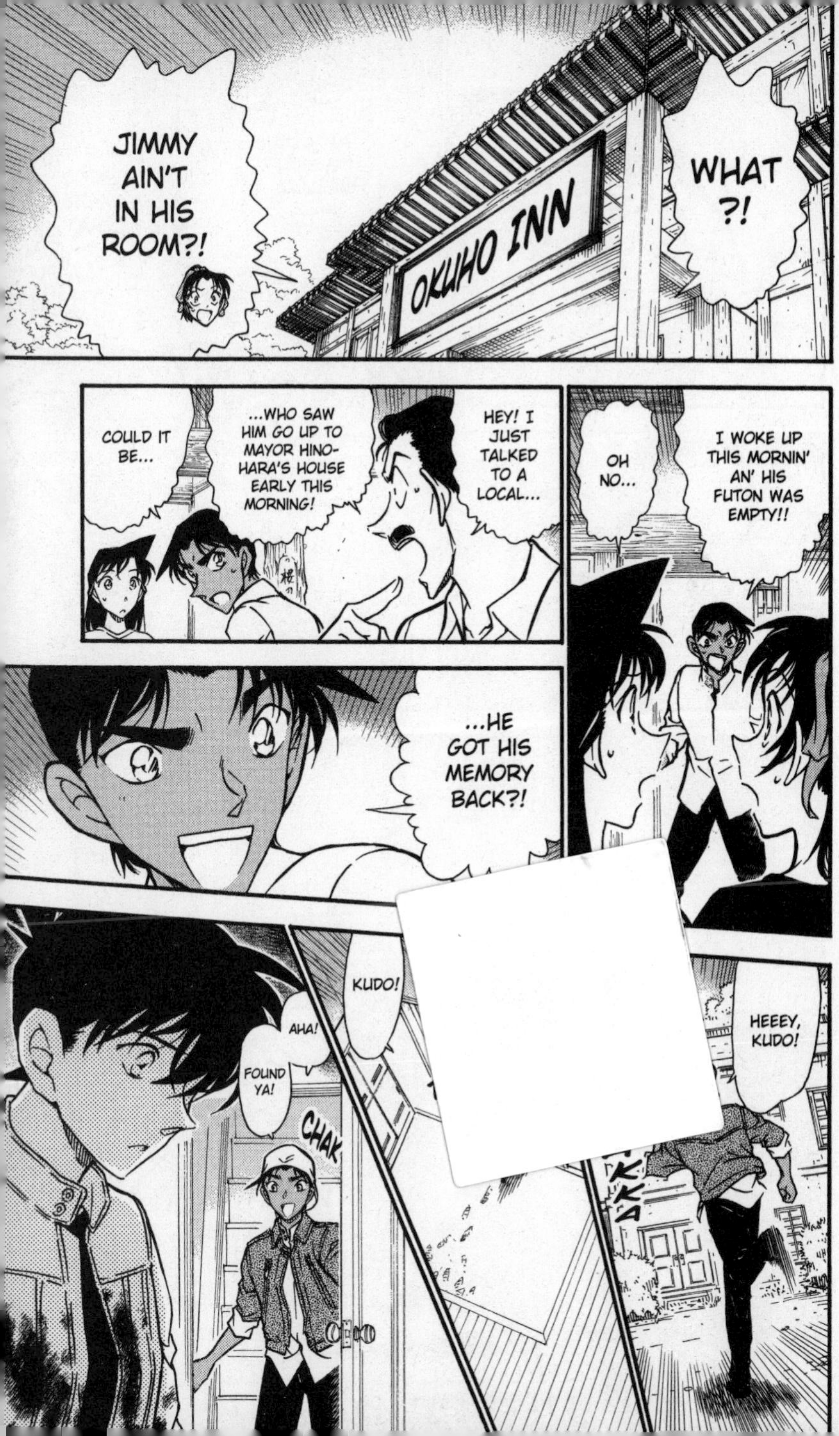
WHAT?!
JIMMY AIN'T IN HIS ROOM?!
OKUHO INN
I WOKE UP THIS MORNIN' AN' HIS FUTON WAS EMPTY!!
OH NO...
HEY! I JUST TALKED TO A LOCAL...
...WHO SAW HIM GO UP TO MAYOR HINO-HARA'S HOUSE EARLY THIS MORNING!
COULD IT BE...
...HE GOT HIS MEMORY BACK?!
HEEEY, KUDO!
KUDO!
CHAK
AHA!
FOUND YA!

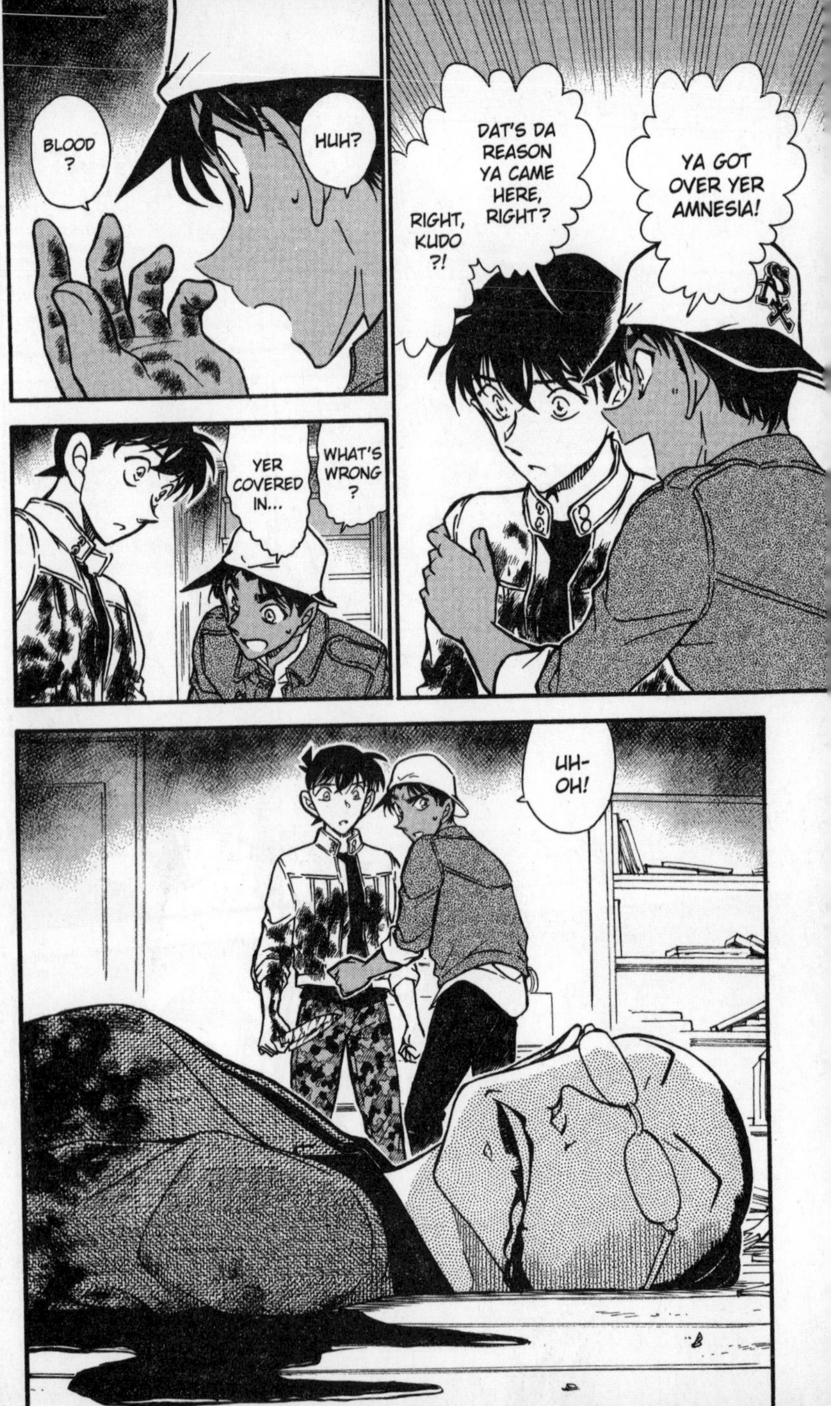
YA GOT OVER YER AMNESIA!
DAT'S DA REASON YA CAME HERE, RIGHT?
RIGHT, KUDO ?!
HUH?
BLOOD ?
WHAT'S WRONG ?
YER COVERED IN...
UH-OH!

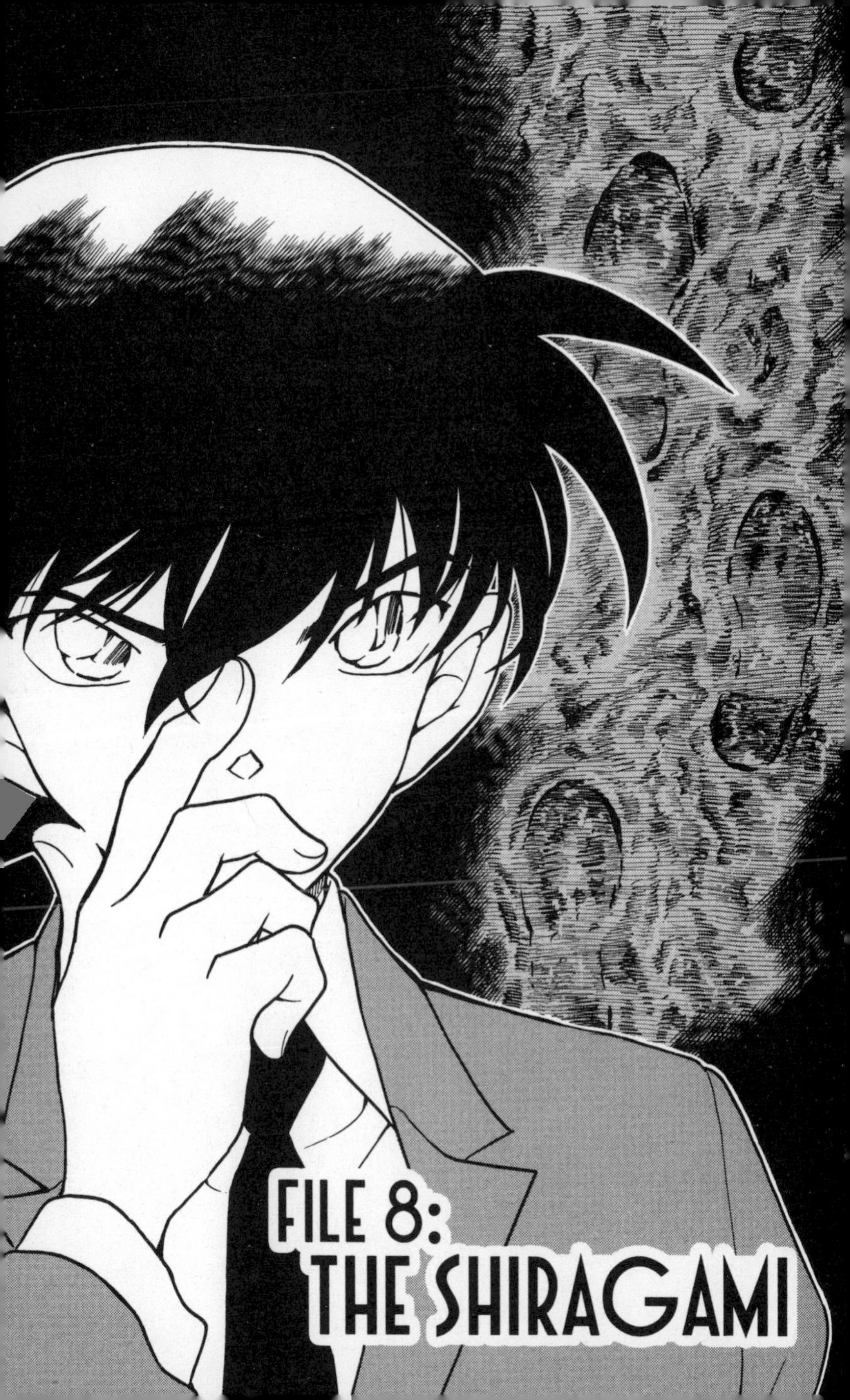
FILE 8:
THE SHIRAGAMI

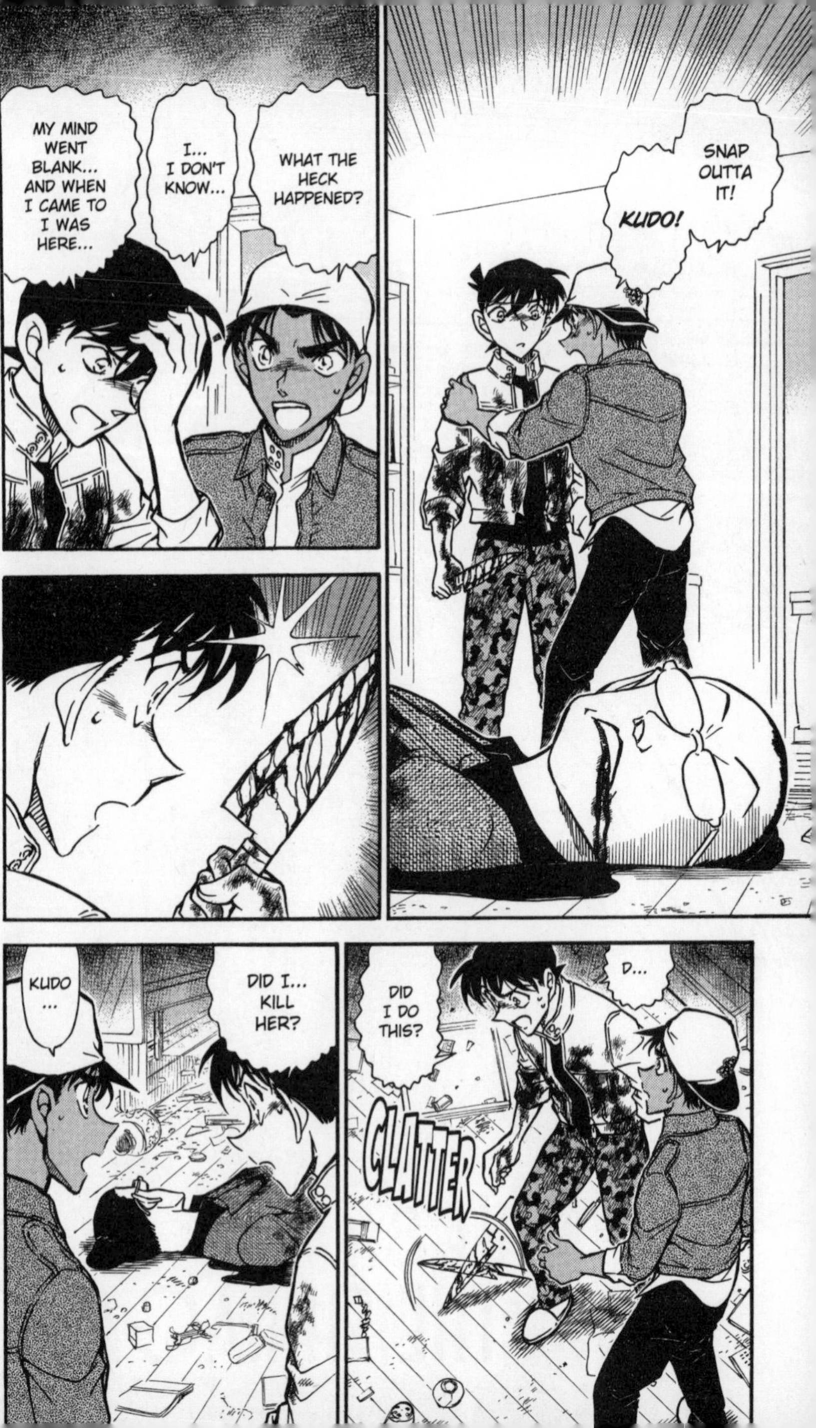
KUDO! SNAP OUTTA IT!
WHAT THE HECK HAPPENED?
I... I DON'T KNOW...
MY MIND WENT BLANK... AND WHEN I CAME TO I WAS HERE...
D...
DID I DO THIS?
CLATTER
DID I... KILL HER?
KUDO...

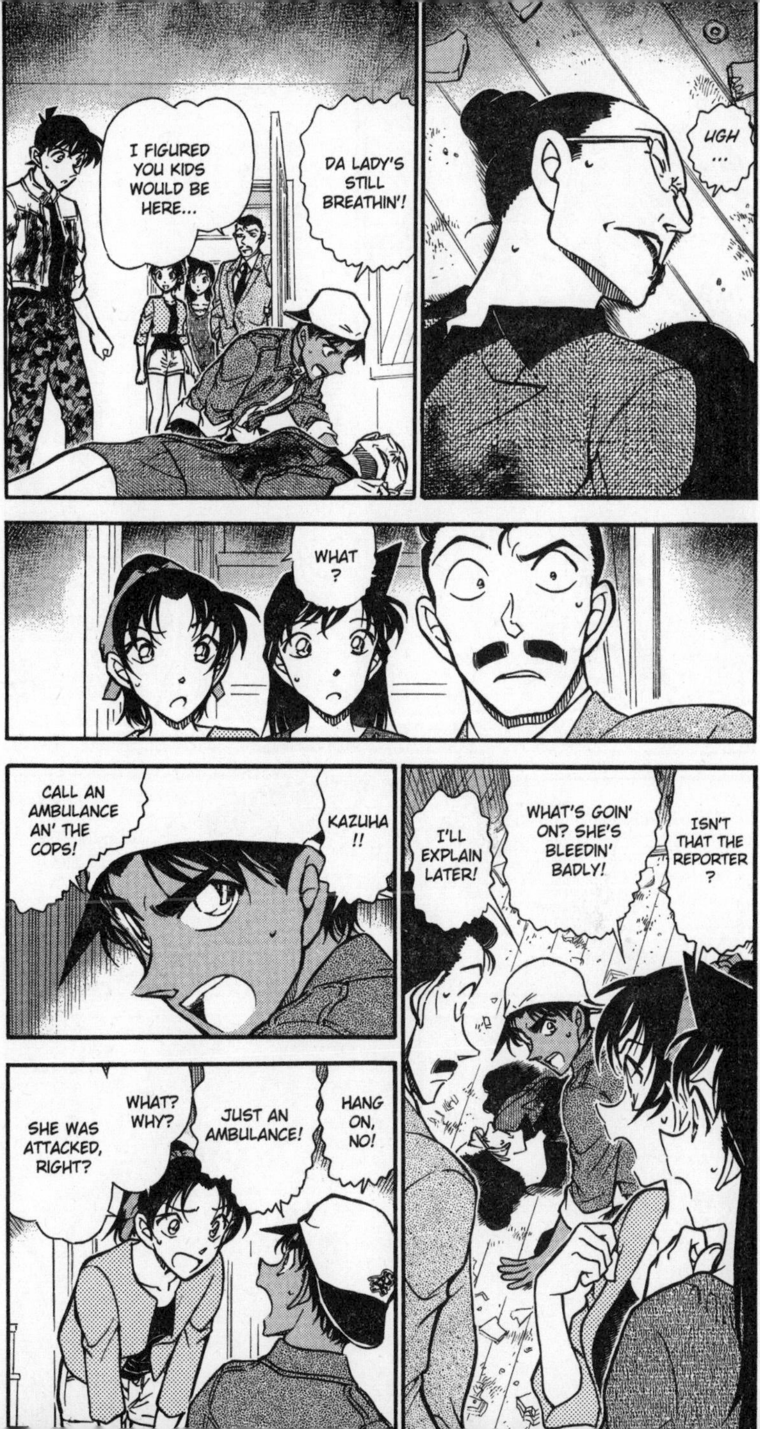
UGH ...
DA LADY'S STILL BREATHIN'!
I FIGURED YOU KIDS WOULD BE HERE...
WHAT ?
ISN'T THAT THE REPORTER ?
WHAT'S GOIN' ON? SHE'S BLEEDIN' BADLY!
I'LL EXPLAIN LATER!
KAZUHA !!
CALL AN AMBULANCE AN' THE COPS!
HANG ON, NO!
JUST AN AMBULANCE!
WHAT? WHY?
SHE WAS ATTACKED, RIGHT?

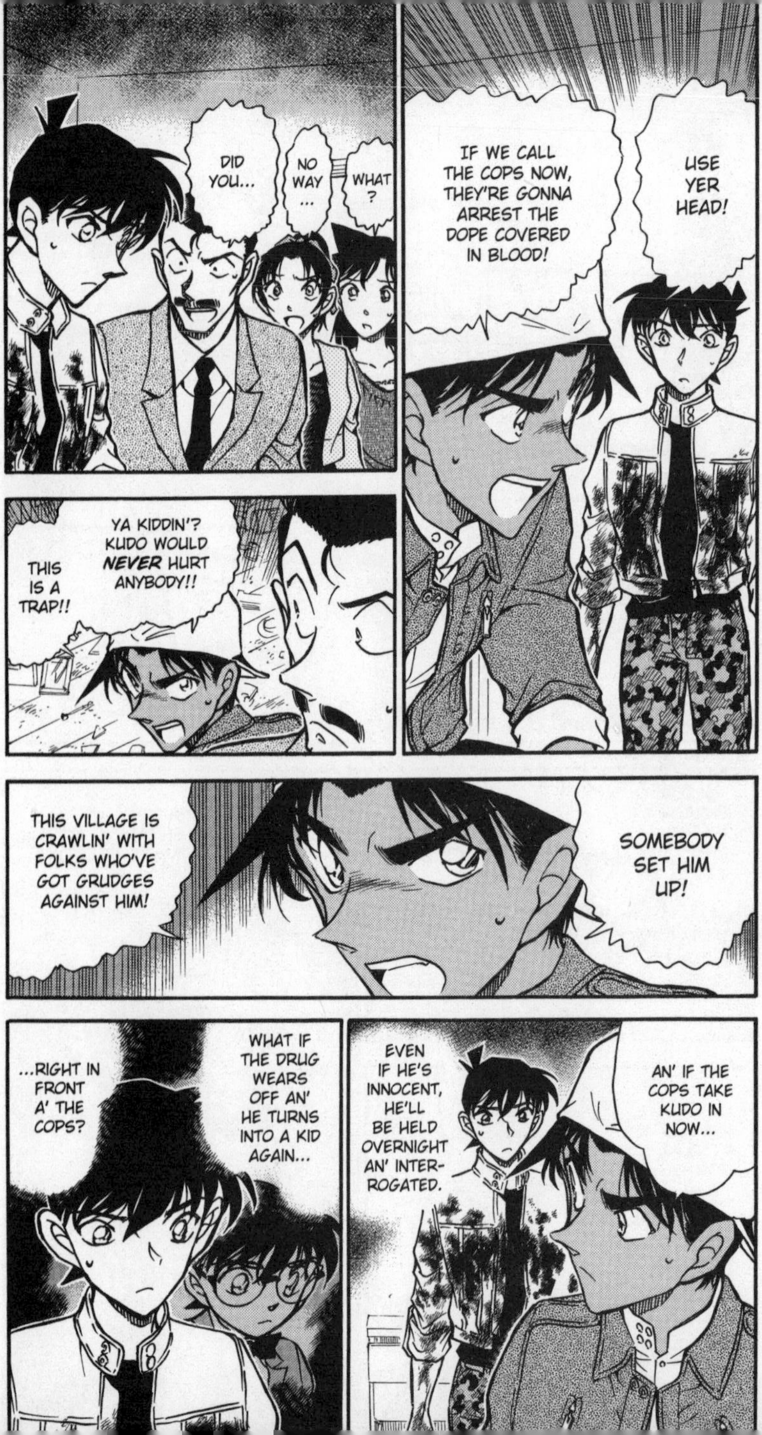
USE YER HEAD!
IF WE CALL THE COPS NOW, THEY'RE GONNA ARREST THE DOPE COVERED IN BLOOD!
WHAT?
NO WAY...
DID YOU...
YA KIDDIN'? KUDO WOULD **NEVER** HURT ANYBODY!!
THIS IS A TRAP!!
SOMEBODY SET HIM UP!
THIS VILLAGE IS CRAWLIN' WITH FOLKS WHO'VE GOT GRUDGES AGAINST HIM!
AN' IF THE COPS TAKE KUDO IN NOW...
EVEN IF HE'S INNOCENT, HE'LL BE HELD OVERNIGHT AN' INTER-ROGATED.
WHAT IF THE DRUG WEARS OFF AN' HE TURNS INTO A KID AGAIN...
...RIGHT IN FRONT A' THE COPS?

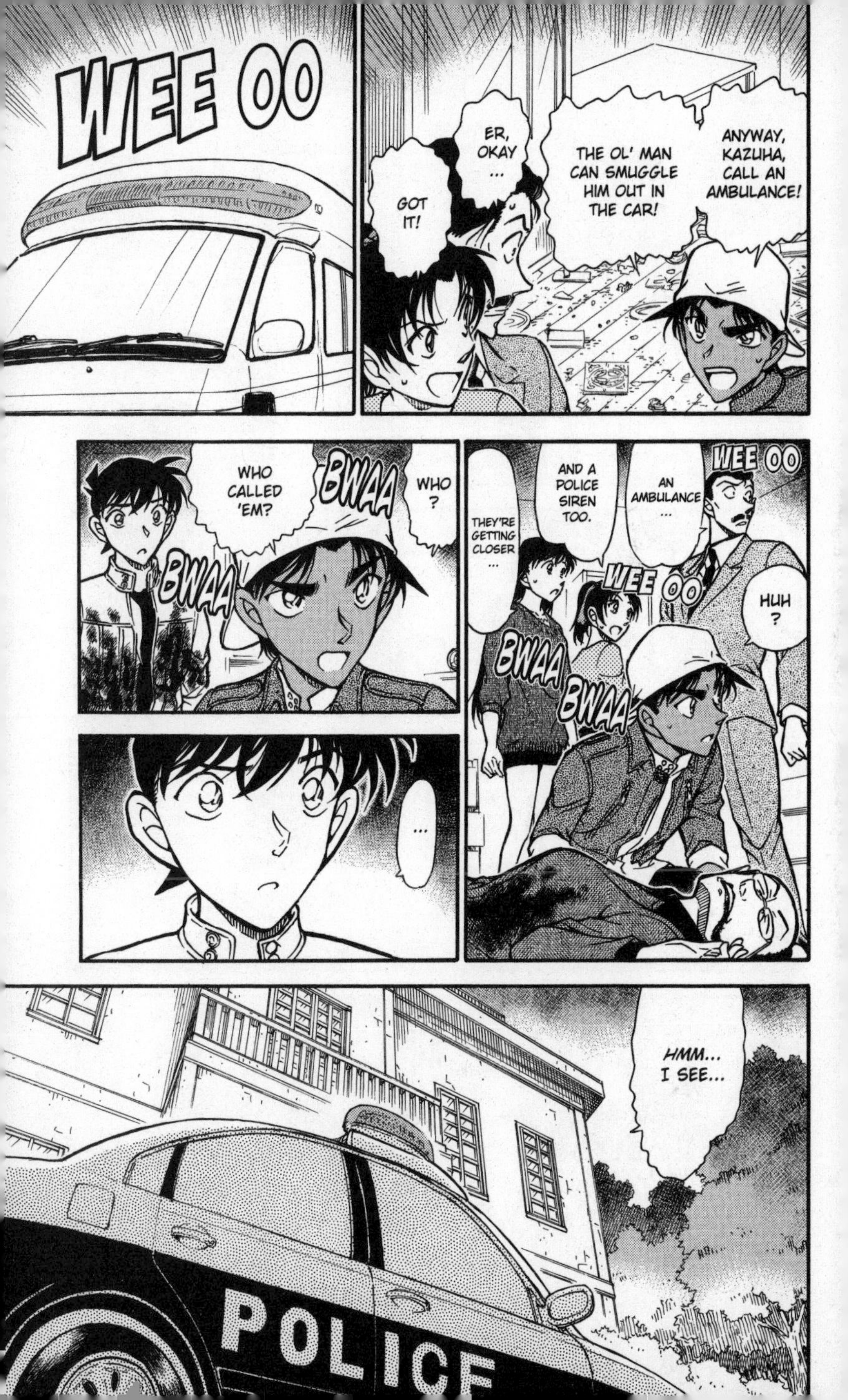
ANYWAY, KAZUHA, CALL AN AMBULANCE!
THE OL' MAN CAN SMUGGLE HIM OUT IN THE CAR!
ER, OKAY ...
GOT IT!
WEE OO
WEE OO
AN AMBULANCE ...
AND A POLICE SIREN TOO.
THEY'RE GETTING CLOSER ...
HUH ?
WEE OO
BWAA
BWAA
WHO ?
BWAA
WHO CALLED 'EM?
BWAA
...
HMM... I SEE...
POLICE

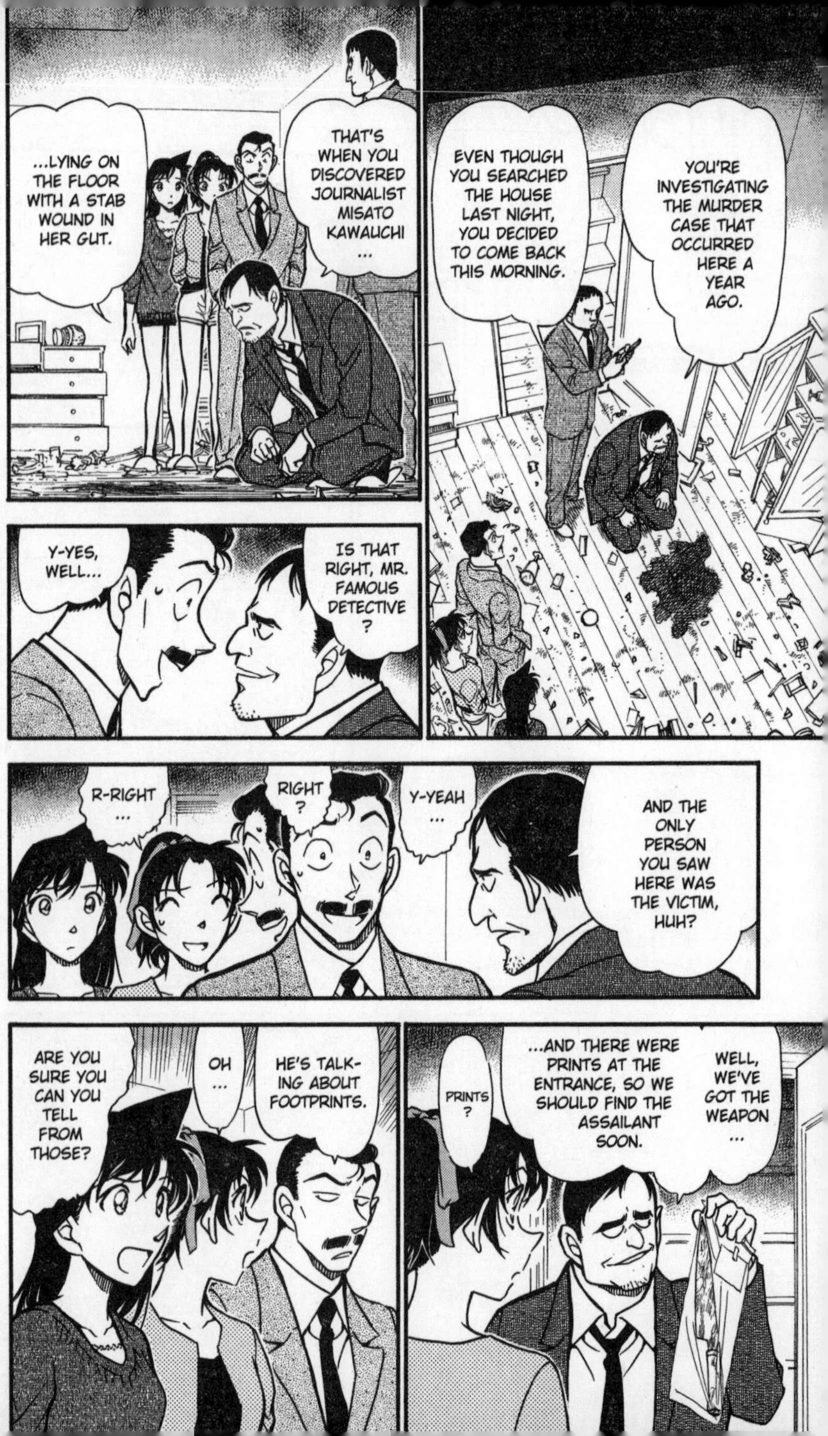
YOU'RE INVESTIGATING THE MURDER CASE THAT OCCURRED HERE A YEAR AGO.
EVEN THOUGH YOU SEARCHED THE HOUSE LAST NIGHT, YOU DECIDED TO COME BACK THIS MORNING.
THAT'S WHEN YOU DISCOVERED JOURNALIST MISATO KAWAUCHI ...
...LYING ON THE FLOOR WITH A STAB WOUND IN HER GUT.
IS THAT RIGHT, MR. FAMOUS DETECTIVE ?
Y-YES, WELL...
AND THE ONLY PERSON YOU SAW HERE WAS THE VICTIM, HUH?
Y-YEAH ...
RIGHT ?
R-RIGHT ...
WELL, WE'VE GOT THE WEAPON ...
...AND THERE WERE PRINTS AT THE ENTRANCE, SO WE SHOULD FIND THE ASSAILANT SOON.
PRINTS ?
HE'S TALK-ING ABOUT FOOTPRINTS.
OH ...
ARE YOU SURE YOU CAN YOU TELL FROM THOSE?

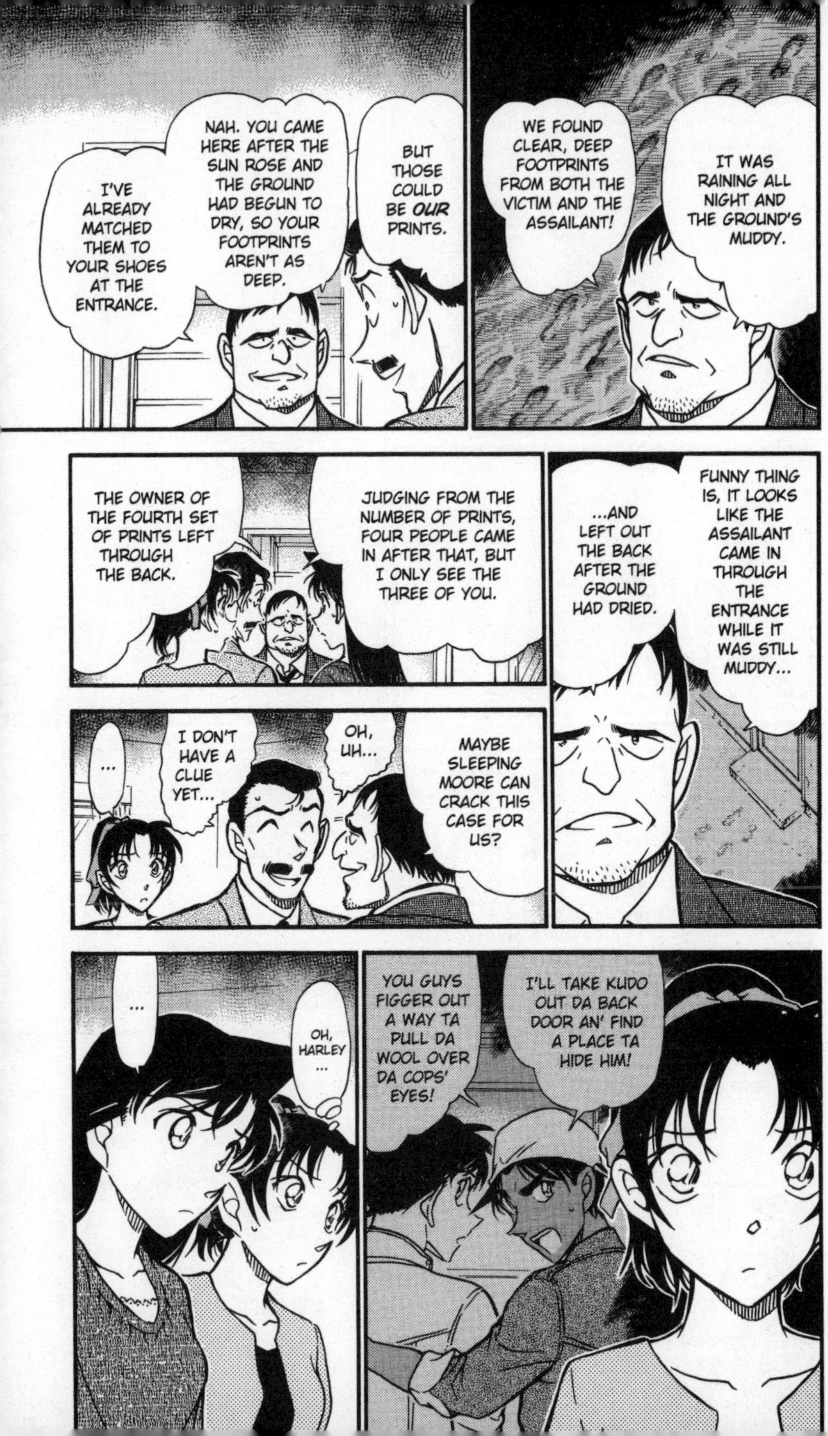
IT WAS RAINING ALL NIGHT AND THE GROUND'S MUDDY.
WE FOUND CLEAR, DEEP FOOTPRINTS FROM BOTH THE VICTIM AND THE ASSAILANT!
BUT THOSE COULD BE *OUR* PRINTS.
NAH. YOU CAME HERE AFTER THE SUN ROSE AND THE GROUND HAD BEGUN TO DRY, SO YOUR FOOTPRINTS AREN'T AS DEEP.
I'VE ALREADY MATCHED THEM TO YOUR SHOES AT THE ENTRANCE.
FUNNY THING IS, IT LOOKS LIKE THE ASSAILANT CAME IN THROUGH THE ENTRANCE WHILE IT WAS STILL MUDDY...
...AND LEFT OUT THE BACK AFTER THE GROUND HAD DRIED.
JUDGING FROM THE NUMBER OF PRINTS, FOUR PEOPLE CAME IN AFTER THAT, BUT I ONLY SEE THE THREE OF YOU.
THE OWNER OF THE FOURTH SET OF PRINTS LEFT THROUGH THE BACK.
MAYBE SLEEPING MOORE CAN CRACK THIS CASE FOR US?
OH, UH...
I DON'T HAVE A CLUE YET...
...
I'LL TAKE KUDO OUT DA BACK DOOR AN' FIND A PLACE TA HIDE HIM!
YOU GUYS FIGGER OUT A WAY TA PULL DA WOOL OVER DA COPS' EYES!
OH, HARLEY ...
...

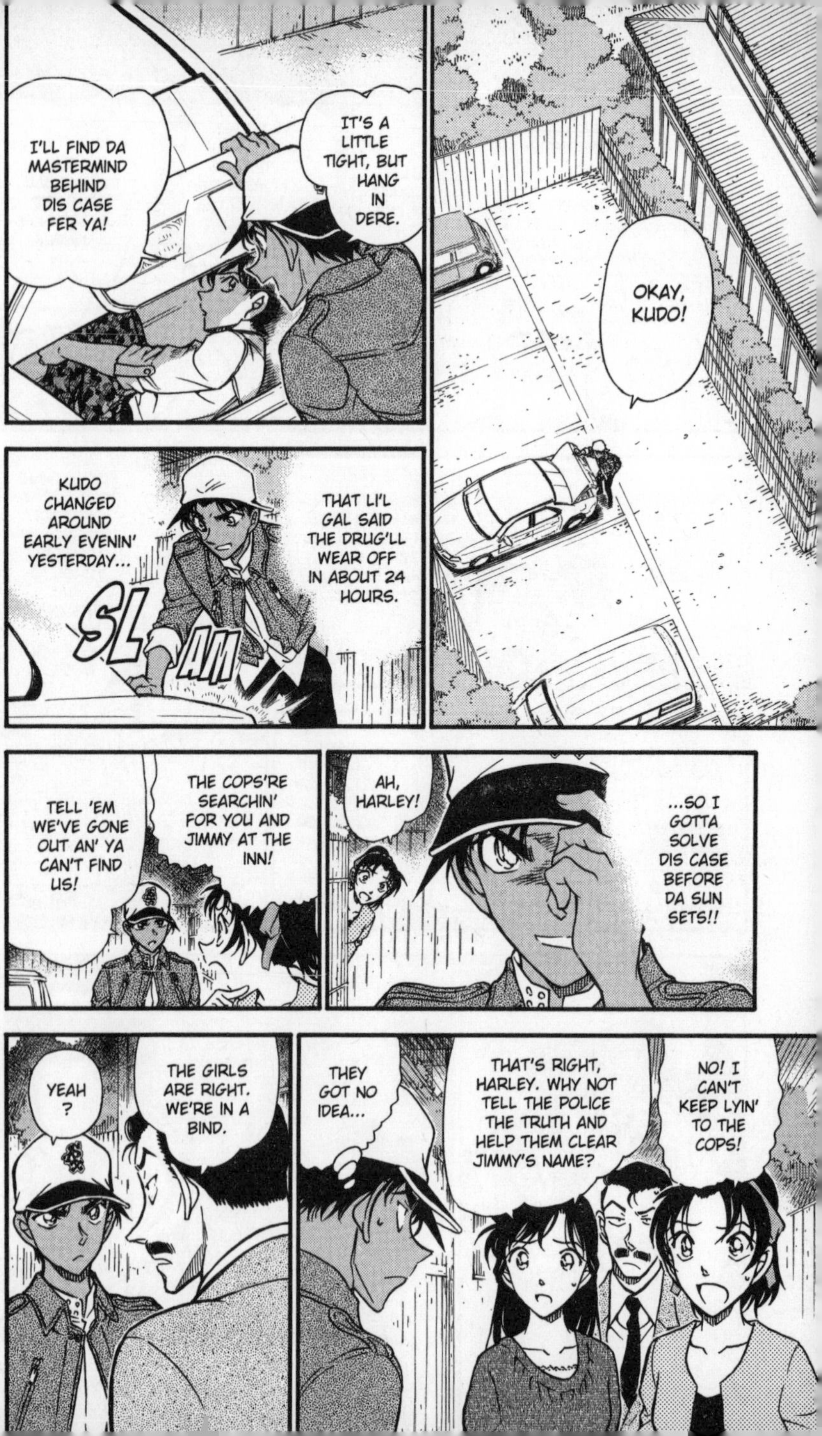
OKAY, KUDO!
IT'S A LITTLE TIGHT, BUT HANG IN DERE.
I'LL FIND DA MASTERMIND BEHIND DIS CASE FER YA!
THAT LI'L GAL SAID THE DRUG'LL WEAR OFF IN ABOUT 24 HOURS.
KUDO CHANGED AROUND EARLY EVENIN' YESTERDAY...
SLAM
...SO I GOTTA SOLVE DIS CASE BEFORE DA SUN SETS!!
AH, HARLEY!
THE COPS'RE SEARCHIN' FOR YOU AND JIMMY AT THE INN!
TELL 'EM WE'VE GONE OUT AN' YA CAN'T FIND US!
NO! I CAN'T KEEP LYIN' TO THE COPS!
THAT'S RIGHT, HARLEY. WHY NOT TELL THE POLICE THE TRUTH AND HELP THEM CLEAR JIMMY'S NAME?
THEY GOT NO IDEA...
THE GIRLS ARE RIGHT. WE'RE IN A BIND.
YEAH ?

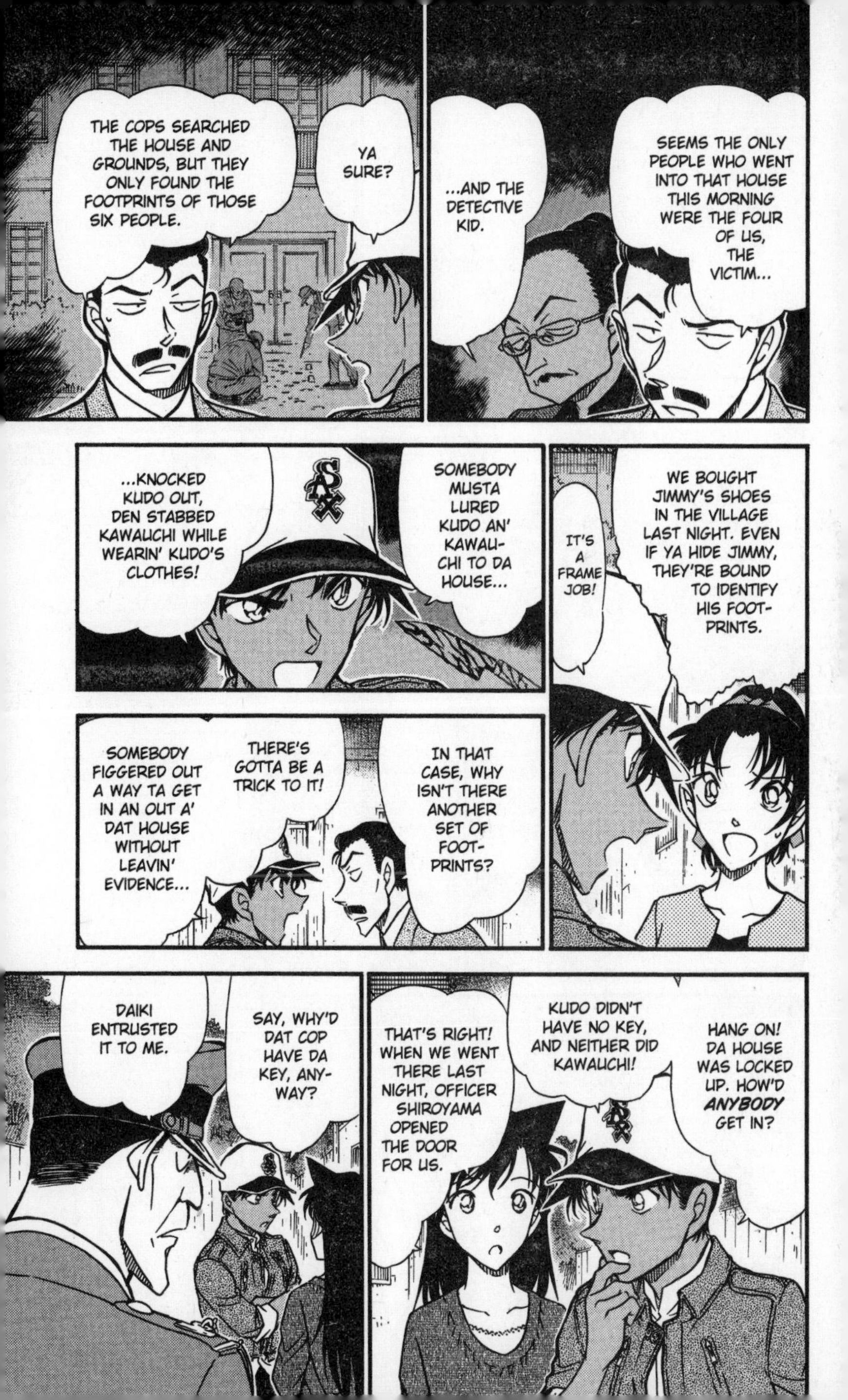
SEEMS THE ONLY PEOPLE WHO WENT INTO THAT HOUSE THIS MORNING WERE THE FOUR OF US, THE VICTIM...
...AND THE DETECTIVE KID.
YA SURE?
THE COPS SEARCHED THE HOUSE AND GROUNDS, BUT THEY ONLY FOUND THE FOOTPRINTS OF THOSE SIX PEOPLE.
WE BOUGHT JIMMY'S SHOES IN THE VILLAGE LAST NIGHT. EVEN IF YA HIDE JIMMY, THEY'RE BOUND TO IDENTIFY HIS FOOTPRINTS.
IT'S A FRAME JOB!
SOMEBODY MUSTA LURED KUDO AN' KAWAUCHI TO DA HOUSE...
...KNOCKED KUDO OUT, DEN STABBED KAWAUCHI WHILE WEARIN' KUDO'S CLOTHES!
IN THAT CASE, WHY ISN'T THERE ANOTHER SET OF FOOTPRINTS?
THERE'S GOTTA BE A TRICK TO IT!
SOMEBODY FIGGERED OUT A WAY TA GET IN AN OUT A' DAT HOUSE WITHOUT LEAVIN' EVIDENCE...
HANG ON! DA HOUSE WAS LOCKED UP. HOW'D ANYBODY GET IN?
KUDO DIDN'T HAVE NO KEY, AND NEITHER DID KAWAUCHI!
THAT'S RIGHT! WHEN WE WENT THERE LAST NIGHT, OFFICER SHIROYAMA OPENED THE DOOR FOR US.
SAY, WHY'D DAT COP HAVE DA KEY, ANYWAY?
DAIKI ENTRUSTED IT TO ME.

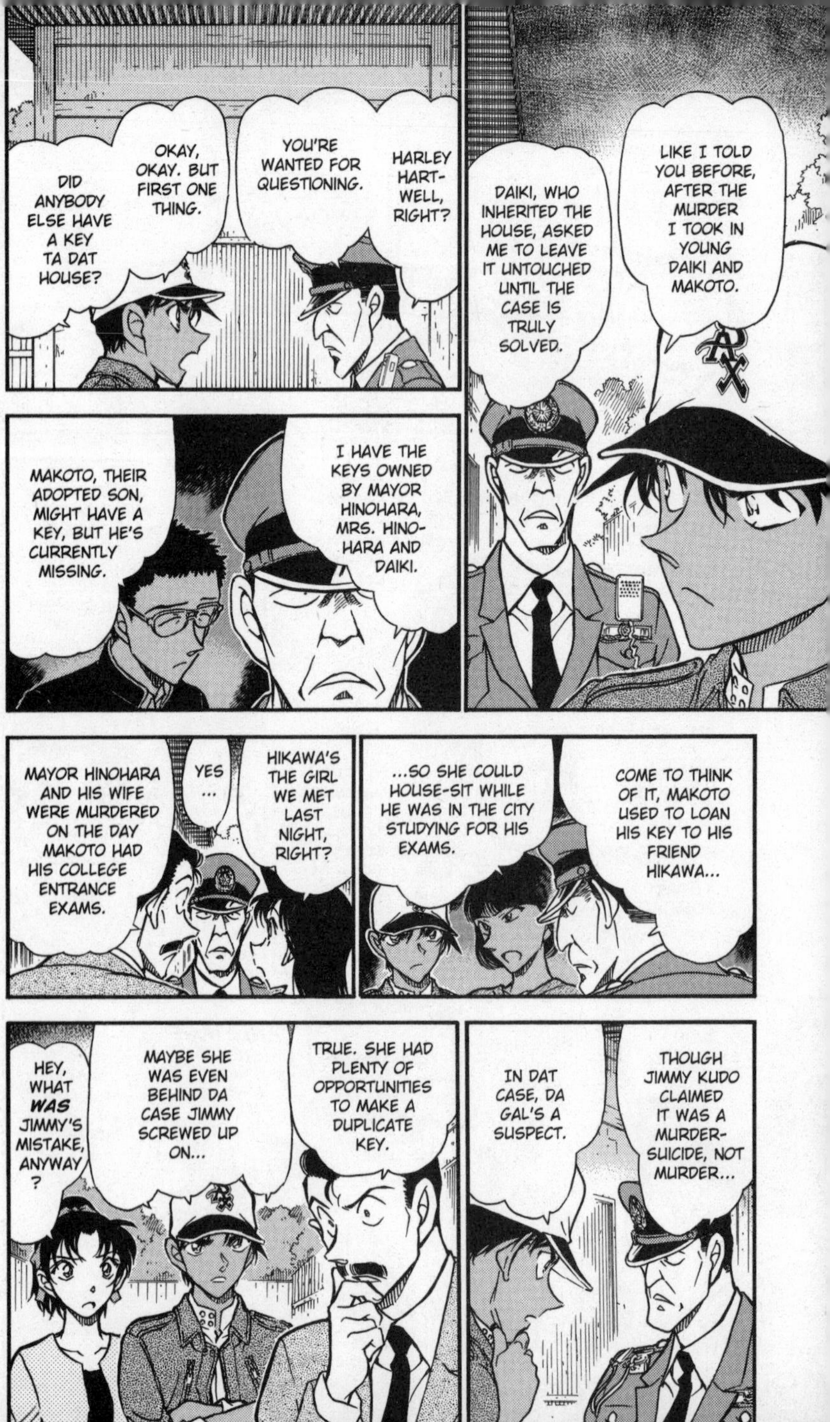
LIKE I TOLD YOU BEFORE, AFTER THE MURDER I TOOK IN YOUNG DAIKI AND MAKOTO.
DAIKI, WHO INHERITED THE HOUSE, ASKED ME TO LEAVE IT UNTOUCHED UNTIL THE CASE IS TRULY SOLVED.
HARLEY HART-WELL, RIGHT?
YOU'RE WANTED FOR QUESTIONING.
OKAY, OKAY. BUT FIRST ONE THING.
DID ANYBODY ELSE HAVE A KEY TA DAT HOUSE?
I HAVE THE KEYS OWNED BY MAYOR HINOHARA, MRS. HINO-HARA AND DAIKI.
MAKOTO, THEIR ADOPTED SON, MIGHT HAVE A KEY, BUT HE'S CURRENTLY MISSING.
COME TO THINK OF IT, MAKOTO USED TO LOAN HIS KEY TO HIS FRIEND HIKAWA...
...SO SHE COULD HOUSE-SIT WHILE HE WAS IN THE CITY STUDYING FOR HIS EXAMS.
HIKAWA'S THE GIRL WE MET LAST NIGHT, RIGHT?
YES...
MAYOR HINOHARA AND HIS WIFE WERE MURDERED ON THE DAY MAKOTO HAD HIS COLLEGE ENTRANCE EXAMS.
THOUGH JIMMY KUDO CLAIMED IT WAS A MURDER-SUICIDE, NOT MURDER...
IN DAT CASE, DA GAL'S A SUSPECT.
TRUE. SHE HAD PLENTY OF OPPORTUNITIES TO MAKE A DUPLICATE KEY.
MAYBE SHE WAS EVEN BEHIND DA CASE JIMMY SCREWED UP ON...
HEY, WHAT ***WAS*** JIMMY'S MISTAKE, ANYWAY?

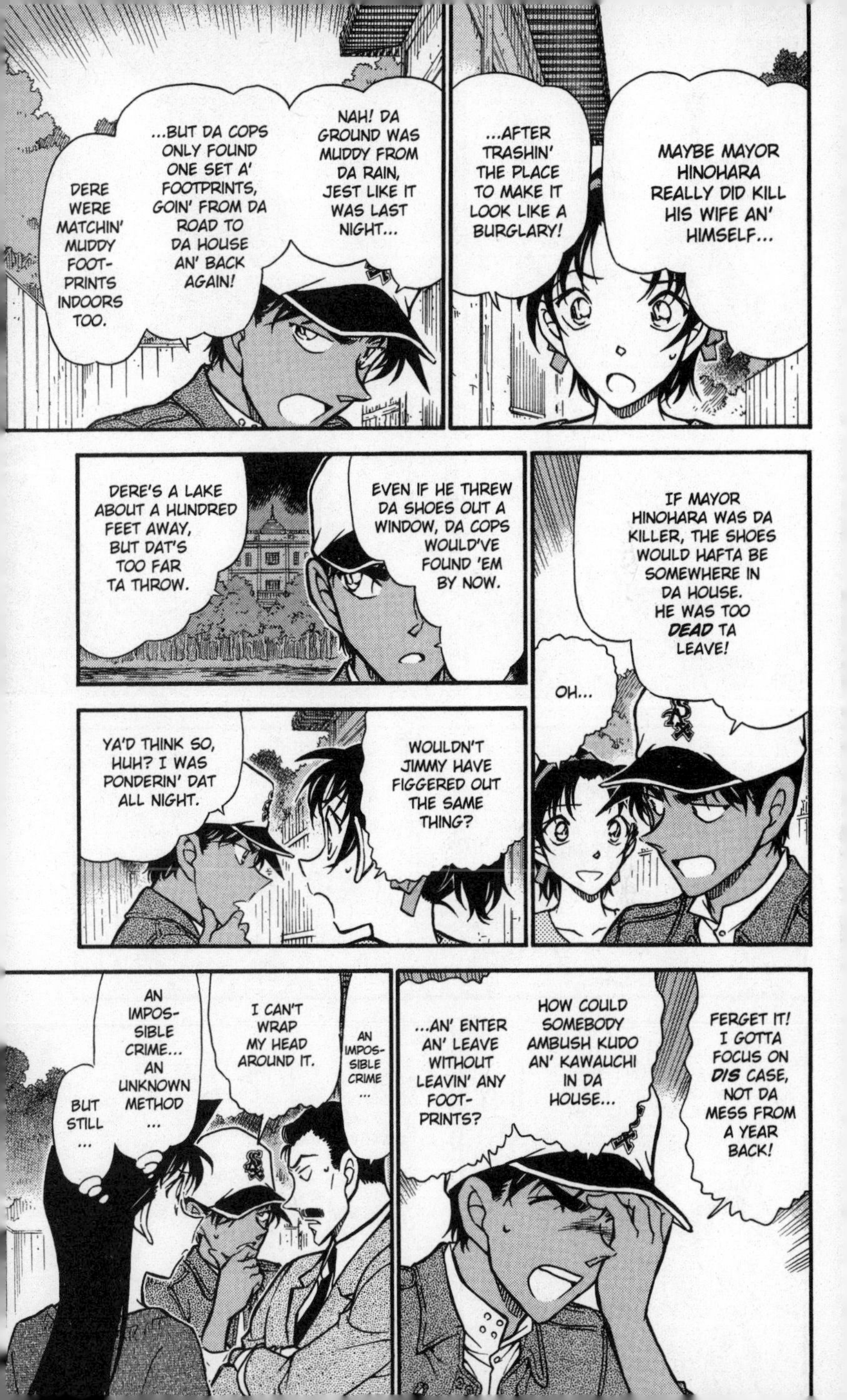

MAYBE MAYOR HINOHARA REALLY DID KILL HIS WIFE AN' HIMSELF...
...AFTER TRASHIN' THE PLACE TO MAKE IT LOOK LIKE A BURGLARY!
NAH! DA GROUND WAS MUDDY FROM DA RAIN, JEST LIKE IT WAS LAST NIGHT...
...BUT DA COPS ONLY FOUND ONE SET A' FOOTPRINTS, GOIN' FROM DA ROAD TO DA HOUSE AN' BACK AGAIN!
DERE WERE MATCHIN' MUDDY FOOT-PRINTS INDOORS TOO.
IF MAYOR HINOHARA WAS DA KILLER, THE SHOES WOULD HAFTA BE SOMEWHERE IN DA HOUSE. HE WAS TOO ***DEAD*** TA LEAVE!
OH...
EVEN IF HE THREW DA SHOES OUT A WINDOW, DA COPS WOULD'VE FOUND 'EM BY NOW.
DERE'S A LAKE ABOUT A HUNDRED FEET AWAY, BUT DAT'S TOO FAR TA THROW.
WOULDN'T JIMMY HAVE FIGGERED OUT THE SAME THING?
YA'D THINK SO, HUH? I WAS PONDERIN' DAT ALL NIGHT.
FERGET IT! I GOTTA FOCUS ON ***DIS*** CASE, NOT DA MESS FROM A YEAR BACK!
HOW COULD SOMEBODY AMBUSH KUDO AN' KAWAUCHI IN DA HOUSE...
...AN' ENTER AN' LEAVE WITHOUT LEAVIN' ANY FOOT-PRINTS?
AN IMPOS-SIBLE CRIME...
I CAN'T WRAP MY HEAD AROUND IT.
AN IMPOS-SIBLE CRIME... AN UNKNOWN METHOD...
BUT STILL...

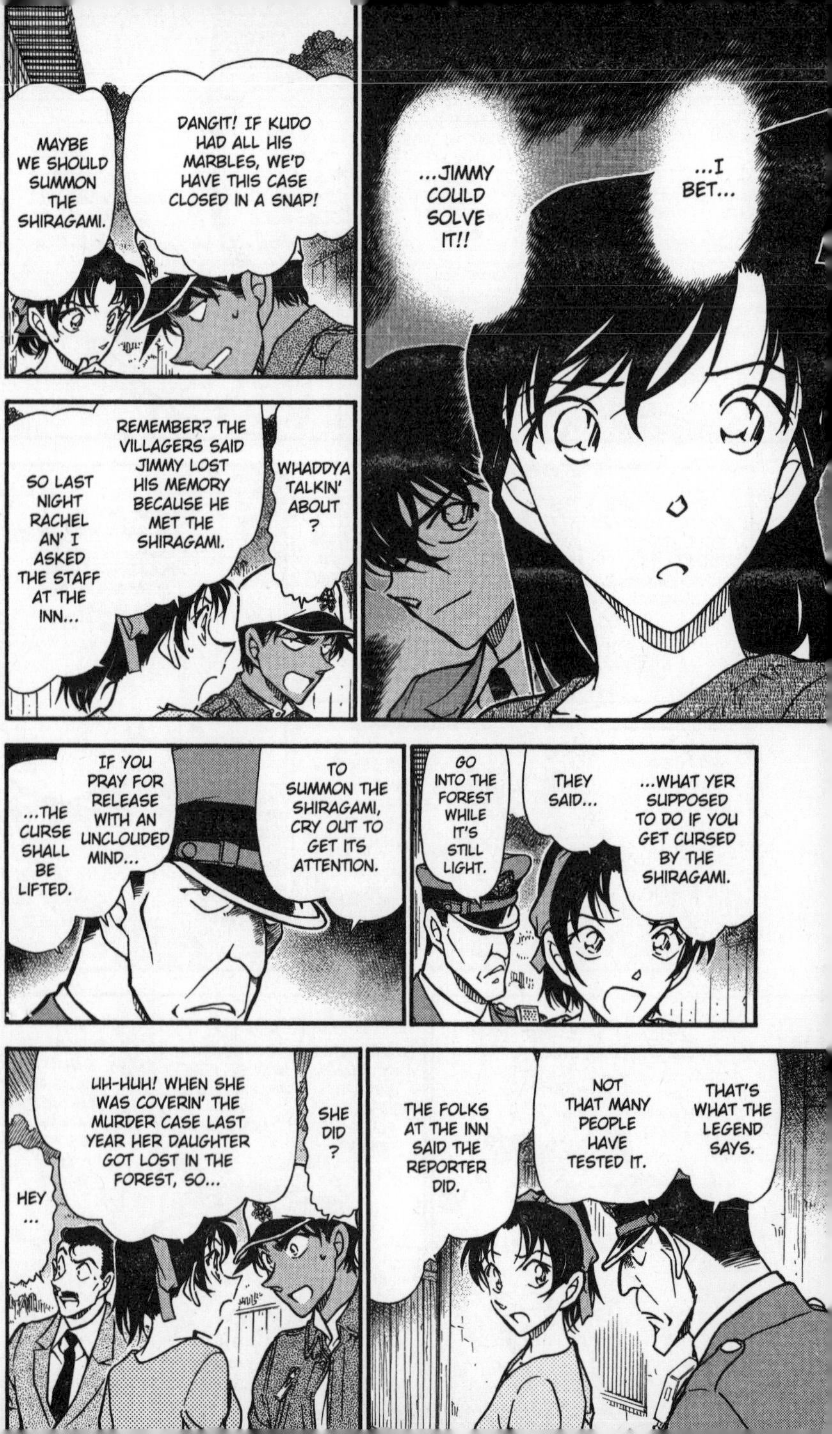
...I BET...
...JIMMY COULD SOLVE IT!!
DANGIT! IF KUDO HAD ALL HIS MARBLES, WE'D HAVE THIS CASE CLOSED IN A SNAP!
MAYBE WE SHOULD SUMMON THE SHIRAGAMI.
WHADDYA TALKIN' ABOUT?
REMEMBER? THE VILLAGERS SAID JIMMY LOST HIS MEMORY BECAUSE HE MET THE SHIRAGAMI.
SO LAST NIGHT RACHEL AN' I ASKED THE STAFF AT THE INN...
...WHAT YER SUPPOSED TO DO IF YOU GET CURSED BY THE SHIRAGAMI.
THEY SAID...
GO INTO THE FOREST WHILE IT'S STILL LIGHT.
TO SUMMON THE SHIRAGAMI, CRY OUT TO GET ITS ATTENTION.
IF YOU PRAY FOR RELEASE WITH AN UNCLOUDED MIND...
...THE CURSE SHALL BE LIFTED.
THAT'S WHAT THE LEGEND SAYS.
NOT THAT MANY PEOPLE HAVE TESTED IT.
THE FOLKS AT THE INN SAID THE REPORTER DID.
SHE DID?
UH-HUH! WHEN SHE WAS COVERIN' THE MURDER CASE LAST YEAR HER DAUGHTER GOT LOST IN THE FOREST, SO...
HEY...

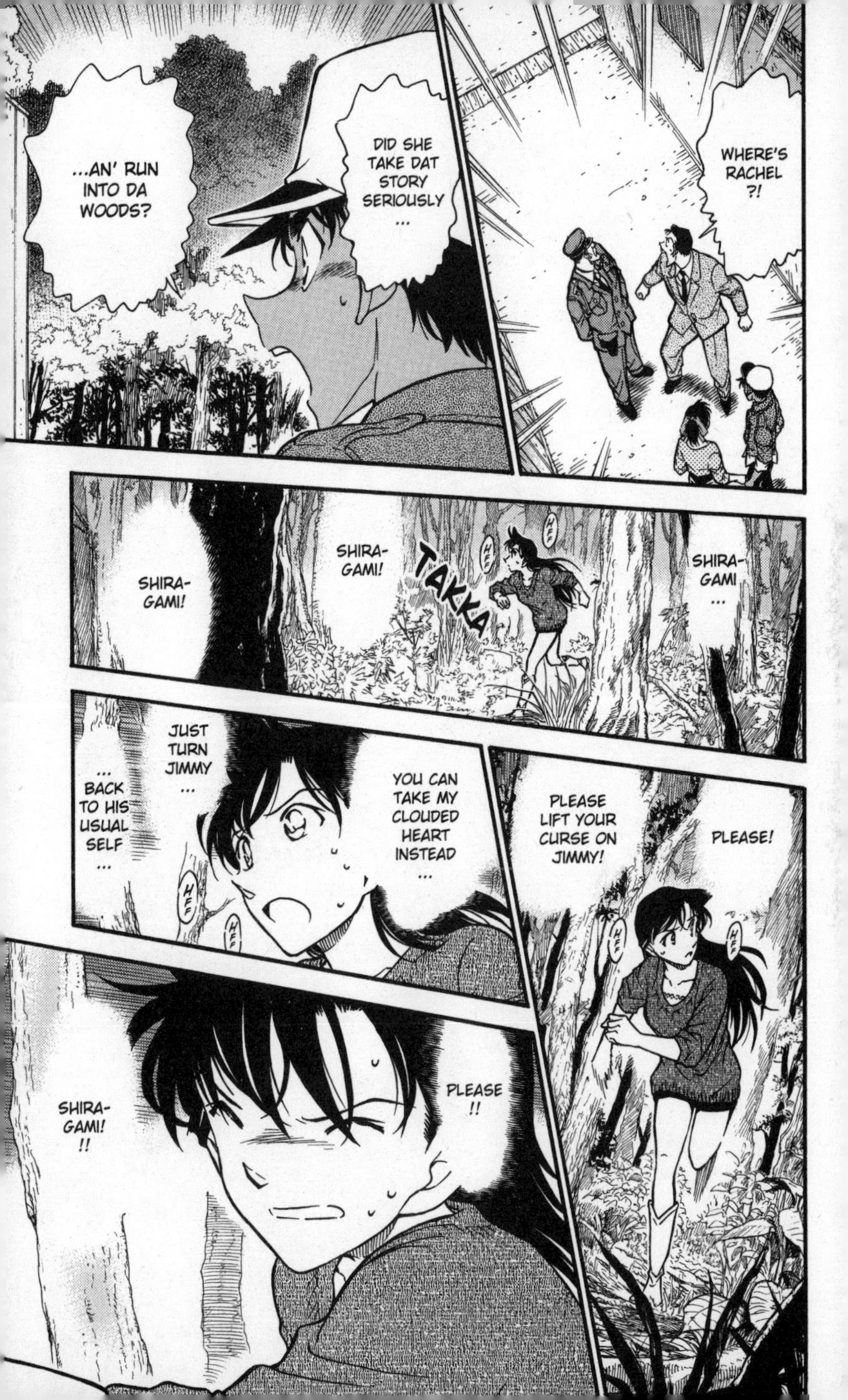
WHERE'S RACHEL ?!
DID SHE TAKE DAT STORY SERIOUSLY ...
...AN' RUN INTO DA WOODS?
SHIRA-GAMI ...
TAKKA
SHIRA-GAMI!
SHIRA-GAMI!
PLEASE!
PLEASE LIFT YOUR CURSE ON JIMMY!
YOU CAN TAKE MY CLOUDED HEART INSTEAD ...
JUST TURN JIMMY ...
... BACK TO HIS USUAL SELF ...
PLEASE !!
SHIRA-GAMI! !!

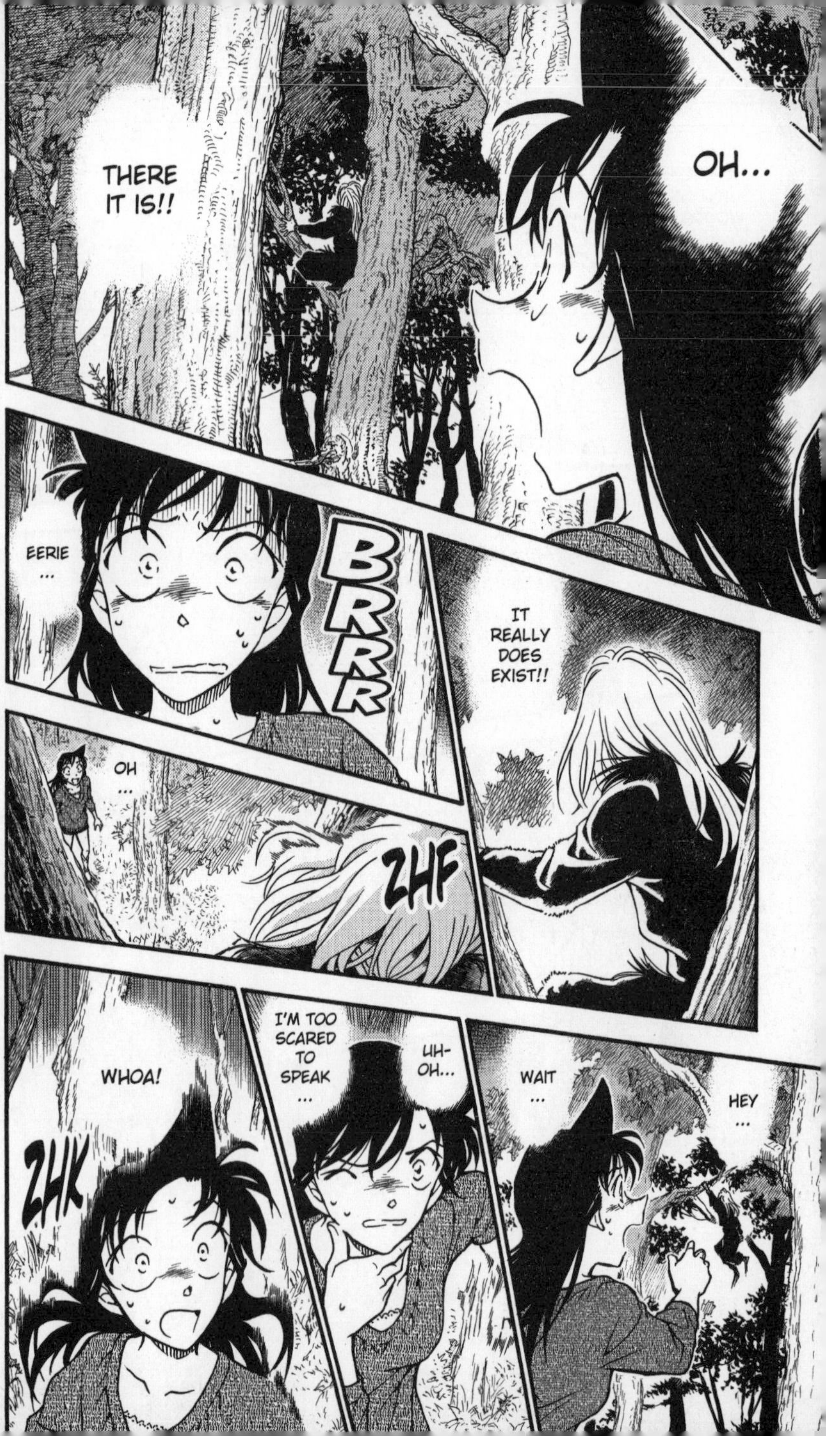
OH...
THERE IT IS!!
IT REALLY DOES EXIST!!
EERIE...
BRRR
OH...
ZHF
HEY...
WAIT...
UH-OH...
I'M TOO SCARED TO SPEAK...
WHOA!
ZHK

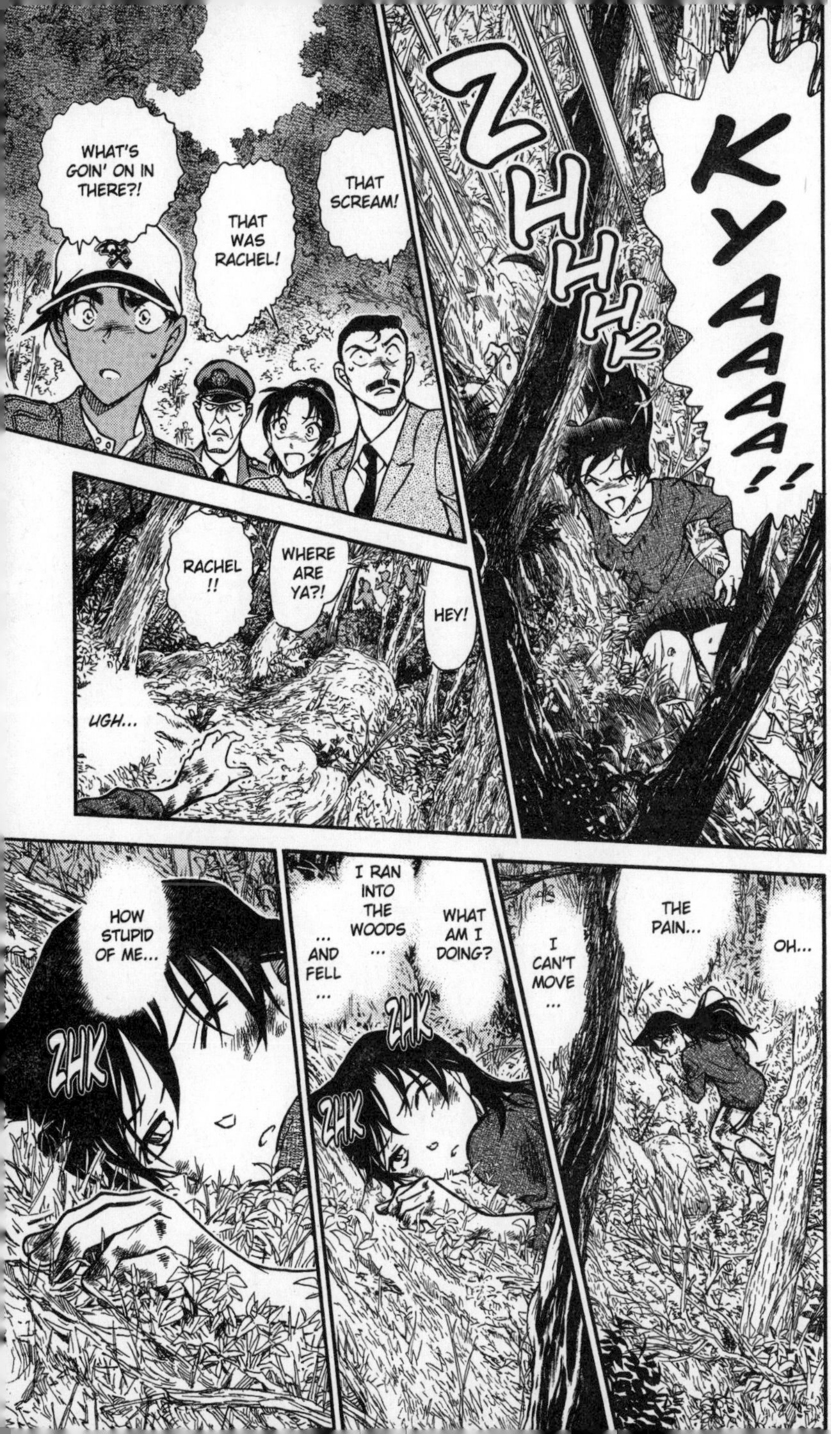
KYAAAA!!
ZHHHK
THAT SCREAM!
THAT WAS RACHEL!
WHAT'S GOIN' ON IN THERE?!
HEY!
WHERE ARE YA?!
RACHEL!!
UGH...
OH...
THE PAIN...
I CAN'T MOVE...
WHAT AM I DOING?
I RAN INTO THE WOODS...
...AND FELL...
ZHK
HOW STUPID OF ME...
ZHK

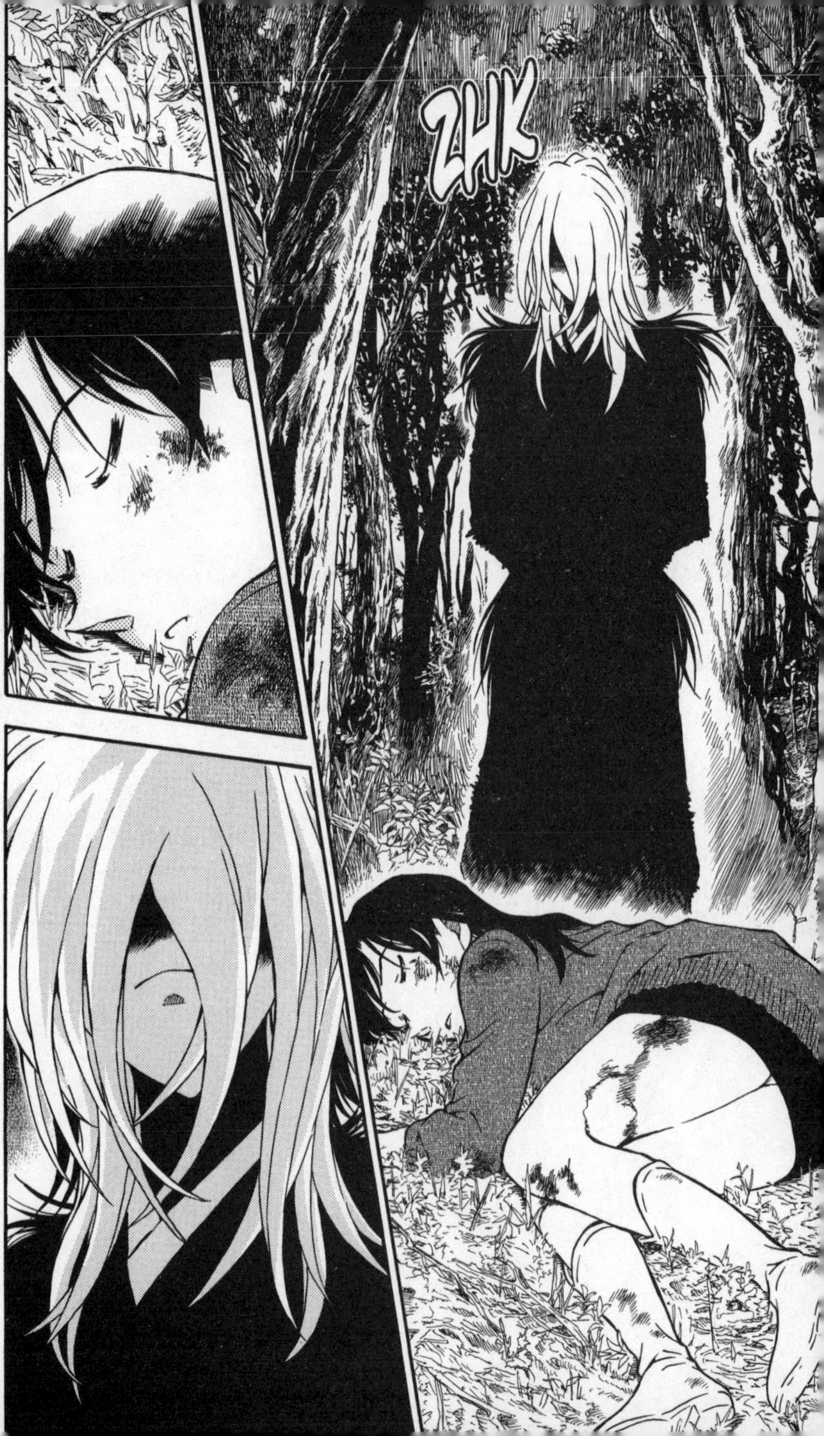
ZHK

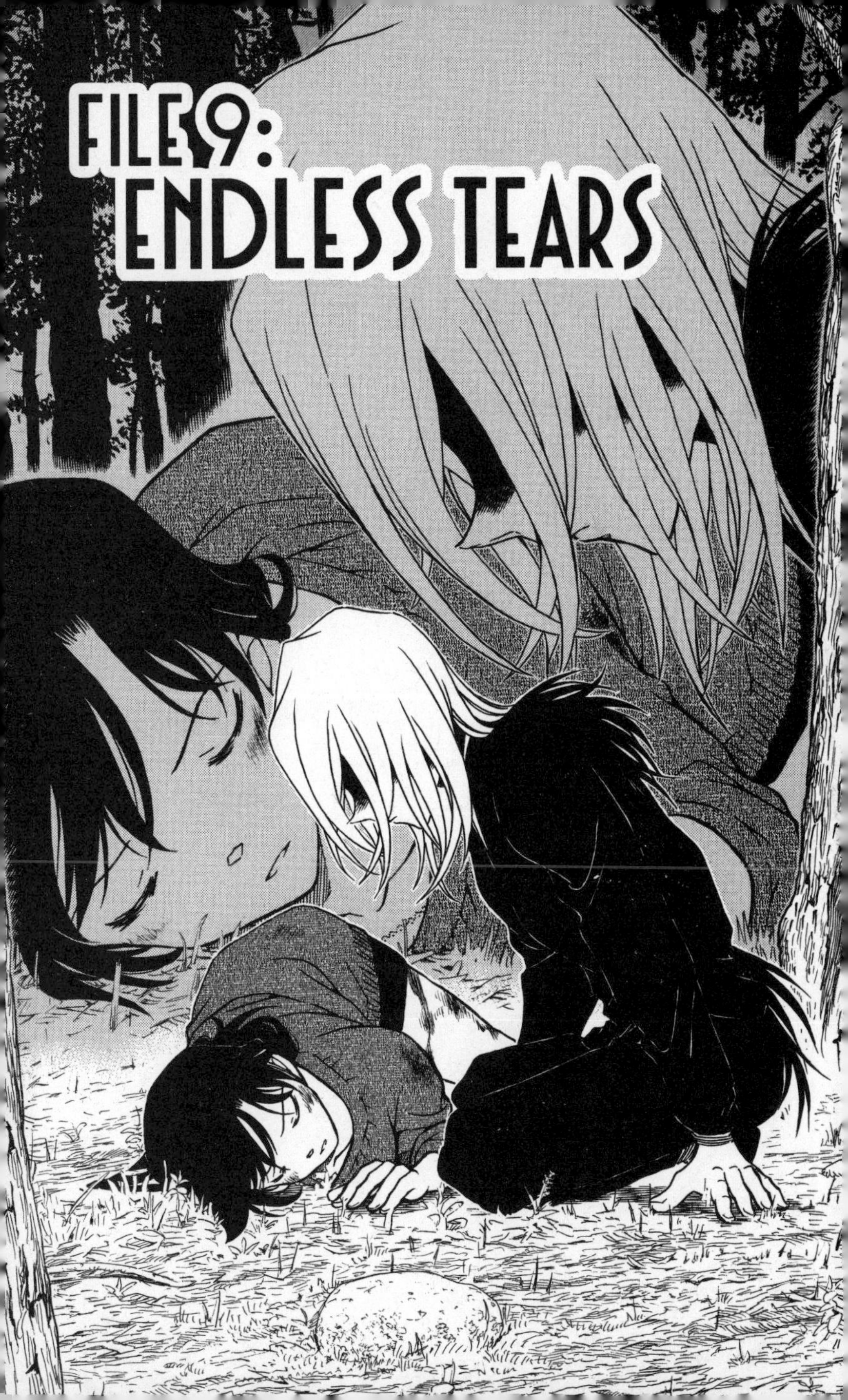
FILE 9:
ENDLESS TEARS

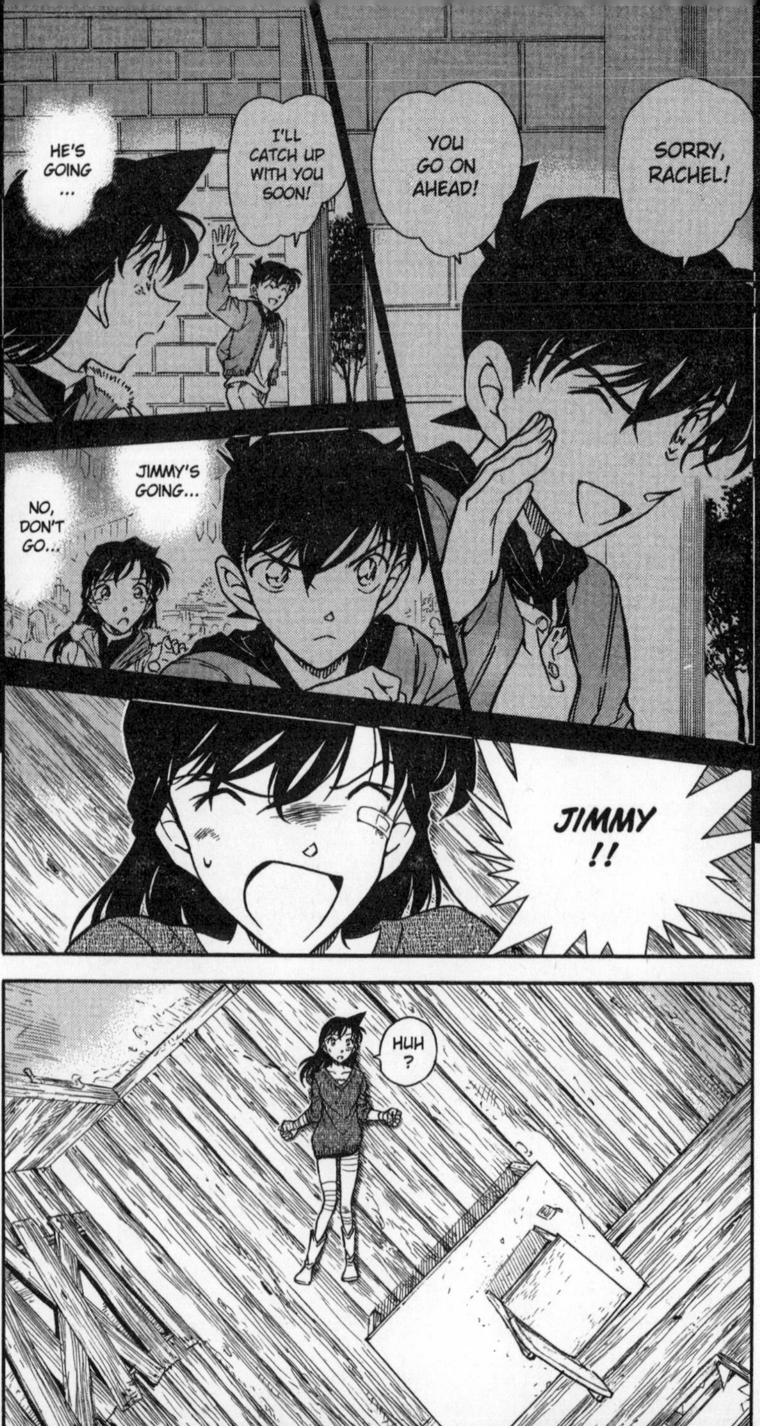
SORRY, RACHEL!
YOU GO ON AHEAD!
I'LL CATCH UP WITH YOU SOON!
HE'S GOING ...
JIMMY'S GOING...
NO, DON'T GO...
JIMMY !!
HUH ?

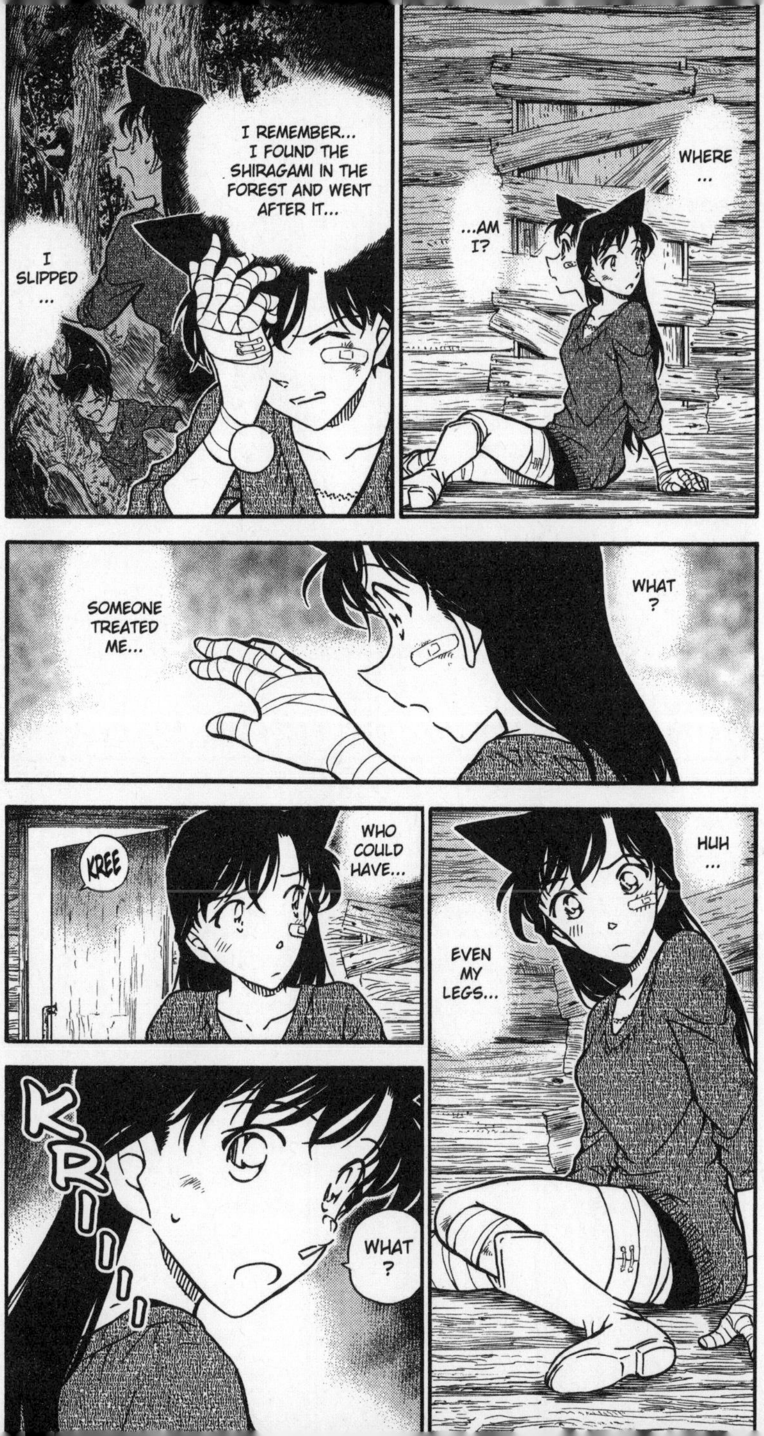

WHERE ...
...AM I?
I REMEMBER... I FOUND THE SHIRAGAMI IN THE FOREST AND WENT AFTER IT...
I SLIPPED ...
WHAT ?
SOMEONE TREATED ME...
HUH ...
EVEN MY LEGS...
WHO COULD HAVE...
KREE
KRIIII
WHAT ?

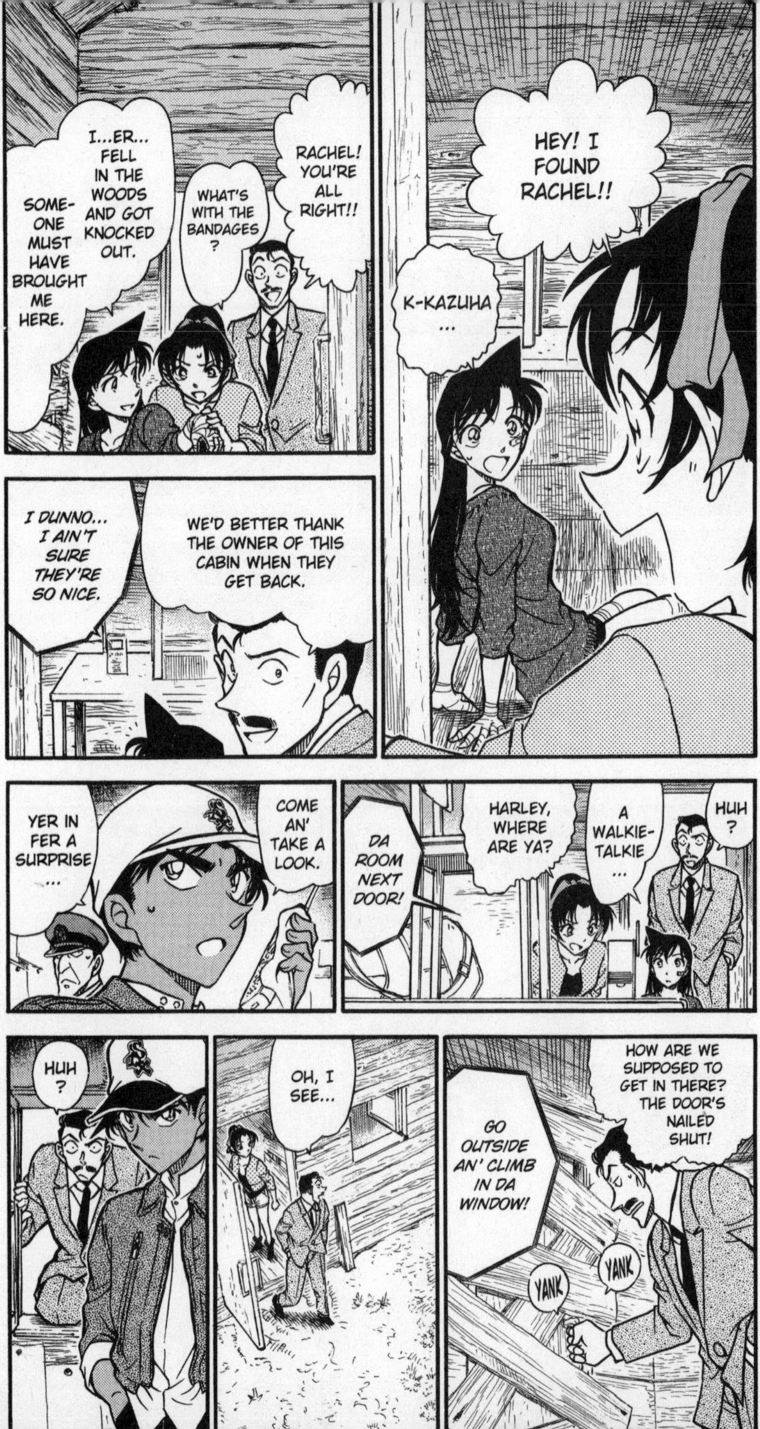
HEY! I FOUND RACHEL!!
K-KAZUHA...
RACHEL! YOU'RE ALL RIGHT!!
WHAT'S WITH THE BANDAGES?
I...ER... FELL IN THE WOODS AND GOT KNOCKED OUT.
SOME-ONE MUST HAVE BROUGHT ME HERE.
WE'D BETTER THANK THE OWNER OF THIS CABIN WHEN THEY GET BACK.
I DUNNO... I AIN'T SURE THEY'RE SO NICE.
HUH?
A WALKIE-TALKIE...
HARLEY, WHERE ARE YA?
DA ROOM NEXT DOOR!
COME AN' TAKE A LOOK.
YER IN FER A SURPRISE...
HOW ARE WE SUPPOSED TO GET IN THERE? THE DOOR'S NAILED SHUT!
GO OUTSIDE AN' CLIMB IN DA WINDOW!
YANK
YANK
OH, I SEE...
HUH?

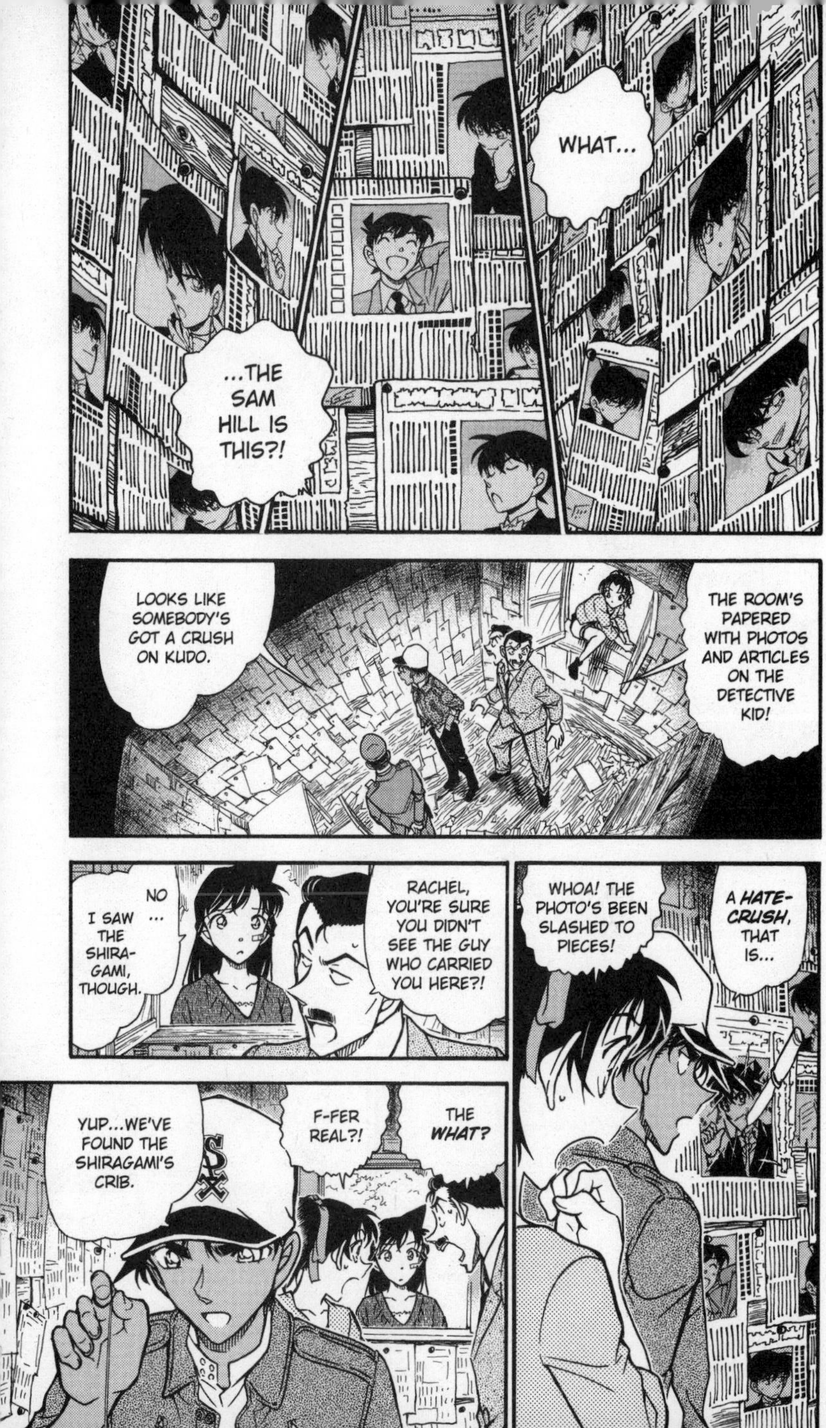
WHAT...
...THE SAM HILL IS THIS?!
THE ROOM'S PAPERED WITH PHOTOS AND ARTICLES ON THE DETECTIVE KID!
LOOKS LIKE SOMEBODY'S GOT A CRUSH ON KUDO.
A *HATE-CRUSH*, THAT IS...
WHOA! THE PHOTO'S BEEN SLASHED TO PIECES!
RACHEL, YOU'RE SURE YOU DIDN'T SEE THE GUY WHO CARRIED YOU HERE?!
NO ... I SAW THE SHIRAGAMI, THOUGH.
THE *WHAT?*
F-FER REAL?!
YUP...WE'VE FOUND THE SHIRAGAMI'S CRIB.

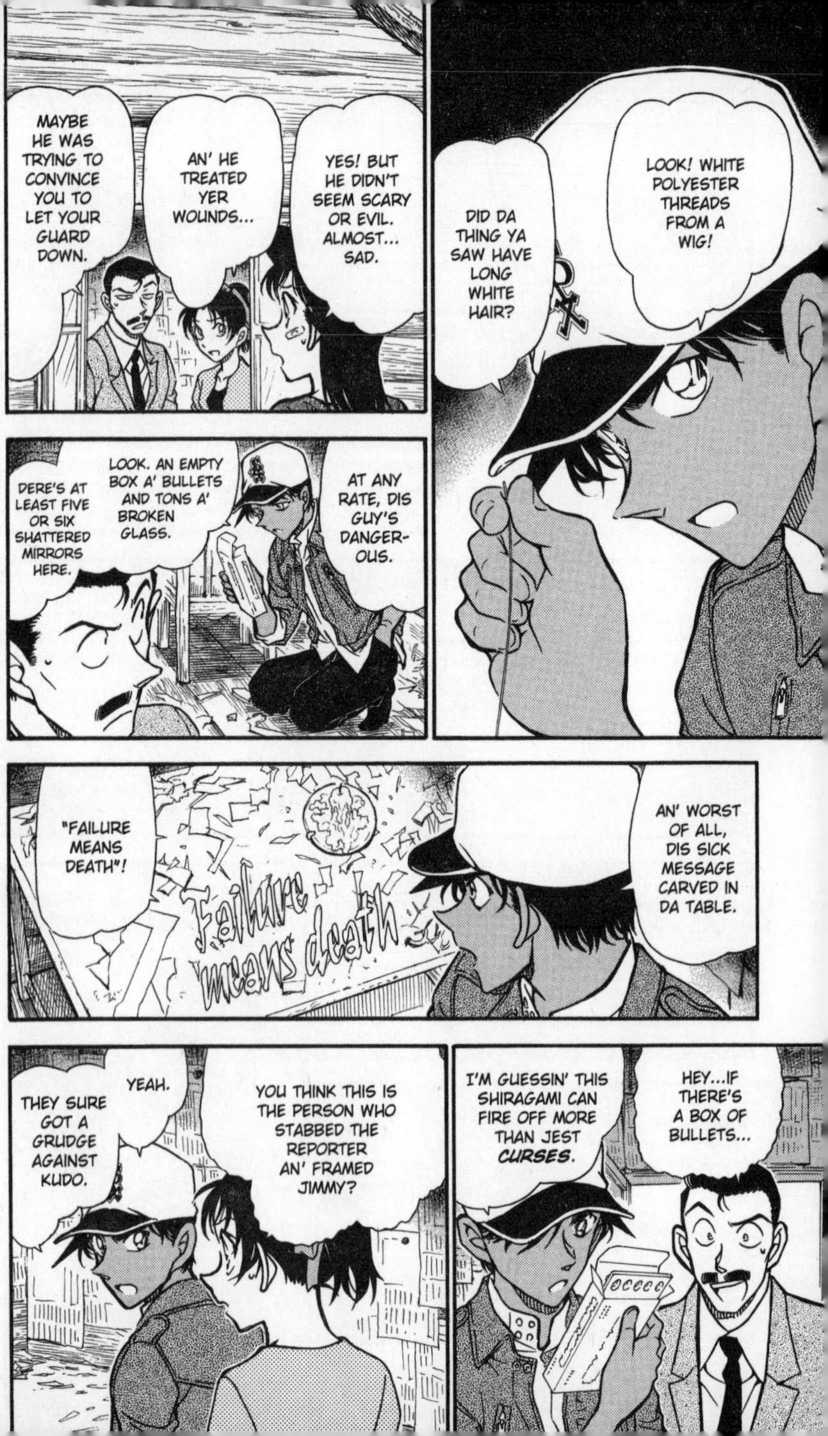
LOOK! WHITE POLYESTER THREADS FROM A WIG!
DID DA THING YA SAW HAVE LONG WHITE HAIR?
YES! BUT HE DIDN'T SEEM SCARY OR EVIL. ALMOST... SAD.
AN' HE TREATED YER WOUNDS...
MAYBE HE WAS TRYING TO CONVINCE YOU TO LET YOUR GUARD DOWN.
AT ANY RATE, DIS GUY'S DANGER-OUS.
LOOK. AN EMPTY BOX A' BULLETS AND TONS A' BROKEN GLASS.
DERE'S AT LEAST FIVE OR SIX SHATTERED MIRRORS HERE.
AN' WORST OF ALL, DIS SICK MESSAGE CARVED IN DA TABLE.
Failure means death
"FAILURE MEANS DEATH"!
HEY...IF THERE'S A BOX OF BULLETS...
I'M GUESSIN' THIS SHIRAGAMI CAN FIRE OFF MORE THAN JEST *CURSES*.
YOU THINK THIS IS THE PERSON WHO STABBED THE REPORTER AN' FRAMED JIMMY?
YEAH.
THEY SURE GOT A GRUDGE AGAINST KUDO.

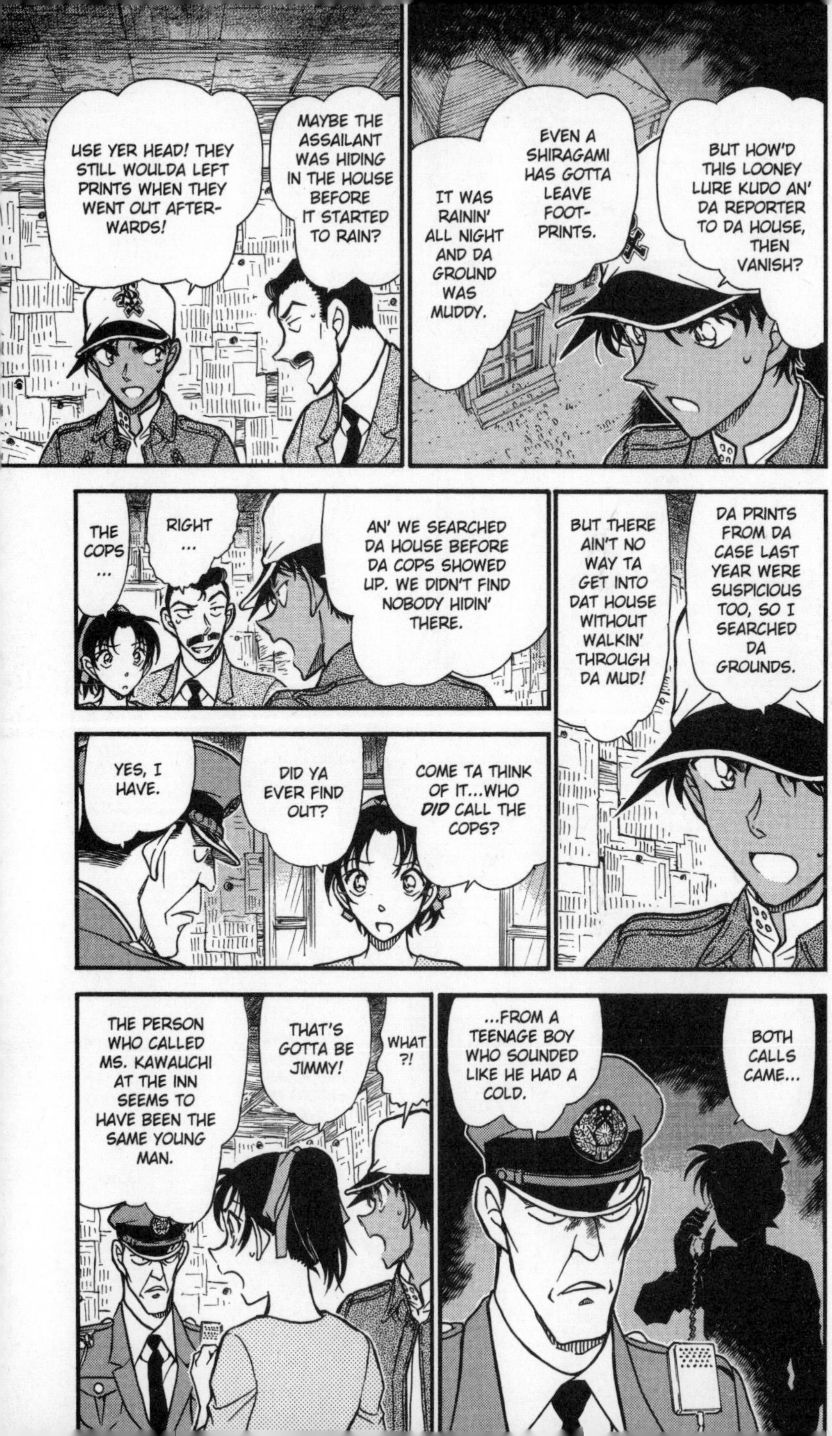

BUT HOW'D THIS LOONEY LURE KUDO AN' DA REPORTER TO DA HOUSE, THEN VANISH?
EVEN A SHIRAGAMI HAS GOTTA LEAVE FOOT-PRINTS.
IT WAS RAININ' ALL NIGHT AND DA GROUND WAS MUDDY.
MAYBE THE ASSAILANT WAS HIDING IN THE HOUSE BEFORE IT STARTED TO RAIN?
USE YER HEAD! THEY STILL WOULDA LEFT PRINTS WHEN THEY WENT OUT AFTER-WARDS!
DA PRINTS FROM DA CASE LAST YEAR WERE SUSPICIOUS TOO, SO I SEARCHED DA GROUNDS.
BUT THERE AIN'T NO WAY TA GET INTO DAT HOUSE WITHOUT WALKIN' THROUGH DA MUD!
AN' WE SEARCHED DA HOUSE BEFORE DA COPS SHOWED UP. WE DIDN'T FIND NOBODY HIDIN' THERE.
RIGHT ...
THE COPS ...
COME TA THINK OF IT...WHO *DID* CALL THE COPS?
DID YA EVER FIND OUT?
YES, I HAVE.
BOTH CALLS CAME...
...FROM A TEENAGE BOY WHO SOUNDED LIKE HE HAD A COLD.
WHAT?!
THAT'S GOTTA BE JIMMY!
THE PERSON WHO CALLED MS. KAWAUCHI AT THE INN SEEMS TO HAVE BEEN THE SAME YOUNG MAN.

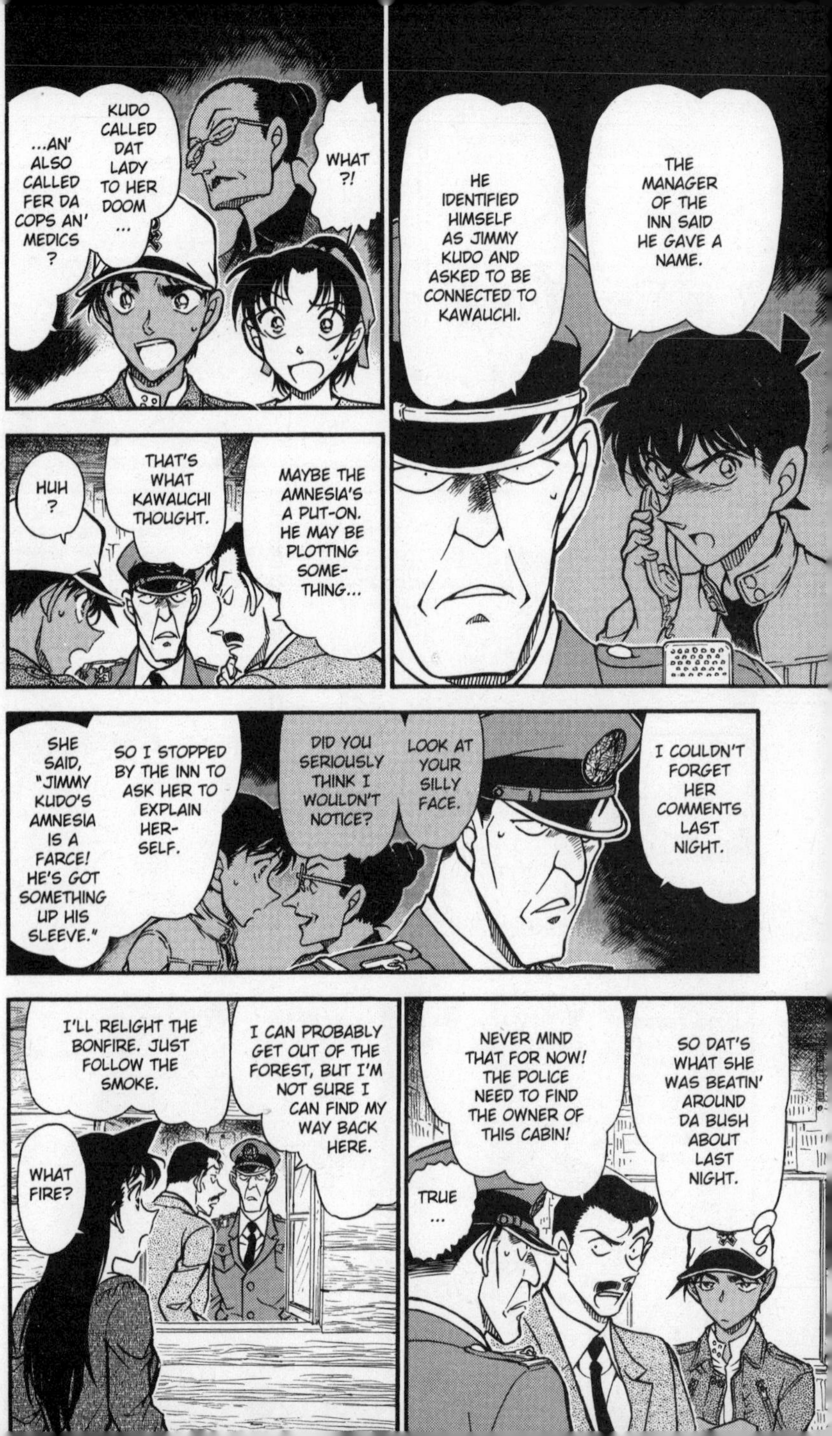
THE MANAGER OF THE INN SAID HE GAVE A NAME.
HE IDENTIFIED HIMSELF AS JIMMY KUDO AND ASKED TO BE CONNECTED TO KAWAUCHI.
WHAT ?!
KUDO CALLED DAT LADY TO HER DOOM ...
...AN' ALSO CALLED FER DA COPS AN' MEDICS ?
MAYBE THE AMNESIA'S A PUT-ON. HE MAY BE PLOTTING SOME-THING...
THAT'S WHAT KAWAUCHI THOUGHT.
HUH ?
I COULDN'T FORGET HER COMMENTS LAST NIGHT.
LOOK AT YOUR SILLY FACE.
DID YOU SERIOUSLY THINK I WOULDN'T NOTICE?
SO I STOPPED BY THE INN TO ASK HER TO EXPLAIN HER-SELF.
SHE SAID, "JIMMY KUDO'S AMNESIA IS A FARCE! HE'S GOT SOMETHING UP HIS SLEEVE."
SO DAT'S WHAT SHE WAS BEATIN' AROUND DA BUSH ABOUT LAST NIGHT.
NEVER MIND THAT FOR NOW! THE POLICE NEED TO FIND THE OWNER OF THIS CABIN!
TRUE ...
I CAN PROBABLY GET OUT OF THE FOREST, BUT I'M NOT SURE I CAN FIND MY WAY BACK HERE.
I'LL RELIGHT THE BONFIRE. JUST FOLLOW THE SMOKE.
WHAT FIRE?

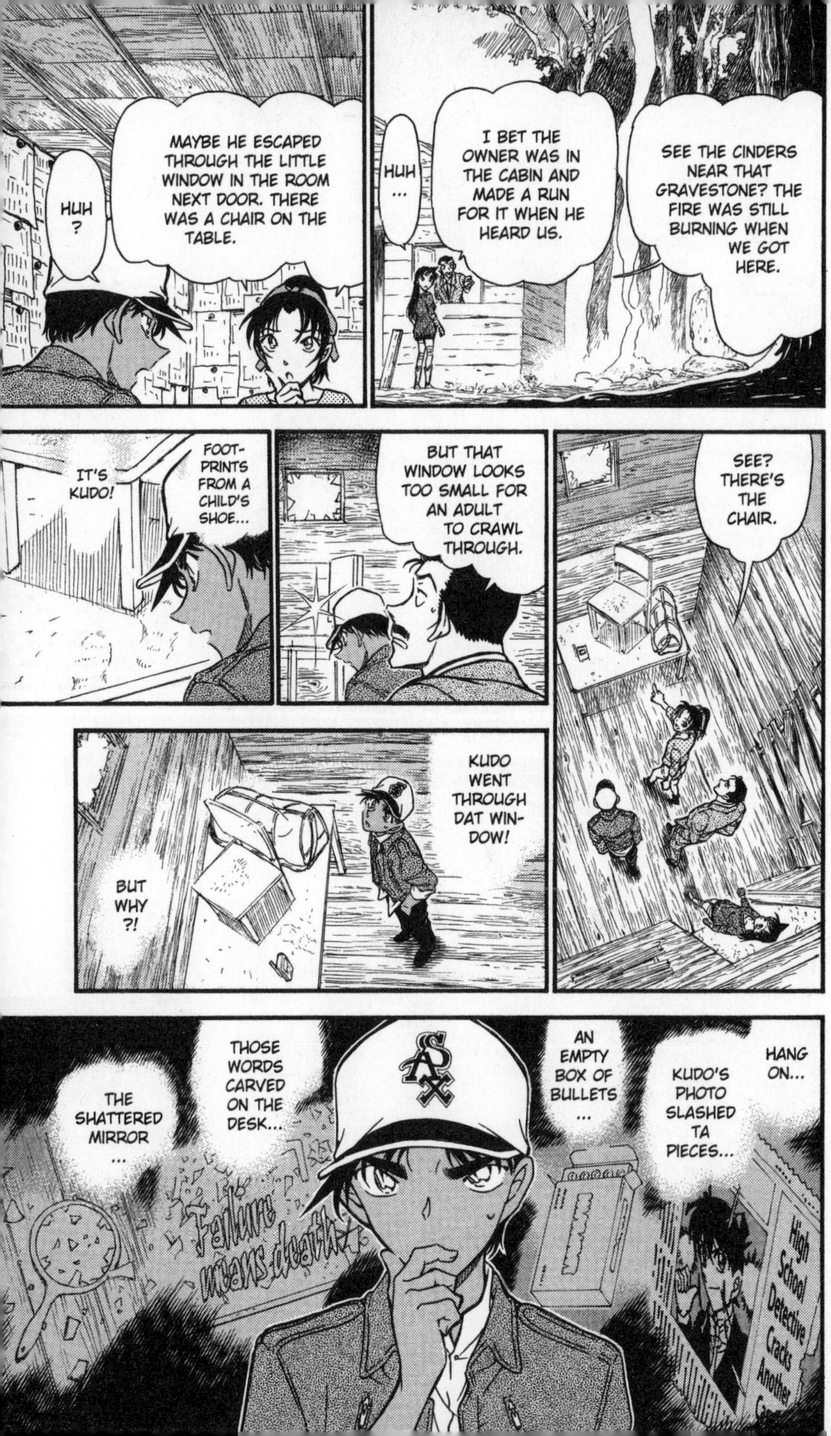
SEE THE CINDERS NEAR THAT GRAVESTONE? THE FIRE WAS STILL BURNING WHEN WE GOT HERE.
I BET THE OWNER WAS IN THE CABIN AND MADE A RUN FOR IT WHEN HE HEARD US.
HUH ...
MAYBE HE ESCAPED THROUGH THE LITTLE WINDOW IN THE ROOM NEXT DOOR. THERE WAS A CHAIR ON THE TABLE.
HUH ?
SEE? THERE'S THE CHAIR.
BUT THAT WINDOW LOOKS TOO SMALL FOR AN ADULT TO CRAWL THROUGH.
FOOT-PRINTS FROM A CHILD'S SHOE...
IT'S KUDO!
KUDO WENT THROUGH DAT WIN-DOW!
BUT WHY ?!
HANG ON...
KUDO'S PHOTO SLASHED TA PIECES...
High School Detective Cracks Another
AN EMPTY BOX OF BULLETS ...
THOSE WORDS CARVED ON THE DESK...
Failure means death!
THE SHATTERED MIRROR ...

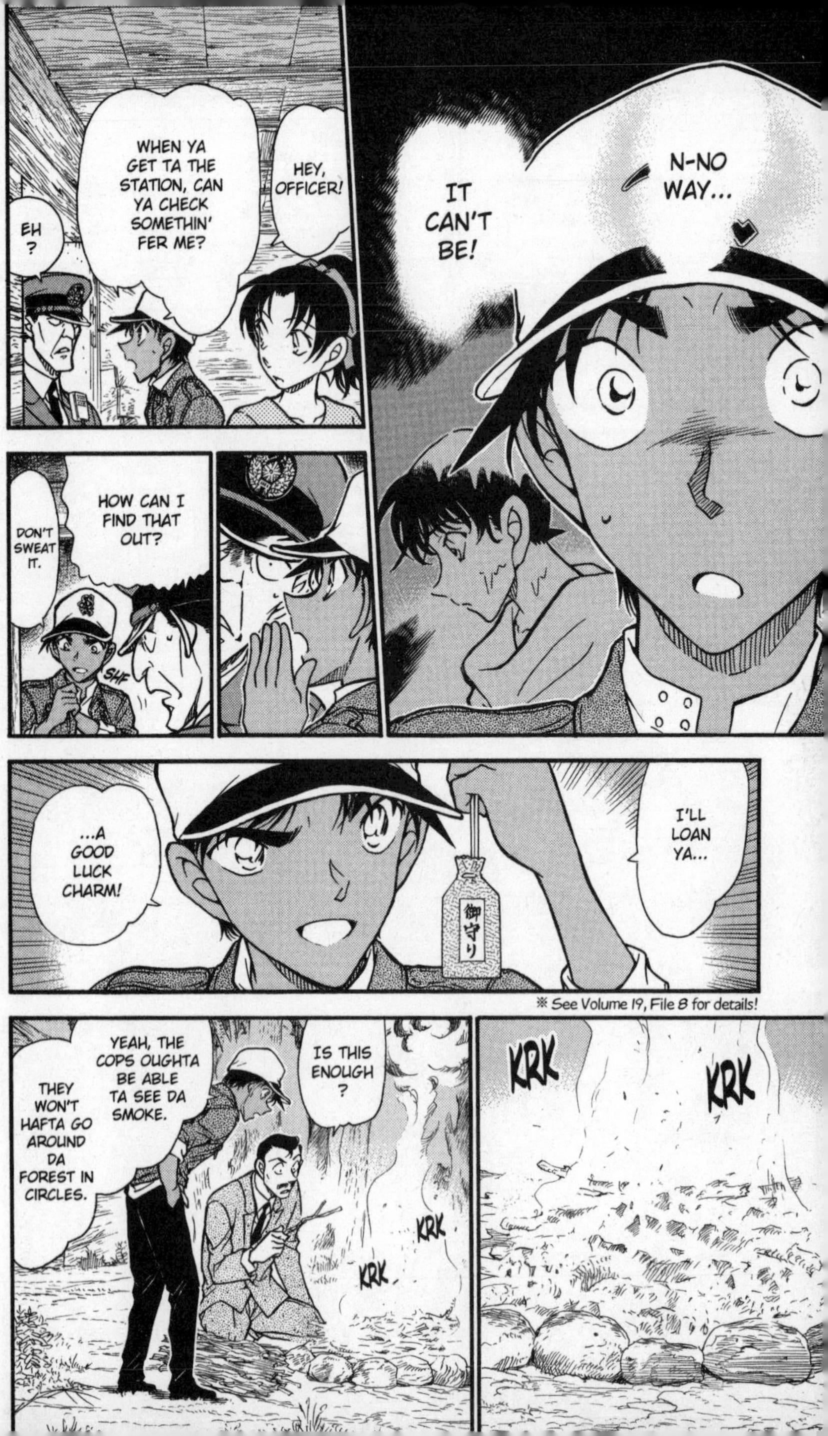
N-NO WAY...
IT CAN'T BE!
HEY, OFFICER!
WHEN YA GET TA THE STATION, CAN YA CHECK SOMETHIN' FER ME?
EH?
HOW CAN I FIND THAT OUT?
DON'T SWEAT IT.
SHF
I'LL LOAN YA...
...A GOOD LUCK CHARM!
御守り
KRK
KRK
IS THIS ENOUGH?
YEAH, THE COPS OUGHTA BE ABLE TA SEE DA SMOKE.
THEY WON'T HAFTA GO AROUND DA FOREST IN CIRCLES.
KRK
KRK
※ See Volume 19, File 8 for details!

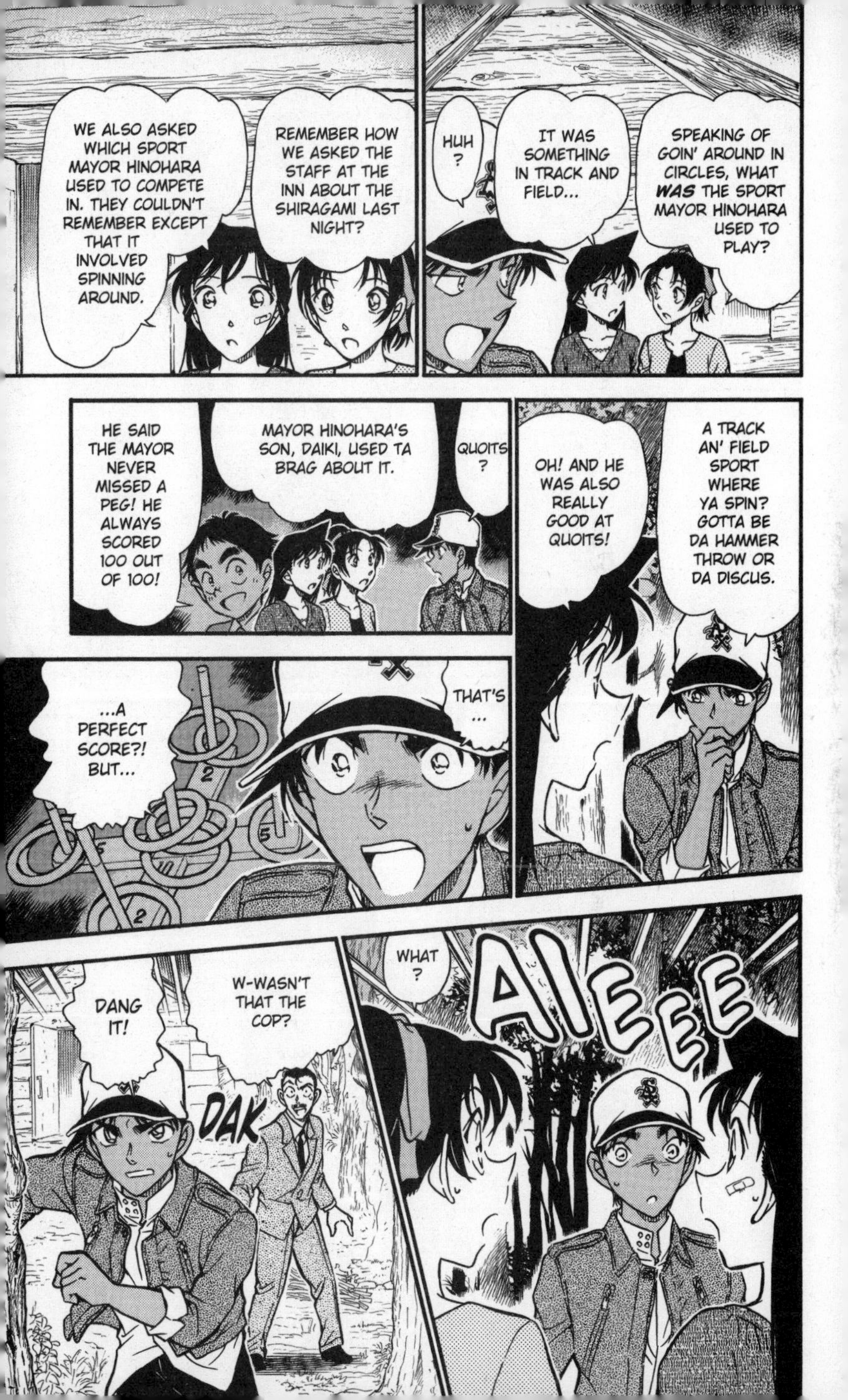
SPEAKING OF GOIN' AROUND IN CIRCLES, WHAT *WAS* THE SPORT MAYOR HINOHARA USED TO PLAY?
IT WAS SOMETHING IN TRACK AND FIELD...
HUH?
REMEMBER HOW WE ASKED THE STAFF AT THE INN ABOUT THE SHIRAGAMI LAST NIGHT?
WE ALSO ASKED WHICH SPORT MAYOR HINOHARA USED TO COMPETE IN. THEY COULDN'T REMEMBER EXCEPT THAT IT INVOLVED SPINNING AROUND.
A TRACK AN' FIELD SPORT WHERE YA SPIN? GOTTA BE DA HAMMER THROW OR DA DISCUS.
OH! AND HE WAS ALSO REALLY GOOD AT QUOITS!
QUOITS?
MAYOR HINOHARA'S SON, DAIKI, USED TA BRAG ABOUT IT.
HE SAID THE MAYOR NEVER MISSED A PEG! HE ALWAYS SCORED 100 OUT OF 100!
THAT'S...
...A PERFECT SCORE?! BUT...
AIEEEE
WHAT?
W-WASN'T THAT THE COP?
DANG IT!
DAK

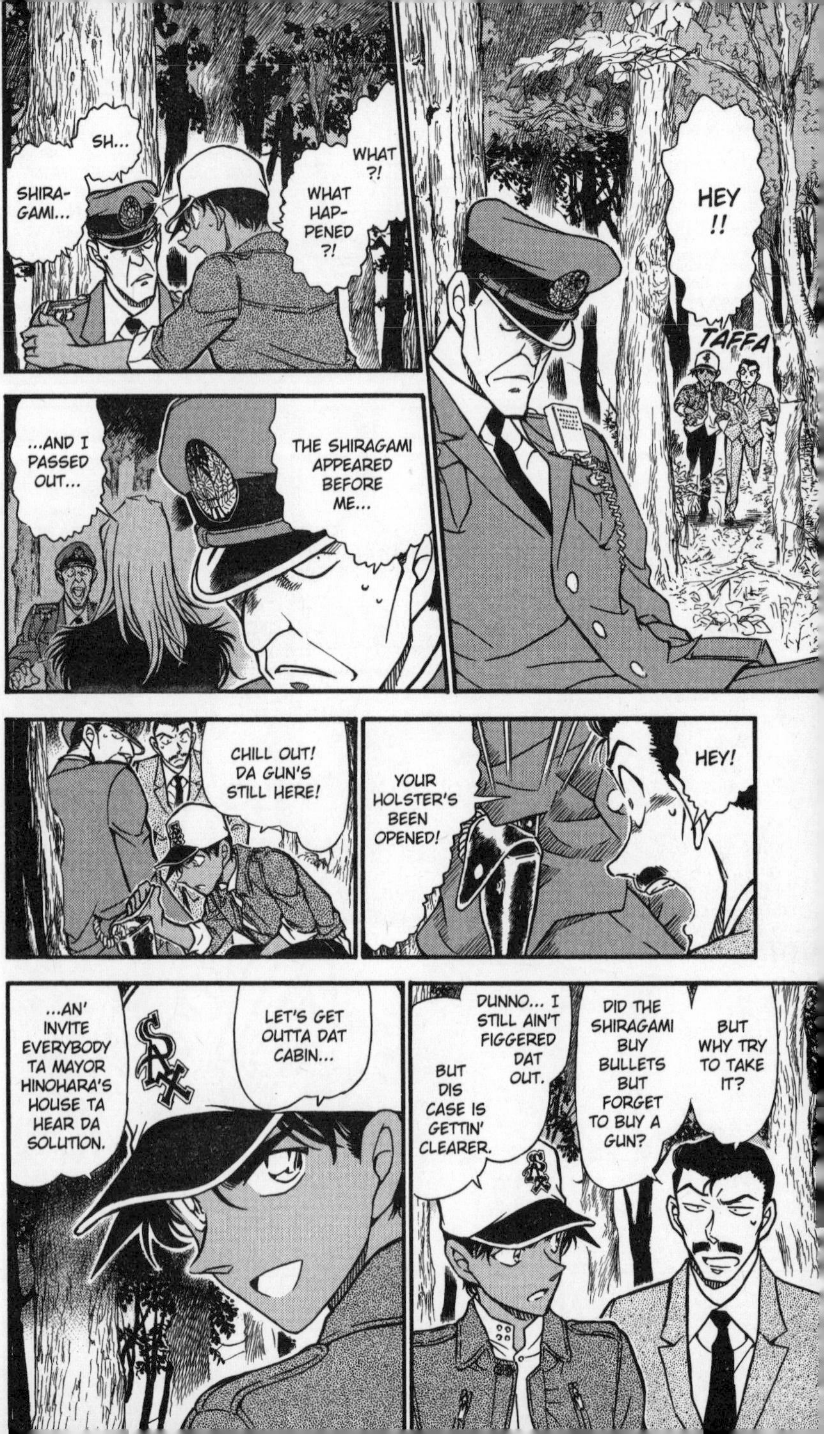
HEY !!
TAFFA
WHAT ?!
WHAT HAPPENED ?!
SH...
SHIRAGAMI...
THE SHIRAGAMI APPEARED BEFORE ME...
...AND I PASSED OUT...
HEY!
YOUR HOLSTER'S BEEN OPENED!
CHILL OUT! DA GUN'S STILL HERE!
BUT WHY TRY TO TAKE IT?
DID THE SHIRAGAMI BUY BULLETS BUT FORGET TO BUY A GUN?
DUNNO... I STILL AIN'T FIGGERED DAT OUT.
BUT DIS CASE IS GETTIN' CLEARER.
LET'S GET OUTTA DAT CABIN...
...AN' INVITE EVERYBODY TA MAYOR HINOHARA'S HOUSE TA HEAR DA SOLUTION.

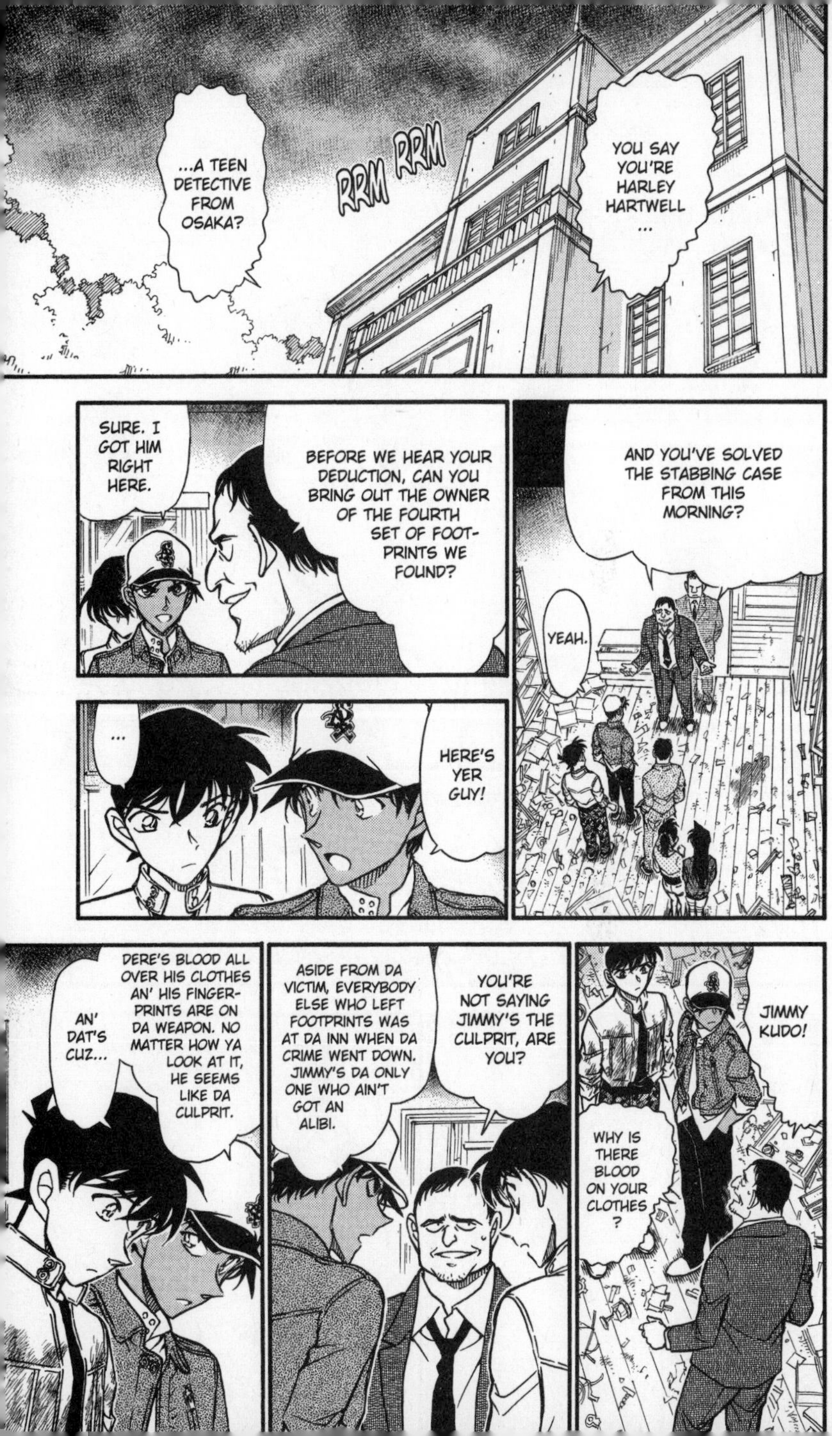
YOU SAY YOU'RE HARLEY HARTWELL...
RRM RRM
...A TEEN DETECTIVE FROM OSAKA?
AND YOU'VE SOLVED THE STABBING CASE FROM THIS MORNING?
YEAH.
BEFORE WE HEAR YOUR DEDUCTION, CAN YOU BRING OUT THE OWNER OF THE FOURTH SET OF FOOT-PRINTS WE FOUND?
SURE. I GOT HIM RIGHT HERE.
HERE'S YER GUY!
...
JIMMY KUDO!
WHY IS THERE BLOOD ON YOUR CLOTHES?
YOU'RE NOT SAYING JIMMY'S THE CULPRIT, ARE YOU?
ASIDE FROM DA VICTIM, EVERYBODY ELSE WHO LEFT FOOTPRINTS WAS AT DA INN WHEN DA CRIME WENT DOWN. JIMMY'S DA ONLY ONE WHO AIN'T GOT AN ALIBI.
DERE'S BLOOD ALL OVER HIS CLOTHES AN' HIS FINGER-PRINTS ARE ON DA WEAPON. NO MATTER HOW YA LOOK AT IT, HE SEEMS LIKE DA CULPRIT.
AN' DAT'S CUZ...

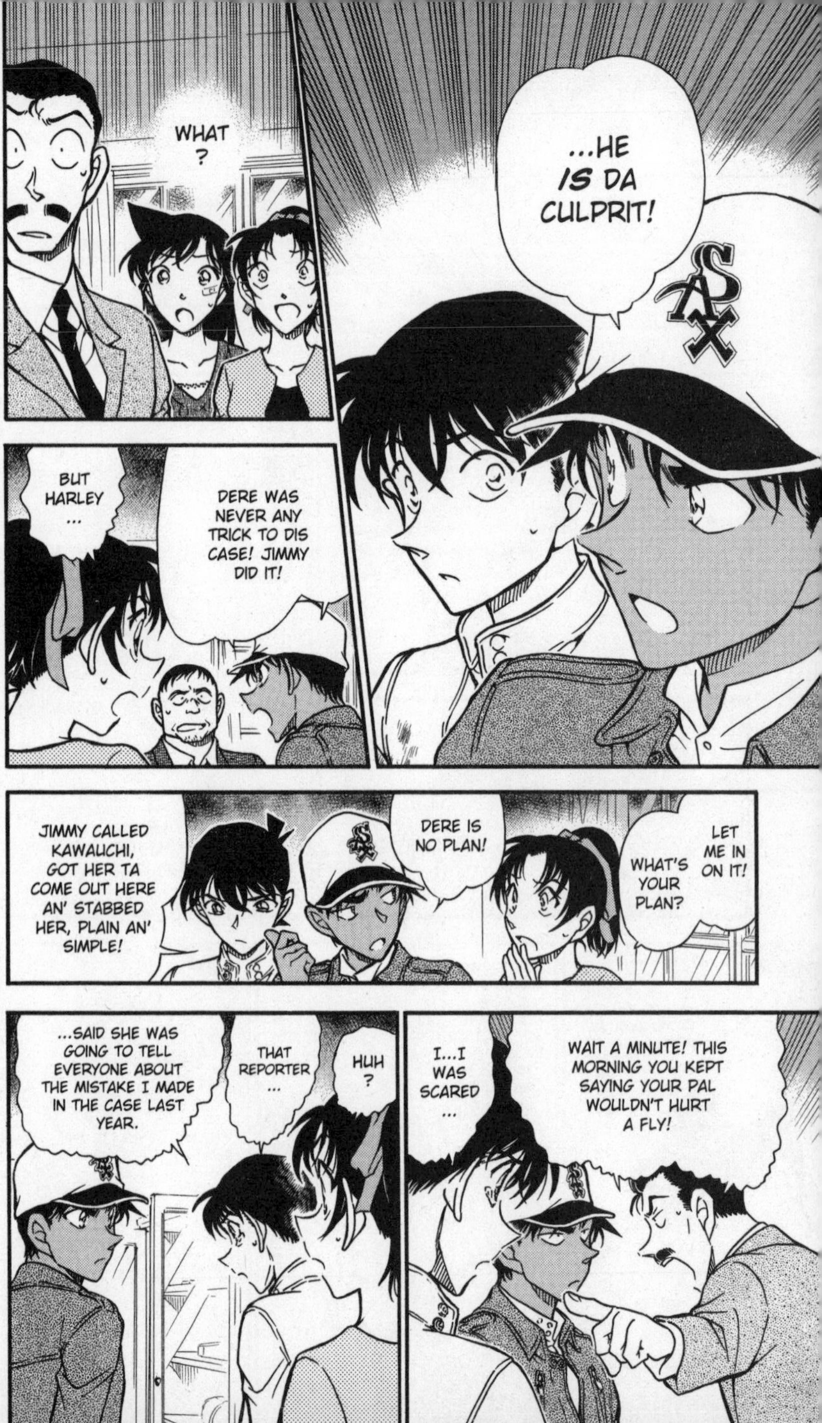
...HE IS DA CULPRIT!
WHAT?
DERE WAS NEVER ANY TRICK TO DIS CASE! JIMMY DID IT!
BUT HARLEY...
LET ME IN ON IT!
WHAT'S YOUR PLAN?
DERE IS NO PLAN!
JIMMY CALLED KAWAUCHI, GOT HER TA COME OUT HERE AN' STABBED HER, PLAIN AN' SIMPLE!
WAIT A MINUTE! THIS MORNING YOU KEPT SAYING YOUR PAL WOULDN'T HURT A FLY!
I...I WAS SCARED...
HUH?
THAT REPORTER...
...SAID SHE WAS GOING TO TELL EVERYONE ABOUT THE MISTAKE I MADE IN THE CASE LAST YEAR.

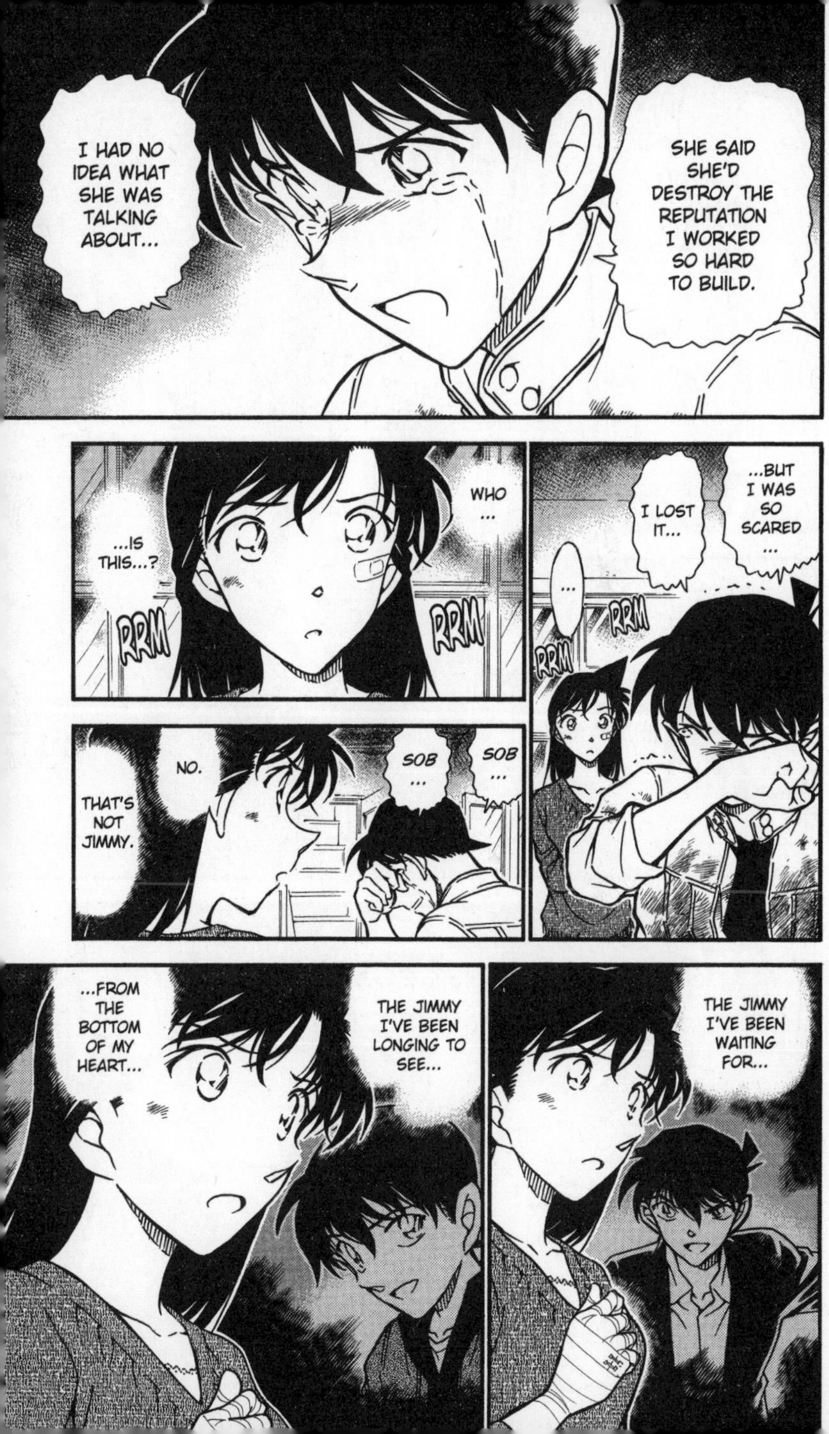
SHE SAID SHE'D DESTROY THE REPUTATION I WORKED SO HARD TO BUILD.
I HAD NO IDEA WHAT SHE WAS TALKING ABOUT...
...BUT I WAS SO SCARED ...
I LOST IT...
...
RRM
RRM
WHO ...
...IS THIS...?
RRM
RRM
SOB ...
SOB ...
NO.
THAT'S NOT JIMMY.
THE JIMMY I'VE BEEN WAITING FOR...
THE JIMMY I'VE BEEN LONGING TO SEE...
...FROM THE BOTTOM OF MY HEART...

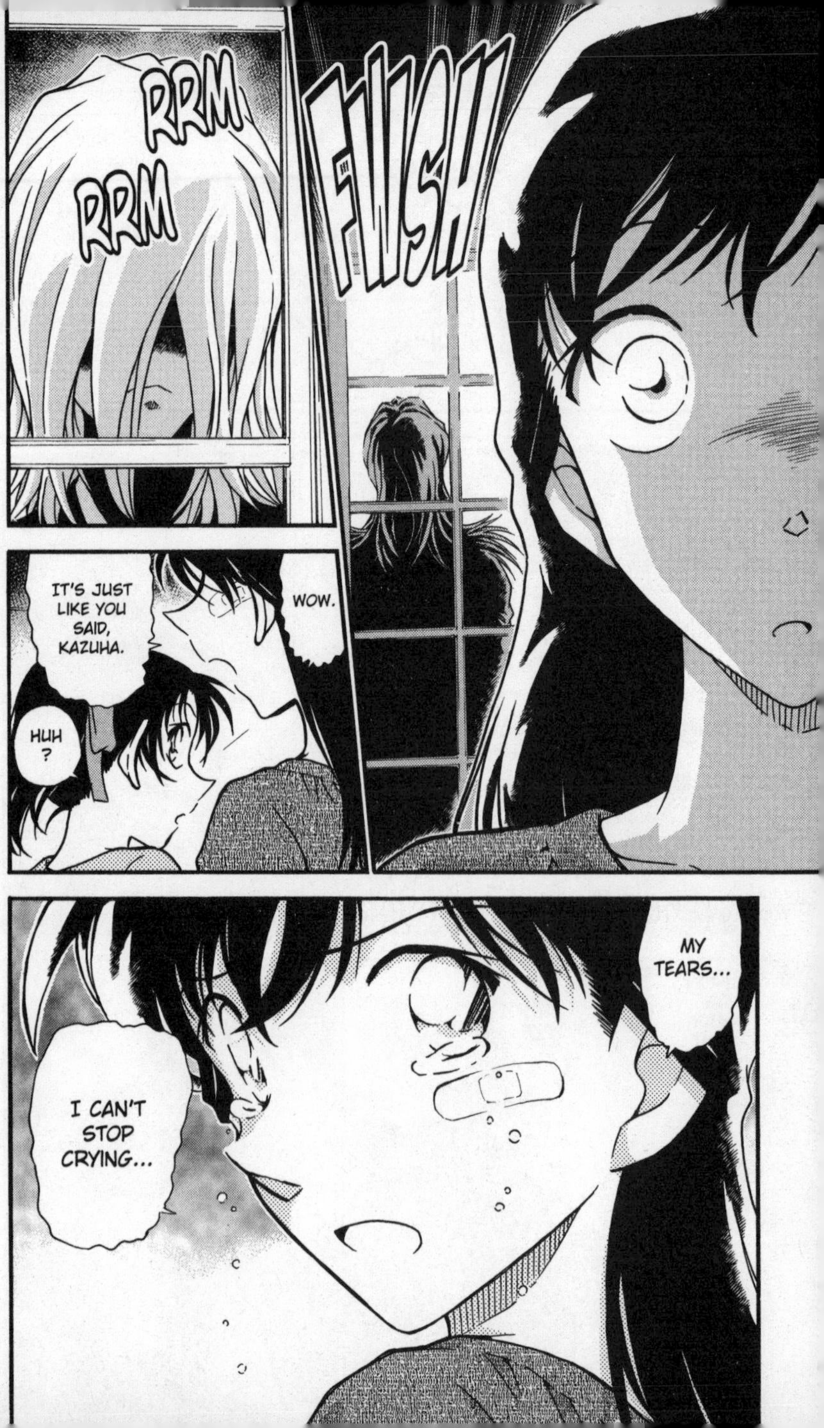
FWSH
RRM RRM
WOW.
IT'S JUST LIKE YOU SAID, KAZUHA.
HUH?
MY TEARS...
I CAN'T STOP CRYING...

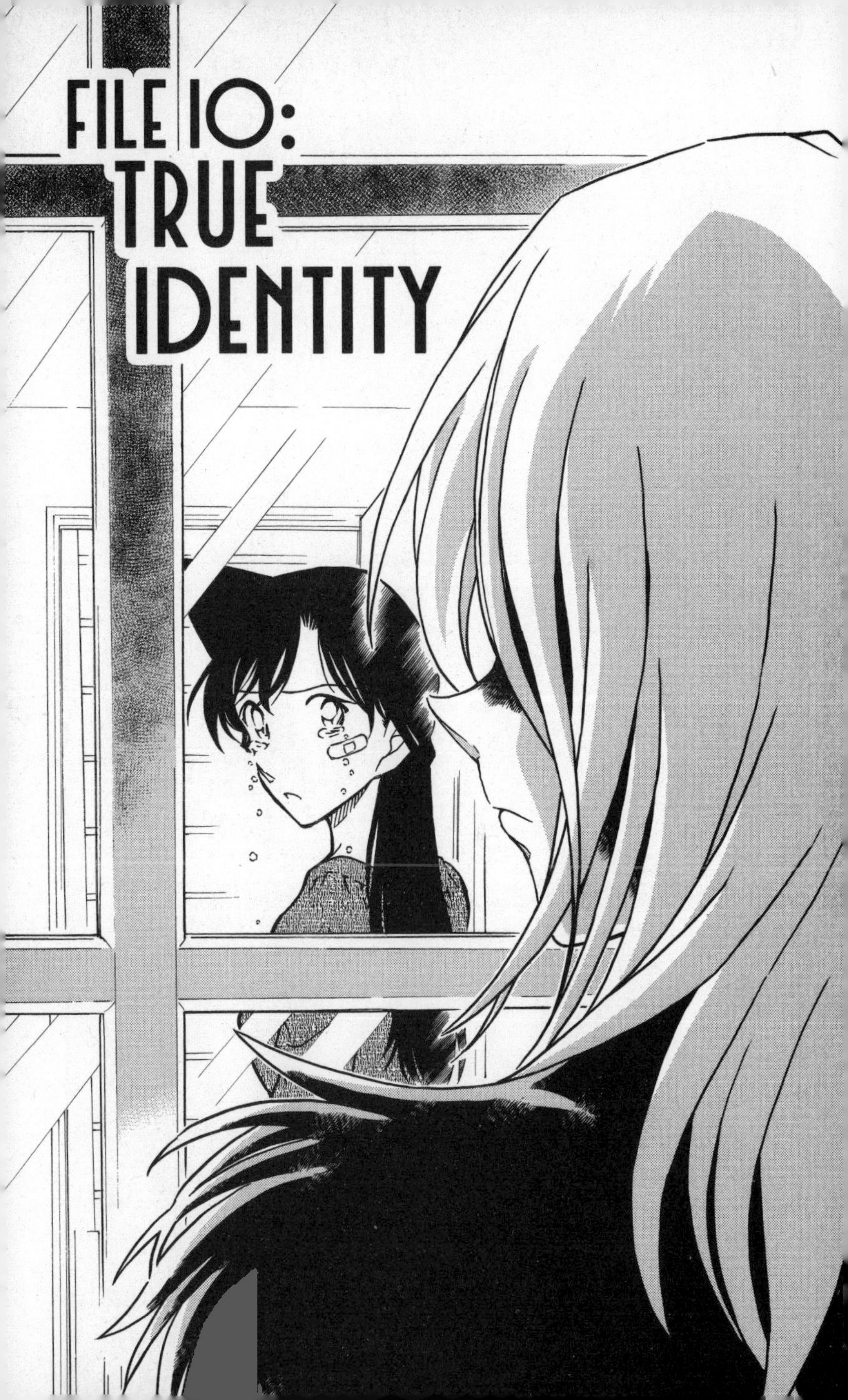
FILE 10:
TRUE
IDENTITY

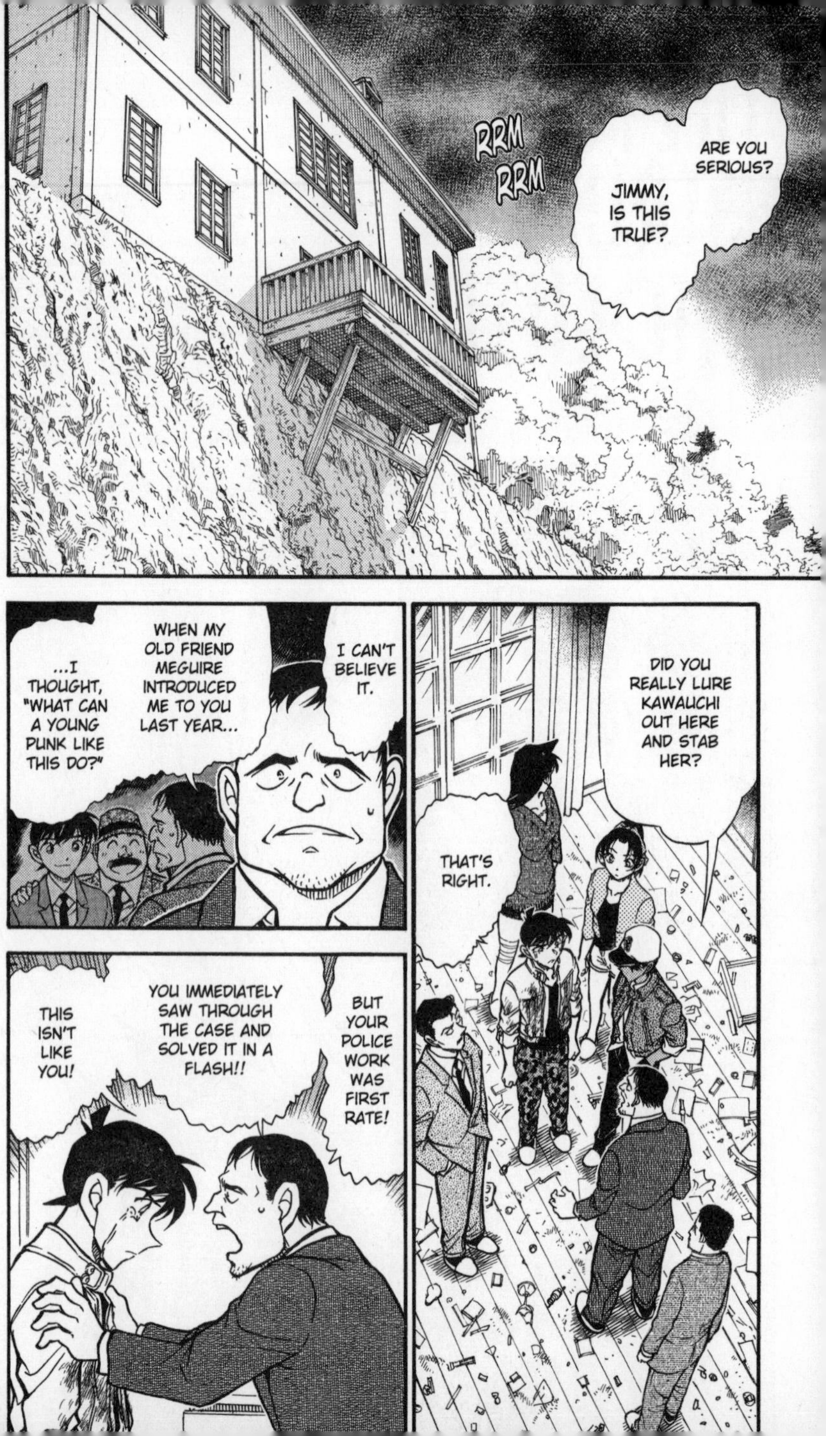
ARE YOU SERIOUS?
JIMMY, IS THIS TRUE?
RRM RRM
DID YOU REALLY LURE KAWAUCHI OUT HERE AND STAB HER?
THAT'S RIGHT.
I CAN'T BELIEVE IT.
WHEN MY OLD FRIEND MEGUIRE INTRODUCED ME TO YOU LAST YEAR...
...I THOUGHT, "WHAT CAN A YOUNG PUNK LIKE THIS DO?"
BUT YOUR POLICE WORK WAS FIRST RATE!
YOU IMMEDIATELY SAW THROUGH THE CASE AND SOLVED IT IN A FLASH!!
THIS ISN'T LIKE YOU!

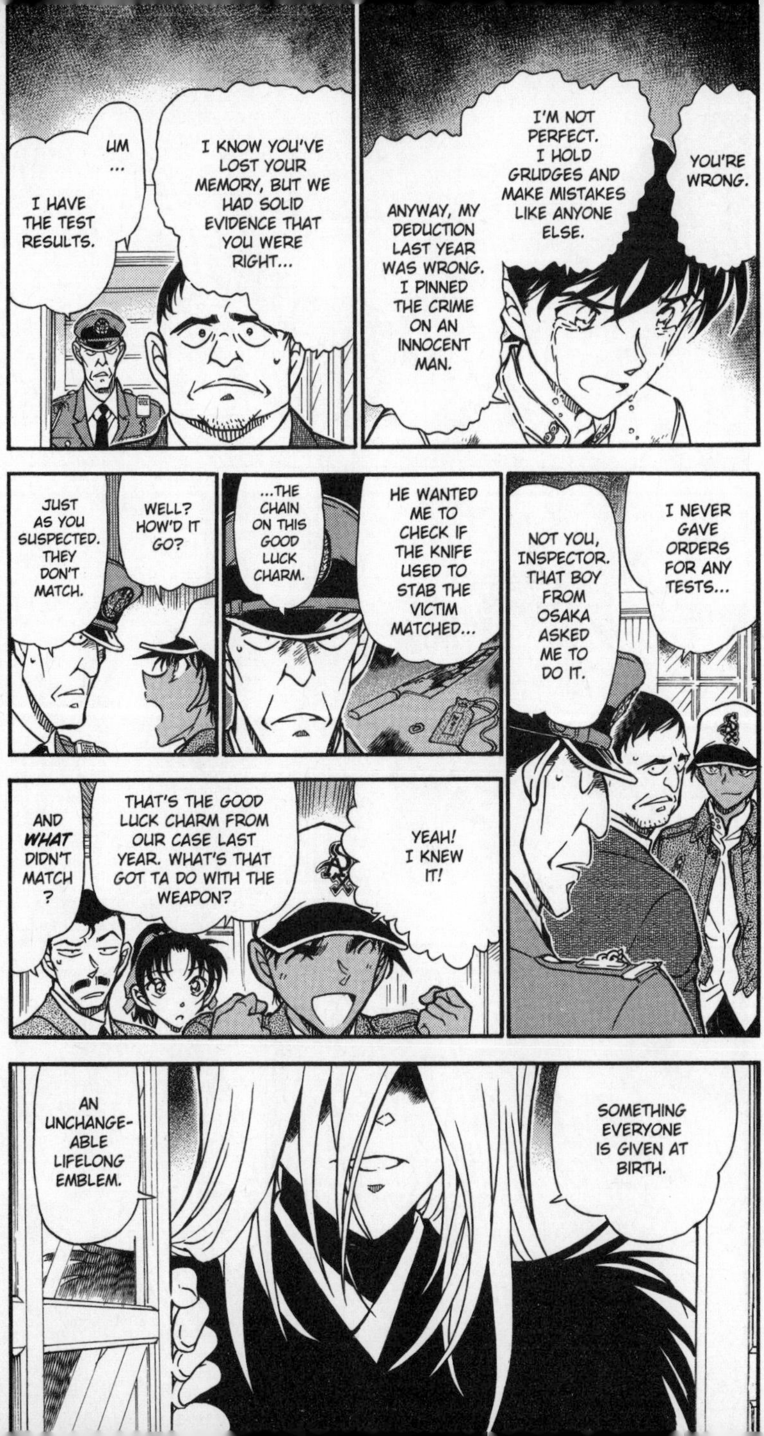
YOU'RE WRONG.
I'M NOT PERFECT. I HOLD GRUDGES AND MAKE MISTAKES LIKE ANYONE ELSE.
ANYWAY, MY DEDUCTION LAST YEAR WAS WRONG. I PINNED THE CRIME ON AN INNOCENT MAN.
I KNOW YOU'VE LOST YOUR MEMORY, BUT WE HAD SOLID EVIDENCE THAT YOU WERE RIGHT...
UM ...
I HAVE THE TEST RESULTS.
I NEVER GAVE ORDERS FOR ANY TESTS...
NOT YOU, INSPECTOR. THAT BOY FROM OSAKA ASKED ME TO DO IT.
HE WANTED ME TO CHECK IF THE KNIFE USED TO STAB THE VICTIM MATCHED...
...THE CHAIN ON THIS GOOD LUCK CHARM.
WELL? HOW'D IT GO?
JUST AS YOU SUSPECTED. THEY DON'T MATCH.
YEAH! I KNEW IT!
THAT'S THE GOOD LUCK CHARM FROM OUR CASE LAST YEAR. WHAT'S THAT GOT TA DO WITH THE WEAPON?
AND *WHAT* DIDN'T MATCH?
SOMETHING EVERYONE IS GIVEN AT BIRTH.
AN UNCHANGEABLE LIFELONG EMBLEM.

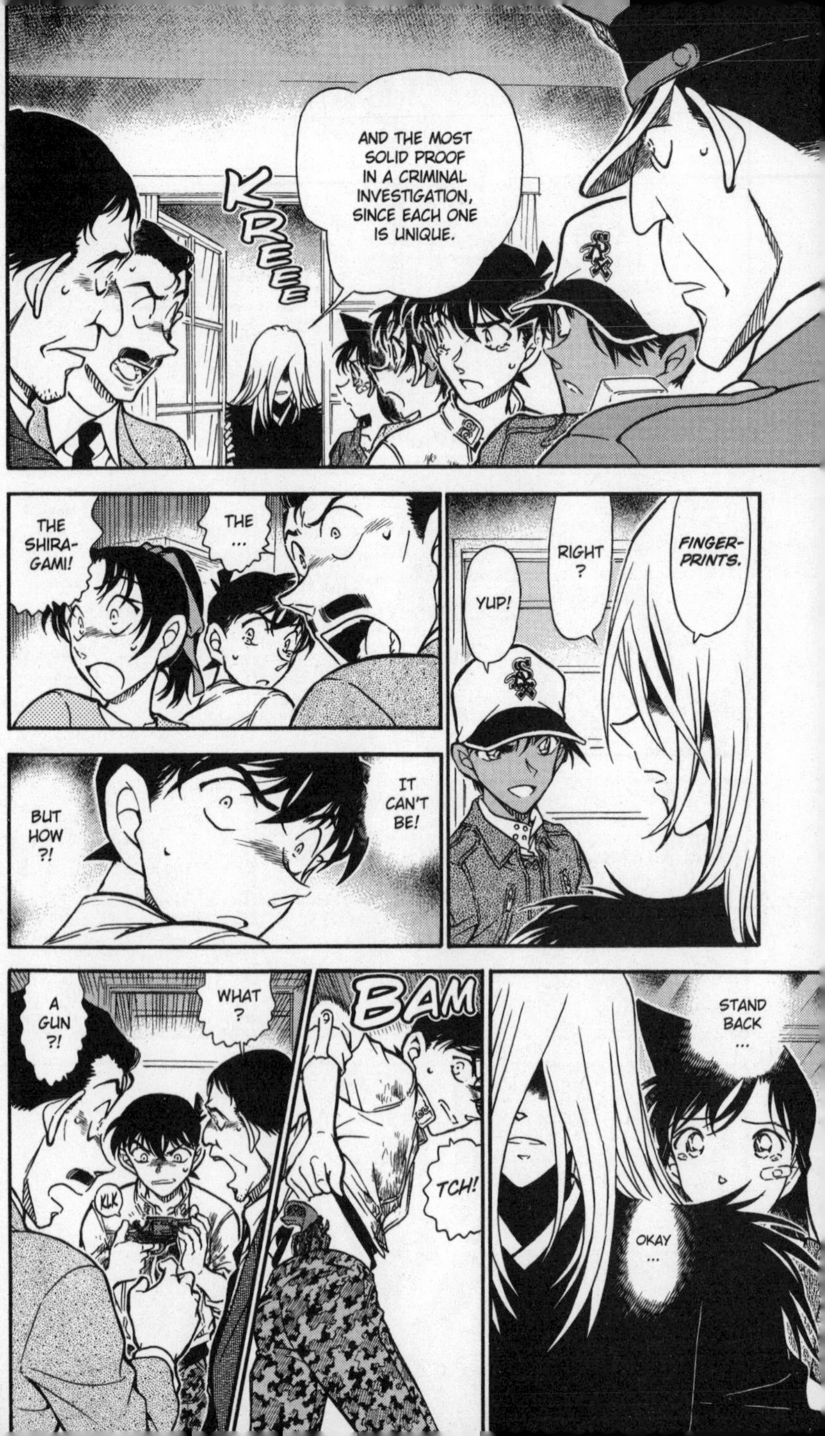
AND THE MOST SOLID PROOF IN A CRIMINAL INVESTIGATION, SINCE EACH ONE IS UNIQUE.
KREEE
FINGER-PRINTS.
RIGHT?
YUP!
THE ...
THE SHIRA-GAMI!
IT CAN'T BE!
BUT HOW?!
STAND BACK ...
OKAY ...
BAM
TCH!
WHAT?
A GUN?!
KLK

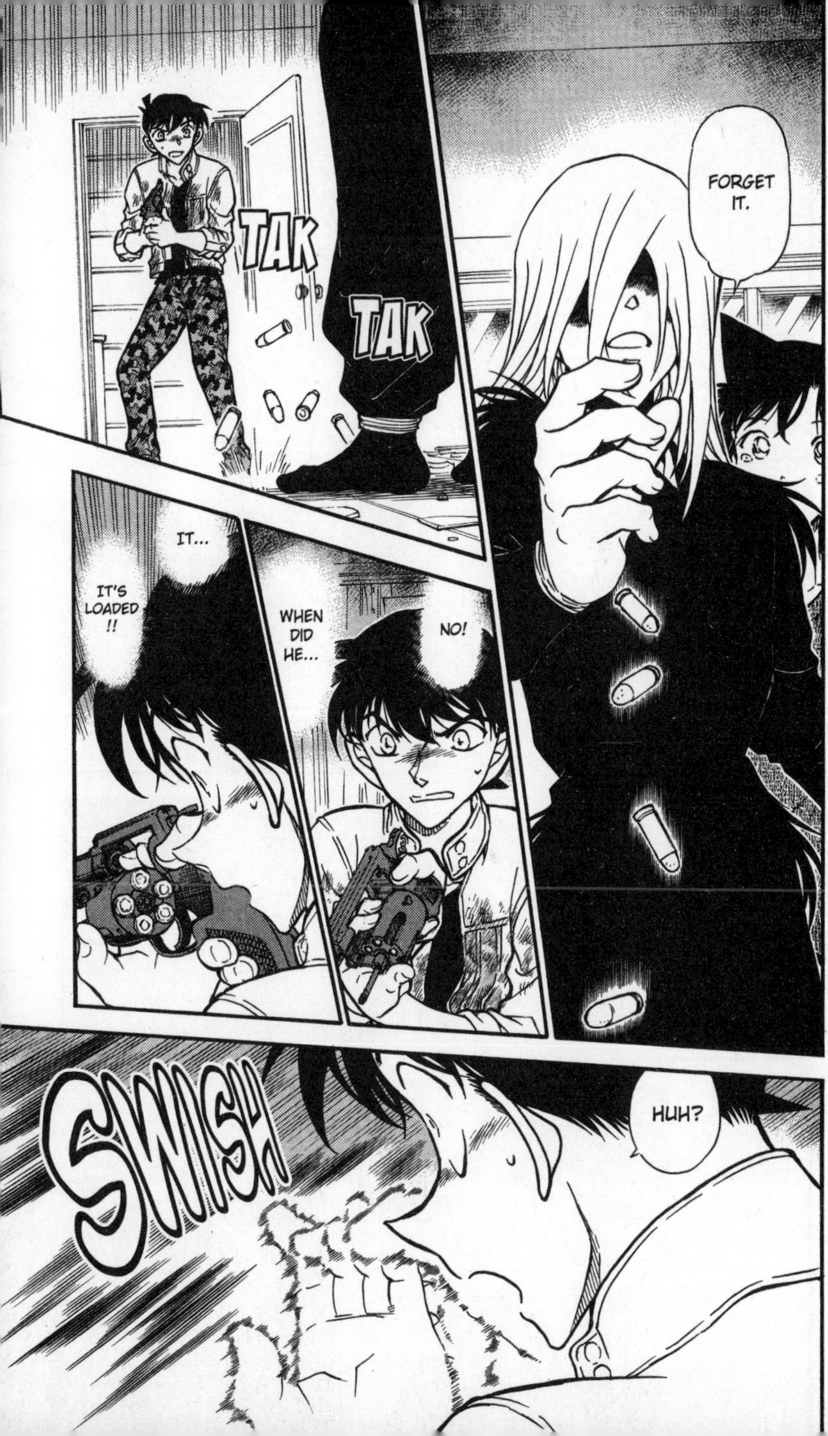

FORGET IT.
TAK
TAK
NO!
WHEN DID HE...
IT...
IT'S LOADED!!
HUH?
SWISH

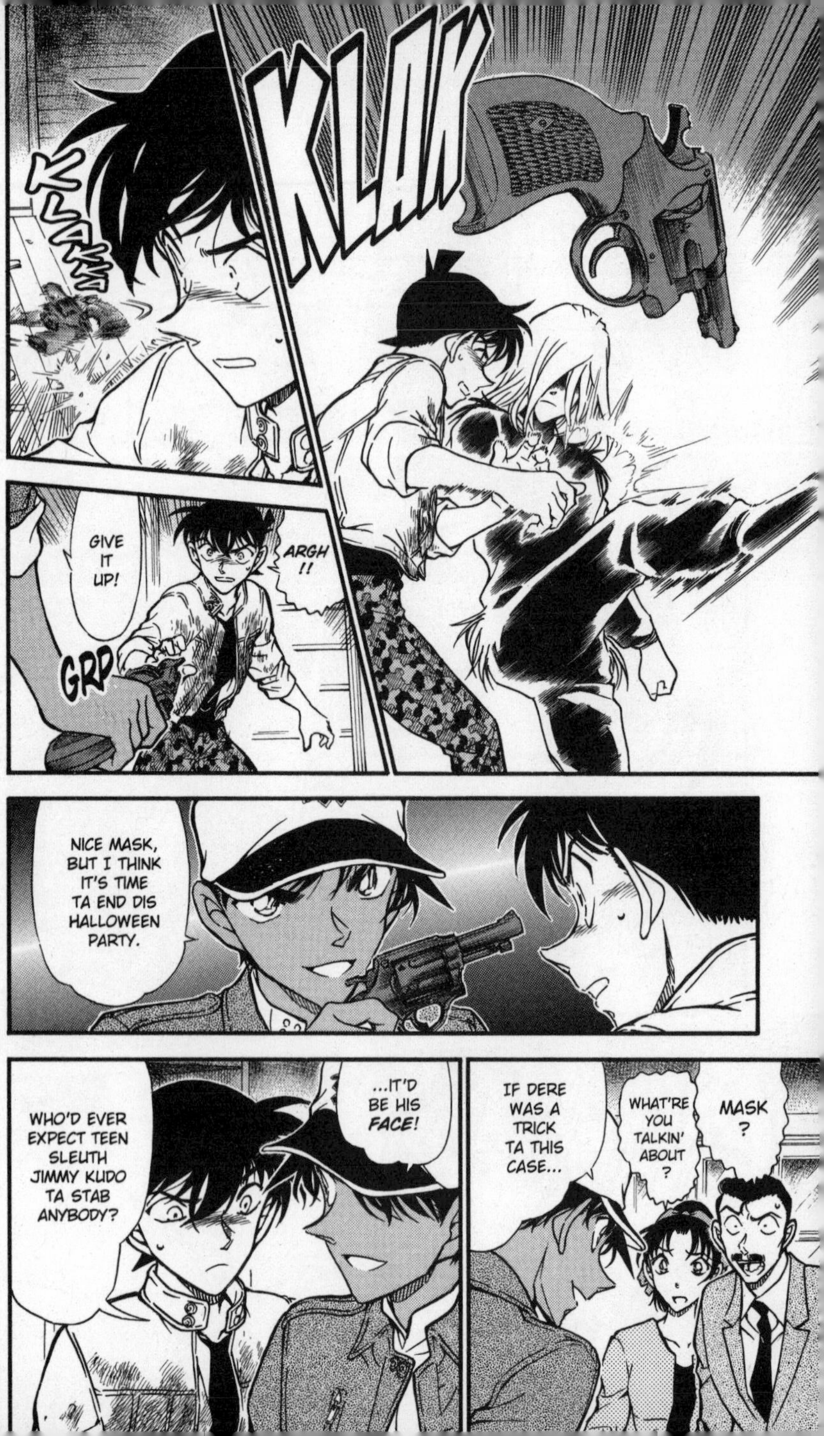
KLAK
KLAKK
ARGH !!
GIVE IT UP!
GRP
NICE MASK, BUT I THINK IT'S TIME TA END DIS HALLOWEEN PARTY.
MASK ?
WHAT'RE YOU TALKIN' ABOUT ?
IF DERE WAS A TRICK TA THIS CASE...
...IT'D BE HIS *FACE!*
WHO'D EVER EXPECT TEEN SLEUTH JIMMY KUDO TA STAB ANYBODY?

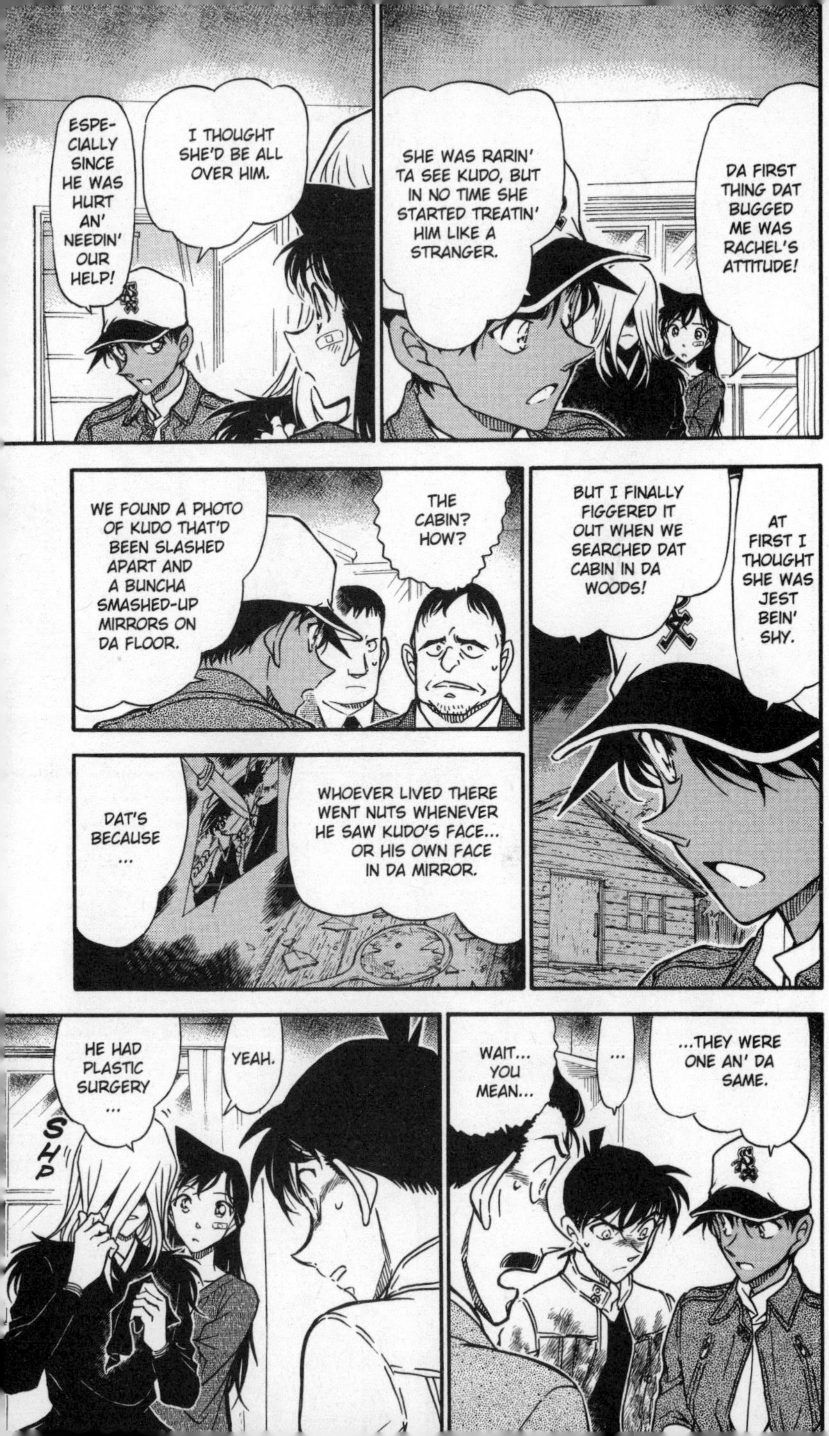
DA FIRST THING DAT BUGGED ME WAS RACHEL'S ATTITUDE!
SHE WAS RARIN' TA SEE KUDO, BUT IN NO TIME SHE STARTED TREATIN' HIM LIKE A STRANGER.
I THOUGHT SHE'D BE ALL OVER HIM.
ESPE-CIALLY SINCE HE WAS HURT AN' NEEDIN' OUR HELP!
AT FIRST I THOUGHT SHE WAS JEST BEIN' SHY.
BUT I FINALLY FIGGERED IT OUT WHEN WE SEARCHED DAT CABIN IN DA WOODS!
THE CABIN? HOW?
WE FOUND A PHOTO OF KUDO THAT'D BEEN SLASHED APART AND A BUNCHA SMASHED-UP MIRRORS ON DA FLOOR.
WHOEVER LIVED THERE WENT NUTS WHENEVER HE SAW KUDO'S FACE... OR HIS OWN FACE IN DA MIRROR.
DAT'S BECAUSE ...
...THEY WERE ONE AN' DA SAME.
...
WAIT... YOU MEAN...
YEAH.
HE HAD PLASTIC SURGERY ...
SHP

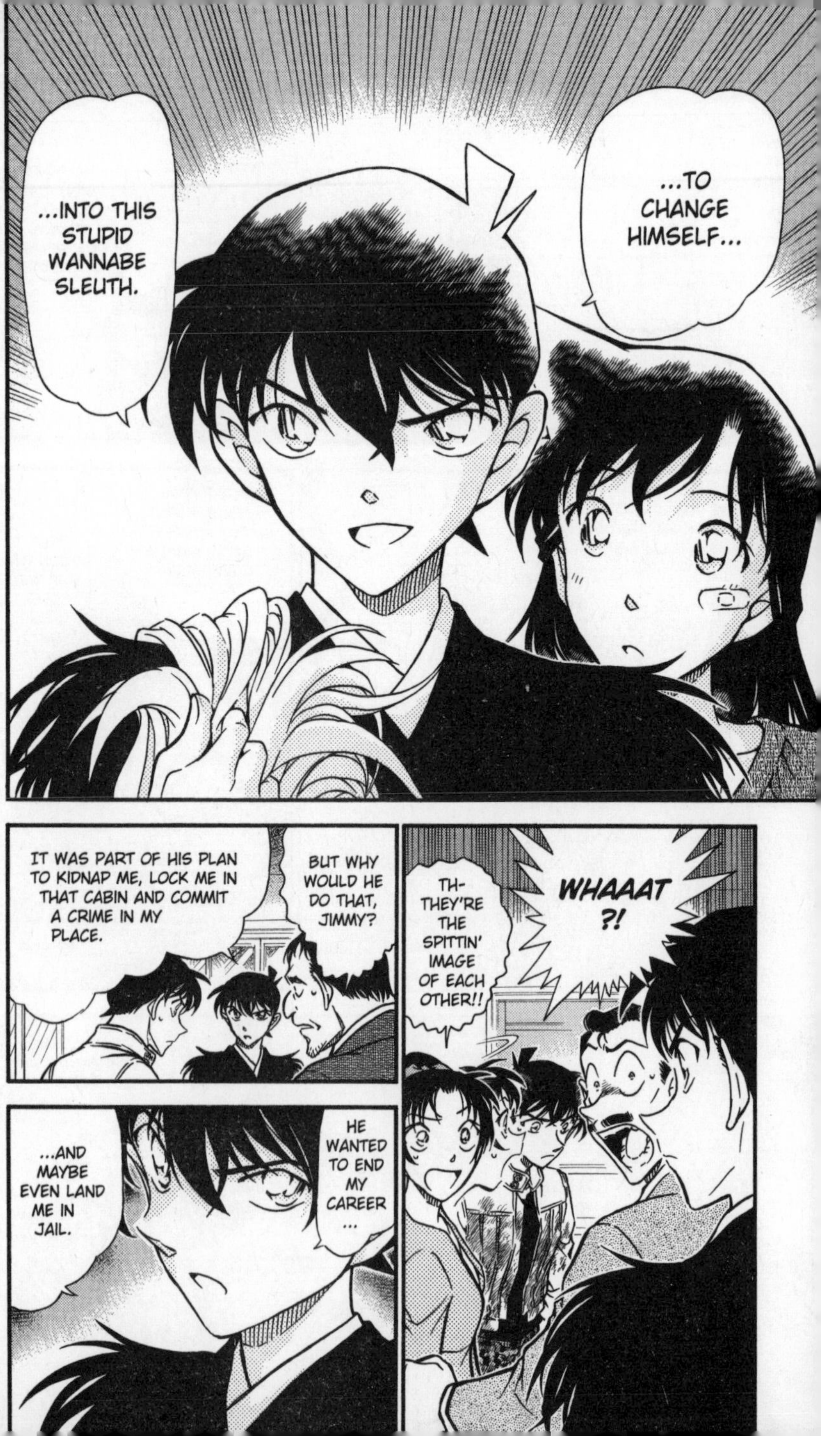
...TO CHANGE HIMSELF...
...INTO THIS STUPID WANNABE SLEUTH.
WHAAAT?!
TH-THEY'RE THE SPITTIN' IMAGE OF EACH OTHER!!
BUT WHY WOULD HE DO THAT, JIMMY?
IT WAS PART OF HIS PLAN TO KIDNAP ME, LOCK ME IN THAT CABIN AND COMMIT A CRIME IN MY PLACE.
HE WANTED TO END MY CAREER...
...AND MAYBE EVEN LAND ME IN JAIL.

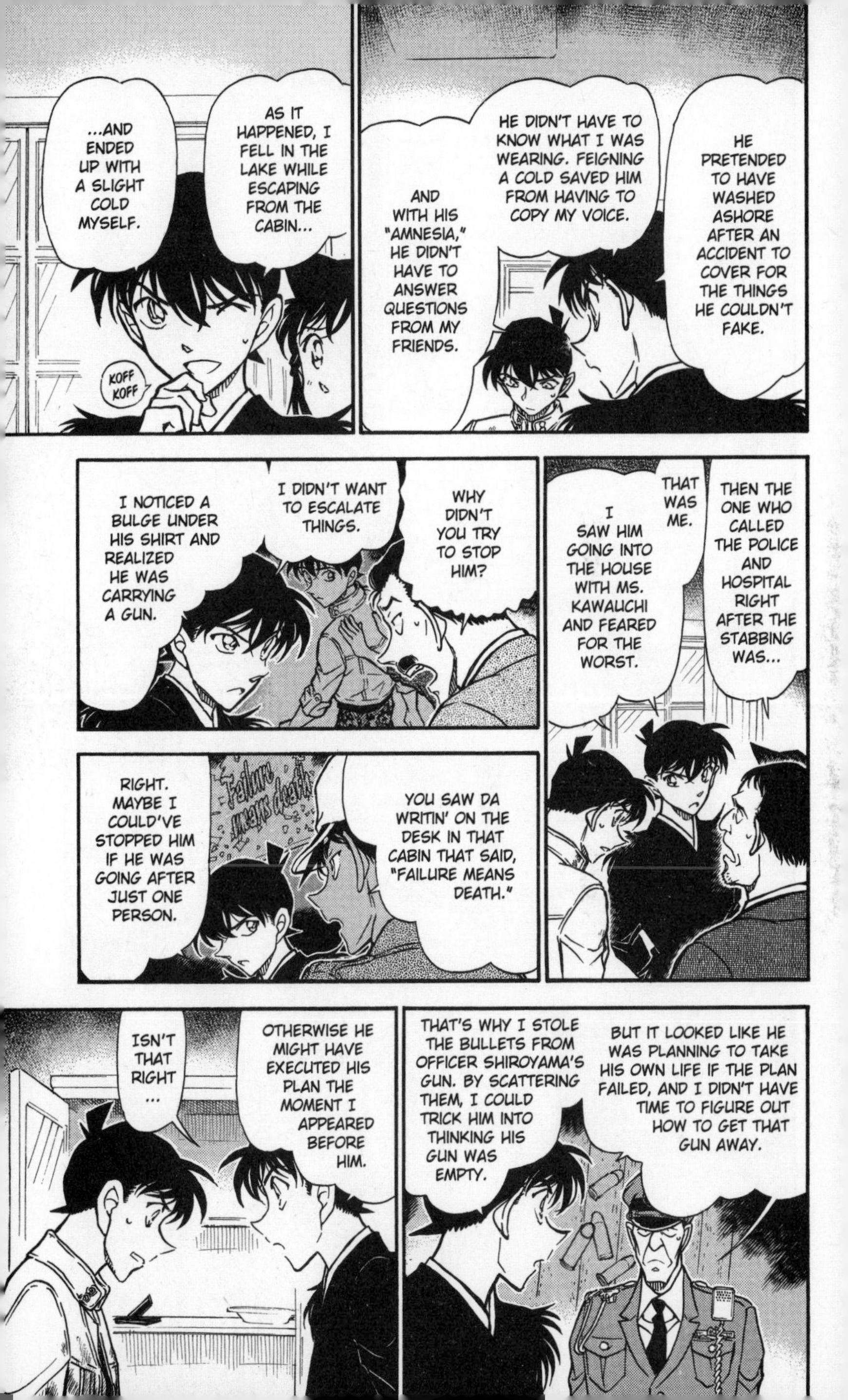
HE PRETENDED TO HAVE WASHED ASHORE AFTER AN ACCIDENT TO COVER FOR THE THINGS HE COULDN'T FAKE.
HE DIDN'T HAVE TO KNOW WHAT I WAS WEARING. FEIGNING A COLD SAVED HIM FROM HAVING TO COPY MY VOICE.
AND WITH HIS "AMNESIA," HE DIDN'T HAVE TO ANSWER QUESTIONS FROM MY FRIENDS.
AS IT HAPPENED, I FELL IN THE LAKE WHILE ESCAPING FROM THE CABIN...
...AND ENDED UP WITH A SLIGHT COLD MYSELF.
KOFF KOFF
THEN THE ONE WHO CALLED THE POLICE AND HOSPITAL RIGHT AFTER THE STABBING WAS...
THAT WAS ME.
I SAW HIM GOING INTO THE HOUSE WITH MS. KAWAUCHI AND FEARED FOR THE WORST.
WHY DIDN'T YOU TRY TO STOP HIM?
I DIDN'T WANT TO ESCALATE THINGS.
I NOTICED A BULGE UNDER HIS SHIRT AND REALIZED HE WAS CARRYING A GUN.
YOU SAW DA WRITIN' ON THE DESK IN THAT CABIN THAT SAID, "FAILURE MEANS DEATH."
Failure means death
RIGHT. MAYBE I COULD'VE STOPPED HIM IF HE WAS GOING AFTER JUST ONE PERSON.
BUT IT LOOKED LIKE HE WAS PLANNING TO TAKE HIS OWN LIFE IF THE PLAN FAILED, AND I DIDN'T HAVE TIME TO FIGURE OUT HOW TO GET THAT GUN AWAY.
THAT'S WHY I STOLE THE BULLETS FROM OFFICER SHIROYAMA'S GUN. BY SCATTERING THEM, I COULD TRICK HIM INTO THINKING HIS GUN WAS EMPTY.
OTHERWISE HE MIGHT HAVE EXECUTED HIS PLAN THE MOMENT I APPEARED BEFORE HIM.
ISN'T THAT RIGHT ...

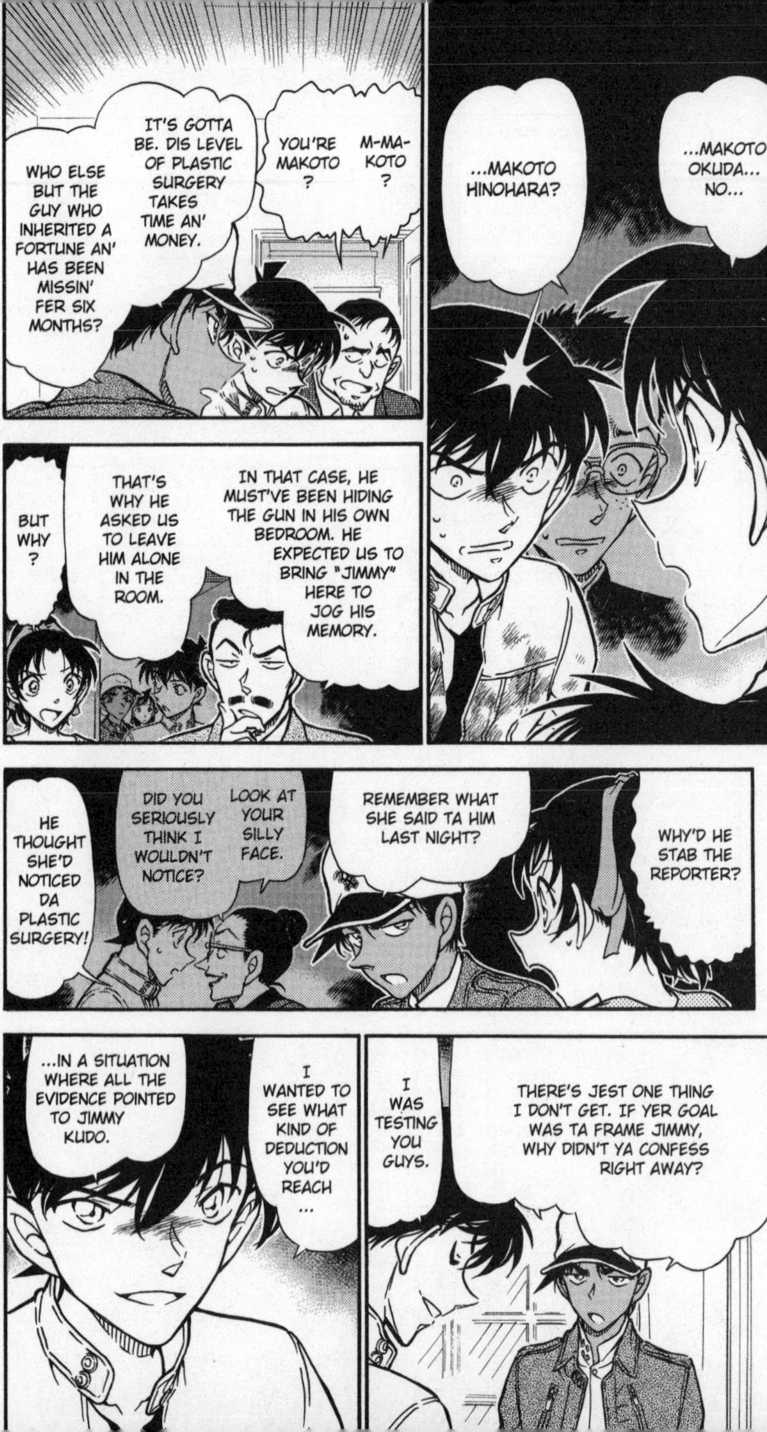
...MAKOTO OKUDA... NO...
...MAKOTO HINOHARA?
M-MA-KOTO?
YOU'RE MAKOTO?
IT'S GOTTA BE. DIS LEVEL OF PLASTIC SURGERY TAKES TIME AN' MONEY.
WHO ELSE BUT THE GUY WHO INHERITED A FORTUNE AN' HAS BEEN MISSIN' FER SIX MONTHS?
IN THAT CASE, HE MUST'VE BEEN HIDING THE GUN IN HIS OWN BEDROOM. HE EXPECTED US TO BRING "JIMMY" HERE TO JOG HIS MEMORY.
THAT'S WHY HE ASKED US TO LEAVE HIM ALONE IN THE ROOM.
BUT WHY?
WHY'D HE STAB THE REPORTER?
REMEMBER WHAT SHE SAID TA HIM LAST NIGHT?
LOOK AT YOUR SILLY FACE.
DID YOU SERIOUSLY THINK I WOULDN'T NOTICE?
HE THOUGHT SHE'D NOTICED DA PLASTIC SURGERY!
THERE'S JEST ONE THING I DON'T GET. IF YER GOAL WAS TA FRAME JIMMY, WHY DIDN'T YA CONFESS RIGHT AWAY?
I WAS TESTING YOU GUYS.
I WANTED TO SEE WHAT KIND OF DEDUCTION YOU'D REACH ...
...IN A SITUATION WHERE ALL THE EVIDENCE POINTED TO JIMMY KUDO.

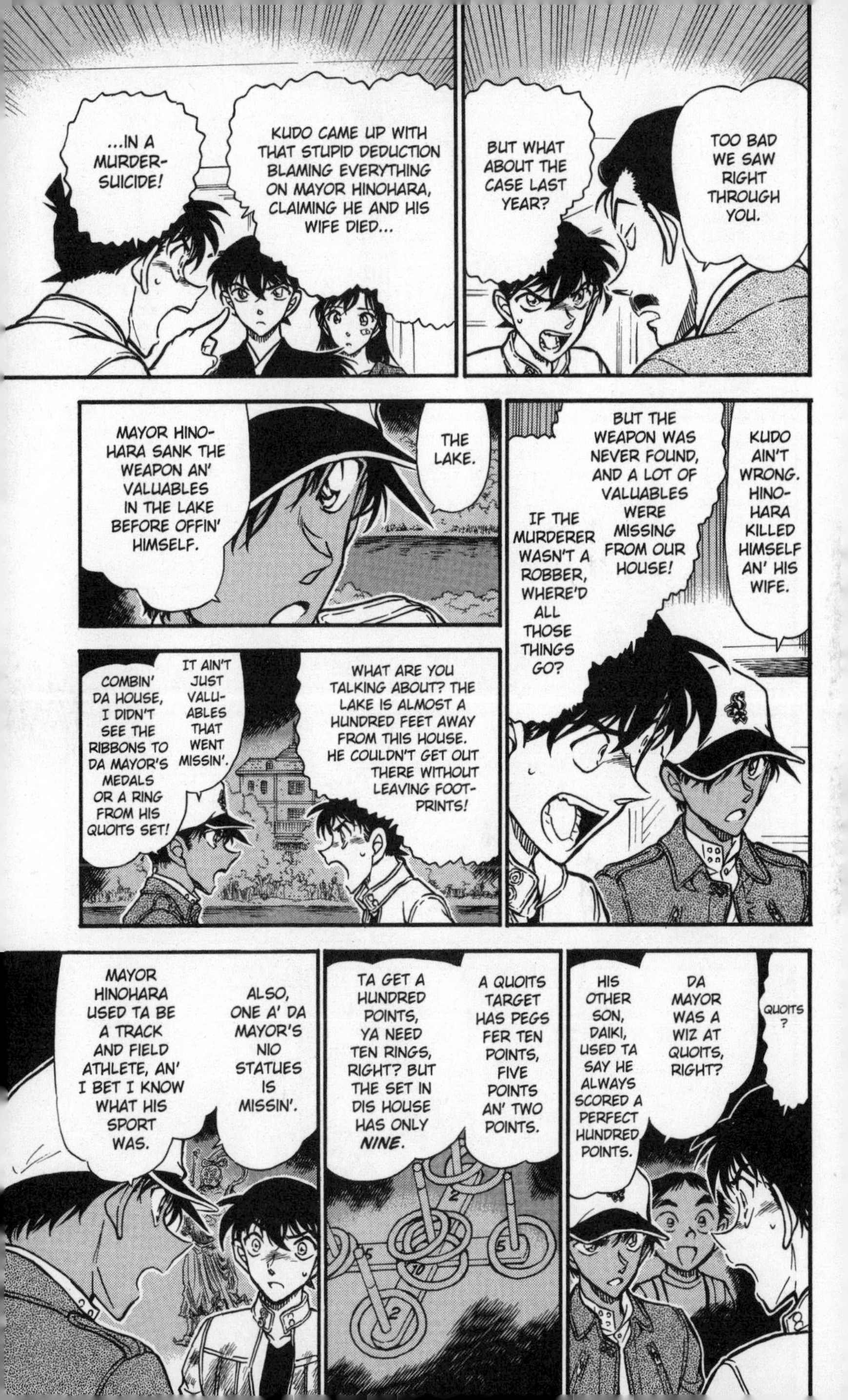
TOO BAD WE SAW RIGHT THROUGH YOU.
BUT WHAT ABOUT THE CASE LAST YEAR?
KUDO CAME UP WITH THAT STUPID DEDUCTION BLAMING EVERYTHING ON MAYOR HINOHARA, CLAIMING HE AND HIS WIFE DIED...
...IN A MURDER-SUICIDE!
KUDO AIN'T WRONG. HINO-HARA KILLED HIMSELF AN' HIS WIFE.
BUT THE WEAPON WAS NEVER FOUND, AND A LOT OF VALUABLES WERE MISSING FROM OUR HOUSE!
IF THE MURDERER WASN'T A ROBBER, WHERE'D ALL THOSE THINGS GO?
THE LAKE.
MAYOR HINO-HARA SANK THE WEAPON AN' VALUABLES IN THE LAKE BEFORE OFFIN' HIMSELF.
WHAT ARE YOU TALKING ABOUT? THE LAKE IS ALMOST A HUNDRED FEET AWAY FROM THIS HOUSE. HE COULDN'T GET OUT THERE WITHOUT LEAVING FOOT-PRINTS!
IT AIN'T JUST VALU-ABLES THAT WENT MISSIN'.
COMBIN' DA HOUSE, I DIDN'T SEE THE RIBBONS TO DA MAYOR'S MEDALS OR A RING FROM HIS QUOITS SET!
QUOITS?
DA MAYOR WAS A WIZ AT QUOITS, RIGHT?
HIS OTHER SON, DAIKI, USED TA SAY HE ALWAYS SCORED A PERFECT HUNDRED POINTS.
A QUOITS TARGET HAS PEGS FER TEN POINTS, FIVE POINTS AN' TWO POINTS.
TA GET A HUNDRED POINTS, YA NEED TEN RINGS, RIGHT? BUT THE SET IN DIS HOUSE HAS ONLY ***NINE***.
ALSO, ONE A' DA MAYOR'S NIO STATUES IS MISSIN'.
MAYOR HINOHARA USED TA BE A TRACK AND FIELD ATHLETE, AN' I BET I KNOW WHAT HIS SPORT WAS.

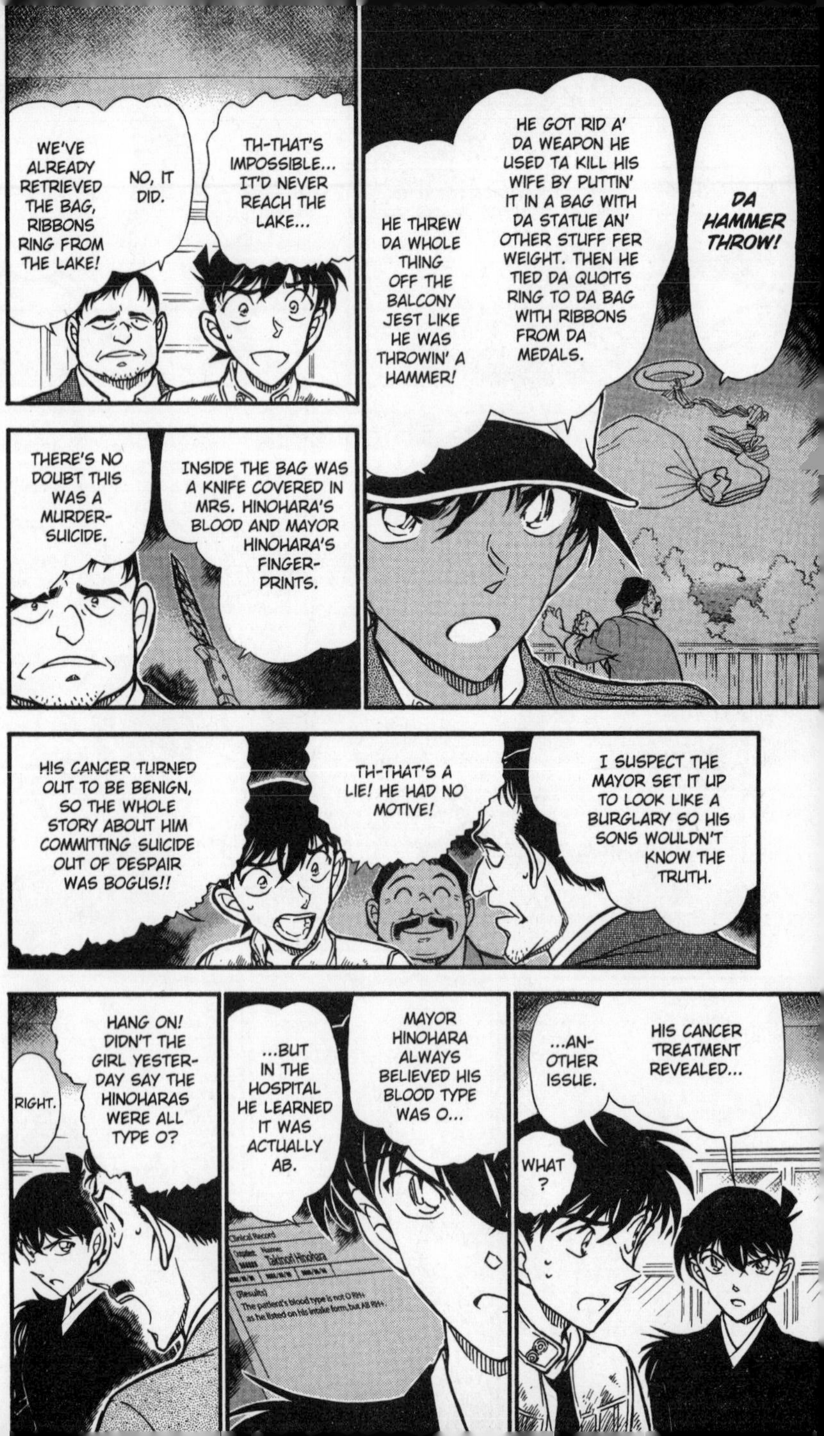
DA HAMMER THROW!
HE GOT RID A' DA WEAPON HE USED TA KILL HIS WIFE BY PUTTIN' IT IN A BAG WITH DA STATUE AN' OTHER STUFF FER WEIGHT. THEN HE TIED DA QUOITS RING TO DA BAG WITH RIBBONS FROM DA MEDALS.
HE THREW DA WHOLE THING OFF THE BALCONY JEST LIKE HE WAS THROWIN' A HAMMER!
TH-THAT'S IMPOSSIBLE... IT'D NEVER REACH THE LAKE...
NO, IT DID.
WE'VE ALREADY RETRIEVED THE BAG, RIBBONS RING FROM THE LAKE!
INSIDE THE BAG WAS A KNIFE COVERED IN MRS. HINOHARA'S BLOOD AND MAYOR HINOHARA'S FINGER-PRINTS.
THERE'S NO DOUBT THIS WAS A MURDER-SUICIDE.
I SUSPECT THE MAYOR SET IT UP TO LOOK LIKE A BURGLARY SO HIS SONS WOULDN'T KNOW THE TRUTH.
TH-THAT'S A LIE! HE HAD NO MOTIVE!
HIS CANCER TURNED OUT TO BE BENIGN, SO THE WHOLE STORY ABOUT HIM COMMITTING SUICIDE OUT OF DESPAIR WAS BOGUS!!
HIS CANCER TREATMENT REVEALED...
...AN-OTHER ISSUE.
WHAT?
MAYOR HINOHARA ALWAYS BELIEVED HIS BLOOD TYPE WAS O...
...BUT IN THE HOSPITAL HE LEARNED IT WAS ACTUALLY AB.
Clinical Record
Takinori Hinohara
(Results)
The patient's blood type is not O Rh+ as he listed on his intake form, but AB Rh+.
HANG ON! DIDN'T THE GIRL YESTER-DAY SAY THE HINOHARAS WERE ALL TYPE O?
RIGHT.

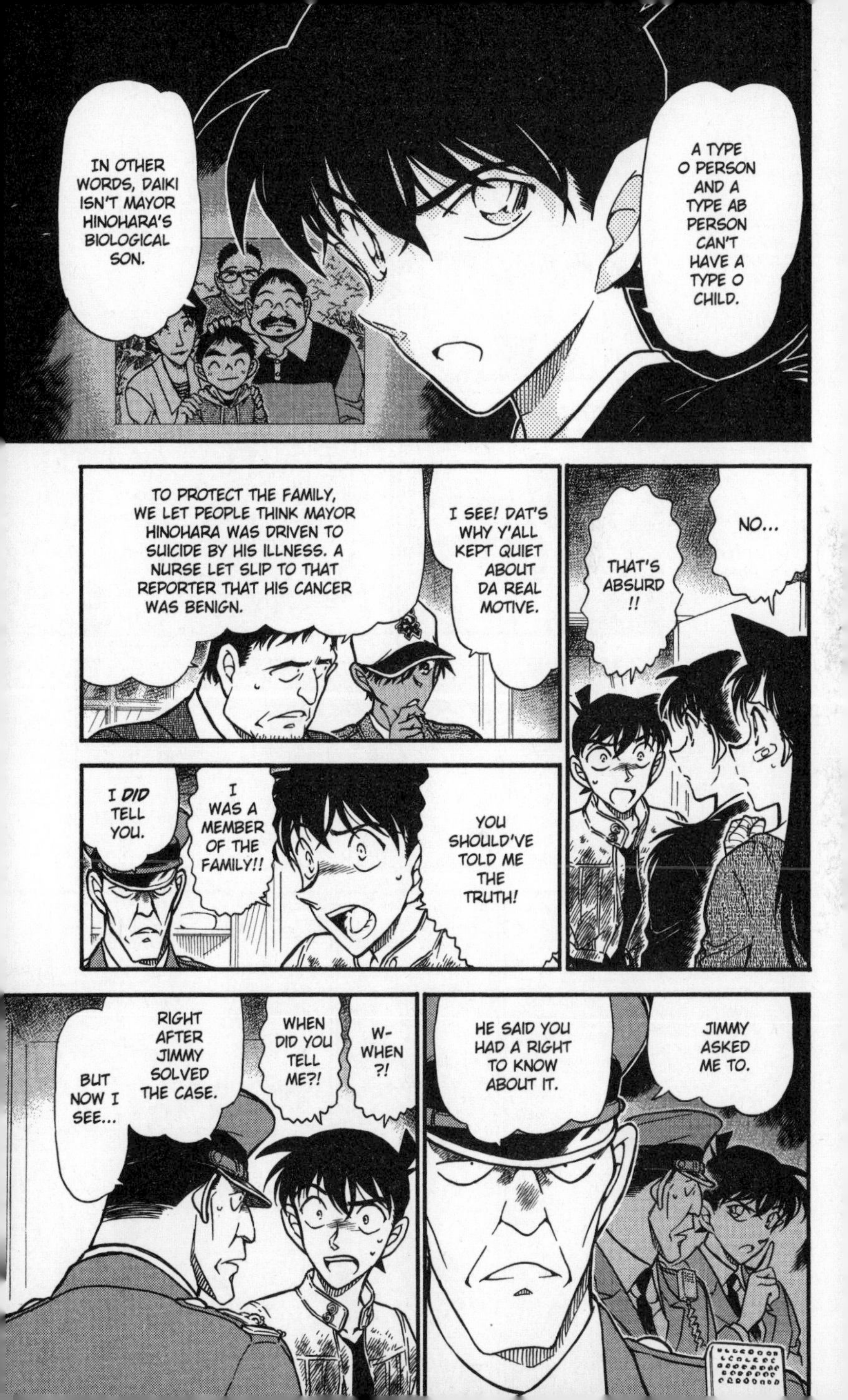
A TYPE O PERSON AND A TYPE AB PERSON CAN'T HAVE A TYPE O CHILD.
IN OTHER WORDS, DAIKI ISN'T MAYOR HINOHARA'S BIOLOGICAL SON.
NO...
THAT'S ABSURD!!
I SEE! DAT'S WHY Y'ALL KEPT QUIET ABOUT DA REAL MOTIVE.
TO PROTECT THE FAMILY, WE LET PEOPLE THINK MAYOR HINOHARA WAS DRIVEN TO SUICIDE BY HIS ILLNESS. A NURSE LET SLIP TO THAT REPORTER THAT HIS CANCER WAS BENIGN.
YOU SHOULD'VE TOLD ME THE TRUTH!
I WAS A MEMBER OF THE FAMILY!!
I *DID* TELL YOU.
JIMMY ASKED ME TO.
HE SAID YOU HAD A RIGHT TO KNOW ABOUT IT.
W-WHEN?!
WHEN DID YOU TELL ME?!
RIGHT AFTER JIMMY SOLVED THE CASE.
BUT NOW I SEE...

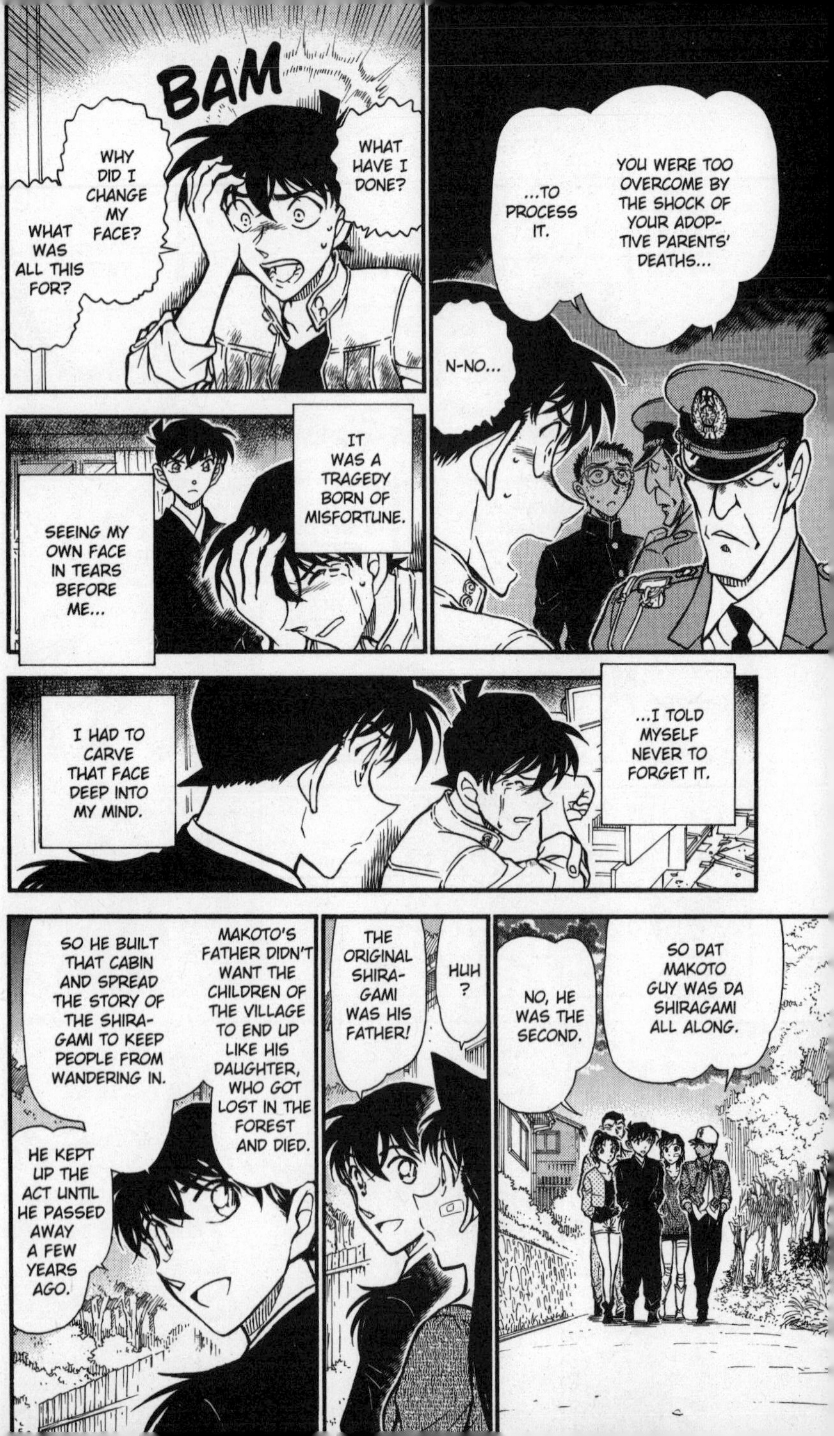
YOU WERE TOO OVERCOME BY THE SHOCK OF YOUR ADOPTIVE PARENTS' DEATHS...
...TO PROCESS IT.
N-NO...
BAM
WHAT HAVE I DONE?
WHY DID I CHANGE MY FACE?
WHAT WAS ALL THIS FOR?
IT WAS A TRAGEDY BORN OF MISFORTUNE.
SEEING MY OWN FACE IN TEARS BEFORE ME...
...I TOLD MYSELF NEVER TO FORGET IT.
I HAD TO CARVE THAT FACE DEEP INTO MY MIND.
SO DAT MAKOTO GUY WAS DA SHIRAGAMI ALL ALONG.
NO, HE WAS THE SECOND.
HUH?
THE ORIGINAL SHIRAGAMI WAS HIS FATHER!
MAKOTO'S FATHER DIDN'T WANT THE CHILDREN OF THE VILLAGE TO END UP LIKE HIS DAUGHTER, WHO GOT LOST IN THE FOREST AND DIED.
SO HE BUILT THAT CABIN AND SPREAD THE STORY OF THE SHIRAGAMI TO KEEP PEOPLE FROM WANDERING IN.
HE KEPT UP THE ACT UNTIL HE PASSED AWAY A FEW YEARS AGO.

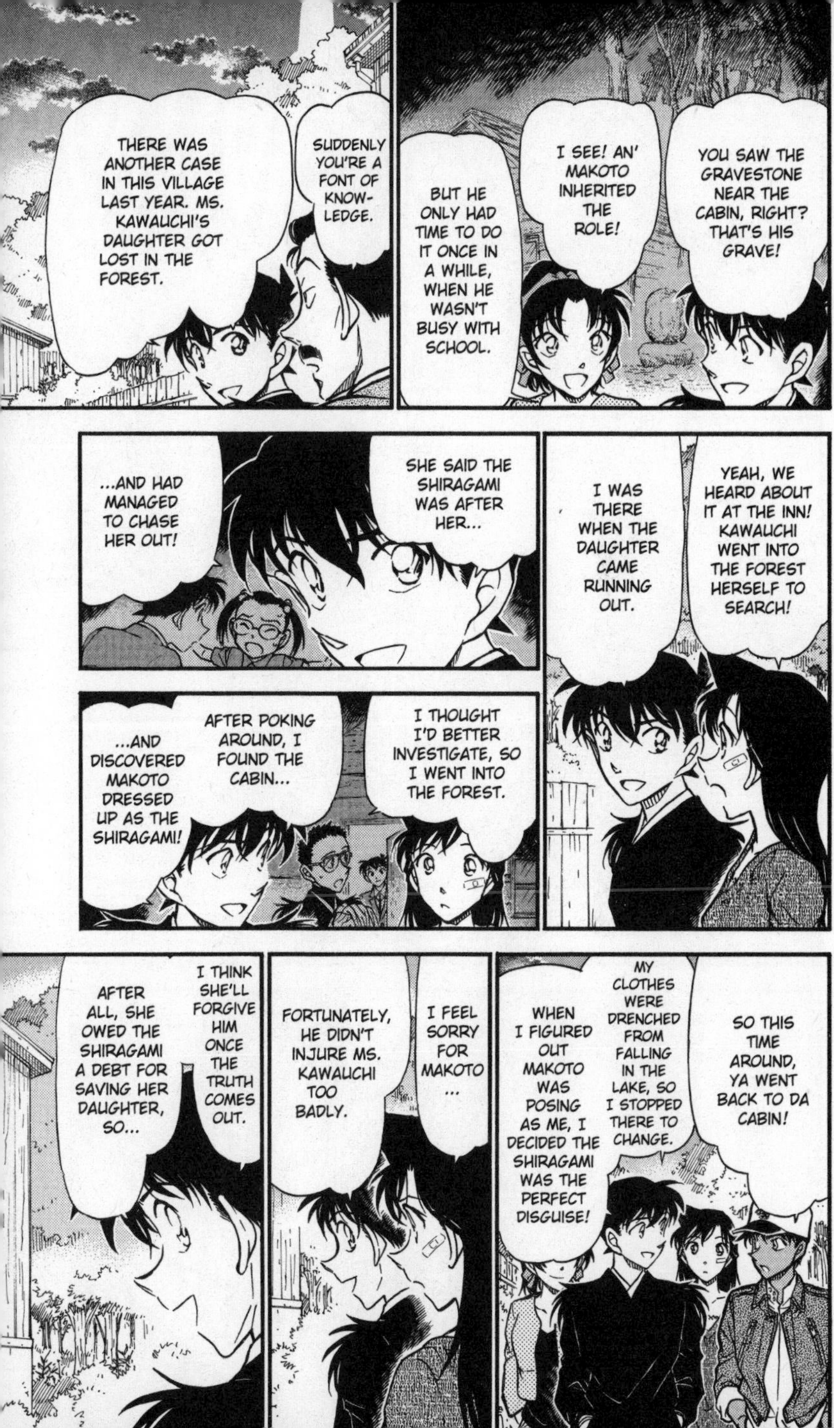
YOU SAW THE GRAVESTONE NEAR THE CABIN, RIGHT? THAT'S HIS GRAVE!
I SEE! AN' MAKOTO INHERITED THE ROLE!
BUT HE ONLY HAD TIME TO DO IT ONCE IN A WHILE, WHEN HE WASN'T BUSY WITH SCHOOL.
SUDDENLY YOU'RE A FONT OF KNOW-LEDGE.
THERE WAS ANOTHER CASE IN THIS VILLAGE LAST YEAR. MS. KAWAUCHI'S DAUGHTER GOT LOST IN THE FOREST.
YEAH, WE HEARD ABOUT IT AT THE INN! KAWAUCHI WENT INTO THE FOREST HERSELF TO SEARCH!
I WAS THERE WHEN THE DAUGHTER CAME RUNNING OUT.
SHE SAID THE SHIRAGAMI WAS AFTER HER...
...AND HAD MANAGED TO CHASE HER OUT!
I THOUGHT I'D BETTER INVESTIGATE, SO I WENT INTO THE FOREST.
AFTER POKING AROUND, I FOUND THE CABIN...
...AND DISCOVERED MAKOTO DRESSED UP AS THE SHIRAGAMI!
SO THIS TIME AROUND, YA WENT BACK TO DA CABIN!
MY CLOTHES WERE DRENCHED FROM FALLING IN THE LAKE, SO I STOPPED THERE TO CHANGE.
WHEN I FIGURED OUT MAKOTO WAS POSING AS ME, I DECIDED THE SHIRAGAMI WAS THE PERFECT DISGUISE!
I FEEL SORRY FOR MAKOTO...
FORTUNATELY, HE DIDN'T INJURE MS. KAWAUCHI TOO BADLY.
I THINK SHE'LL FORGIVE HIM ONCE THE TRUTH COMES OUT.
AFTER ALL, SHE OWED THE SHIRAGAMI A DEBT FOR SAVING HER DAUGHTER, SO...

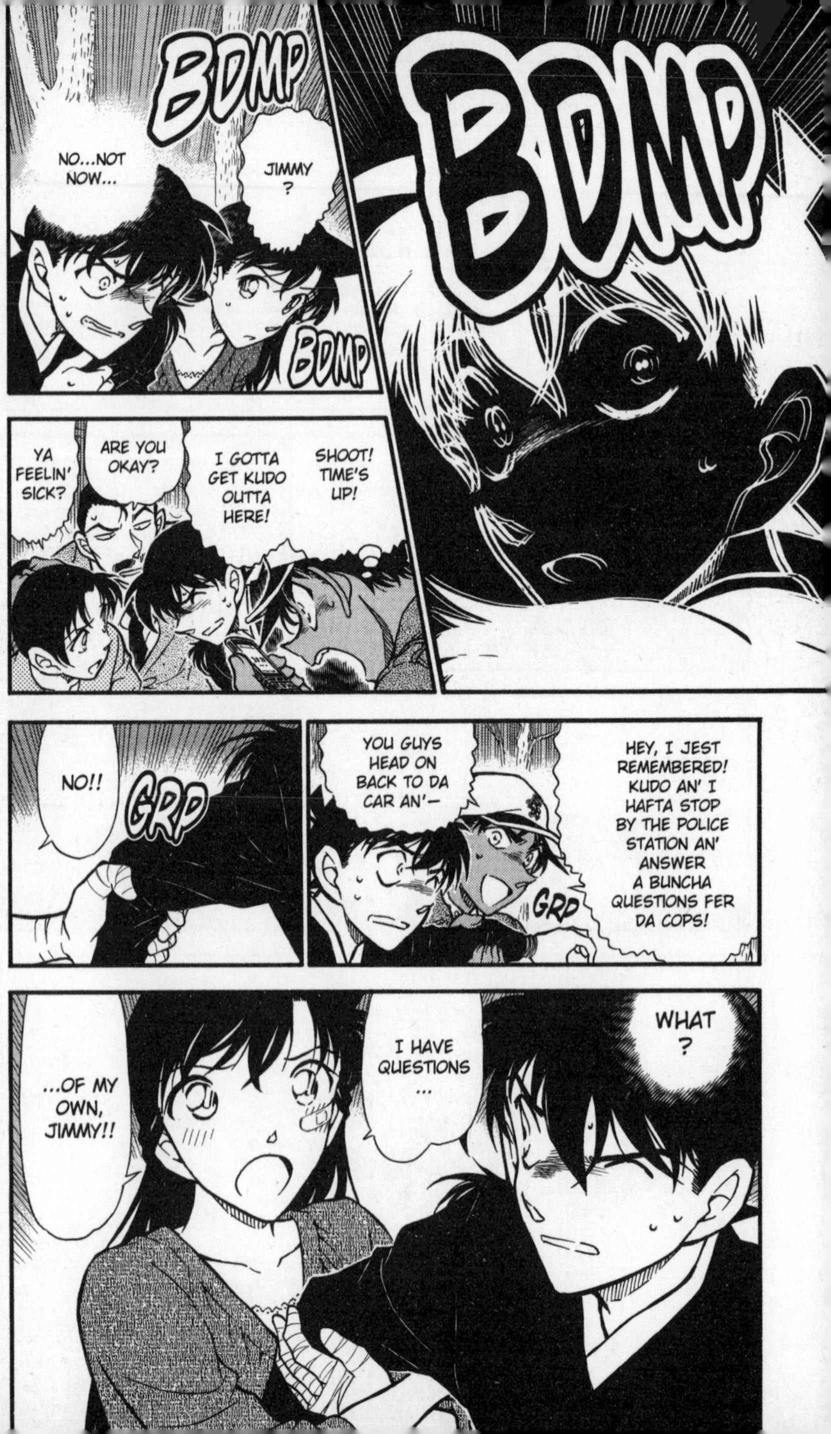
BDMP
BDMP
JIMMY?
NO...NOT NOW...
BDMP
SHOOT! TIME'S UP!
I GOTTA GET KUDO OUTTA HERE!
ARE YOU OKAY?
YA FEELIN' SICK?
HEY, I JEST REMEMBERED! KUDO AN' I HAFTA STOP BY THE POLICE STATION AN' ANSWER A BUNCHA QUESTIONS FER DA COPS!
YOU GUYS HEAD ON BACK TO DA CAR AN'—
GRP
GRP
NO!!
WHAT?
I HAVE QUESTIONS...
...OF MY OWN, JIMMY!!

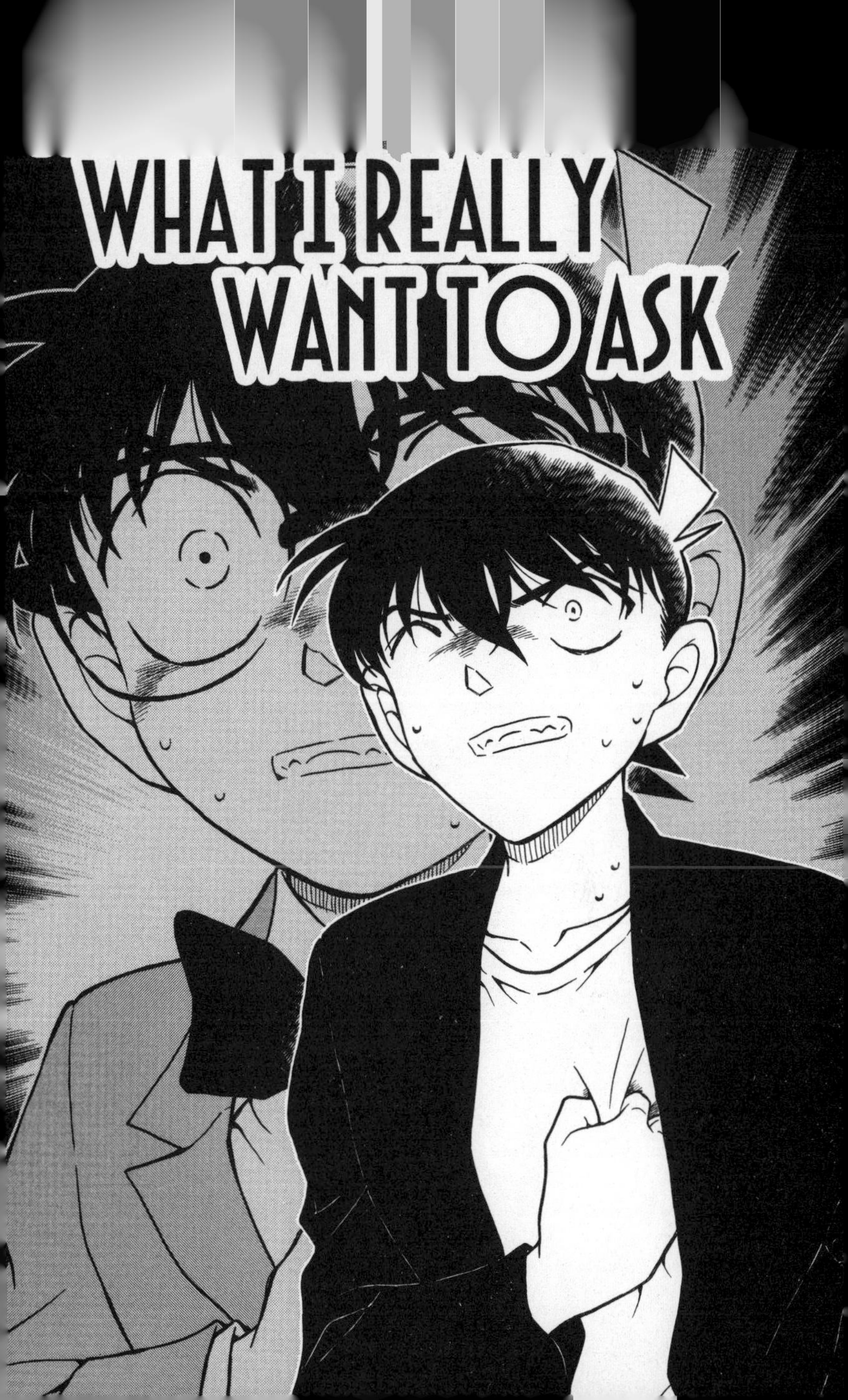
WHAT I REALLY
WANT TO ASK

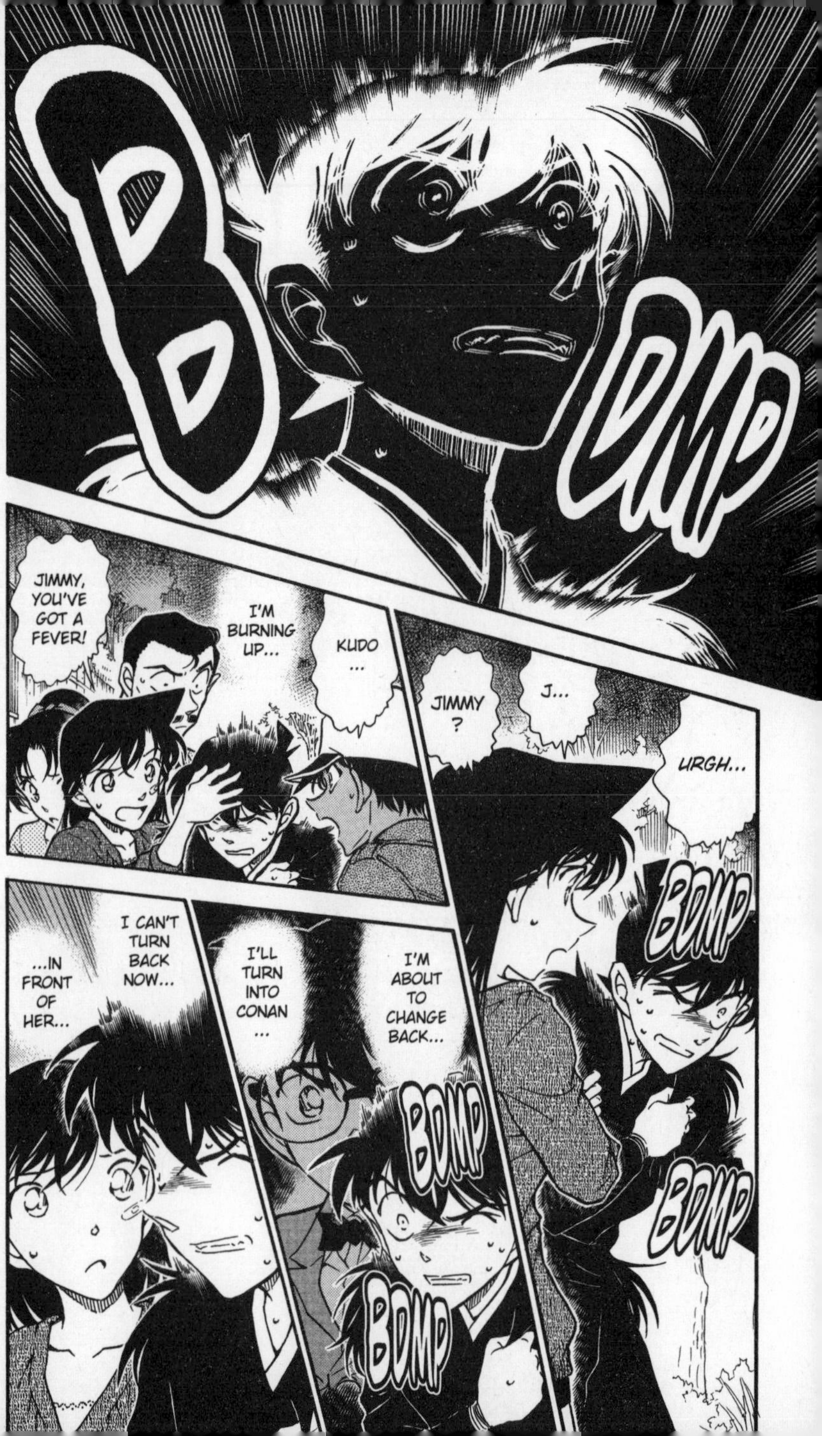
BDMP
J...
JIMMY?
URGH...
BDMP
BDMP
KUDO...
I'M BURNING UP...
JIMMY, YOU'VE GOT A FEVER!
I'M ABOUT TO CHANGE BACK...
I'LL TURN INTO CONAN...
BDMP
BDMP
I CAN'T TURN BACK NOW...
...IN FRONT OF HER...

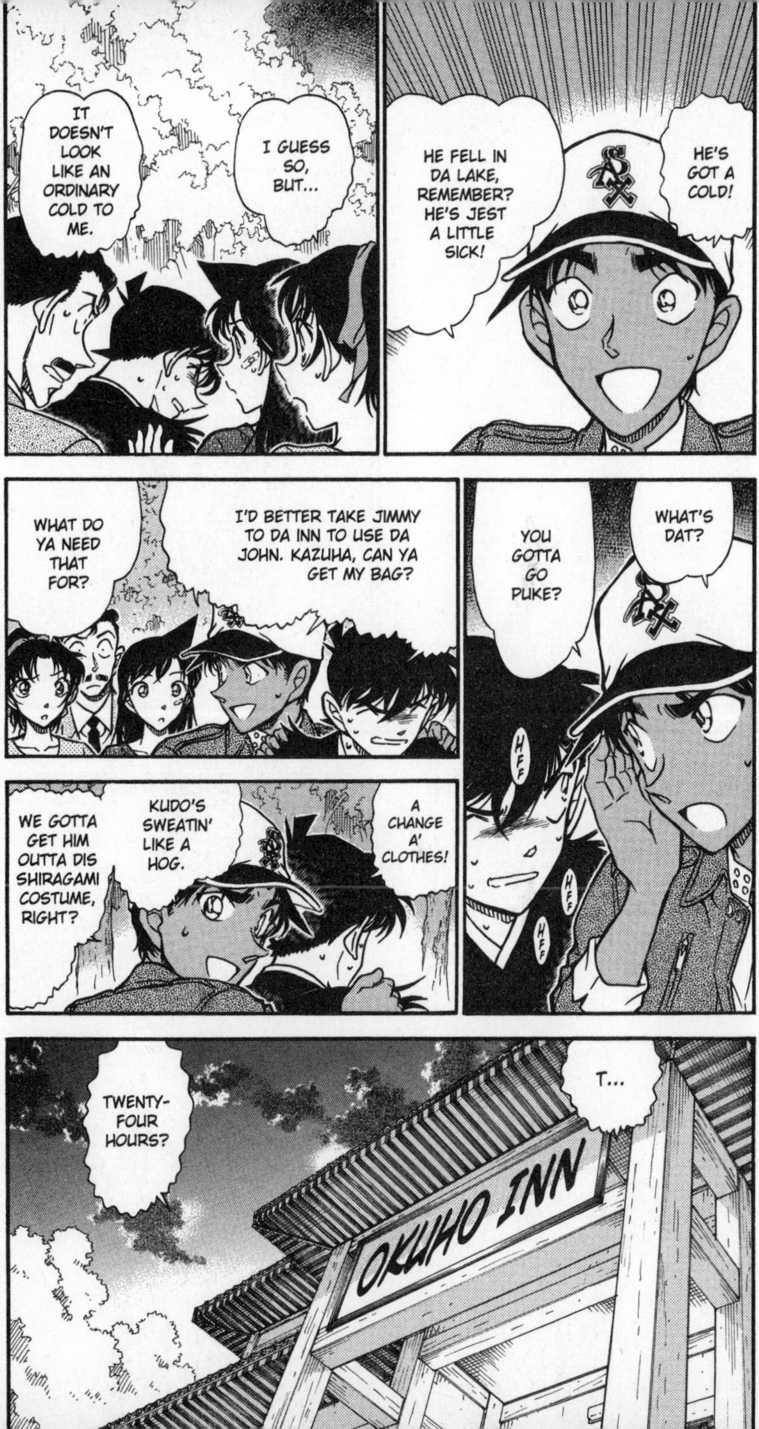
HE'S GOT A COLD!
HE FELL IN DA LAKE, REMEMBER? HE'S JEST A LITTLE SICK!
I GUESS SO, BUT...
IT DOESN'T LOOK LIKE AN ORDINARY COLD TO ME.
WHAT'S DAT?
YOU GOTTA GO PUKE?
HFF
HFF
HFF
I'D BETTER TAKE JIMMY TO DA INN TO USE DA JOHN. KAZUHA, CAN YA GET MY BAG?
WHAT DO YA NEED THAT FOR?
A CHANGE A' CLOTHES!
KUDO'S SWEATIN' LIKE A HOG.
WE GOTTA GET HIM OUTTA DIS SHIRAGAMI COSTUME, RIGHT?
T...
TWENTY-FOUR HOURS?
OKUHO INN

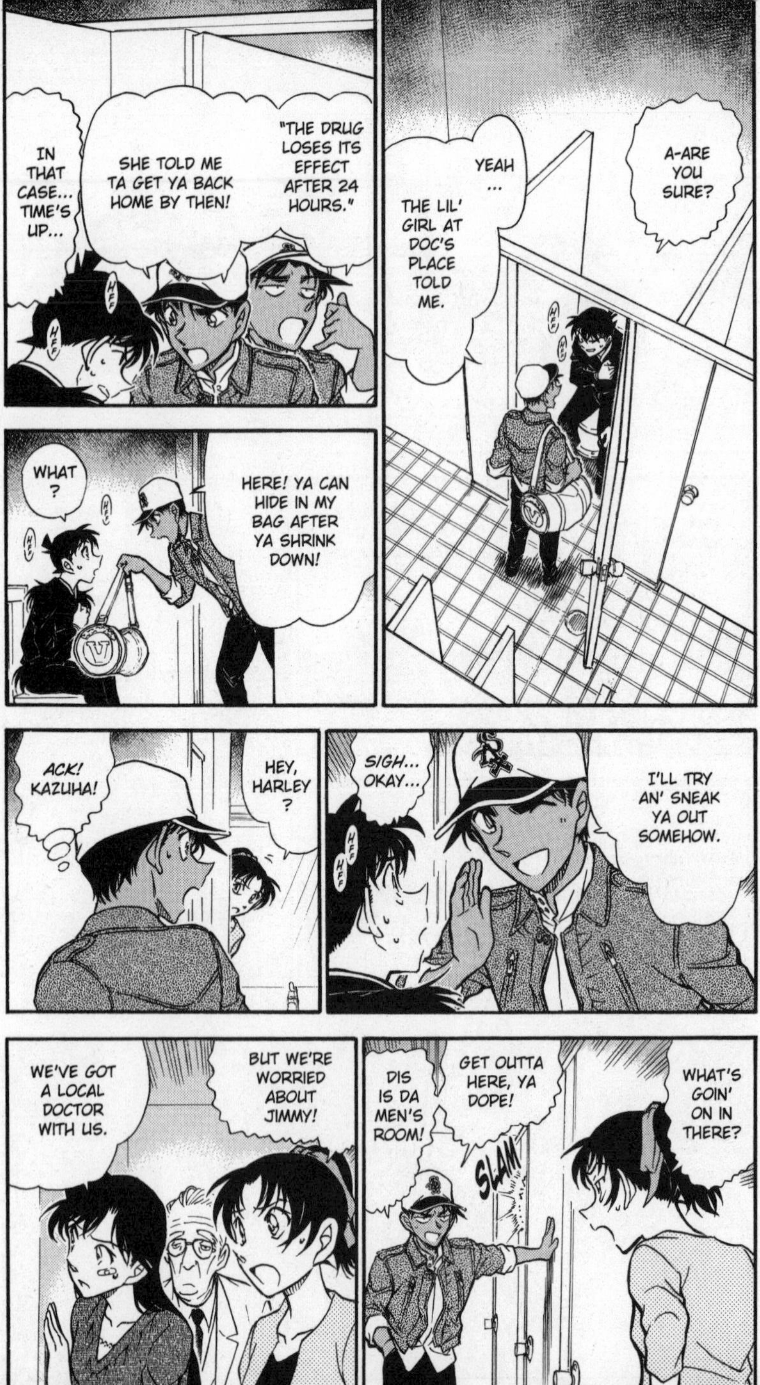
A-ARE YOU SURE?
YEAH ...
THE LIL' GIRL AT DOC'S PLACE TOLD ME.
HEFF
HEFF
"THE DRUG LOSES ITS EFFECT AFTER 24 HOURS."
SHE TOLD ME TA GET YA BACK HOME BY THEN!
IN THAT CASE... TIME'S UP...
HEFF
HEFF
HERE! YA CAN HIDE IN MY BAG AFTER YA SHRINK DOWN!
WHAT ?
HEFF
HEFF
I'LL TRY AN' SNEAK YA OUT SOMEHOW.
SIGH... OKAY...
HEFF
HEFF
HEY, HARLEY ?
ACK! KAZUHA!
WHAT'S GOIN' ON IN THERE?
GET OUTTA HERE, YA DOPE!
DIS IS DA MEN'S ROOM!
SLAM
BUT WE'RE WORRIED ABOUT JIMMY!
WE'VE GOT A LOCAL DOCTOR WITH US.

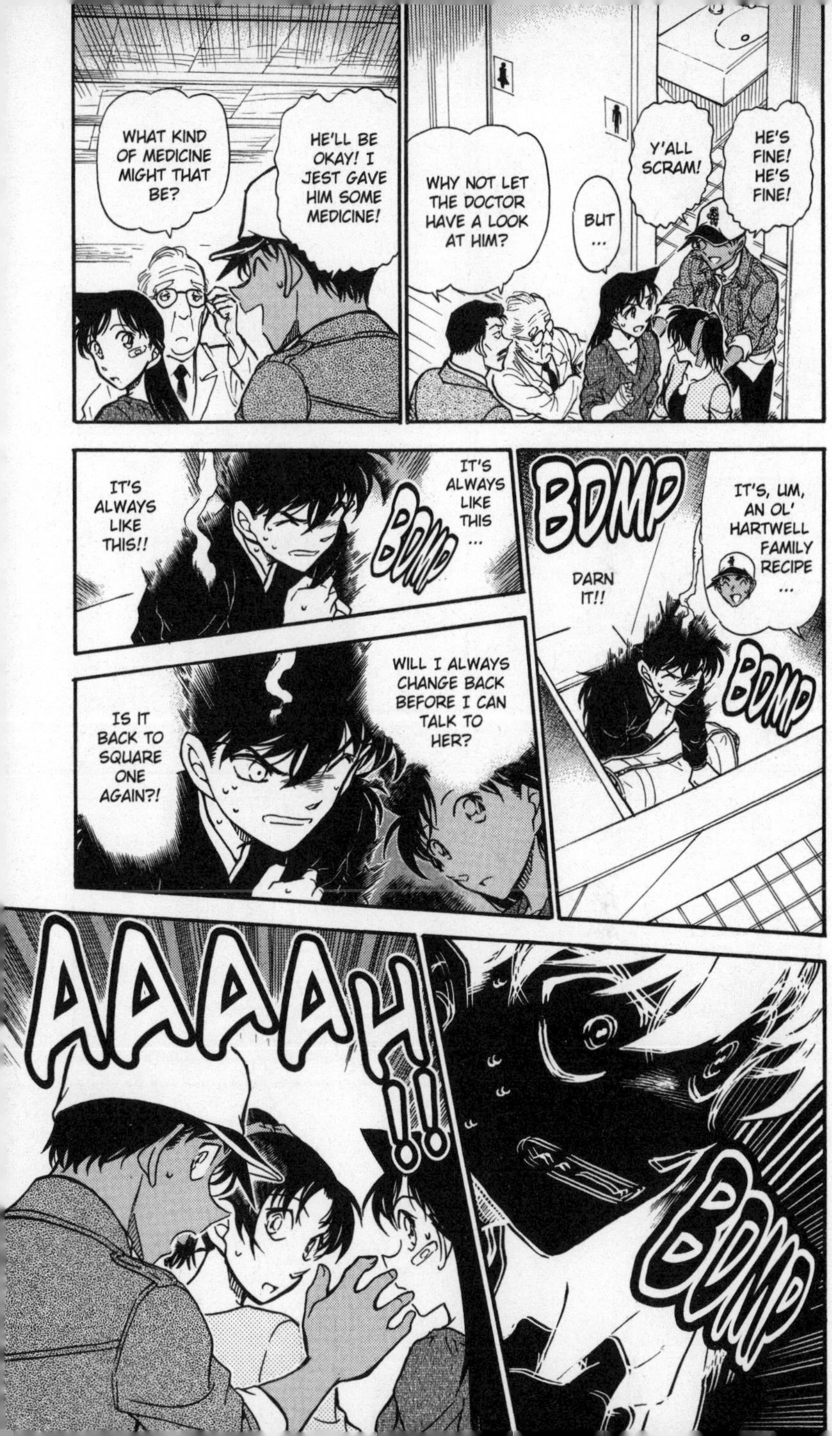
HE'S FINE! HE'S FINE!
Y'ALL SCRAM!
BUT ...
WHY NOT LET THE DOCTOR HAVE A LOOK AT HIM?
HE'LL BE OKAY! I JEST GAVE HIM SOME MEDICINE!
WHAT KIND OF MEDICINE MIGHT THAT BE?
BDMP
IT'S, UM, AN OL' HARTWELL FAMILY RECIPE ...
DARN IT!!
BDMP
BDMP
IT'S ALWAYS LIKE THIS ...
IT'S ALWAYS LIKE THIS!!
WILL I ALWAYS CHANGE BACK BEFORE I CAN TALK TO HER?
IS IT BACK TO SQUARE ONE AGAIN?!
BDMP
AAAAH!!!

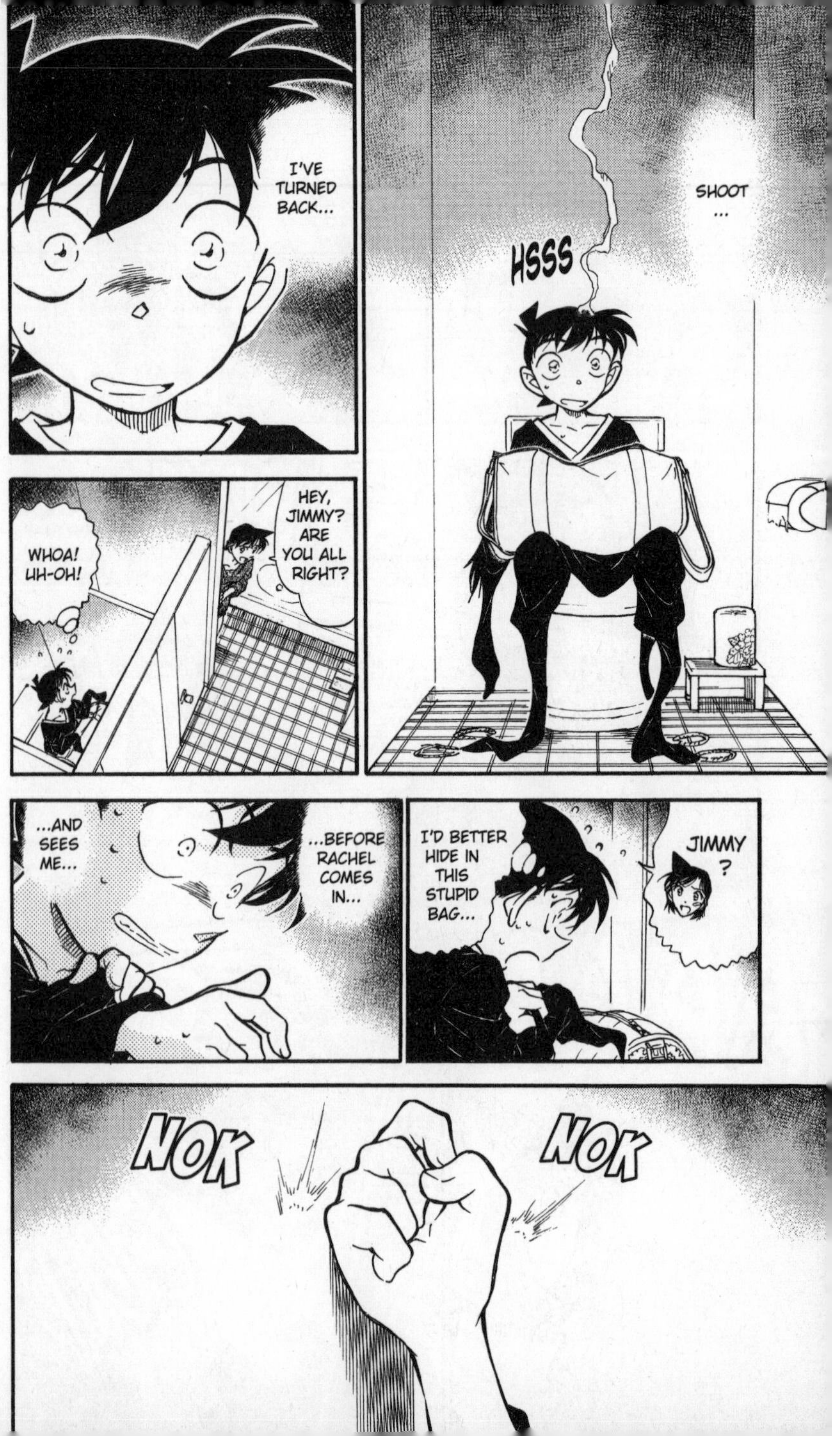
SHOOT ...
HSSS
I'VE TURNED BACK...
HEY, JIMMY? ARE YOU ALL RIGHT?
WHOA! UH-OH!
JIMMY ?
I'D BETTER HIDE IN THIS STUPID BAG...
...BEFORE RACHEL COMES IN...
...AND SEES ME...
NOK
NOK

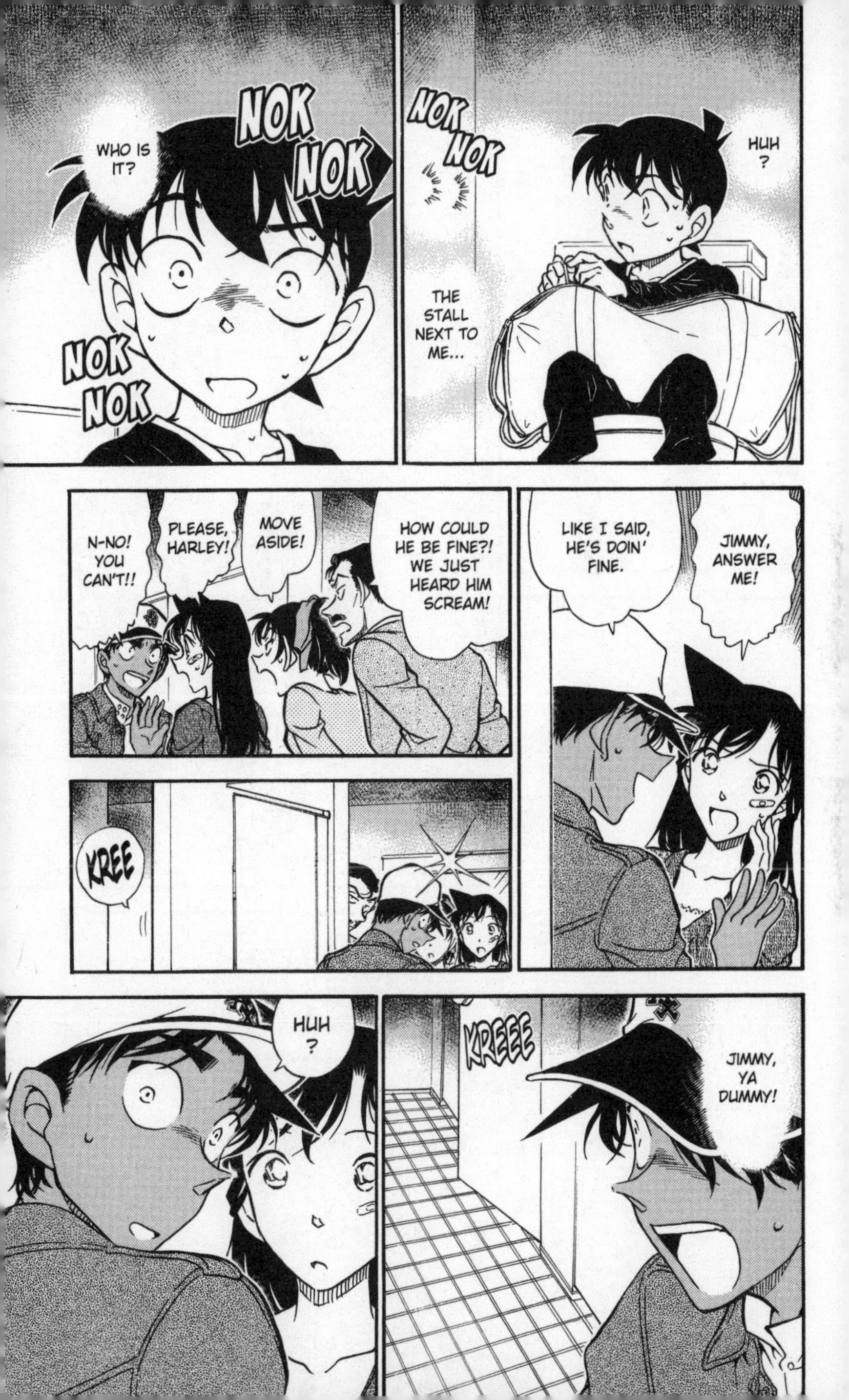
HUH ?
NOK NOK
THE STALL NEXT TO ME...
NOK NOK
WHO IS IT?
NOK NOK
JIMMY, ANSWER ME!
LIKE I SAID, HE'S DOIN' FINE.
HOW COULD HE BE FINE?! WE JUST HEARD HIM SCREAM!
MOVE ASIDE!
PLEASE, HARLEY!
N-NO! YOU CAN'T!!
KREE
KREEE
JIMMY, YA DUMMY!
HUH ?

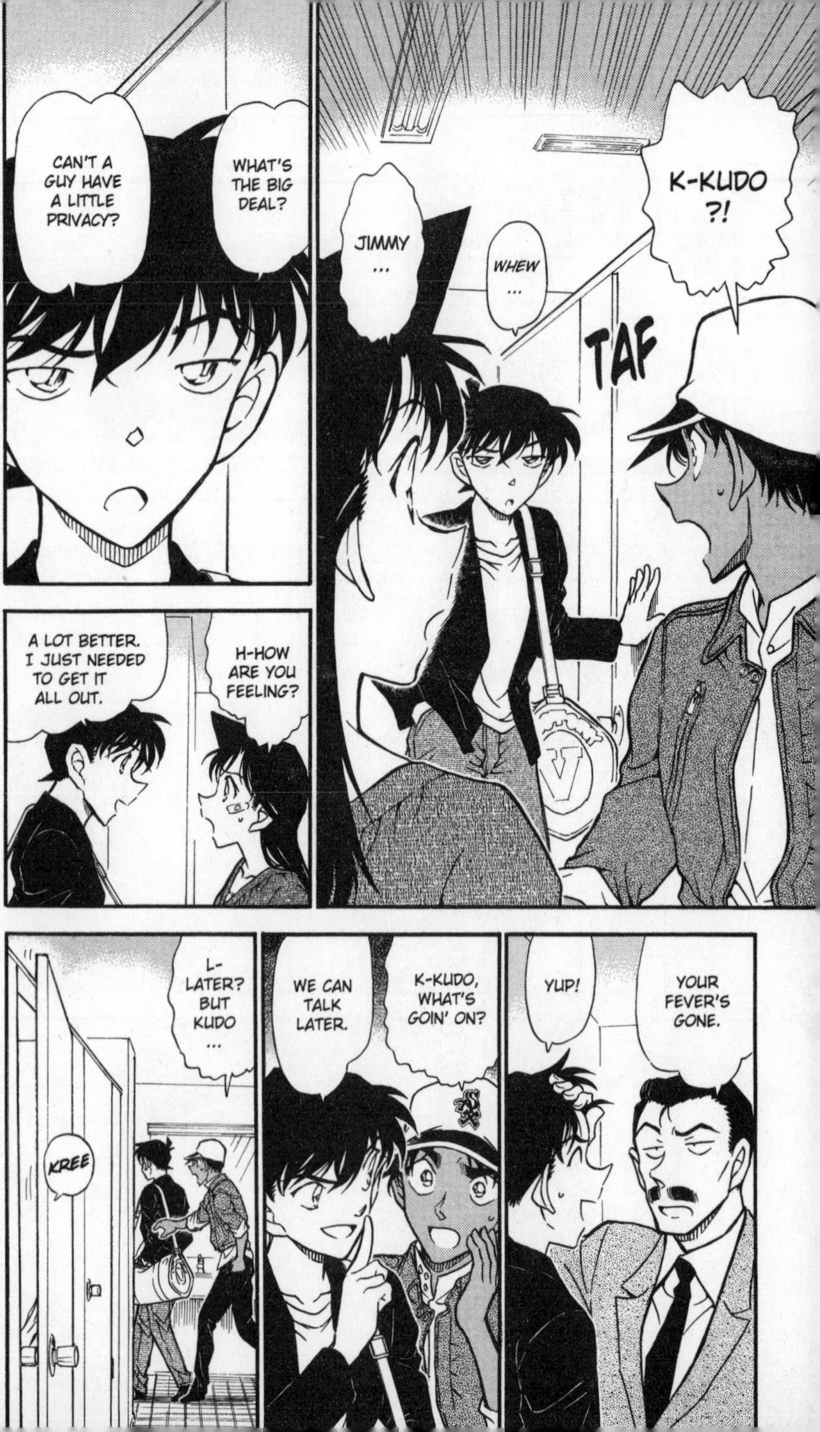
K-KUDO ?!
TAF
WHEW ...
JIMMY ...
WHAT'S THE BIG DEAL?
CAN'T A GUY HAVE A LITTLE PRIVACY?
H-HOW ARE YOU FEELING?
A LOT BETTER. I JUST NEEDED TO GET IT ALL OUT.
YOUR FEVER'S GONE.
YUP!
K-KUDO, WHAT'S GOIN' ON?
WE CAN TALK LATER.
L-LATER? BUT KUDO ...
KREE

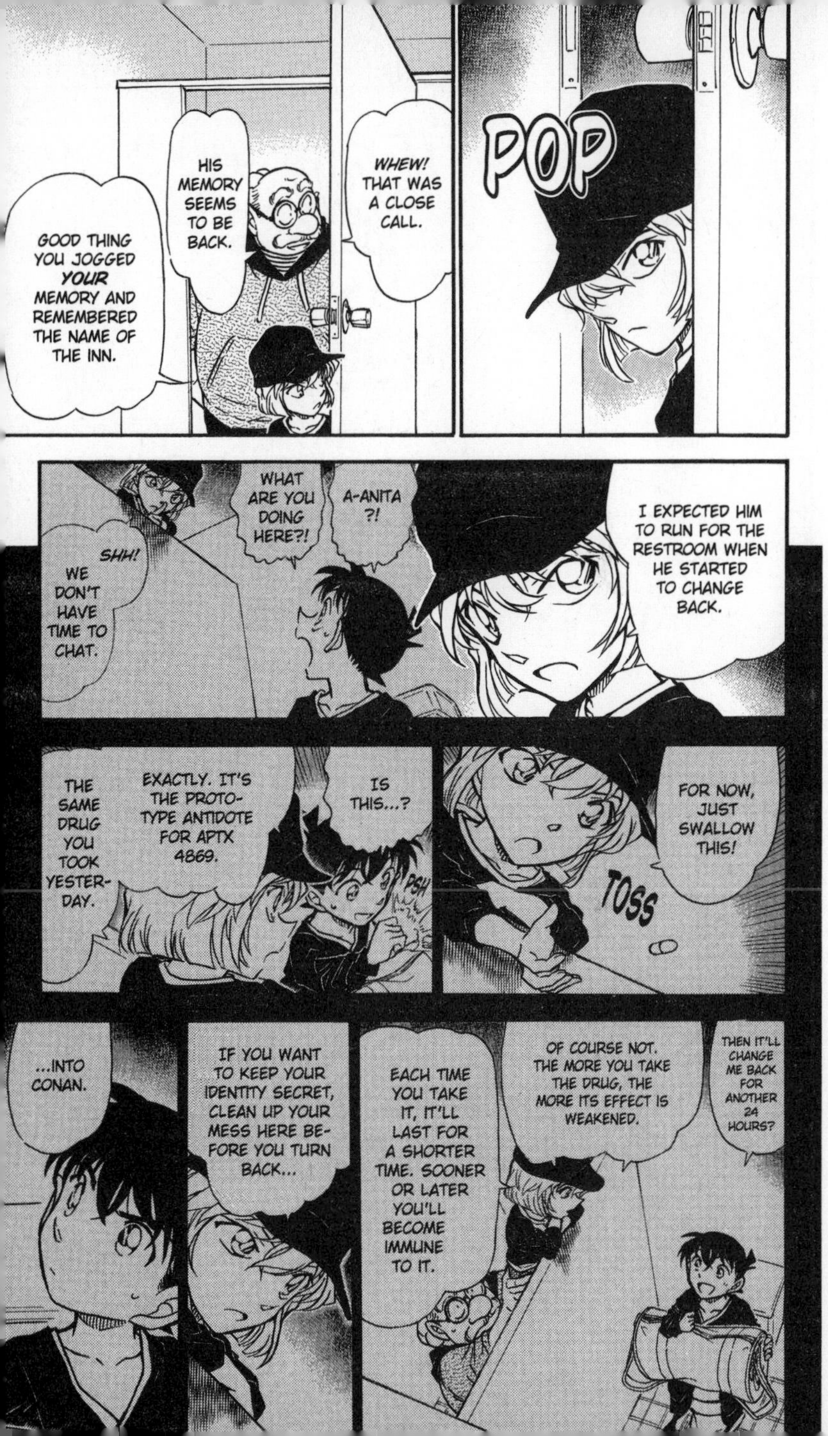
POP
WHEW! THAT WAS A CLOSE CALL.
HIS MEMORY SEEMS TO BE BACK.
GOOD THING YOU JOGGED YOUR MEMORY AND REMEMBERED THE NAME OF THE INN.
I EXPECTED HIM TO RUN FOR THE RESTROOM WHEN HE STARTED TO CHANGE BACK.
A-ANITA?!
WHAT ARE YOU DOING HERE?!
SHH! WE DON'T HAVE TIME TO CHAT.
FOR NOW, JUST SWALLOW THIS!
TOSS
IS THIS...?
PSH
EXACTLY. IT'S THE PROTOTYPE ANTIDOTE FOR APTX 4869.
THE SAME DRUG YOU TOOK YESTERDAY.
THEN IT'LL CHANGE ME BACK FOR ANOTHER 24 HOURS?
OF COURSE NOT. THE MORE YOU TAKE THE DRUG, THE MORE ITS EFFECT IS WEAKENED.
EACH TIME YOU TAKE IT, IT'LL LAST FOR A SHORTER TIME. SOONER OR LATER YOU'LL BECOME IMMUNE TO IT.
IF YOU WANT TO KEEP YOUR IDENTITY SECRET, CLEAN UP YOUR MESS HERE BEFORE YOU TURN BACK...
...INTO CONAN.

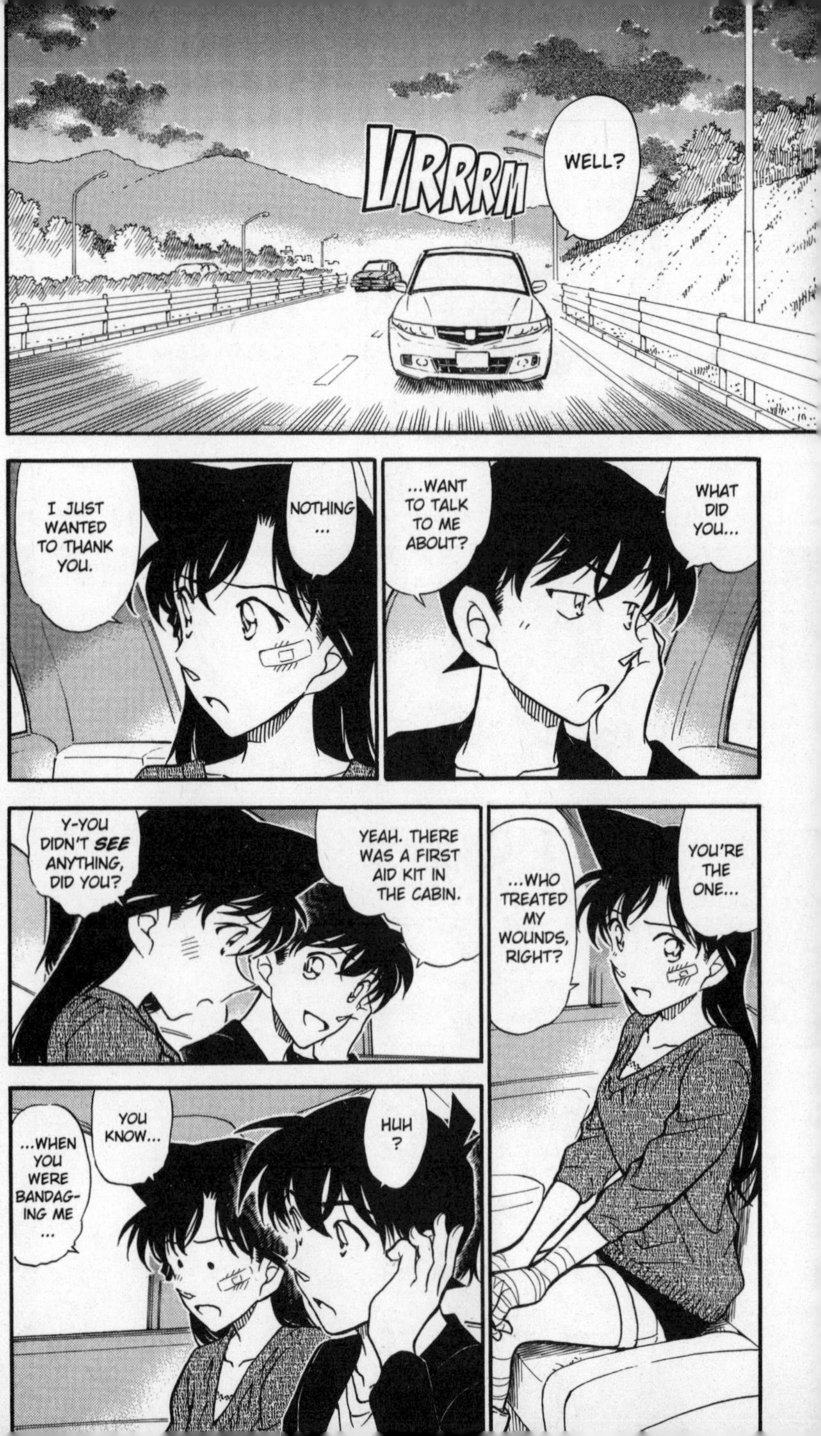
VRRRM
WELL?
WHAT DID YOU...
...WANT TO TALK TO ME ABOUT?
NOTHING...
I JUST WANTED TO THANK YOU.
YOU'RE THE ONE...
...WHO TREATED MY WOUNDS, RIGHT?
YEAH. THERE WAS A FIRST AID KIT IN THE CABIN.
Y-YOU DIDN'T **SEE** ANYTHING, DID YOU?
HUH?
YOU KNOW...
...WHEN YOU WERE BANDAGING ME...

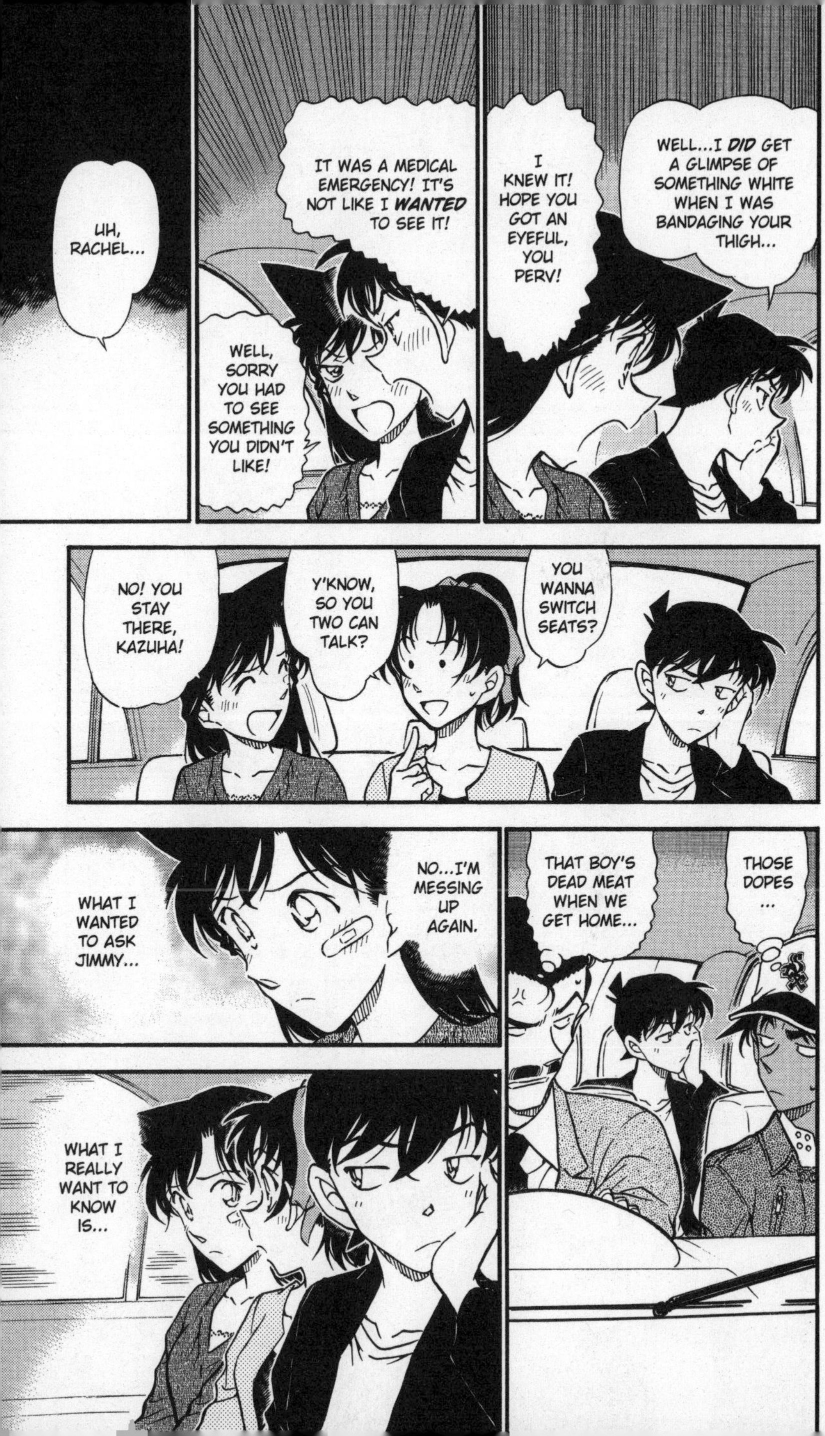
WELL...I DID GET A GLIMPSE OF SOMETHING WHITE WHEN I WAS BANDAGING YOUR THIGH...
I KNEW IT! HOPE YOU GOT AN EYEFUL, YOU PERV!
IT WAS A MEDICAL EMERGENCY! IT'S NOT LIKE I WANTED TO SEE IT!
WELL, SORRY YOU HAD TO SEE SOMETHING YOU DIDN'T LIKE!
UH, RACHEL...
YOU WANNA SWITCH SEATS?
Y'KNOW, SO YOU TWO CAN TALK?
NO! YOU STAY THERE, KAZUHA!
THOSE DOPES...
THAT BOY'S DEAD MEAT WHEN WE GET HOME...
NO...I'M MESSING UP AGAIN.
WHAT I WANTED TO ASK JIMMY...
WHAT I REALLY WANT TO KNOW IS...

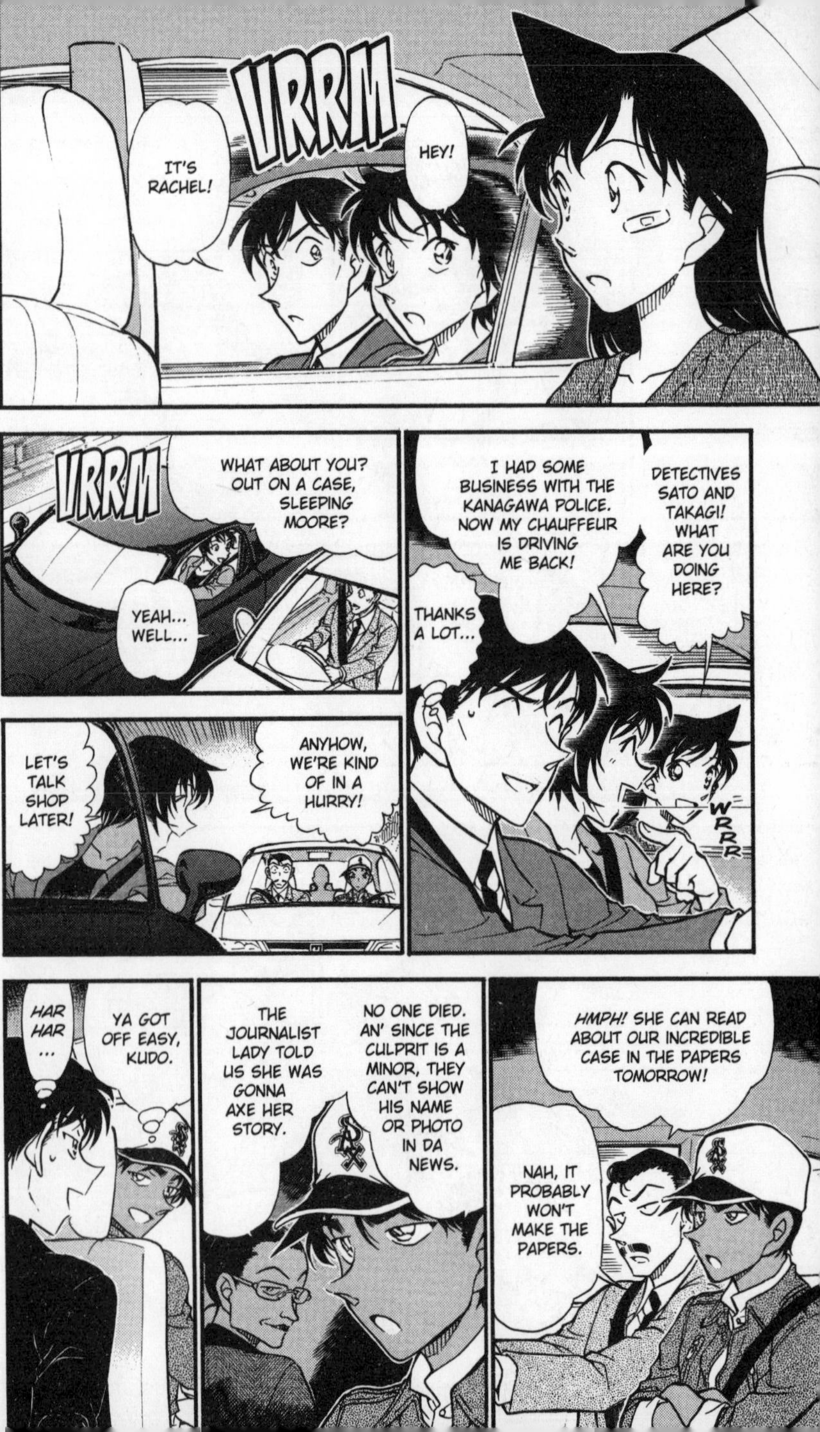
HEY!
VRRM
IT'S RACHEL!
DETECTIVES SATO AND TAKAGI! WHAT ARE YOU DOING HERE?
I HAD SOME BUSINESS WITH THE KANAGAWA POLICE. NOW MY CHAUFFEUR IS DRIVING ME BACK!
THANKS A LOT...
WRRR
WHAT ABOUT YOU? OUT ON A CASE, SLEEPING MOORE?
VRRM
YEAH... WELL...
ANYHOW, WE'RE KIND OF IN A HURRY!
LET'S TALK SHOP LATER!
HMPH! SHE CAN READ ABOUT OUR INCREDIBLE CASE IN THE PAPERS TOMORROW!
NAH, IT PROBABLY WON'T MAKE THE PAPERS.
NO ONE DIED. AN' SINCE THE CULPRIT IS A MINOR, THEY CAN'T SHOW HIS NAME OR PHOTO IN DA NEWS.
THE JOURNALIST LADY TOLD US SHE WAS GONNA AXE HER STORY.
YA GOT OFF EASY, KUDO.
HAR HAR ...

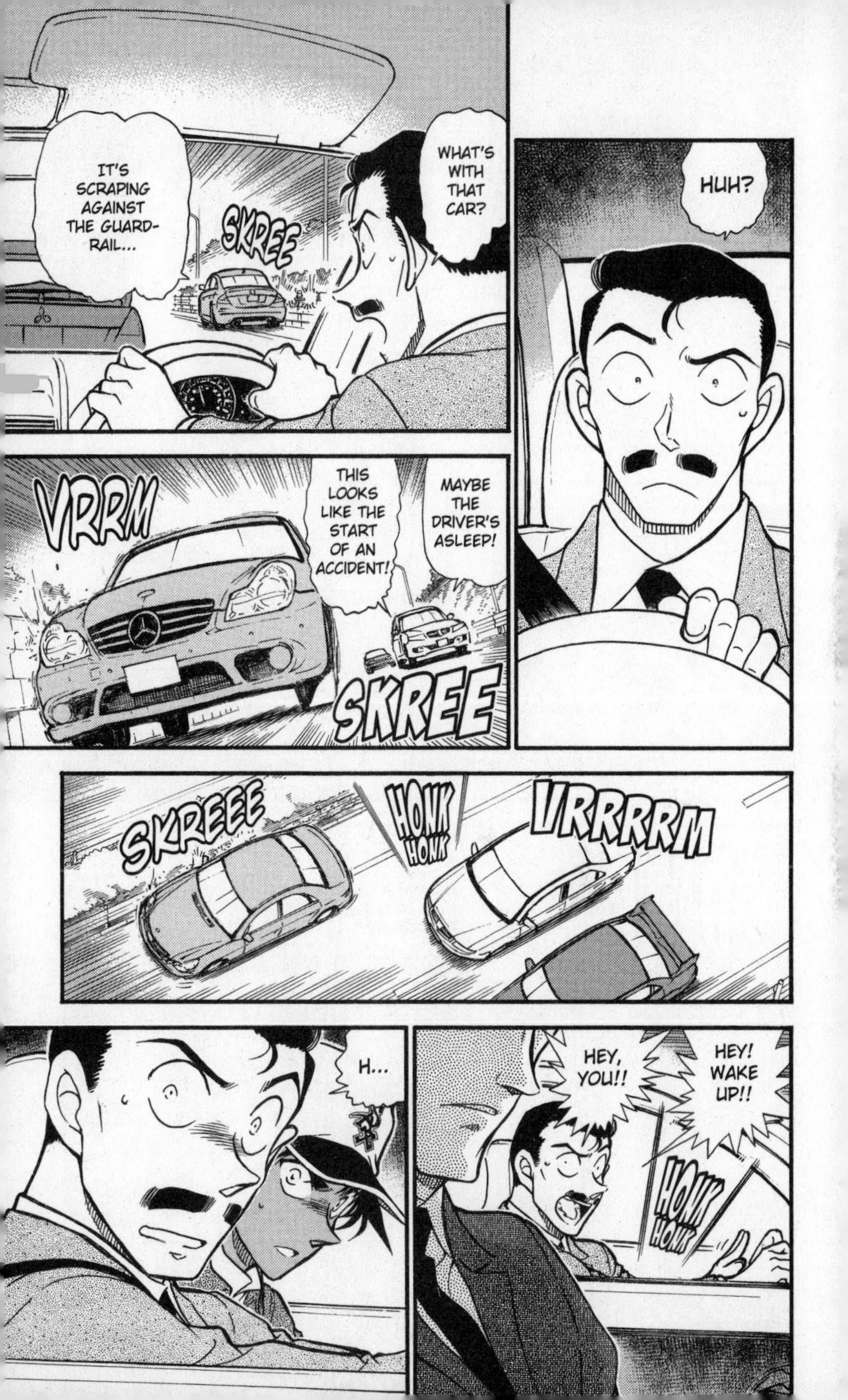
HUH?
WHAT'S WITH THAT CAR?
IT'S SCRAPING AGAINST THE GUARD-RAIL...
SKREE
MAYBE THE DRIVER'S ASLEEP!
THIS LOOKS LIKE THE START OF AN ACCIDENT!
VRRM
SKREE
VRRRRM
HONK HONK
SKREEE
HEY! WAKE UP!!
HEY, YOU!!
HONK HONK
H...

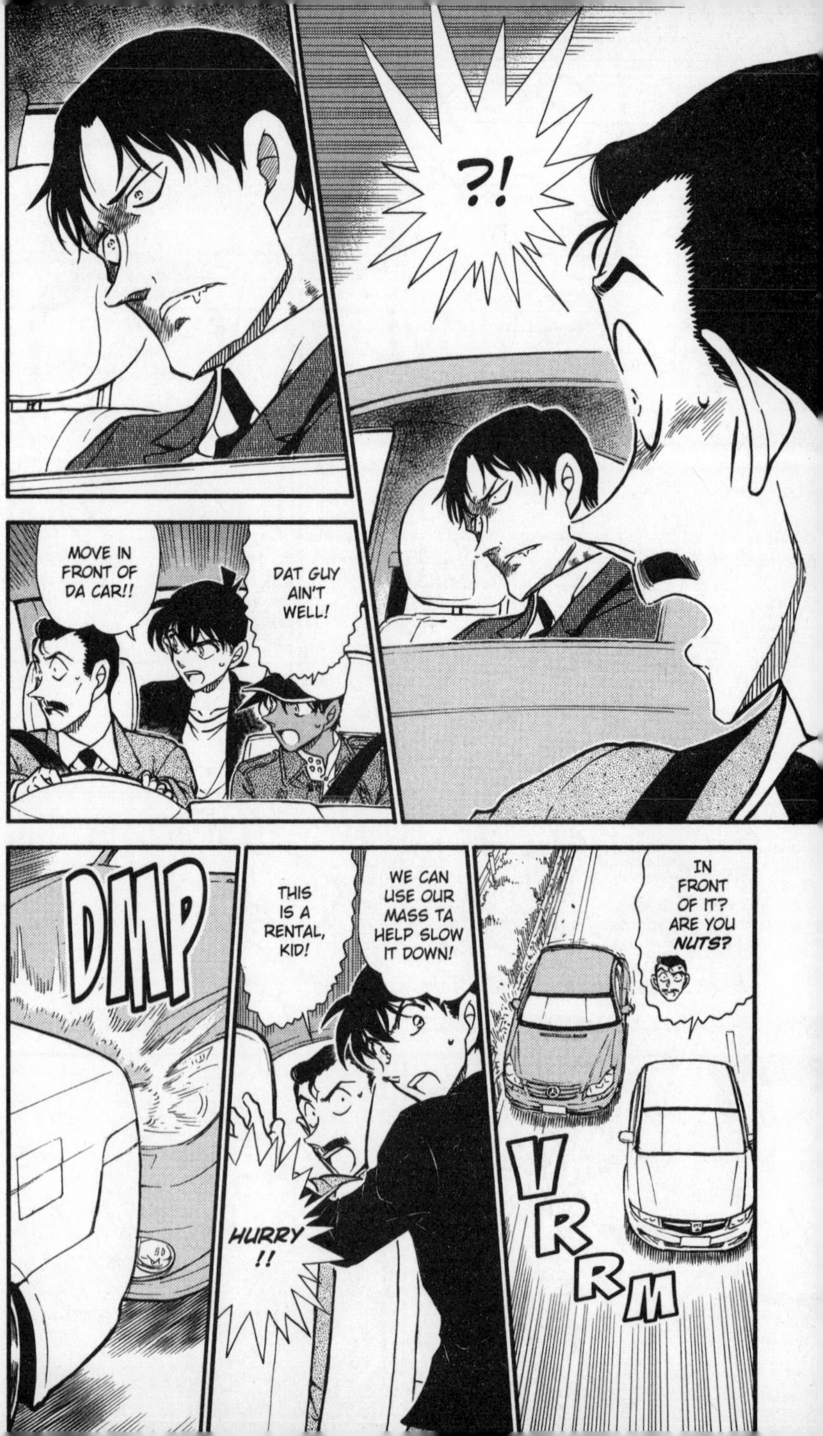
?!
DAT GUY AIN'T WELL!
MOVE IN FRONT OF DA CAR!!
IN FRONT OF IT? ARE YOU ***NUTS?***
VRRM
WE CAN USE OUR MASS TA HELP SLOW IT DOWN!
THIS IS A RENTAL, KID!
HURRY!!
DMP

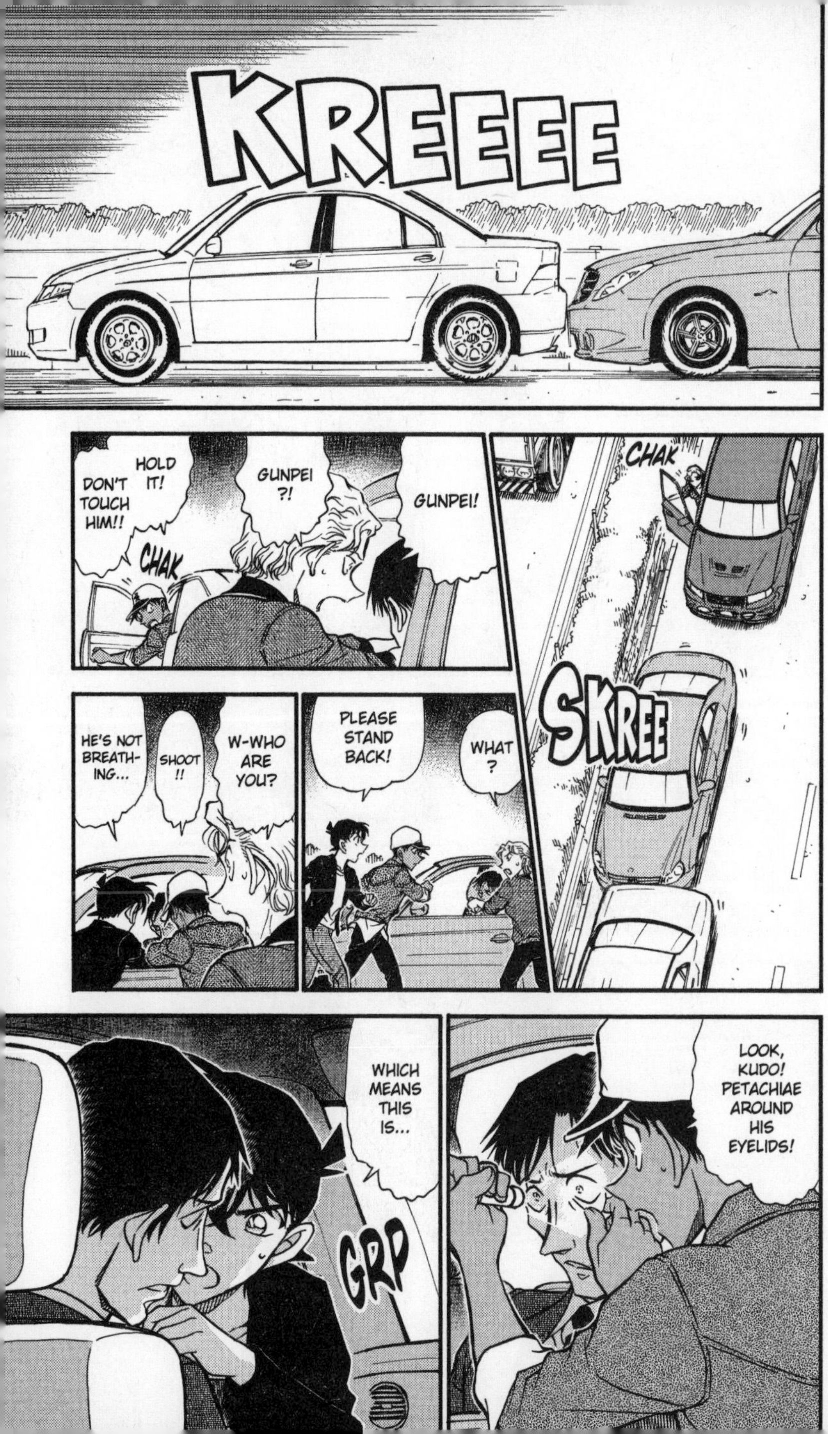
KREEEE
CHAK
SKREE
GUNPEI!
GUNPEI ?!
HOLD IT! DON'T TOUCH HIM!!
CHAK
WHAT ?
PLEASE STAND BACK!
W-WHO ARE YOU?
SHOOT !!
HE'S NOT BREATH-ING...
LOOK, KUDO! PETACHIAE AROUND HIS EYELIDS!
WHICH MEANS THIS IS...
GRP

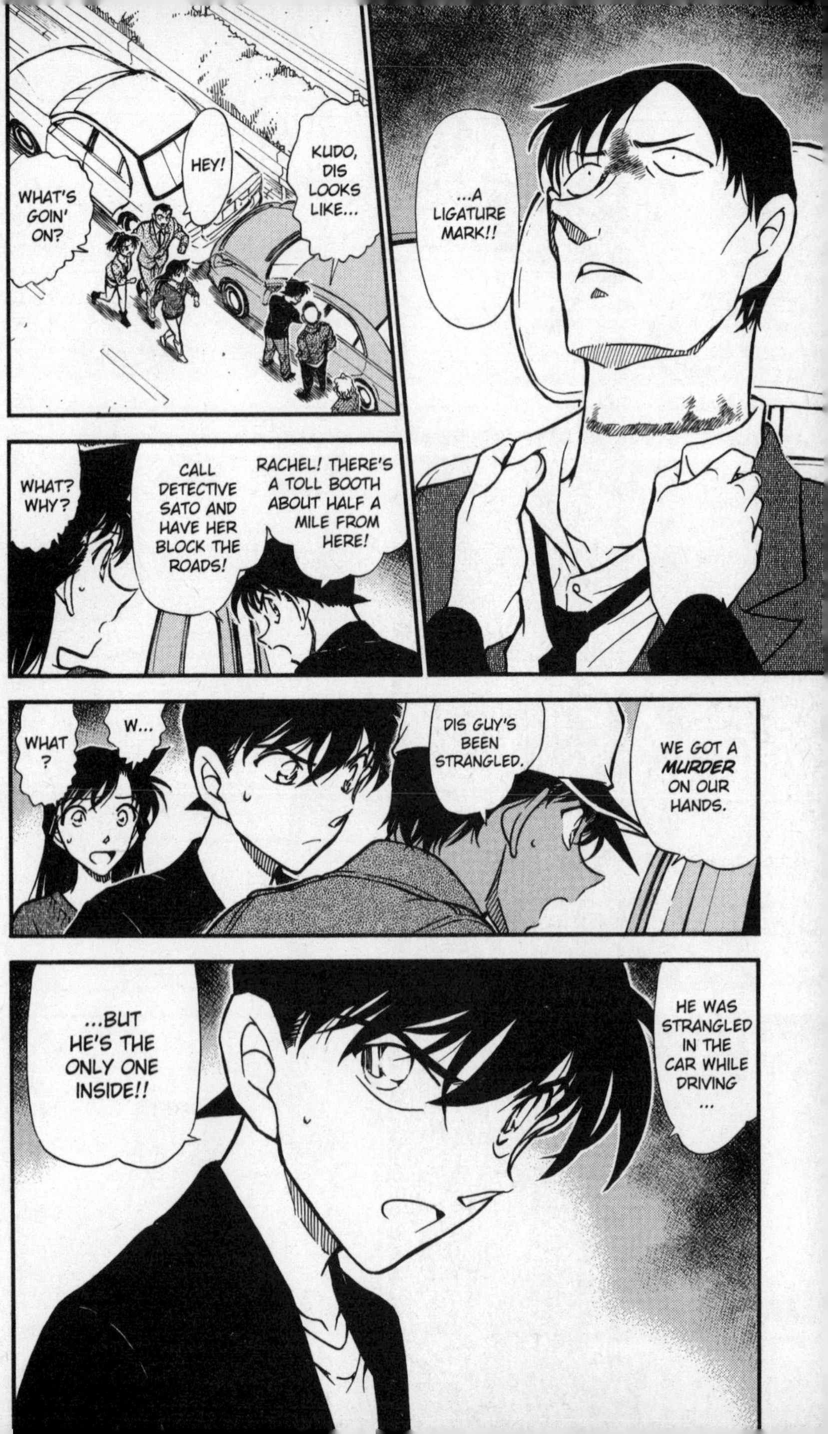
...A LIGATURE MARK!!
KUDO, DIS LOOKS LIKE...
HEY!
WHAT'S GOIN' ON?
RACHEL! THERE'S A TOLL BOOTH ABOUT HALF A MILE FROM HERE!
CALL DETECTIVE SATO AND HAVE HER BLOCK THE ROADS!
WHAT? WHY?
WE GOT A MURDER ON OUR HANDS.
DIS GUY'S BEEN STRANGLED.
W...
WHAT?
HE WAS STRANGLED IN THE CAR WHILE DRIVING...
...BUT HE'S THE ONLY ONE INSIDE!!

Hello, Aoyama here.

The other day I went to get a new cell phone. They told me I could save money by applying for a special discount service, so I decided to go for it. They asked me what my last phone bill was so they could explain how cheap it would be after the discount, and I said... "Sixteen yen."* I barely use my cell phone! So there was no point to getting the special service...heh.

*About 16 cents.

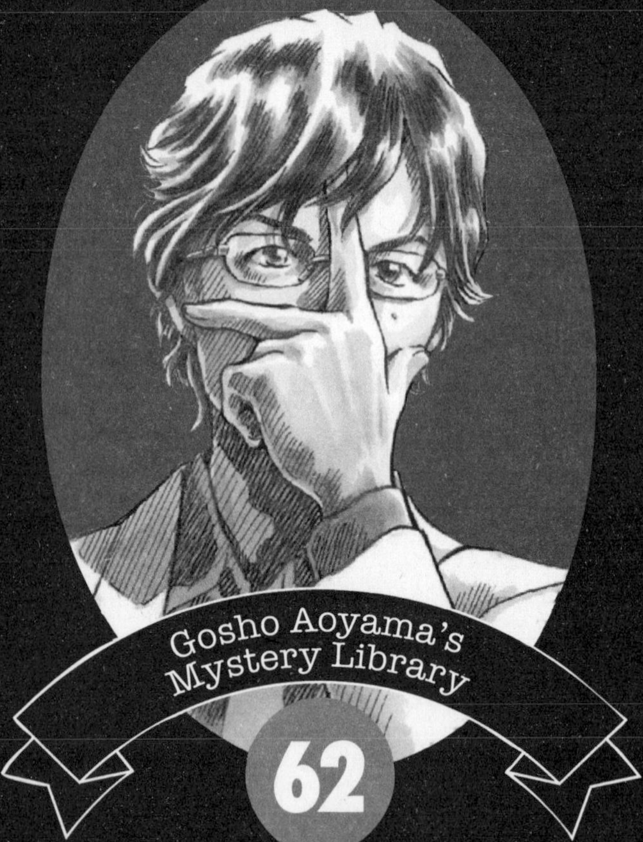
Gosho Aoyama's
Mystery Library
62

MANABU YUKAWA

Scientific know-how is a must for criminal investigators, but “Detective Galileo,” a.k.a. Manabu Yukawa, is an extreme example! He's an associate professor in the physics department of the Teito University School of Science and Engineering. Though he certainly looks brainy with his tall frame, glasses and pale complexion, he's pretty athletic too. His only weakness is children. Detectives Shunpei Kusanagi and Kaoru Utsumi of the Metropolitan Police bring him baffling cases involving seemingly supernatural elements like spontaneous human combustion, out-of-body experiences and ESP. His talent for solving mysteries in his head, using pure logic, has earned him the nickname “Galileo.”

His author, Keigo Higashino, is a former engineer. He started writing the series because he always wanted to “make use of my scientific knowledge to create a novel.” My big brother is a scientist too. He helps me out with the gimmicks in *Case Closed*, but he's not as cool as Yukawa. *Heh...*

I recommend *Burn*.